DATE DUE

OC '00			
OC 4 '03			
MX 72 '08			

DEMCO 38-296

IN DEFENSE OF HUMAN CONSCIOUSNESS

IN DEFENSE OF
HUMAN
CONSCIOUSNESS

Joseph F. Rychlak

AMERICAN PSYCHOLOGICAL ASSOCIATION
WASHINGTON, DC

Riverside Community College
Library
4800 Magnolia Avenue
Riverside, California 92506

Published by
American Psychological Association
750 First Street, NE
Washington, DC 20002

Copies may be ordered from
APA Order Department
P.O. Box 92984
Washington, DC 20090-2984

In the UK and Europe, copies may be ordered from
American Psychological Association
3 Henrietta Street
Covent Garden, London
WC2E 8LU England

Permissions to quote from copyrighted material appear on page 329.

Typeset in Goudy by EPS Group Inc., Easton, MD

Printer: Data Reproductions Corporation, Auburn Hills, MI
Jacket Designer: Anne Masters Design, Washington, DC
Technical / Production Editor: Edward B. Meidenbauer

Library of Congress Cataloging-in-Publication Data
Rychlak, Joseph F.
    In defense of human consciousness / by Joseph F. Rychlak.
       p.   cm.
    Includes bibliographical references and indexes.
    ISBN 1-55798-421-2 (acid-free paper)
    1. Consciousness.   2. Apperception.   3. Human information processing.
    I. Title.
    BF311.R93   1997
    153—dc21   97-3877
                                                                                 CIP

British Library Cataloguing-in-Publication Data
A CIP record is available from the British Library

Printed in the United States of America
First edition

To my grandchildren:
Joseph, Lindsey, Susanna, Mary Helen, and Sally Rychlak
Robert and Scott Stilson

CONTENTS

LIST OF FIGURES

ACKNOWLEDGMENTS

I was greatly helped in this effort by the manuscript readings and critical comments of Karen Cox, Kristin Lang, Nancy Norman, Haroldas Subačius, and Karin Stronck. Del Jenkins generously gave me the fruits of his insightful thinking, as did Tracy Henley and Chuck Dill. There were many other brief encounters with students and colleagues too numerous to detail, but I would like to single out Gavin Lew and Danilo Ramirez for their critical interest and trenchant observations. As in all my writing efforts, my wife Lenora played an invaluable role as editor and morale booster. I would also like to thank Mary Lynn Skutley, Beth Beisel, and Ed Meidenbauer for their support and editorial efforts in bringing the manuscript to print.

J. F. R.

INTRODUCTION

When I was a boy there was a phrase that we used when we felt it necessary to assert our individuality in disagreements with our playmates. If challenged with something like "Oh yeah, who says so?" we responded with "Me, myself, and I." This assertive retort affirmed our personal consciousness; it conveyed that we were willing to take responsibility for the view that we had selected to defend in the face of alternative possibilities. It never occurred at the time that I was merely mouthing linguistic conventions "shaped into" me by my cultural milieu regarding how to behave in a childhood dispute. I took these words pretty seriously as really belonging to me—representing my conscious state of mind. This was not like pretending, where conviction could be role-played for effect. Nor was it like playing a game, or going to a party, where you were indeed aware of certain social rules to be followed. But today I am told by my social-constructivist colleagues—highly competent scholars—that this conviction of personal identity was merely an illusion. Indeed, "I" as a decision-making, conscious individual never really existed (and still don't!).

As I came into this profession out of an interest in the psychology of an individual human being (myself, really) and not statistical probabilities concerning collectives, it naturally frustrates me to hear such things—as it turns out, "all over again." That is, there is nothing new in this social-constructivist claim that people are mere pawns in the cultural milieu. Leading psychologists like B. F. Skinner and Clark Hull made this point decades ago. In effect, today's computer modelers are repeating the same thing in the name of a supposed "cognitive revolution" taking place in psychology. I see no revolution whatsoever in the basic human image being advanced, and frankly marvel at the willingness these information-processing theorists have to tack something called consciousness onto their views. The truth is, there is no need for consciousness in such theories if we mean by this term what "us kids" and our parents meant by it years ago—and what I think the average person means by it today.

The formal positions taken by academic psychologists and related social scientists concerning human behavior are not aimed at trying to capture the commonsense understanding of what it means to be conscious, or to have a sense of personal responsibility and self-determination. "Real people" know what is involved here, but the academicians have the arrogant attitude that this commonsense understanding is founded on mere "folk" psychology, which is tantamount to saying that it is illusory or mythological and therefore its tenets are unworthy of scientific consideration. Even so, the popular view of the psychologist continues to be that of someone who tries to find out how people function *as people*, as individual organisms that are more than simply a collection of chemicals, tissues, and physical energies. I have found that even professional colleagues in various specialties tend to think of psychologists as studying the dynamics of behavior, the choices that people make, and the self-selected goals that they try to reach. Some psychologists do indeed want to capture the grandeur of being human, the victories and foibles of a unique behavioral pattern that seems at times to rise above the natural course of events. But the truth is that in reaching for scientific status the academicians assume (sometimes reluctantly) that their professional role is to frame human beings along the same lines that their kin in the physical sciences have used to frame inanimate, bloodless objects and events.

The founders of modern psychology took so readily to the language of natural science that they narrowly limited the kind of terminology that could be used in the study of human beings. This was unfortunate, because it so happens that in order to explain consciousness of the kind real people believe in, we have to reach back into history and resurrect descriptive terminology that was allowed to die—indeed, was put to death—during the rise of natural science. It was once considered proper to include descriptions and explanations in science that bore the stamp of the reasons "why" objects existed and events took place. Ancient physical accounts of philosophers like Aristotle therefore suggested that items and actions in nature occurred for a reason and served a discernible purpose in the overall scheme of things.

Centuries later, after they had been wound into theology, such purposive explanations came into direct conflict with the rise of empirical science. Some rather unfortunate but inevitable developments were the consequence, such as Galileo's house arrest and forced recantation on the matter of whether the earth rotated around the sun (as he believed) or the sun rotated around the earth (as Biblical accounts depicted). Because theological beliefs were presumably divinely inspired and therefore reflected the deity's creative intentions, science could not violate such prescriptive understandings. From this time forward (roughly the 16th and 17th centuries), proper empirical scientists specifically threw out all references to purpose and intention in their descriptive accounts. This rigorous attitude came to be known as Newtonian science.

When modern scientific psychology was born in the late 19th century, the tail end of this Newtonianism still enjoyed hegemony in the physical sciences. As a result, the early psychologists were expected to conform to the strictures of this worldview if they sought acceptance into the family of sciences. This materialistic outlook was not easy to embrace for a psychologist interested in the human mind. A person's body was obviously physical and possibly even mechanical in nature, but surely this was not true of the mind. The mind seemed to have unique features, the most prominent of which was most assuredly consciousness. Psychologists in academia, where science was highly prized, were therefore forced into a kind of hybrid career status, caught between the poles of a Cartesian dualism that has separated mind from body to this very day. A small minority struggled to sustain interest in the mind. But the vast majority of psychologists were only too ready to focus on bodily functions and altogether dismiss concerns over the mind, which came to be identified with "spirit" and other things too mysterious for words.

The ancient language of purposes and intentions has never returned to scientific psychology, even though it can be shown that modern physical science is open to such designations. The Newtonian belief in a free-standing reality, functioning independently of the conceptualizing scientist, is no longer tenable in today's scientific community. The post-Newtonian scientist recognizes that his or her approach, viewpoint, theoretical paradigm, and so forth, plays an immense role in what can and will be learned in the laboratory. Psychology has lagged behind other modern scientific disciplines on this score, for it continues to insist that people are pawns under the direction of biological and sociological forces that presumably strip them of their capacity to behave according to conscious free will.

In the popular imagination, human agency is not understood as former "shapings" directing behavior totally without some form of self-influence by the person who can freely select from among one or more possibilities open at the moment. But this manipulative shaping view is how modern Newtonianism—parading as behaviorism, social constructivism, mechanism, cognitive psychology, information-processing, and a host of other such "scientific" accounts—conceptualizes human behavior and cognition: as merely a more complex assemblage of the forces that move inanimate things about, like rocks rolling down hills or changes in the weather. People facing the challenge of crossing a busy street under a time pressure do not see their free will in this manner.

They sense the tug of alternative possibilities, and consciously estimate the risks in crossing through moving traffic to reach their important appointment on time.

The response to this disparity between how psychologists explain behavior and how people understand their behavior is frequently something like this: "All sciences redefine the person's naive understanding of the subject matter under study. Biology and physiology introduced new terminology to account for physical processes that common sense does not have an inkling of to begin with." Although this is true, we should remind ourselves that these sciences rarely *explain away* the item under study in framing their reconceptualizations of commonsense experience. The process of digestion may have had many quaint commonsense theories explaining it that scientific investigation negated or clarified, but digestion per se was not drummed out of existence in the explanation. Yet this is precisely what occurs in psychology's treatment of the human being, where consciousness and free will are wrung out of the account in the name of scientific clarification. Lacking proper terminology to make the case, the easy way out here is simply to dismiss the annoying concept altogether. This is not clarification but assassination.

I believe that what is needed today is an enlightened return to the terminology that was jettisoned in science 300 years ago for a good reason but is now under continued repression for a bad reason (i.e., to defend the Newtonian status quo). This terminological resurrection has been a long-term goal of mine, eventuating in what I call logical learning theory (LLT). From the perspective of LLT, people are intentional organisms, behaving for reasons that are either consciously or unconsciously affirmed. People are accepted as agents, capable of free will. Having carefully developed this theory and submitted it to rigorous empirical tests for over 30 years, I think it is about time to apply it to an examination of consciousness. Can LLT provide a clear definition of human consciousness? Can it help us to understand what such consciousness means in everyday behavior as well as in some of the less popular topics pursued by academics like hypnotism, lucid dreaming, conscience, channeling, meditation, and self-identity? Do computers possess consciousness like we do, and if not, why not? Can we be consciously or unconsciously influenced by sociocultural forces that are not themselves initiated by individuals? Does thought originate in unconsciousness, as the founders of psychoanalysis claimed?

These are the kinds of questions I wanted to answer in a book on consciousness because I believe they encompass what puzzles us about this uniquely human aspect of our lived experience. No one has the final answer on such an important topic, but we can sharpen our thinking on it if we are willing to make a slight effort to broaden our image of humanity. This broadening will significantly raise our consciousness on the topic. I can guarantee this much, and only hope that such consciousness-raising will prove instructive to the reader's self-understanding. I hold out this hope because I continue to believe in the validity of concepts like self, individual, and person.

1

IN SEARCH OF A GROUNDING

Thomas Aquinas was famous for his dictations, sometimes keeping three secretaries busy on different topics at the same time. He once sat down to rest only to fall asleep and continue his dictation, which a secretary duly recorded for posterity (Carruthers, 1990, p. 7). Carl G. Jung (1963) found himself drafting a series of strange fantasies during his self-analysis. He wondered at the time "What am I really doing?", for surely there was nothing here of a clearly scientific nature. Whereupon a *feminine* voice from within said "It is art" (p. 185). Jung went on to challenge and carry on a tumultuous debate with what he found to be an opinionated female identity speaking from within his psyche. Jean Piaget (1973) could recall very clearly an incident that occurred when he was about 5 years old. It seems he was the target of a kidnapping, but thanks to the bravery of his nanny, who was attending to him at the time, they fought the thief off. Piaget retained a "very precise, very detailed, and very lively memory" (p. 143) of this harrowing experience into his adulthood—even after it was established by a letter of confession from the nanny that it had never happened.

It is often dramatic events like these that attract people to the study of psychology and related disciplines. There is a fascination with such unusual and atypical forms of behavior. The basic dynamic going on in such events is presumably not consciousness, but unconsciousness or the so-called influence of the unconscious on the conscious. If I had begun this chapter with a handful of experiences drawn from routine consciousness, like feeling an itch on one's nose or deciding after some deliberation to take up tennis, it would lack the dramatic "hook" through which I hoped to "reel-in" the reader's interest—and I might add, the reader's *conscious* interest. But if the interested reader fails to appreciate that a hook has been put in place, can one say that he or she is actually conscious of what is occurring? Maybe it is unconsciousness that is being reeled-in. This contrast between consciousness and unconsciousness is not simply a play on words. Consciousness somehow delimits the meaning of unconsciousness, and vice versa. There is an implicit tie here, a dimension of meaning that reflects unity; but, along with this unity, there is also an opposing difference in meaning that must not be overlooked.

Chapter 1 consists of two broad sections. The first section takes up a thematic survey of the various meanings that have been attributed to consciousness as well as several important technical terms that the reader must grasp in order to tackle the intricacies of the subject matter in the chapters to follow. The second section of Chapter 1 presents four grounds on which any explanation of consciousness may be positioned, either singly or in combination. I will be selecting one of these grounds on which to make my case, but I shall confront the other groundings at various points as well. It is important to know precisely where we stand at the outset, and a clear recognition of our ground will enlighten the effort to follow.

THE MEANINGS OF CONSCIOUSNESS:
A THEMATIC

No concept in psychology or psychiatry enjoys (or suffers) greater ubiquity than consciousness, whose meaning regularly bumps into itself masquerading as insight, intention, choice, regression, suggestion, possession, and a host of other terms framed to capture the psychic life of human beings. Due to this multiplicity of usage I am forced to undertake the study of consciousness thematically. Thus, if I hope to clarify our understanding, I must find some way in which to limit the coverage of the themes that might otherwise be considered. More of this later. For now, I want simply to survey the major themes that have been thrust before readers when consciousness is under consideration. Combined with this thematic overview, I will introduce several conceptual issues that necessarily arise in the study of consciousness and that I will be making use of throughout this book.

Awareness and Its Causes

The most common theme in the literature on consciousness is undoubtedly that of *awareness* (Farthing, 1992, p. 6; Klein, 1984, p. 6; Natsoulas, 1983, p. 29). To be aware of something going on, either inside or outside of one's bodily locus, is to be conscious. The precise way in which we are to think about awareness is not always clarified in such definitions. For example, there is the problem of a false awareness, as in "seeing" the proverbial ghost when passing a graveyard after dark (White, 1964, p. 60). Is this an awareness? A clinician might consider the ghost to be a projection from the unconscious. But how can the unconscious—presumably unaware to begin with—bring on such a ghostly awareness? Another source of awareness is said to be the emotions. Langer (1964) thought of consciousness as the general mode and depth of feeling that "marks a creature's mental activities as a whole at a given time" (p. 20). Clinicians refer to this total awareness as being "in touch" with one's feelings—or one's genuine feelings, because false awareness of an emotional mood can also occur. But does the person decide what is a genuine mood consciously or unconsciously?

This reference to decision brings up our first conceptual issue in the study of consciousness: *causation.* We must broaden our understanding of what a cause "is" because since about the 17th century a narrowing of this concept from four to one or two meanings has taken place. Although Aristotle (384–322 BC) was not the first to use these four meanings, he was the first to list and name them as the *material, efficient, formal,* and *final* causes. In broad terms, materials are the substances of things, as in bronze statues or silver bowls. Efficiency effects have to do with change—how things move or come to rest. Forms are discernible patterns—such as the pattern typifying the essence of all those figures known as a triangle, including their geometrical measurements. And finality is the intention, purpose, or reason why anything exists or is taking place. The word we translate from the Greek as cause is *aitiá,* which conveys the idea of responsibility, so that in following Aristotle's usage we would be trying to assign responsibility for why a specific item existed or one event rather than another occurred. Such attributions necessarily take us into the question of *determinism.* The word "determine" devolves from a Latin root meaning "to set limits" on what exists or takes place. Each cause creates its own type of determinism (Aristotle, 1952e, p. 128).

To concretize the causal meanings a bit, I will analyze the game of billiards in terms of such determinants. A *material cause* sets limits on the substantial utensils used in this game, such as the resiliency of the cushions on the billiard table. If such cushions were stuffed with straw they would greatly limit the rolling about of the billiard balls on the table. A rubber cushion is much preferred for it makes many more banking alternatives possible. The *efficient cause* sets limits on the directions that a thrust of motion takes, as when the cue ball, impelled by the player's cue stick, connects with yet another ball being targeted. This efficient-cause impetus is therefore responsible for why the targeted ball moves in one direction on the table rather than the many other ways that it might have moved (reflecting thereby a limiting determination).

But there is the game itself to consider, with certain rules to be followed, a scoring procedure, and so on. The *formal cause* is responsible for the abstract pattern known as the game. Aristotle thought of the formal cause as the *essence* of anything, a difficult notion to circumscribe. The essence is often captured by a distinctive style or shape, which is another way of referring to pattern, order, or organization—in other words, to formal causation. We do no great violence to Aristotle's theory by saying that the way in which billiards is played—as opposed to the playing of tennis, for example—is determined by the formal-causation of its rules.

There is also the fact that people play with the intention to win the game. To describe the game of billiards completely I would have to take such motivation into consideration. This feature of the game, which gets at the reason why it exists in the first place, is what Aristotle named the *final cause*. A final cause is *that* (reason, intent, hope, wish, etc.) *for the sake of which* something now exists or is in the process of being carried out or completed. The Greeks referred to a reason or intention as involving the *end* being sought (e.g., to win the game). The Greek word for end is *telos*; therefore any account taking the goal, purpose, intention, aim—that is, "end"—into consideration is called a *teleological* (or *telic*) explanation. A *teleology* is a theoretical explanation that employs final causes. So, the players purposely limit what takes place by accepting and sticking to the rules (though these can be changed). Their wishes and intentions are responsible for the outcome as the game of billiards is carried to its conclusion.

Now, what kind of determinism occurs when the person is aware? What cause would be responsible for awareness? I believe that we should be looking along the lines of formal and final causation to explain awareness. These two conceptualizations go together. As a matter of fact, the formal cause is a necessary (but not sufficient) ingredient for final causation to occur. The strategy carried out by the billiards player is a formal cause; and the fact that the player behaves for the sake of *this* strategy—as opposed to *that* different strategy—is a final cause. It is impossible to think of a "pure" final cause that is not preliminarily dependent upon some formal cause pattern like this. If I now decide to get up from my desk in the study and have something to eat in the kitchen, there is a patterned layout "for the sake of which" I will move in order to carry out my intention. The door out of this room is "over there" and not "over here." I am aware of this patterning and so I leave the room successfully. This is how I understand awareness: it has something to do with teleological actions like intentions or purposes.

However, traditional psychological explanation has been almost exclusively of a material- and an efficient-cause variety. Stimulus–response (S-R) psychology is an efficient-cause explanation, and the same goes for modern computer analogues (see Rychlak, 1991). The stimulus acts as an antecedent trigger that brings about the response in strictly an efficient-cause manner, like a first billiard ball colliding with a second (inputs and outputs of computer models work the same way). Given this scenario, it is not surprising to find S-R psychologists referring to conscious awareness as "a process which intervenes between stimuli and responses" (Spielberger, 1962, p. 76). This is like saying that the process of awareness intervenes between efficient causes and their effects. It is almost routine today to hear that consciousness is that which "mediates our experience" (Baenninger, 1994, p. 806). This concept of intervention or mediation suggests both the notion of a clear signal and the previously established store of responses having relevance to this clear signal. Signal awareness is like a sunny day, with no fog. On a clear day, when the stimulus is presented it can easily be picked up by the receptor. If awareness is present the connection between stimuli in experience and responses being made by the mechanism (person) are sure to relate. Without awareness we have a foggy day and such connection is not as likely to come about.

To give an example of such awareness, when my telephone rings I must be conscious of this stimulus in order to respond appropriately. I must be aware of what the ring signifies, and what to do when I hear the stimulating ring. I pick up the receiver and begin talking, which involves other mediators such as the language and attitudes that I have been shaped into outputting at times like this. The person on the other end of the line continues to send stimuli my way, and I reply in ongoing conversation. This continuing facilitation of stimulus-to-response is said to be consciousness. But just because I am conscious of what is occurring and what to do about it does not mean that I am behaving teleologically. According to traditional S-R explanations, all I am doing is responding and mediating without intention or purpose. Behavior is exclusively dependent on material and efficient causation. There is no formal–final causation to consider as a basic determiner of my actions on the behavioristic or S-R model.

Both Process and Content

Another theme in this literature holds that "consciousness always has contents" (Farthing, 1992, p. 7). This is actually a recognition that the term consciousness can take on two different meanings—referring to either a process or a content. By a *process* I mean a discernible, repeatable course of action on the basis of which some item under description and explanation is believed to be sequentially patterned. By a *content* I mean an ingredient that is produced, conveyed, or otherwise employed by a process. To use a physical example, William Harvey (1578–1657) discovered that the vascular process takes a circular route in which the heart's muscles provide the motor power to pump various contents around the body through the arteries, veins, and capillaries. Blood's constituents like white and red corpuscles are the primary contents being pumped, of course, but wastes, foreign proteins, clots, and other unwanted contents are also circulated through the vascular system.

A mental process might be a stereotyped line of reasoning in which, given that certain presumptive meanings are believed, certain predictable inductions or deductions are automatically drawn. These meanings would represent the contents, or distinctive ingredients that have been produced, conveyed, or otherwise employed by this reasoning process. We call these meanings *ideas*, and they can change from one line of thought to another. Indeed, this is the crucial difference between all processes and their contents: *Contents change, but the processes that create or employ them remain the same.* We might be thinking about billiards one moment and the eating of a banana split in the next. The study of consciousness as a process would therefore involve trying to understand how things "work" in this process without specifying the meanings or actions involved in such working.

This process–content distinction has relevance for the question of awareness. When we are aware of something taking place does this refer to the process of consciousness, or to the contents being conveyed by consciousness? It could be that the question of awareness is irrelevant when we are speaking of the process of consciousness. We do not have to be aware of our digestive process to know that certain foods (contents) just do not mix well. All we need do is concentrate on the contents eaten and the digestive process will take care of itself. Analogically, all we need do is concentrate on the ideas (meanings) passing before us and the consciousness process conveying these meanings will take care of itself (totally outside of our awareness).

Intentionality and Selectivity

A familiar theme in the literature of consciousness suggests that it is closely tied to *intentions*, including the selection of alternatives. Searle (1985) has noted how it is often impossible to "carve off" (p. 34) a conscious state from the intentionality of a belief or a desire. Consciousness is thus invariably "about something" (Farthing, 1992, p. 6); it involves preferences, desires, and aspirations that are being pursued. The teleologist views these as ends "for the sake of which" behavior is selectively intended. Another word for this capacity to influence one's behavior intentionally is *agency.* The agent is an organism that behaves or believes in conformance with, in contradiction to, in addition to, or without regard for environmental or biological determinants. In more popular parlance, human agency is called *freedom of the will* or simply *free will.*

As I explained in the Introduction, the traditionally mechanistic psychologist, relying on material and efficient causation, would not be so ready to admit agency into her or his description of human beings. The fact that a person's consciousness may influence the direction of behavior is interpreted by the mechanist as the person using language in mediational fashion. Human beings can use words as signs to represent items in their experience, particularly those that involve pleasure or pain. Language provides a rich storehouse of word-signals, ready for use as mediators or so-called discriminative stimuli, permitting the individual to operantly respond in a manner that appears to be intentional although it is not (Skinner, 1974, p. 76). Former word-responses made to stimuli—in efficient-cause fashion—can be retained in memory and serve as cues in the present. Dollard and Miller (1950) called these previously learned words *cue-producing responses* and referred glowingly to their utility in behavior:

> Through their capacity to mediate learned drives and rewards, verbal and other cue-producing responses [words, statements, images, etc.] enable the person to respond foresightfully to remote goals [pseudo-intention]. They free him from the control of stimuli immediately present in the here and now, provide a basis for sustained interest and purpose, and are the basis for the capacity for hope and reassurance. (p. 219)

To give an example of this theorizing, if a woman knows that every time there is a man to compete against she tries harder than when there is a woman, she is manifesting this "insight" based on cue-producing responses serving as mediators. She tells herself something like "I just try harder when men are my competition," and is therefore conscious of what is taking place. She might also grasp this difference in her effort through non-verbal imagery (e.g., seeing herself behave differently in such mixed-gender situations without framing actual words). But if she cannot use words (cue-producing responses) or images to frame this relationship between the gender of her competition and the motivation to try harder, we witness unconscious behavior. There is simply no mediation taking place in her course of behavior at this point (Dollard & Miller, 1950, pp. 198, 250). The driving force is there, but the woman is unaware of its presence. An observer can see and record her performance differential between the sexes quite readily. Her consciousness or lack of it is irrelevant so far as her measurable performance is concerned.

Identity, Selfhood, and Introspective Explanation

A theme closely related to intentionality is that of identity and self-hood, concepts that are unessential to mechanists but vital to teleologists. After all, if there is an intention being expressed it would seem to follow that there is an identity or self expressing it. As John Dewey (1859–1952) said: "The self not only exists, but may know that it exists; psychical phenomena are not only facts, but they are facts of consciousness" (Dewey, 1893, p. 1). A self that knows it exists is manifesting a capacity for *reflectivity* or *reflexivity*; that is, it can turn back and consciously observe itself thinking as well as examine the assumptions of its thought contents. Terms other than self may be used to describe this psychic identity, such as ego, subject, the person, the individual, and so on—all of which stand for an originating source that frames or construes intentions (i.e., thought contents). And as this construing continues, there is a certain knowledge (awareness) to be gained reflexively about the identity involved. There is a "recognition by the thinking subject of its own acts and affections" (Natsoulas, 1983, p. 35).

When reflexivity is in the picture, a distinction may be drawn between consciousness and awareness. This difference is suggested in the root meanings of these words. The word *consciousness* is from the Latin *conscio* and *scire*, meaning "to know." Awareness, on the other hand, takes Anglo-Saxon roots from the word *waere*, meaning "cautious" or "watchfully alert." Awareness thus suggests a more expectant, evaluative concern, possibly transcending the known to imply what might yet occur or is about to be realized, recognized, or admitted. If this concern were directed inwardly, to the above mentioned source of intentionality, we would probably be referring to what is commonly termed the *conscience*. Conscience and consciousness actually share theological origins, a significant fact that I will enlarge upon in Chapter 3 (Potts, 1980). As Natsoulas (1983) correctly observed, "Properly qualified, the Latin *conscio* served frequently in speaking of *sharing guilty knowledge with oneself about oneself*" (p. 23; italics in original). Whether it is at ease or sensing guilt, the conscience seems dependent upon awareness. As Eric Fromm (1962) once said, "how can I have a good conscience if I am not aware of anything" (p. 52).

An important issue arising here has to do with the perspective or point of view taken by any explanation. There are two contrasting slants that we can take in framing an explanation of anything that we come upon in life. We can look "at" the item or "with" it. When we look at it, we take the vantage point of an observer and offer our descriptive analysis in third-person terms (e.g., "that, it, him, them, their, etc."). This is not just a matter of grammar. We are taking an *extraspective* (moving outward) approach to the understanding and description of whatever it is that we are out to explain. We make no effort to understand or explain things from the perspective of our targeted item of interest. The physical sciences (at least since the 17th century) have taken the extraspective perspective exclusively. In accounting for how it is that the earth circumnavigates the sun each 24-hour period, the physical scientist is not going to suggest explanations from the point of view of either the earth or the sun. Forces in a field engulfing both of these bodies are sufficient to account for their patterned relationship.

When we now turn to an account written from the perspective of the object of our interest, we frame our concepts in an *introspective* manner (moving inward). This results in first-person terminology ("I, me, us, we, our, etc."). We no longer limit our meanings to terms that exclusively favor the observer's point of view. We draw our terminology from the convenience of the item under consideration. The old adage that we should not judge someone until we have walked a mile in his or her shoes is framed introspectively. We must see things from within a person's life context. Once again, this is not a question of mere grammatical usage. Modern psychologists who consider themselves phenomenologists or existentialists frequently criticize their colleagues for refusing to consider the point of view of the human beings they study, preferring instead to foist pet theories with arbitrary measurements onto experimental participants (Valle & Halling, 1989). This is an example of introspectively oriented psychologists criticizing their extraspectively oriented colleagues for the mechanistic concepts used by the latter to explain human behavior. The philosopher and ethicist, Charles Taylor (1989), brought the identical issue to light in the following, where he is discussing the unwarranted dismissal of important terms by an observer regarding a human being's need for self-understanding:

> What are the requirements of "making sense" of our lives? These requirements are not yet met if we have some theoretical language which purports to explain behaviour from the observer's standpoint but is of no use to the agent in making sense of his own thinking, feeling, and acting. Proponents of a reductive theory may congratulate themselves on explanations which do without these or those terms current in ordinary life, e.g., "freedom" and "dignity," . . . But even if their third-person [extraspective] explanations were more plausible than they are, what would be the significance of this if the terms prove ineradicable in first-person, non-explanatory uses? Suppose I can convince myself that I can explain people's behaviour as an observer without using a term like "dignity." What does this prove if I can't do without it as a term in my deliberations about what to do, how to behave, how to treat people, my questions about whom I admire, with whom I feel affinity, and the like? (p. 57)

Now, what do we make of our concept of self or selfhood in light of these contrasting theoretical perspectives? The word *self* draws on Anglo-

Saxon roots meaning that there is a *sameness* in the behavior of a person over time. Looked at from the introspective perspective, the following case might be made: We are conscious of having a self because we find "ourselves" showing up each morning as we step out into the world among other selves (who contrast with us in various ways), and our *memory* establishes that we are confronting the same life scenario today that faced us yesterday (developing out of an even more remote continuity). It is important to stress memory because this concept frequently enters the discussion on the assumption that to be conscious requires that one remember what has occurred. Many of these memories are of "our" responsibilities. There are challenges to consider and choices to be made involving both positive and negative possibilities for the future. There are doubts and indecisions shot through all of this. We are now clearly walking in our own shoes.

On the other hand, an extraspective explanation of our behavior might suggest that the word "self" is just another one of those mediating cue-producing word responses that have been fed into the mechanical sequence of efficient causation that makes up behavior. The human being, the person under such "shaping" from the cultural environment, learns various words enabling him or her to speak about such things as selves as well as other supposedly teleological concepts like purpose and intention. Later, when these environmentally shaped people are seen behaving and giving reasons for their behavior, we find them using such teleological word-meanings to account for why they behave as they do. Even though they use words having the "sound" of conscious intentionality and decision making, the truth is they are actually behaving in efficient-cause fashion thanks to these now mediating cue-producing responses. These words run off mechanically; they are not expressions of a person who has the telic capacity to self-reflexively examine things and make decisions free of such efficient-cause determinism.

Harré (1984) has a view along this line, holding that the self is nothing but a linguistic convention. Harré suggests that people believe they have selves after being taught words framing a theory of personhood by their culture. From such learned word-contents they fashion a belief in their own selfhood (p. 214). The self thus represents more of an effect than a cause of anything in the behavioral realm. Consciousness is fashioned through the same cultural influence:

> Consciousness ... is not some unique state, but is the possession of certain grammatical models for the presentation to oneself and others of what one knows by inter- and intrapersonal perception. These models provide the structures by which I can know that which I am currently feeling, thinking, suffering, doing, and so on, that is, they provide the wherewithal for an organization of knowledge as mine. (p. 214; italics in original)

Despite my assertions to the contrary, Harré would doubtless consider the distinction between intro- and extraspection to be grammatical in nature. He would understand these concepts as mediating contents that I had learned in the acculturation process. My view is that the perspective taken in framing an explanation of behavior is up to the theorist in question, who can formulate contents reflecting either a first- or third-person rendering. In Chapter 2 I will outline the learning process that makes such personal choices possible. I will also return to the role of language and cultural influence on consciousness in Chapter 9 (where I will look at Harré's social constructionism in greater detail).

Lockean Versus Kantian Reflexivity

There is an important sub-theme of the identity or selfhood thematic that I would like to take up at this point. On first consideration, it might seem that self-reflectivity (or reflexivity) has to be introspectively formulated, but actually this is not true. We can contrast the philosophers John Locke (1632–1704) and Immanuel Kant (1724–1804) on this point. Locke's (1690/1952) reflection was termed an *internal sense* (p. 121), paralleling the sensory inputs passively received and recorded from external sources—as when the retina of the eye is stimulated via some light source to see a hand moving in front of it. Through such passive observation we could learn, for example, how our beating heart works by X-raying its ongoing process. We could even tape an electronic picture of the heart as it beats "over there" in our bodily functioning, enabling us to view it repeatedly and in great detail. Although Locke held that the mind carries on thinking, doubting, believing, and reasoning, these processes are made known to us by looking "at" them as they take place, analogous to observing the beating heart. We do not "look with" or "look through" these processes. Lockean reflectivity is therefore an extraspective viewing of an efficiently caused thought process as it takes place. What is learned in such extraspective observation is that thought is continually directed by cultural shapings such as imitating what others do, or using certain linguistic conventions to characterize things.

On the other hand, in his understanding of reflectivity, Kant (1788/ 1952) invites an introspective exploration because there is always a fundamental implication here that what is perceived depends on a framing point of view (p. 99). We are always looking "with" or "through" an introspective process—grasping its meaningful "slant" on things. Lockean reflection emphasizes knowing what *is* taking place, not what might *otherwise* be taking place, all circumstances remaining the same. Kant makes it clear that thought involves taking a position and that a reflexive intelligence knows that positions can be transcended and examined pro and con—and even reformulated without additional influences from sensory input (as the Lockean formulation would require). Thus, taking in an internal sensory experience by observing the mind reasoning "over there" can be instructive, but it does not capture what is meant by an introspective formulation of reflectivity. To give a concrete example of this point, the social-learning theorist Bandura (1979) once defined reflectivity as follows:

> There is no great mystery about what *reflective* means. Reflective thought refers to thoughts about one's thoughts. By operating on what they know, people can derive knowledge about things that extend beyond their experiences and generate innovative courses of action. (p. 439; italics in original)

This is an extraspective formulation of reflexivity (I will use this latter spelling henceforth). The definition of "thoughts about one's thoughts" fits the Lockean view better than the Kantian, suggesting as it does a kind of mediation going on within the processing of ideas. Locke would have considered such thoughts about thoughts to be complex ideas made up of simpler ideas. Asking oneself "Let's see, what did I decide to do about this problem last night?" is a thought about a thought—a mental effort to put oneself back on track. But there is no real sense of a transcendence taking place here, an examination of the sort, "Now that I have mulled it over, that decision last night had some flaws" or "Why do I always cook up these stupid problems when they just bring me headaches?" The essential point of a concept like reflexivity is to capture the thinking organism as central to the thought process, and as always capable of questioning, rejecting, or seeing alternatives to what is being thought about.

Sometimes there are no real thoughts about other thoughts going on, yet an unexpressed alternative is making itself known to the person. People occasionally know that even though everything appears all right, something is wrong, or something is missing. This is not a question of looking "at" anything taking place, but sensing that an alternative understanding of things is likely to occur. People also know that what they are doing is not necessarily the only or even the best alternative. They can sense a probable error even though they cannot say why. We know from studies on children as early as the first grade that they can distinguish between test items that they are almost certainly answering correctly and those that they are probably answering incorrectly (Pressley, Borkowski, & Schneider, 1987). The latter are not always pure guesses; it is a matter of knowing when an error is more or less probable. Some children are incapable of making this metacognitive judgment, of course.

Although humans can report on such evaluations of their efforts, they do not actually have thoughts about such thoughts until they reflexively ask themselves "I wonder why I can sometimes tell when an answer is either right or probably wrong." Children may not pose such questions, but adults surely do. And only a self-reflexive and potentially transcending intellect *knows that it does not know* and hence that something other than what is taking place could (might, should, etc.) be taking place. I believe that only an introspective formulation can genuinely capture this kind of self-conscious experience.

The Collective

By acknowledging the tie between consciousness and conscience I have already begun to address the fact that a collective theme is to be found in this literature. Both guilt and shame issue from actions that we have carried out in relation to others. We blush or feel uneasy because we know that someone else knows or may discover our transgression, awkwardness, or vulnerability. There is a collective awareness into which our personal awareness invariably feeds. Probably the most pronounced depiction of a collective consciousness is Thomas Hobbes's *Leviathan* (1651/1952), in which the state is pictured as a huge, artificial person made up of many other people. Hobbes (1588–1679) interpreted consciousness as follows: "When two or more men know of one and the same fact, they are said to be *conscious* of it one to another; which is as much as to know it together" (p. 65).

Emphasis is often placed on such sharing of knowledge, thereby heightening the identity or consciousness of a certain group. For example, Marxian theory holds that there is a social process that is moving toward an inevitable end, whether or not the individuals caught up in this movement are conscious of it (Marx, 1952a, p. 10). But, at the same time, to facilitate the revolutionary changes called for in the class struggle, raising the proletariat's class consciousness is salutary (p. 63). This matter of "raising the consciousness" of a collective (e.g., racial- or sexual-group) identity has been widely disseminated and often serves today as the rationale for holding public demonstrations. We shall take a closer look at the relationship between personal and collective consciousness in Chapter 9.

Psychology has many sociocultural interpretations of consciousness. Harré's (1987) cultural theory of the self is of this nature. An even better example is Asch's (1952) *social consciousness*, which he viewed as functioning interpersonally depending on the participants in the relationship (p. 252). Asch wanted to avoid human descriptions tied solely to individuals, whom he felt were being pictured as isolated from one another, but he also rejected notions of the group mind. Social consciousness is born when two people take cognizance of each other in an interpersonal context, and perceiving that they share this common environment, interact with mutual expectancies concerning what will follow (pp. 161–162).

Sometimes, people are described as thinking collectively in what might be termed an unconscious manner. Jung held that this was the natural state of primitive humanity: "Primitive man does not think his thoughts, they simply *appear* in his mind. Purposive and directed thinking is a relatively late human achievement" (1958, p. 312; italics in original). Primitives thus projected their emotions onto what they took to be a reality, and such moods were readily swayed by the group. In this sense, the primitive's thinking was "being thought" by the group rather than personally. There were no ego-identities at this early date in human development. In effect, primitives were perpetually unconscious. When they began to recognize the contribution to experience made by their emotions, primitives moved from an exclusively collective identity to an individual identity living within a collective. This was the birth of consciousness, which retained both a collective and a personal aspect (I will revisit Jungian theory in Chapters 4 and 9).

The question of whether collective influences are always unconscious naturally leads to a discussion of normative influences. Do people conform to norms consciously? There are also more specialized normative influences in the approach taken by those who work in some realm of human endeavor such as science. The eminent historian of psychology, Edwin Boring (1950), relied on the concept of the *Zeitgeist* to present his analysis of such an influence on his discipline:

> Discovery and its acceptance are ... limited also by the habits of thought that pertain to the culture of any region and period, that is to say, by the *Zeitgeist*: an idea too strange or preposterous to be thought in one period of western civilization may be readily accepted as true only a century or two later. (p. 3)

This would imply that a Zeitgeist is similar to Kuhn's (1970) *paradigm*, which is a universally recognized formulation that has been empirically proven so that it now acts as a model for scientists, who seek to flesh out all of its implications (p. viii). New paradigms, which may negate older models, arise at various times in history to bring about alterations in "the historical perspective of the community" (p. ix). The shift from the Ptolemaic geocentric universe to the Copernican heliocentric universe is an example of such a change in paradigmatic formulation. Although dramatically changing the worldview, this shift took place entirely consciously—but not without overt suppression by Ptolemaic adherents, as when Galileo was forced to recant his Copernican views while sentenced to house arrest by the churchmen of the Inquisition.

Boring's understanding of the Zeitgeist is therefore as a conscious influence, a habitual style of thinking being carried on in one age when it might never have been entertained in another. But the history of this concept reveals that it was introduced by Romanticist sociocultural theorists of the 19th century who thought of it as an *unconscious* influence on the thinking of the collective. The Romanticists were revolting against the rationalistic social philosophies of their era, arguing that everything influencing thought cannot be pinpointed through such concrete logical reasoning. Becker and Barnes (1952) summed things up this way:

> The basic premise of the historical philosophy of Romanticism was the doctrine of the gradual and unconscious nature of cultural evolution. The unique organic unity and development of all forms of national culture was stressed. There was a decided mystical strain in the thinking of the Romanticists; they maintained that the unconscious creative forces operated in a mysterious manner which defied rationalistic analysis. It was held that all were subject to the operation of these inscrutable forces of psychic power which went to make up the *Zeitgeist* (the spirit of the age). (p. 487)

The historical origin of Zeitgeist would surely contradict Boring's interpretation of this concept. As a true "group mind" concept, the Zeitgeist is to be understood as influencing the thinking of a group unconsciously, similar to Jung's collective unconscious in the psychic life of the individual. Of course, Jung's theory holds that influences from the collective unconscious can be averted by the individual, who can "refuse to listen" (1953b, p. 81) to what is being suggested. This is not usually a wise choice, of course, because it frequently leads to interpersonal tension and ultimately some form of personal maladjustment. Jung had to find a way for the personal conscious to communicate with the collective unconscious. As our opening comments to this chapter indicate, he was successful in doing so by personifying his unconscious attitudes in the form of a female (a patient he was then seeing in therapy). But this female was actually an archetypal figure from his collective unconscious—his *anima*, or contrasexual identity—and he benefited from the turbulent exchange that followed. The Zeitgeist concept has no such techniques for putting its meaning in touch with the individual members of a collective. It functions supra-individually.

Wakeful Activity

Consciousness under this final thematic refers to the normal wakeful activity of a biological organism. This seems to be an unassailable distinction—consciousness is wakefulness and unconsciousness is loss of this state due to sleep, fainting, being drugged, suffering physical brain trauma, and so forth. But as we shall see in later chapters, things do not work out this clearly. To take just one example for now, if we can recall our dreams—or, more dramatically, if we can intentionally influence the course of our dreams while we are having them (see Chapter 8)—then how can we say that we are unconscious during sleep? Such recollections and thematic manipulations suggest consciousness. Note once again that memory plays a significant role in our assessment of consciousness.

Natsoulas (1983) observes that the heavily biological interpretation on which wakeful activity is based "seems to be the latest sense of the word [i.e., consciousness] to enter the English language" (p. 48). Of course, other terms may have been used for this meaning in ancient times. We know, for example, that memory—a term that we have seen winding its way into the interpretations of consciousness—was considered to have a biological basis. Galen (c. 130–200) placed memory in the posterior ventricle of the brain (Carruthers, 1990, p. 50). Biological interpretations of consciousness abound in modern times. Wakefulness is probably just as prevalent as awareness in today's theorizing on consciousness. Farthing (1992) notes that the meanings of consciousness as awareness and as wakefulness are not always consistent—as when one may be aware of a dream while in the unconscious state of sleep—and that consequently he avoids the latter usage in favor of the former (p. 8).

A classical definition within the current thematic is Hebb's (1972) suggestion that a person or animal is conscious when experiencing a "normal waking state and responsive to . . . [the] environment" (p. 248). Bunge (1980) advanced an even more explicitly biological definition of consciousness:

> We shall postulate that a conscious event is a brain activity consisting in monitoring (recording, analyzing, controlling, or keeping track of) some other brain activity, much as a voltmeter measures the electromotive force between two points of an electric network. . . . Conscious events are then activities of certain (probably rather large) neural systems. (p. 175)

Bunge distinguished between awareness and consciousness as follows: Awareness involves an organism registering what goes on or has happened to it in the environment (including its inner physical environment); consciousness involves the organism being aware of its own brain processes (p. 174). Thus, awareness is limited to sensation whereas consciousness requires that the organism have intelligence (p. 175). There is a definite Lockean formulation of reflexivity in this extraspective formulation of consciousness.

Bunge's introduction of sensation versus intelligence can be taken further, even into the question of animate versus inanimate life. That is, occasionally we run across the contrast of consciousness–unconsciousness versus nonconsciousness (Klein, 1984, p. 5). The inanimate objects of life—rocks and plants—are said to be *nonconscious*. But do plants, for example, have sensations? Tropisms suggest that they do, as when a sunflower follows the sun's path across the sky each day. Plant leaves shrink away from fire as if they were feeling great pain. Some people believe that plants have higher growth rate and longevity when they are treated as if they were conscious. Some even talk to their plants and play music for them.

I have introduced a number of descriptive terms that will play a vital role in the chapters to follow. There are many ways in which consciousness has been interpreted. Consciousness cannot really be separated from other issues of great significance in psychology, like the nature of selfhood, intentionality, interpersonal influence, conscience, and wakeful activity. Each of these issues brings its unique conceptual baggage to our journey of discovery and understanding. What can we say of consciousness that will satisfy our quest in terms of these diverse yet ramifying formulations? I have tried to find a way to organize this analysis of consciousness that will avoid the easy temptation to slip back and forth amidst what may be fundamentally unresolvable, hence confounding issues in our understanding of human behavior. To avoid this temptation, I will seek suitable ground on which to carry our work forward.

A LEVEL GROUND ON WHICH TO STAND

The Latin words from which "explanation" devolve are *ex* and *planare*, meaning "to make level or plain." This suggests bringing claims on knowledge down to a kind of rock-bottom "given" that is clear to everyone. This level grounding is common to all who participate in the exchange of ideas—reminding us of those entrepreneurs who talk about wanting a "level" playing field when they compete with others for access to a desirable market. The allusion to a market is not inappropriate here because there *is* a "market" for ideas in all realms of knowledge. Scholars compete to dominate such markets, "sell" their ideas, reap both financial and status rewards from appreciative "customers," and then celebrate their success as "idea merchants." But, as my thematic study suggests, there is no common playing field for those of us engaged in the examination of consciousness. Things are pretty muddled and overlapping in the theories here, and we are left wondering how to proceed.

Theory, Method, and Certainty

At this point I think I should draw the important distinction between a theory on the one hand and the method used to prove it on the other. A *theory* is a "series of two or more constructions (abstractions, concepts, items, images, etc.) that have been hypothesized, assumed, or even factually demonstrated to bear a certain relationship, one to the other" (Rychlak, 1988, p. 520). Hypothesizing that meticulousness in adulthood is due to a harsh toilet training in childhood is a Freudian theoretical tie of one concept (meticulousness) to another (toilet training). A *method* is the "means or manner of determining whether a theoretical construct or proposition is [held to be] true or false. . . . Methods are vehicles for the exercise of evidence" (pp. 515–516). How do we prove that meticulous adults have had a harsh toilet training in childhood?

Extensive philosophical analysis has pretty well established that there are two fundamental ways to prove anything, based upon contrasting interpretations of truth—*coherence* and *correspondence*. A theoretical claim may be said to be true if it hangs together clearly, is internally consistent, or fits smoothly into our initial assumptions (coherence). Alternatively, something is true if it meets with our repeated observations or ongoing experience even though we might not be able to say precisely "how" this observed regularity comes about (correspondence).

Correspondence tests are empirical in nature and are basic to the scientific method, resulting in what is called *validating evidence*. In contrast, a coherence test of plausibility relies on *procedural evidence* (Rychlak, 1981, p. 77). Plausibility and coherence are what we mean by common sense. Common sense dictates that if you walk out in the rain without appropriate protection you will get wet. In the final analysis, we all look for some commonsense grounding on which to frame our beliefs (i.e., our theories). We can appreciate that when scientists conduct experiments they are necessarily making preliminary selections as to the grounds on which their work is to be understood. Even the grounds that they may have considered and rejected are not therefore "wrong"—without assuming yet another ground on which to justify this negative evaluation (via procedural evidence). The ground provides a broad background within which several specific theories may be framed and tested.

Unfortunately, this very breadth of the ground ensures that a certain error of logic always hounds the scientific method. To state that "If my theory is correct, then the experimental data will array as I predict, in XYZ fashion," and find as predicted that the empirical data do indeed array in XYZ fashion, does not permit the scientist to conclude "My theory is *necessarily* correct!" To do so would be to commit the logical fallacy of *affirming-the-consequent* of an *If-then* line of reasoning. This would be like reasoning, "If a human being, then a mortal being" and, finding a mortal standing before one, concluding that this is necessarily a human (i.e., affirm the consequent or second major term of the initial proposition). It would be improper to conclude that this mortal being is *necessarily* human because many organisms other than humans are mortal—and could be standing before us. The meaning of mortal is quite broad. The fallacy of affirming-the-consequent stipulates the fact that it will always be possible for some other explanation to account for any empirically observed fact pattern.

This loss of certainty in validation is not fatal for the scientific method, of course. It has not prevented scientists from curing polio or putting people on the moon. It merely alerts us to the fact that some conceptualizer always has to make a decision as to which fundamental grounding will be used in the sequence of theory formation and testing.

The grounds are never "out there" in the hard data but "in here" as assumptive frameworks.

If we who theorize appreciate that we never attain certainty in validating our theories we will be in a better position to see that alternative groundings that explain such empirical evidence can be complementary. To *complement* is to fill out or make up for what is lacking in any theoretical understanding of a subject—including the explanation of data arraying in a predicted (expected, anticipated, etc.) XYZ fashion. I think history establishes a handful of grounds that can be used individually, yet serve a complementary role in theory generation and the empirical validation which follows. I would suggest four such grounds: *Physikos*, *Bios*, *Socius*, and *Logos*. This is not an exhaustive list. Other grounds might be fashioned in the future. But for now I believe that explanations of consciousness can employ a principle of complementarity relying on these four grounds (Rychlak, 1993).

Physikos

The *Physikos* ground is taken most directly from physical science, where an effort has been made to explain inanimate events in terms of energic processes, such as gravitation or conservation of energy (constancy). A ground cannot be considered a ground unless it has a distinctive process of this sort. It is the *process* that distinguishes one ground from another. Each process employs or produces distinctive contents, which are the items targeted for explanation. In physics or astronomy, for example, a basic process like gravitation suggests that some presumed attraction and action at a distance holds the planets in sequentially patterned orbits as they fall through space within force fields. The planets are contents within gravitation, targeted for explanation by this process—which could also be employed to explain raindrops falling from the sky (as other contents of this same process!). Indeed, the eminent behaviorist, Clark Hull (1884–1952) once referred to the "beautiful" raindrop analogy that his colleague Albert P. Weiss had coined:

> We may start with the assumption that every drop of rain in some way or other gets to the ocean. . . . Anthropomorphizing this condition we may say that it is the *purpose* of every drop of rain to get to the ocean. Of course, this only means that virtually every drop *does* get there eventually. . . . Falling from the cloud it may strike the leaf of a tree, and drop from one leaf to another until it reaches the ground. From here it may pass under or on the surface of the soil to a rill, then to a brook, river, and finally to the sea. Each stage, each fall from one leaf to the next, may be designated as a *means* toward the final end, the sea. . . . Human behavior is merely a complication of the same factors. (Hull, 1937, p. 2)

So here is an extraspectively framed, efficient-cause account of how human beings are moved by the same physical forces that bring rain droplets to earth. Little wonder that Hull could view consciousness as due to mediating, cue-producing responses that mechanically intervene between a stimulus and its response. He never for a moment considered behavior from the introspective perspective. This mechanistic bias was common among behaviorists. For example, John B. Watson (1878–1958), the oft-cited father of behaviorism, once said "*let us try to think of man as an assembled organic machine ready to run*" (1924, p. 216; italics in original). It is obviously difficult if not impossible to capture interpretations of consciousness as awareness, intentionality, or identity on the ground of the *Physikos*. This ground seems best suited to explanations of nonconsciousness.

Bios

Our next ground is closely related to the *Physikos* kind of explanation. The difference appears to be that the *Bios* explanation relates more specifically to animate life than does the *Physikos* explanation—although some theorists might dispute this. The *Bios* ground places emphasis on the physical substance of animate organisms. The processes of the *Bios* include things like genetics, physiology, and organic systems. In an article entitled "What Psychology Is About" the psychologist and brain scientist Donald Hebb (1974) stated flatly that "*Psychology is a biological science*" (p. 72; italics in the original). Hebb goes on to bring a *Socius* emphasis on his commentary relying primarily on Darwinian tenets to make this case, as well as on the fact that there is an interaction between heredity and environment in the organic development of human beings (p. 73). This interaction can be observed and described extraspectively because, so far as Hebb is concerned, "Introspection is a dead duck" (p. 73). Drawing on the wakeful-activity interpretation of consciousness, Hebb suggests that thought is a physically "integrative activity of the brain" (p. 75) that overrides reflexive responses to control behavior in ways other than through direct sensory stimulation. Hence, "Free will . . . has a physiological basis" (p. 75).

The great compatibility of *Physikos* and *Bios* grounds stems from the fact that both of these types of explanation rely heavily on processes of a material- and efficient-cause nature. Sometimes they even share the same process. For example, chemical reactions can take place in both of these realms. Any formal-cause patterning that might be used in *Physikos* or *Bios* theoretical explanations is reduced to such underlying considerations. Thus, the funnel cloud of a tornado has a distinctive pattern, but one that has been whipped-up from below by the material substances and energic forces of the natural environment. Without these material and efficient causes the funnel cloud would not exist. The circulatory system of a living organism is similarly constituted of tissues and fluids that are themselves built up—in material- and efficient-cause fashion—from individually discernible cells. British philosophy fostered this concept of an atomic substrate entering materially and energically into everything that exists. This atomic model has had immense influence on the development of psychology as a science and is readily identified in the theorizing of Hebb.

Technically, neither *Physikos* nor *Bios* explanations should admit of final-cause meanings. But here is where these two groundings occasionally part ways. Sometimes the theoretician relying on the *Bios* wishes to capture purpose in the animate behavior of living organisms. Although I do not believe that this kind of biologically oriented theorist ever really captures the teleology of a human being, there is at least the presumption that she or he is doing something of the sort. Often, such *Bios* formulations of a final-cause nature stem from the influence of Galenic medicine, which calls them *vitalisms*. Galen had suggested that there were God-created vital spirits, which were enlivening forces that interacted with the ebb and flow of blood to stimulate life and influence its course. Note that this is an extraspective teleological explanation in which the deity's will has presumably created and now regularly directs the biological realm's functioning through the instrumentality of material and efficient causation. Religionists also believe that the deity influences the course of physical events, but this is not predicated on some intrinsic vitalistic principle shot through all of material existence. It is just that a supreme being can intervene in anything, at any time.

I think it is fair to say that final-cause meanings are more likely to be considered relevant to a theorist relying on *Bios* than on *Physikos* grounds—simply because animate, biological organisms often seem to be working toward ends. Hull might not see this need for telic commentary in psychological theorizing, but I think we could cite the "purposive behaviorist," E. C. Tolman (1886–1959) as an example of someone who wanted to move toward a final-cause explanation while retaining his commitment to the *Bios* ground so precious to the scientific rigors of behaviorism (see Tolman, 1967).

Socius

Our next ground departs from the physical complexities we have been considering to view the person in terms of group relations and sociocultural influences. This is the *Socius* grounding of explanation in which the processes that are invoked include socialization, cultural shaping, historicism, and even political collectivism. Berger (1963) has drawn an interesting contrast between the famous sociologists Èmile Durkheim (1858–1917) and Max Weber (1864–1920). Durkheim stood more solidly on the *Socius* ground than Weber: "Durkheim emphasized that society is a phenomenon *sui generis*, that is, it confronts us with a massive reality that cannot be reduced to or translated into other terms" (p. 91; italics in original). The social order is entirely independent of the individual and cannot be explained in terms of the latter. Durkheim did not wish to see social explanations being tied to psychological theories of the person (p. 91). For Durkheim, the person is shaped by autonomous social forces that are beyond his or her influence. His concept of *anomie* (loss of normative influence) captures what happens to individual behavior when the structure of a social order breaks down, as in high-crime regions of a city. The focus here is primarily on the collective, which then secondarily influences the individual. Weber, on the other hand, was more psychologically oriented in his theorizing, and in his concept of *charisma* captures the reverse circumstance—of *certain* individuals influencing the collective (p. 128). Charismatic leaders—that is, individuals with an "extraordinary quality" giving them an almost magical power of influence over others (Bendix, 1962, p. 299)—not only create but regularly change the patterned order of the social system. Durkheim viewed such person-centered theorizing, however limited, as giving in to psychology. Berger (1963) has this to say about a seeming paradox between the individual as both socially influencing and influenced: "The Durkheimian and Weberian ways of looking at society are not logically contradictory. They are only antithetical since they focus on different aspects of social reality" (p. 128). I will return to the Weber–Durkheim divergence in Chapter 9 preliminary to taking an in-depth look at social constructionism.

Theories of collective influences tend to gravitate to the extraspective perspective. Probably the best example of such extraspection in psychology is the work of B. F. Skinner (1904–1990), whom we mentioned above. Skinner actually situated his theory on both a Darwinian *Bios* ground and a *Socius* ground. I will discuss this theory, contrasting it with Edelman's theory of natural selection in Chapter 5. Skinner (1971) spoke derisively of "autonomous man" (p. 19), for in his scheme of things all selective choices were carried out by a kind of Durkheimian social reality that "not only prods or lashes, it *selects*" (p. 18; italics in original). In fact, according to Skinner, "consciousness is a social product" (p. 192).

Of course, although Skinner places great emphasis on the collective his specific theory of learning focuses on the individual organism. The collective is required by Skinnerian learning theory because something outside of or other than the individual must shape her or his ongoing behavior. Skinner did not like to base explanations entirely on *Bios* groundings. He appreciated that there was always something going on inside the "black-box" person. But, he also believed that this was not the proper realm of study for the psychologist (Skinner, 1977). He liked to think of himself as a behavior analyst, and employed a sophisticated actuarian's outlook concerning the tracking and predicting of behavior. The *Socius* ground is widely used in psychology and related social sciences today (see Chapter 9). Actually, if one does not want to explain behavior on the basis of individual agents who are capable of self-direction and personal choice, then there are two possibilities open—either reduce the direction that behavior takes to biology (genes, etc.) or to the supra-individual shaping forces of society. For those behaviorists who like Skinner do not wish to speculate on biological mechanisms per se, the only route open is to become social psychologists. And so many of them have.

Logos

The final ground on which theories are based may be called the *Logos*, which deals with the patterned order (and disorder) of experience. The word "logos" devolves from the Greek meaning *word*, but also conveys the meanings of *reason*, *speech*, *definition*, and *principle* (Reese, 1980, p. 314). Heraclitus used the term in 500 BC to describe what he took to be a kind of shaping power—a power to pattern events—occurring in the universe analogous to the reasoning power of the human being. Natural events were patterned and continually repatterned into similarities, differences, opposites, and so on. The *Logos* obviously promotes the meaning of formal causation, and this patterned order can be captured either extraspectively or introspectively. This is a unique characteristic of the *Logos*: It is the only one of the four grounds that readily adapts to the introspective as well as the extraspective theoretical perspective.

An independent universe moving in patterned order is an extraspective formulation of the *Logos*. One could ask "Is this order fundamental to reality, or is it the result of some other, more basic influence?" Traditional Newtonian science had the efficient cause at the base of all experience, so that patterning was the "effect" of such underlying, thrusting "causes" issuing from a palpable, *Physikos* grounding (Rychlak, 1994, pp. 6, 27). Motion was thus basic to pattern—as in the example of the funnel cloud of a tornado taking its shape through colliding air pressures and material particles. But modern science has found it necessary to replace efficient causation at the base of reality with formal causation. Subatomic physics was the first area of extraspective investigation to suggest that pattern may be basic to motion rather than vice versa. Thus, Niels Bohr (1885–1962) concluded that no mechanical (i.e., efficient cause) explanation of the stability of an atom's structure can be given (1934, p. 40). We must rely on mathematical approximations of actions that are decidedly *not* like the Newtonian efficient causes. And as for the material-cause substances of an atom's structure, Werner Heisenberg (1901–1976) had this to say: "In modern quantum theory there can be no doubt that the elementary particles will finally also be mathematical *forms*" (Feuer, 1974, p. 166; italics added).

This extraspective commentary along *Logos* lines has become the standard fare of modern science, where efficient and material causation are not ignored, but neither do they have the status that they once did as basic explanations (see the overview of scientific experimentation in Chapter 3). As for some more recent manifestations of *Logos* theorizing in science we can point to the theoretical physicist, David Bohm (1987), who postulated an "implicate order" (p. 14) in events that functions both in subatomic fields and in the functioning of human reasoning. The mathematician-physicist, Roger Penrose (1989) has also suggested that consciousness is a product of some quantum patterning process. Although such extraspective formulations grounded in the *Logos* are important, I do not believe that they will provide a satisfactory understanding of the kind of consciousness that we all sense in our daily lives.

For the latter, more personally psychological experience, we must turn to the introspective theoretical perspective. When the psychologist, Franz Brentano (1838–1917) criticized natural scientists for not capturing the true nature of the *mental act* (1874/1973, pp. 98, 100) he was leveling an introspectively framed criticism at the Newtonians of his day. Brentano used the word consciousness as synonymous with mental act because he felt that both of these concepts get at the intentionality of human reasoning (p. 102). The mental act was Brentano's process, to be used in framing explanations on the basis of a *Logos* ground. Human intelligence seeks relational patterns leading to meaningful ends. We rely on the four directions of the compass to locate our position on a trip across strange lands to find an interesting tourist attraction. Indeed, the very concepts of *intellect* and *intelligence* take Latin roots from "perceiving" or "gathering together" the various (introspectively understood) relations that occur among and between life experiences, resulting in patterned meanings having implications as well as the knowledge to make choices among them.

The personality theorist, George Kelly (1905–1967), named his process *construction* or *construing* (1955, pp. 50–55), theorizing here on the ground of an introspectively conceived *Logos* in which constructs were said to be patterned by the person from contrasting elements. If a young girl finds her teacher to be just as devious as her mother is, and this pattern of behavior is the direct opposite of her best friend who is always open and sincere, she might well frame a construct of "sneakiness" based on this contrast. This dimensional contrast might then be used to assess and categorize others for the rest of her life as either sneaky or sincere. Of course, if her evaluations went the other way she might have framed a construct of "sincerity" that would place her friend at this end of the contrasting dimension and her mother and teacher at the other. This conceptual alignment of judged behavior is not precisely a stereotype, because it is a unique or subjective mental formulation framed and used by an individual. Social stereotypes may not be initially framed by the person holding them, who has been taught these biasing outlooks by others (possibly requiring a *Socius* explanation).

As I noted in the Introduction to this volume, modern physical scientists have become just as aware of something like an introspectively conceived *Logos* in their work as have psychologists like Brentano or Kelly. Physicists now refer to themselves as "participators" (Zukav, 1979, p. 29) in the study of external reality. What physical scientists have to offer as participators is their framing assumptions, their points of view, and their logical ordering of the material under study. This is what Albert Einstein (1879–1955) was getting at when he wrote the following: "Experience remains, of course, the sole criterion of the physical utility of a mathematical construction. But the creative principle resides in mathematics. In a certain sense, therefore, I hold it true that pure thought can grasp reality, as the ancients dreamed" (Einstein, 1934, p. 18).

CONCLUDING COMMENT

The thematic survey has surely shown *consciousness* is not easily pinned down. We may begin a study of consciousness with meanings like alertness and vigilance in mind, but very quickly such intimations dissolve into a host of unexpected but highly relevant considerations. We will have to decide what sort of causation is involved, whether we are faced with a process, a content, or both, and assess the desirability of thinking about consciousness from either an introspective or an extraspective stance. There is the important matter of the ground on which to situate our understanding. Add to this the need to take a position on the question of human identity and agency as opposed to some entirely mechanical social manipulation or biological reduction and we have arrived at what the old movie comedian, Oliver Hardy, would have called a "fine mess."

But we need not despair. The challenge of understanding the broad range of consciousness can be achieved. It was the force of historical commentary and speculation regarding this concept, the mixture of different theories for different purposes, that put us in our current predicament. The way out is to provide a stable background theory equal to the task of accounting for the many facets at issue, as well as to match up with alternative theories that have made claims on our much-traveled conception. This background theory must be thorough even as it is realistic in the sense of not attempting too much. It is pointless to try describing something in *Logos* terms if this concept is intrinsically and unalterably captured by the *Bios* ground alone. A theorist may limit his or her account to any one of the four complementing grounds and leave the others for colleagues to use as they see fit. Not everyone would agree with this suggestion. For example, although Edelman (1992) argues against simple-minded reductionism (p. 166), he considers neurobiology so important that he cannot see psychology declaring its autonomy from biology (p. 177). Mind is based on matter (p. 109) so how can anyone dare to theorize on the *Logos* ground independent of the *Bios* ground?

I plan to do precisely this. Like so many of my *Logos*-oriented colleagues I have learned that when we begin mixing both *Logos* terms and *Bios* terms into our theories, the former meanings are twisted into and thus are lost to the language of the latter. As I am not trying to dismiss or in any way discourage framing *Bios* ideas I have elected to use the phrase *psychic consciousness* to describe the realm of understanding that will be pursued in this volume. In this sense, the phrase includes *both* consciousness and unconsciousness as a psychic relation of meaning in which one end of this dimension delimits the other. This practice of combining both ends of the relation in a shortened version avoids writing "psychic consciousness/unconsciousness" each time I am referring to this full dimension. But in Chapter 2 there will be a distinction drawn between the conscious and unconscious ends of this psychic relation, and in this case the phrase "psychic consciousness" will be used in a more restrictive sense. It will always be possible to judge from the context of presentation whether the phrase "psychic consciousness" is referring to the entire dimension of consciousness–unconsciousness or simply to one end of this dimension.

I use the word "psychic" in the simple dictionary sense of "that which has to do with mind." Psychic meanings are therefore not based on the physical but draw exclusively from the *Logos* grounding. There is nothing mysterious or spiritual being implied in a psychic account of the sort presented in this volume. As it can become boring, I will not always use the word "psychic" to modify consciousness in the material under consideration, but this usage should be presumed at all unspecified times. When some other interpretation of consciousness is intended I will specify it. For example, we will look at *Bios* and even *Physikos* explanations of consciousness (see esp. Chapters 5 and 7).

In the Introduction I noted that my theory is termed logical learning theory (LLT; see the Glossary for quick reference to LLT terminology). It stands squarely on the *Logos* ground and is a teleological formulation. The procedure we will now follow begins with the presentation of LLT in Chapter 2, followed by an explanation of psychic consciousness in light of its concepts, and then as succeeding chapters unfold we will broaden our understanding even as we assess the applicability of our framing theory in light of the many issues that present themselves. It would not do for a theory professing to account for psychic consciousness to deviate so far from other formulations that two entirely different phenomena would seem to be under consideration. Logical learning theory will not be in complete agreement with other approaches to consciousness, but the relevance of its criticisms and alternative formulations will always be clear and therefore hopefully instructive. What we are engaged in here with other theories is nothing less than a conceptual struggle over our understanding of human nature.

2

SHIFTING GROUNDS TO
THE LOGOS

From my first psychology classes I found it impossible to take seriously my teachers' explanations of human behavior. I caught onto their rules of explanation quickly enough—that genuinely "scientific" psychologists were supposed to think about people like quasi-engineers describing the workings of machines. This involved using material- and efficient-cause conceptions framed from the extraspective perspective. But I just could not think about the *psyche* (mind, executive, etc.) in this *Physikos—Bios* manner. This mechanistic strategy of explanation seemed too contrived; it failed to consider the *Logos* aspects of behavior. I believed that to explain people humanly demanded an introspective formulation, one that captured the intentionality of their behavior through formal and final causation. Over 30 years ago, I began fashioning such a theory and with the help of students and colleagues have since that time enlarged and scientifically tested it through well over 100 empirical research experiments. As noted in the Introduction and at the close of Chapter 1, I must spell out its tenets at this point to provide a proper background for understanding not only psychic consciousness but a truly human form of behavior in general.

LOGICAL LEARNING THEORY

In the first chapter, I noted that *logos* derives from the Greek, where it conveys the meaning of *word* as well as *reason, speech, definition,* and *principle.* I also underscored the formal-cause nature of this concept. Logos has played an immensely important role in the history of ideas. Stone (1989) observed the following about this rich concept:

> A thousand years of philosophic thought are embodied in a term [i.e., logos] that begins by meaning 'talk' in Homer, develops into 'Reason'—with a capital R, as the divine ruler of the universe—in the Stoics, and ends up in the Gospel of St. John—by a subtle borrowing from biblical sources—as the creative Word of God, His instrument in the Creation. (p. xi)

I will be using logos (or *Logos,* when referring to the grounding of an explanation) to capture the essential difference between a teleological and a mechanistic view of human behavior, memory, and perception. As learning plays a role in all such human actions, it is right and proper to name my view *logical learning theory* (LLT).

I do not wish to be technically detailed in this volume, but there are several concepts that must be mastered before we can get into the meat of things. For the sake of those in the profession of psychology or related social sciences I will cite certain of my published experiments for immediate reference. For a detailed treatment of LLT, I recommend *Logical learning theory: A human teleology and its empirical support* (Rychlak, 1994). This is my "magnum opus," containing over 750 references, most of which are empirical studies having relevance to LLT. There is always new terminology to grasp in any new theory, of course. I hate to burden the reader with new theoretical lingo, but as I noted in Chapter 1, if you frame your line of theorizing using another person's (e.g., a mechanist's) terminology, you wind up saying what this person clearly understands all right, but this is only because you are conveying what he or she already knows. Although I came to use this very point in LLT—that people must already "know in order to know"—it was not pleasant to feel trapped by the conceptual terminology of colleagues who were getting me to say what I did not intend to say just so they would listen to me. So, in this chapter I want to walk the reader through the fundamental concepts of LLT in a reasonably discursive fashion, with the promise that these concepts are essential in the chapters that follow.

Logic

What is *logic* anyway? Logic is frequently viewed as dealing with reasoning that leads to the truth. Michael Polanyi (1968) put it this way: "I call 'logic' the rules for reaching valid conclusions from premises assumed to be true" (p. 42). Now, to a psychologist who hopes to cover the full range of human behavior, irrational as well as rational, this understanding of logic is not very helpful. Many lines of conscious thought are not assumed by the thinker to be true, and indeed, are frequently intentionally fanciful and beyond plausibility. Furthermore, Polanyi's definition could be understood extraspectively, as when we might generate rules for syllogistic reasoning to be written on a blackboard entirely without consideration of the phenomenal viewpoint of the person who follows the rules. John Stuart Mill (1806–1873) defined logic as the process of inducting from "known truths to the unknown" (1843/1974, p. 12). Mill then helped the introspectively oriented psychologist when he added: "Existence, so far as Logic is concerned about it, has reference only to phenomena; to actual, or possible, states of *external or internal consciousness*, in ourselves or others" (p. 604; italics added).

The slippery thing about a "known truth" is that it must be grasped by someone, which means that it has been consciously evaluated (as true) by an intellect. In centuries past, people believed that truth could be garnered through a sweep of experience entirely independent of the mind doing the sweeping. The role of perceptual bias and alternative understanding in the targeting of such truth was greatly underestimated. Truth is a judgment of certainty concerning some beliefs relative to others. This judgment results in what philosophers term an *apodictic* truth. As a psychologist, I find that even an apodictic truth exists only because there are reasoners who render its certainty, whereas others may reject it. This turns me into a relativist, but only partially for I claim that the relativism is limited to the meaningful content and not the process of logical reasoning per se. Kapp (1942) supports me here when he quotes from the 17th century work by Arnauld and Nicole (i.e., *The Art of Thinking*) known as the Port Royal logic: "The greater part of the errors of men ... arise much more from their reasoning *on* false principles, than from their reasoning wrongly *from* their principles" (pp. 79–80; italics in original).

I think this venerable insight is absolutely correct, resting as it does on our process–content distinction. The specific beliefs that people embrace differ, and the resultant errors, misunderstandings, and disagreements that flow from the premises (principles, assumptions, beliefs, etc.) occur because of these precedents that take thought in different directions with a sense of necessity that can also parade as certainty. The person's beliefs are also likely to be heavily weighted with affective significance. The concept of the self-fulfilling prophecy rests on some such capacity. People can watch the same football game and yet "see" entirely different rule infractions taking place on the playing field depending on their team allegiance (Hastorf & Cantril, 1954). Quite obviously, their *logical process* is the same whether favoring team A or team B. They think alike just as they focus their eyes alike. But the meanings they frame as the truth of what it is they are seeing is not to be found in this perceptual process. Such *meaning-contents* are relative to the assumptive perspective framed initially, and we psychologists can view things from either side as "true"—unless we wish to assume a third, self-styled "objective" perspective. And so we would now have a third, "relative truth" to report. But the process called perceiving (thinking, cognizing, etc.) is *not* relative; it is demonstrably the same for all.

Therefore, as used in LLT, logic is the study of formal- and final-cause patterning in human reasoning, whether this eventuates in what is considered truth, an arbitrary truth, or no truth at all (falsehood). We expect an aspect of logic to involve the "illogic" of moving from arbitrary, questionable, flatly incorrect premises to equally damaged conclusions. The responsibility of LLT is to explain the process that moves sound or unsound thought along. The specific thought contents are not its responsibility for they can be anything imaginable. I next move to a consideration of the process that has been used in traditional psychological explanations.

Association–Mediation

In Chapter 1, I considered the mechanist's attitudes regarding intentionality and selectivity in human behavior. American psychology has been greatly influenced by British philosophy, a tradition that stresses empiricism and associationism. Sir Francis Galton (1822–1911), who carried this tradition into empirical studies of people and inspired several early American psychologists, expressed the view that the human being "is little more than a conscious machine, the larger part of whose actions are predicable" (1884/1971, p. 6). What made the person predictable was the fact that all behaviors—including ideas—were joined together by lawful *associations*. Study these patterns of association and you can predict what the person will do. These associations were thought to be links imprinted right into the physical substance of the brain, which was known to use electrical impulses. Thus, any formal-cause organization of behavior that seemed to be carrying out a final-cause intention was actually nothing more than a series of such blind (because unintended) associations following out an efficient-cause sequence.

The basic idea here is that events flow from antecedents to consequents in efficient-cause fashion (recall the analysis of billiards in Chapter 1). If a large number of dominoes are set on end in a series, and if the first in line is then flicked over, a succession of clicking sounds takes place as they tumble over in sequence. We can even alter the pattern of dominoes from a straight line to curves and zigzags so that a most fascinating course of action takes place, especially if we are willing to arrange many hundreds of dominoes. Looked at from afar (i.e., extraspectively), such patterns taking shape almost suggest that there is an intelligence carrying them out intentionally "at the moment"—drawing out some kind of meaning as the clicking proceeds. Well, this is essentially how the associationists view the brain-processing of human beings, although the efficiently caused patterning within the neurons of the brain is assumed to occur via transmitted electrical impulses and not bumping dominoes. Patterns of meaningful relations are brought about by mechanical links between ideas, not by any final-cause intentionality of the person doing the thinking. The particular brain pattern being formed may be inborn (via genes, DNA, etc.) or it may have been shaped into the person's organic constitution by efficiently caused inputs in early life experience.

It is this shaping from past experience that brings us to *mediation*. I used this term in Chapter 1 in an exclusively mechanical, efficient-cause sense even though mediation can be thought of teleologically, as when someone is trying to bring two disagreeing parties together. A negotiator meeting with labor and management during a strike serves such a mediational role. This negotiator qua mediator might ferret out the assumptions underlying the conflicting sides and try to find some common end (telos) for the sake of which the dispute could be resolved. The disputants may be so lost in the details that they fail to see a beckoning way out of their gridlock having mutual benefit. But there is also a form of mediation that does not address such assumptive understandings, intentions, and ends.

It is possible to think of a purely mechanical process taking place between events as a mediator of those events. A simple lever serves in such a mediational capacity, whereby a downward pressure applied at one end results in a force of lift at the other end. The mediational influence varies depending on the placement of the lever on the fulcrum. Another form of mechanical mediation occurs when a thermostat in an automobile engine opens or closes depending on the temperature of the coolant in the radiator, allowing for greater or lesser circulation of the coolant through the engine while it is running.

The first kind of mediation is telic, engaging formal and final causation, whereas the second kind is mechanical, founded entirely on material and especially efficient causation. Mediation theory in psychology has relied exclusively on this latter form of explanation. I essentially defined mediation in Chapter 1 as an efficient-cause influence acting as a stimulus in the present by former responses. An old response (e.g., a learned word response like "mother") can be used today as a stimulus (e.g., when the child calls the mother for help). This is how I will continue to use the concept in this volume. In traditional learning theories, mediation occurs over the passage of time. That is, intrinsic to a concept of efficient causation is the notion that something acting earlier in a sequence (the initial domino's bump) moves something along later in the sequence of action (succeeding dominoes). In classical learning theories we always cite the

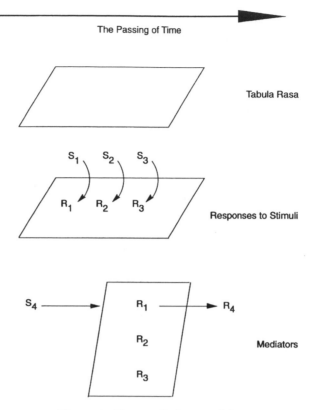

The Passing of Time

Tabula Rasa

S_1 S_2 S_3

R_1 R_2 R_3 Responses to Stimuli

S_4 ⟶ R_1 ⟶ R_4

R_2 Mediators

R_3

Figure 1. The mediation model.

initiating or antecedent force as the stimulus and the resultant motion as the response. In more recent years, computer modeling has shifted these terms to input (antecedent) and output (consequent), but the efficient-cause nature of such action has not changed. I will take up computer modeling of consciousness in Chapter 7. Figure 1 presents a schematization of the mediation model.

Note that at the top of Figure 1 there is a time line symbolizing the fact that this model relies on the passing of linear time to account for what takes place. Immediately below the time line is a parallelogram labeled a *tabula rasa*. This concept dates from Aristotle but was used prominently by John Locke. The tabula rasa symbolizes the blank, initial state of the mind: a blank sheet of paper or a waxed tablet, ready to be inscribed by pencil or stylus respectively. The source of this inscription is certain forces orig-inating in the external world. The next schematization depicts such ex-ternal influences being etched upon the tabula rasa. These influences are depicted as different stimuli (S1, S2, S3), recorded on the blank-sheet mind as different responses (R1, R2, R3). Stimuli occur first in time flow, fol-lowed by responses. Finally, at the bottom of Figure 1 we have the process of mediation presented. In this case, an entirely new stimulus (S4) relies on the help of the previously recorded responses (R1, R2, R3) to facilitate yet a later response (R4). I have used "stimuli" and "responses" in Figure 1, but, once again, it would not change the efficient-cause nature of this process to refer to these as inputs and outputs, respectively.

This mediation model may help explain how language might be learned and used, following the theory of cue-producing responses that was introduced in Chapter 1. According to this theory, the newborn child possesses a tabula-rasa intellect (except for certain innate reflexes, of course). As stimulations enter from the environment (S1, S2, S3) they provoke certain responses (R1, R2, R3). Language sounds amounting to words would be shaped or molded thanks to the continual encouragement (reinforcements) of parents. In time, the infant can form the sound "ma ma." By keeping close to the child when such a response ("ma ma") is voiced, the mother can become the stimulus for this word through sheer association. It is strictly such *frequency* and *contiguity* of events (mother stimulus and "ma ma" response) that accounts for the connecting or patterning that takes place in the mediation model. Purpose or intention are not required in this extraspectively framed style of explanation. Once this word-response is learned (let's consider it R2), the child can not only retain it in memory, but use it now as a cue-producing response to facilitate any subsequent stimulus–response or input–output sequence that might arise.

For example, assume the child is hungry or otherwise discomforted. This discomforting stimulation (S4) can be resolved to the child's satisfaction (positive reinforcement) by employing the learned response (R2) of "ma ma" to call for help. Other words could then make the child's needs understood (R1, R3) so that the mother could meet them, enabling the child to respond (R4) with satisfaction to the need at hand (e.g., by eating, etc.). And, of course, this process of mediation goes on throughout life, accounting for increasingly complex human learnings including those "thoughts about thoughts" that I argued in Chapter 1 were not truly reflexive.

The most significant aspect of the mediation process is that it does not actually shape (create, generate, etc.) the contents it uses to move things along over time. It is like a complex conveyor belt, assembling items that have been initially formed elsewhere and then accepting their influence on what will be constructed over time. The sound of "ma ma" was purely reflexive, made as a natural response to the maturation of the vocal apparatus. The mother then shaped the child's connection between her image and this sound by being close to the child and showing attention when it was used. The mediation process is never an originating source of the fundamental contents that influence what takes place as time goes by. Along this line, it is interesting to note that Locke once referred to ideas as being formed externally and entering mind through the senses. He said "The senses at first let in particular ideas, and furnish the yet empty cabinet" (Cranston, 1957, p. 266). Ideas are "let in," making them like pre-shaped cups being placed into a tea cabinet. One wonders how such an idea-content could represent or convey a distinctive meaning. One would think that meanings are framed and expressed rather than received "all of a piece" like this—which brings up another issue in LLT.

Meaning–Oppositionality

Even though the falling dominoes "enact" patterns instrumentally through their motions, there is no creative intelligence directing them at the moment of such action. The patterns have been designed intelligently by the person who arrayed the dominoes, but once they are in proper order the rest of the action is a fait accompli. With all of the talk today of information processing and artificial intelligence, we can be lulled into the belief that computing machines are somehow creating meanings in their information processing. This is not true, of course. They carry out the patterned meanings of their programs in the same fait-accompli sense that our dominoes enact their prearranged patterns. Claude Shannon, often called the "father" of information-processing theory, stated flatly that the engineering process utilizing "information" has nothing to do with the meaning of any message being communicated (Shannon & Weaver, 1962, pp. 3, 99). In Chapter 7, I will take up Shannon and other founders of information processing in computers, robots, and related cybernetic machines.

A quick check with the dictionary tells us that the word meaning derives from the Anglo-Saxon roots of "to wish" and "to intend." There is an unquestioned teleological "meaning of meaning" involved here. When we look up the meaning of an unknown word in the dictionary we rely on words that we already know to create a context of meaning that can then be extended to the unknown word. We do not know the meaning of "apodictic," but when we look it up in our dictionary, we can use our knowledge of words we already know to grasp its definition. This is what I meant earlier when I said that LLT holds that one must already know in order to know. Now, the printing on the page of the dictionary that records the meaning of apodictic is presented extraspectively. It just stands there, as if etched upon some tabula rasa area. However, as we engage this meaning, learn the word, and then subsequently use it to express an idea we "wish" or "intend" to convey, the "meaning of meaning" shifts to an introspective perspective. We are not now moving previously input words along in efficient-cause fashion, as the mediation model would have it. We are using the words to express our introspectively framed points of view, preferences, and so forth. The words are our tools, our instruments used to fashion and express our intentions. People can use essentially the same words to express conflicting points of view (see Chapter 9).

It strikes me that the latter kind of process—a teleological process—would require the concept of psychic consciousness to round it out. On the other hand, the necessity of consciousness in a mediating machine process is, to put it mildly, problematic (I will get back to this suggestion in Chapter 7). Even more striking is the fact that meanings are always ready to break out in ways that would drive a machine process to lock-up. Meanings are not limited to what "is" under processing. They just as often rely upon what "is not" under processing. We sometimes learn more from information that is *not* being communicated than from what *is* being communicated. People exchange information like this all of the time. "Why didn't Todd mention the fact that I forgot to call him last night? He must *really* be mad at me." Meanings are pulled hither and yon by contradictions, negations, contrasts, and contrary opinions of all sorts—sometimes held to by the same person. "I hate her but I can't live without her." Mediating machines do not act like this, because they do not "work" this way as a process.

Logical learning theory places considerable emphasis on oppositionality in the processing and learning of meaningful materials (for empirical support, see Rychlak & Barnard, 1993; Rychlak, Barnard, Williams, & Wollman, 1989; Rychlak & Williams, 1984; Rychlak, Williams, & Bugaj, 1986; Slife, Stoneman, & Rychlak, 1991). We could also refer to this oppositionality as *dialectics* or *dialectical reasoning* (Aristotle, 1952f, p. 143; see Chapter 7 for greater detail on this concept). But the essential point is that some meanings that are distinctly different from each other are still united in this peculiarly oppositional manner. For example, the meaning of *left* is not a unipolar designation that has through frequent repetition over time been contiguously associated to *right* by some kind of extraneous linkage. The meaning of left–right frames a bipolarity from the outset, a dimension in which one pole (left) intrinsically delimits hence enters into the very definition of the other pole (right), and vice versa. We cannot really know what either pole means unless we also grasp its opposite (contrary, contradiction, negation, or contrast). The mathematician, Jacob Bronowski (1958) referred to this capacity to oppose things into those that are alike and those that are not as "the foundation of human thought" (p. 22). According to LLT, human reasoning is shot through with such oppositionality, both in its underlying process and in the contents that this process generates or creates. Words are contents in this process, expressing meanings like "left" and "right" or "good" and "bad." We next turn to an examination of the logical process that produces them.

Predication

We are now entirely within the realm of the *Logos*, looking for a process that will help us understand the framing and conveying of meanings, including opposite meanings. We do not want to use the extraspec-tively framed, quasi-mathematical logic adopted by those who accept only sound reasoning and dismiss it when it is "illogical." To explain the psychic dimension of conscious–unconscious we must include a kind of "implica-tion to the opposite" in our account (Rychlak & Barnard, 1996). We re-quire this oppositionality because we will be exploring the phenomenal realm, where all sorts of convoluted meanings arise that might be called illogical even though a pattern of contrariety (contradiction, contrast, etc.) is discernible in what is being meaningfully expressed. Can this opposi-tional pattern be a part of the *Logos*, and to that extent a form of logic after all? Also, our model will have to be completely introspective, as if we are examining ourselves. From the LLT perspective, we are always walk-ing in our own shoes.

Predication is frequently discussed in terms of language *syntax*, which necessarily leads to an extraspective analysis as if we were considering grammatical rules fashioning sentences on a blackboard ("out there") rather than the understanding of those who expressed the sentence mean-ings in the first place ("in here"). A sentence includes in its structure a subject, verb, and object. Plato (c. 427–347 BC) discussed predication from this perspective in the *Sophist* dialogue. He clarified how we use words (nouns, verbs, etc.) to frame predications in making statements about anything (1952c, p. 576). The subject of the sentence is predicated by the combination of the verb and the object, which is often termed the *complete predicate*. Plato also noted that we can "predicate many names of the same thing" (p. 569). To reduce this scheme to its essentials, we might take as an example the sentence "John is reliable." The subject of the sentence here, "John," is under the predication of "is reliable." In LLT terms, we would describe John as the *target* of a meaning-extension. The meaning of reliability is being intentionally extended to John. As Plato suggested, we could extend other meanings to John as well—that he is also unassuming, a hard worker, and so on. But none of these descriptive predicates of John are "his" exclusive property. We can name other people who are reliable, unassuming, and hard workers.

This joining of predicate to target is not a linking of free-standing meanings. It is an extension of one meaning to the other, engulfing and enriching the latter by the former. The resultant introspectively understood pattern of meaning can be written down extraspectively as a sentence. But what is essential here is not language syntax. There are syntactical ways in which to array sentences other than the familiar "subject-verb-object" alignment (see Ultan, 1969). What is important is the semantics involved, the meanings being patterned from one locus to another in the cognitions of the person doing the predicating. Looked at introspectively, we *must* predicate in order to enrich our target with meaning. We have something

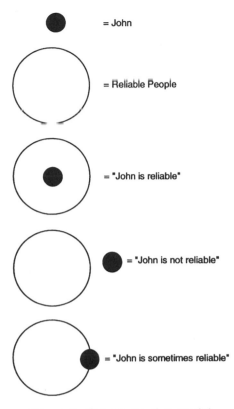

Figure 2. The predication model.

to say about John, so we target him for meaning-extension. Figure 2 presents the predication model, schematized in terms of Euler circles.

Reading from the top down in Figure 2, note that the target, John, is listed first as a small, darkened circle. Next, the predicate meaning (reliable people) to be extended to John is presented as a larger circle. The difference in size of our circles symbolizes that the meaning being employed as the predicate always takes on a broader scope in the process than does the target. This more encompassing circle could have been labeled as simply the abstract quality of "reliability" but the reference to people—in this case, one person—brings out the fact that there are others besides John who can be captured by this category. Incidentally, the term *category* devolves from the Greek word *katēgorein*, which means "to predicate" (Yartz, 1984, p. 147). Aristotle (1952a) pointed to the "wider expanse" of a predicating genus in relation to its species (p. 8).

Logical learning theory holds that this is a fundamental characteristic of human cognitive processing, to move introspectively from a broader to a narrower realm in meaning-extension (for empirical support, see Rychlak & Rychlak, 1991; Rychlak, Stilson, & Rychlak, 1993). The "move" is accomplished in patterning, so that it is instantaneous and outside of any linear time's passage. There is no efficient-cause "push" to this patterning. Patterns shift their relations, generating meanings without being shaped into what they represent. A rough analogy to this patterning would be the kaleidoscopic phenomenon. We rotate the end of the kaleidoscope and the cut-glass bits therein tumble about. The rotation and tumbling is all due to efficient causation. But the resultant pattern made-up by the *relations between* the variously colored glass pieces is not "shaped" by the rotation of the cylinder. These relations must be understood as a fortuitous or chance affair; but as a pattern per se, there is no doubt that they represent a formal-cause phenomenon.

Assume now that people can jumble about the patternings of meaning at will as they reason along, moving inside or outside of Euler-like predicating circles, renaming the meanings of the circles, or "dreaming up" odd combinations of patterned possibilities. The resultant meaning-extensions from the broader, encircling realms of meaning would most assuredly have their "impact," even though this would not be due to an efficient-cause thrust. The weight of logical organization would be all that would occur as one meaningful realm *immediately* (not mediately) patterned with another to infer or imply something, or negate it altogether.

The first such patterned relation in Figure 2 is the middle design in which we find the smaller circle labeled John situated within the broader circle to convey the meaning that "John is reliable." John is enriched by the meaning of reliability (or "all reliable people known"). It is important to appreciate that in the predication model John is not "placed" within the category. Rather, the category—its meaning—is extended to the target known as "John." I sometimes speak of predication as similar to putting on a pair of glasses. Put on rose-colored glasses and your world is suddenly rosy. The problem with this heuristic is that in real life, glasses adapt what is being input rather than actually creating what is seen. Glasses alter the incoming sensations to enlarge them, or they may screen out harmful light rays. The emphasis is still being placed on input, which of course takes us back to mediational modeling (e.g., placing teacups into the Lockean cabinet). In the predication model we want to capture a more active, creative role for thinking and perceiving.

The next pattern of Euler circles in Figure 2 is the "John is not reliable" arrangement in which the meaning of reliability is no longer patterned onto John. The larger circle symbolizing reliability or reliable people is present, but its encircling meaning of reliability no longer extends to the target of John. It is easy to overlook the fact that an oppositionality has been brought into the predicational model at this point. In tracing the more comprehensive realm of meaning (i.e., the larger Euler circle) in the predicational model we necessarily involve the "inside versus outside" of the meaning being symbolized, a point I will be enlarging upon shortly (in Figure 3). Logicians framing Euler circles extraspectively are prone to miss or ignore this "inside versus outside" issue because they are interested in the meaning encircled and not the meaning being excluded. The excluded is usually irrelevant to the point they are making.

But this outside is never irrelevant to an introspectively oriented anal-ysis, because it is an even broader realm of meaning that *also* enriches targets with meaning. If we are bringing to bear the meaning of reliability in our ongoing experience, extending it to this or that person but specifi-cally avoiding John, it follows logically that we do not consider him to be a reliable person. We are, in effect, extending the meaning of nonreliability (unreliability) to him: This is an example of the oppositional implication that I referred to above. The final arrangement at the bottom of Figure 2 symbolizes that "John is sometimes reliable." The darkened smaller circle here straddles the line tracing the larger Euler circle, symbolizing that John cannot be clearly characterized on this question of reliability. Sometimes he is reliable, sometimes he is not.

Here is LLT's formal definition of the process of *predication*:

> The logical process of affirming, denying, or qualifying precedently broader patterns of meaning in sequacious extension to narrower or targeted patterns of meaning. The target is the point, aim, or end (telos) of the meaning-extension.

The words *precedent* and *sequacious* convey the idea of meaning-extension as understood introspectively. These are exclusively formal-cause notions, capturing the fact that if certain patterns of meaning are aligned in thought, those affirmed initially in this logical ordering (precedents) extend their meaning *necessarily* to the targeted meanings that follow. The word sequacious conveys a slavish compliance to what has preceded in the patterning of meanings within the *Logos*. We can think of the old saw here: "If it has a beak, feathers, webbed feet, and quacks like a duck, it *is* a duck!" The precedents (feathers, webbed feet, quacking) sequaciously extend to the meaning of "duck." Thus, when we encompass the meaning of a target (like John) with the meaning of reliability, this target is slavishly compliant in accepting the meaning so patterned or extended. Even if this attribution is objectively wrong, looked at from the introspective perspec-tive of the person who subjectively patterned this belief into existence, John *is* a reliable person. Note that the term *sequacious* captures what is meant by deductive logic (formal-cause determinism): Given "this" (prec-edent) "that" necessarily (sequaciously) follows.

There is no time bar in Figure 2, as there is for the mediation model of Figure 1. This signifies that time is irrelevant to predication. The pred-icating meaning of reliability does not occur first in time and thereby ef-ficiently cause John to be endowed by this meaning on the order of billiard balls or dominoes bumping each other about. The effects of predication occur immediately, *not* mediately! Once the proper meanings are aligned, the resultant meaning "is there" in the pattern that takes form with the alignment. If we do not like to look at any one pattern in the kaleidoscope we give it another turn and see what the glass pieces tumble up for us. A similar "total effect" impression directs our selections in arranging an attractive wardrobe. Once the coordination of colors and clothing styles "work" they do so as a total pattern of good taste (as viewed by the person involved). Alter one piece of the pattern, and the total effect is instantly lost. We of necessity move things around in arranging our wardrobes, employing thereby efficient causation in lifting things, laying them out for viewing, trying them on, and so on. But the efficient cause in this case is a mere instrumentality, a way of assembling the best coordination of attire—which "jumps out" at us in formal-cause fashion immediately as it is achieved. The same thing may be said to occur in thought, whereby we try various notions "on for size" until we hit upon a "good" idea and adopt it as "that" (reason) "for the sake of which" we carry things forward.

I am not implying that a logical sequence, like the syntactic array of a sentence, reflects efficient causation. It does not. Neither are the steps of the traditional *syllogism* (i.e., major premise, minor premise, conclusion) an efficient-cause sequence. Nor are mathematical solutions brought about by efficient causation. The causation in all these endeavors is formal. We are dealing here in the *Logos*, and require a process that is suitable to this realm of patterns signifying meanings. There are many possibilities for meaning creation in the *Logos*, and they are always generated by the predicational process.

It is unfortunately easy to confuse the process of predication in Figure 2 with the contents that this process generates and conveys. That is, in order to speak of predication we have to use certain contents. We select words like *John*, *is*, and *reliable* to convey the meaning intended. When we now refer to the broader circle of Figure 2 as representing reliability or reliable people it is easy to forget that there are *two* aspects involved here—the larger circle per se, and the meaningful contents (reliable, reliable people) being conveyed by this circle. The word *predicate* (or predication) thus takes on two meanings. As a *noun*, it refers to the content (i.e., reliable) that is being ascribed to the target, but as a *verb* it relates to the logical process in which a precedent meaning is affirmed and extended sequaciously to a target.

This separation of process from content in predication presages a distinction made in LLT between *generic* and *delimiting oppositionality*. The former refers to process and the latter to content. Figure 3 presents a schematization of this distinction using the Euler circles. Note that Figure 3 begins at the top with a model of the predication process as a darkened target within the broader realm of some predicating meaning (identical to the "John is reliable" pattern of Figure 2). Immediately below this in Figure 3 we find only the larger Euler circle depicted, with a looping, double-

Predication

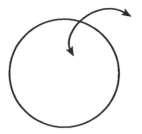

Generic Oppositionality of
Process Reflecting:

Inside — Outside
Same — Different

Reliable — Unreliable

Delimiting Oppositionality
of Word Content

Reliable — Shy

Non-Oppositionality of
Word Content

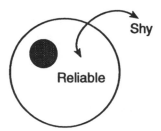

Combined Generic Oppositionality
and Non-Oppositionality

(Process + Content)

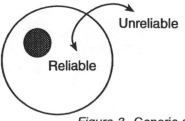

Combined Generic Oppositionality
and Delimiting Oppositionality

(Process + Content)

Figure 3. Generic and delimiting oppositionality.

headed arrow stretching across its boundary line. Think of this looping arrow as pointing to locations where contents that are either *inside* or *outside* of the larger (predicating) Euler circle are positioned. Alternatively, think of the two arrow heads as pointing at contents that are either the *same* (i.e., all found inside the large circle) or *different* (i.e., all found outside the large circle).

The inside–outside relationship is oppositional. It is termed a "generic" oppositionality in LLT because it is common to all predications, whether or not they are involved in conveying opposite word contents like true–false, tall–short, and so on. In other words, generic oppositionality highlights the fact that the predicating (larger) Euler circle of Figure 2 must have both an inside and an outside. Predication as a process always involves such generic oppositionality. This opposition cannot be escaped; it must intrude on the predicating realm of meaning (via the inside–outside or inclusive–exclusive distinction).

When nonopposite words are involved with the two ends of the looping arrow of Figure 3 we are likely to refer to contents inside this circle as being the "same" and those assembling outside the circle as "different." Words like reliable, dependable, and trustworthy might be framed inside the larger Euler circle, indicating that these are really all conveying the same behavioral tendency (i.e., they are synonymous words). Different descriptors falling outside the predication might be words like sensitive, intense, and thoughtful; these are meanings which do not delimit and thereby enter into the definitions of reliable, dependable, and trustworthy. Even so, thanks to the generically oppositional reasoning process it is possible to draw distinctions between such groupings of words, predicating some as having essentially the same meaning and citing others as being different.

Many psychologists would consider all oppositionality to fall under this designation, interpreting opposite word contents as merely "very different" from each other. Although it is true that "left" is very different from "right," there is a delimitation in meaning taking place here that is not true when "left" is paired with "up." The latter words are nonopposites even as they are very different in meaning. But the meaning of "left" delimits and therefore literally enters into the meaning of "right" in a way that words with different meanings (e.g., left vs. up) do not.

The next two items in Figure 3 are examples of the kind of word contents that we are now considering. The pairing of "reliable" and "unreliable" is an example of delimiting oppositionality, for it is impossible to understand one of these word meanings without understanding its opposite. The two words delimit and thus engage each other's meaning in a way that the words "reliable" and "shy" do not. The latter two words are merely different.

The final pair of schematizations in Figure 3 combine the contents of reliable–shy and reliable–unreliable with the process of generic oppositionality. Note that the darkened target has been returned to the predicating realm of meaning labeled "reliable." Reliability is being extended to the target (assume this is John once again). But in one case "shy" has been placed outside the predicating Euler circle and in the other "unreliable" has been placed there. This difference in the outside labelings schematizes the fact that there is an underlying generic oppositionality making judgments of *both* same–different (reliable–shy) and delimiting oppositionality (reliable–unreliable) possible. For example, let's say that I have three male associates: Bruce, Gregg, and Joe. Assume that I was asked to characterize these men as to their predominant personality trait. I might say that Bruce and Gregg were both notably reliable, and Joe was basically a shy person. On the other hand, I might have said that Gregg and Bruce were reliable but Joe was unreliable. Even though the first comparison drawn gets at mere difference (reliable vs. shy) and the second at stark opposition (reliable vs. unreliable), both of these content descriptors are made possible by the generic oppositionality of the underlying process. This same process logically arrays different kinds of content comparisons. We must always keep this process–content distinction in mind.

In LLT terms, predication and intentionality are identical notions. To behave intentionally is to behave for the sake of certain *affirmations* of meaning (rather than others), targeting them to some end (telos). This is how thought is directed or psychically determined. To affirm is the psychic equivalent of drawing the larger Euler circle in relation to some target— taking a meaning and using it as a wider meaning to be extended to a narrower realm called the *target*. In our example, John was targeted and the meaning of reliability affirmed for extension to him (Figure 2). We selected this meaning and attributed it to him as an *understanding-intention*. Our understanding of John is now enriched with the meaning of reliability. Nothing overt in our behavior needs to follow once we have formed this new opinion of John.

It is also possible to frame *action-intentions*, which are affirmed meanings targeting certain overt (hence observable) actions. An action-intention here might be our willingness to recommend John for a job based on the positive quality we have extended to him. Understanding-intentions presage and get action-intentions underway like this. Accidental or nonintentional behaviors take place, of course. But in the main, LLT holds that people are intentional organisms. They intend with purpose, which is to say they sequaciously extend meanings they have framed precedently— mostly for the attainment of positive ends, but not always. Final causation, which makes intention possible, is not always "good" by any means. People aim for some pretty nasty (short-term or long-term) ends in life.

When we consider a predication such as "John is reliable" or "Reliable people make good employees," we can refer to the total statement as a *premise*. It is common for authors to refer to premising as tantamount to predicating. As I have noted earlier, the syllogism encompasses a major premise (e.g., All humans are mortal), minor premise (e.g., This person is a human) and a sequaciously deduced conclusion (i.e., This person is mortal). We tend to think of premises as the beginning or preliminary statements in a line of reasoning. But, of course, even the conclusion here can be called a premise. An alternative way of describing oppositionality is to say that any premise can be challenged (negated, rejected, questioned, contradicted, etc.). So, we could say the premise "Reliable people make good employees" can be challenged by the contradiction "Reliable people do not always make good employees." We need not frame this contradiction in words. Thinking can go on through imagery. We can "see" people behaving reliably—as in meeting a deadline or paying back a debt.

Telosponse, Tautology, Analogy, Learning

Traditional learning theories have used the extraspectively framed, efficient-cause concepts of stimulus–response or input–output to describe behavior. Logical learning theory offers the introspectively framed, final- or formal-cause concept of the *telosponse* (derived from *telos*) to parallel such mechanistic accounts of behavior. To telospond is to affirm a premise (encompassing a predication) and behave covertly or overtly for the sake of the meaning affirmed rather than its opposite (i.e., a contrary, contradiction, contrast, or negation). The telosponder takes a position in affirming the premise, and although this initial position is open to alternatives, once affirmed the meaning predicated is extended by way of formal-cause determinism. We may ponder what to do—which coat to purchase, what book to read, and so on—but once we have settled on an alternative our patterned course is set. The same is true for belief: what to believe, the attitude to take, the hope for some possible occurrence. Naturally, we can be influenced in such selections. Setting the grounds for the sake of which we are being determined is not always our personal decision. We can be influenced by others for any of a number of reasons. But it is equally true that individuals can and do stand against the influence of others. In place of the frequency–contiguity principles of mediational learning theories, LLT relies on the *principle of tautology* to explain how premises are brought forth as understanding- and action-intentions. Tautology can be defined as a *patterned relation of identity* occurring between meaningful referents. This patterning is not dependent on time's passage; it occurs immediately once the meaningful organization is aligned. This formal-cause conception can be understood in either an extraspective or an introspective manner. For example, take Gertrude Stein's famous tautology "A rose is a rose is a rose." If we frame it extraspectively as "If a rose [over there] then a rose, reappearing," we are likely to find the statement redundant, at best a suggestion of the existence of a rose over time. But we can recast this introspectively as "If [I appreciate] a rose then a rose [-quality obtains] henceforth." In the latter instance, what is made known as a meaningful predication (i.e., a rose-quality) can be analogized to other aspects of ongoing experience — such as describing a rosy outlook on life or the rosy cheeks of an acquaintance. Meaning is under creation at this point.

For meaning to be extended logically, it is necessary for something like a tautology to occur in predication. This repetitive extension of a known meaning to an unknown (or lesser known) target is at the very heart of the predicational process. The meaning of reliability is tautologized with the meaning of John — not strictly one-to-one, of course, but partially or analogically. The *analogy* is a relation of only partial identity (a limited tautology). There is generic oppositionality underlying an analogy because we always have the portion that is analogous (same) and the portion that is disanalogous (different) (see Figure 3). We have never tasted a grapefruit, but expect it to be similar to an orange, which we have tasted many times. We find there is an analogous identity shared by these citrus fruits, but there are fairly prominent differences as well. We might not think of this in terms of a dimension of analogy–disanalogy, preferring instead to speak about the similarities and differences of the fruits. But our thoughts are indeed analogies, based ultimately on the generic oppositionality inherent in the predicational process.

When the person is comfortable enough with the former target (grapefruit) to use it now as a predicate extending to a new target (e.g., a lemon), *learning* has taken place. Thus, through full and partial tautologies (i.e., analogies) the person enriches his or her understanding-intentions and makes increasingly complex action-intentions possible. Logical learning theory explains the initial thinking of an infant in this tautologizing fashion. Because LLT holds that the person must know in order to know, it would seem to follow that we require inherited ideas — known at birth! — to get this pro forma view of mind underway in the first place. How can meaning be extended by the infant from the tabula-rasa nothing to something in experience? At this point we must once again remind ourselves of the process–content distinction. What is inherited is a certain process and *not* certain contents. Inherited ideas (concepts, schemata, etc.) would be such contents (see Neisser, 1992, p. 6).

Logical learning theory holds that predication (verb usage) is underway at birth, but the very first contents of this process are items tautologized of themselves. The infant, in the first hours of life, conceptualizes "a nipple is a nipple" as it roots at the mother's breast for nourishment. Obviously, the word "nipple" is not involved in this introspective awareness of a budding psychic consciousness. But if we were to express this awareness as a sentence, "nipple" would be located in both the subject (target) and predicate location: "A nipple is a nipple." The tautological extension of meaning here would quickly result in a stable grasp of what nipple means. We might even view this as a concept or construct of "nippleness."

Now we have our first precedent taking shape: a recognized identity that has been made known through learning so that further knowing is possible. Many such tautologies take place as initiating meanings (e.g., orifices modeled on the ear or a nostril, etc.). The infant is then in the position of taking this known identity and using it to analogize to other aspects of experience. The framing of metaphors is a further manifestation of this analogical capacity that humans have from birth, thanks to the predicational process (see Lakoff, 1987). The maternal nipple serves as a predicating frame of reference (prototype, etc.) as succeeding meaning-extensions to items, examined in light of the predicate meaning of "nippleness," take place. Over the early months of life, the infant begins sucking any other items that, like the nipple, are capable of being sucked. Some of these items, such as the thumb, are similar to the nipple: "A thumb is a nipple" or "A thumb has nippleness." Other items, like clothing, neither look, feel, nor taste like mother's nipple. This signifies that meanings "outside the broader circle" (not nipple-like) are used to enrich the target *even as* the meanings "inside the broader circle" (nipple-like) are under tautological identification as well (as per Figure 3).

Logical learning theory does not have to postulate innate ideas (i.e., contents) in order to account for the pro forma intelligence of human beings. What is present at birth that enables the bringing forward of such content-meanings is a predicational process. First the process, then the creation of many different content-meanings (i.e., ideas) by this same process. In contrast to John Watson's recommendation that we think of the person at birth as an organic machine, ready to run (see Chapter 1), LLT suggests that we think of the newborn as a predicating processor ready to affirm and extend content-meanings. But there is one more aspect to this predicational process that we have to consider.

Affective Assessment

In Chapter 1, I argued that reflexive self-examinations are more than simply "thoughts about thoughts." We now have a better grasp of how this introspective self-examination is possible. In telosponding, or in framing predications, we always can reason to the opposite of the meanings we are affirming at the moment. Human reasoning affords a kind of "distance" from what is being thought about at any point in the logical ordering— also called the *protopoint*. The protopoint is the locus of the initial affirmation in a logical sequence. So, if someone thinks "I need a vacation," the logical affirmation extends the meaning of vacation to a personal identity ("I") at a protopoint. If asked, the person might recall the protopoint as "when" he or she got the idea to consider a vacation. Protopoints offer the thinker units of organization, breaking up thoughts into distinctive segments of a logical sequence even though the flow of meaning in predication is continuous. One of the unique aspects of LLT is the claim that whenever any meaning-content is under affirmation at the protopoint, there is a kind of dual predication taking place. Not only is the predicate meaning of vacation being extended to personal identity, but there is another, even more abstract predication taking place concurrently. This is a purely cognitive evaluation of preference (Rychlak, Flynn, & Burger, 1979). It is called an *affective assessment*; here is the definition of this concept:

> Affective assessment (affection) is an innate capacity to transcend and reflexively evaluate the meanings of one's cognitive contents, characterizing them as either liked (positive evaluation) or disliked (negative evaluation). Such evaluations occur concurrent with the framing of all premises, and are not usually singled out for consideration by the telosponding person.

Transcendence per se draws on generic oppositionality—a rising above or beyond the wider Euler circles of Figures 2 and 3. But the focusing of such preferential judgments on the meaning of specific cognitive contents draws on delimiting oppositionality. Affective assessment is therefore a further manifestation of delimiting oppositionality. We render a preferential evaluation of the concept of *vacation* even as we frame it in relation to ourselves when we think "I need a vacation." Targets are also affectively assessed, of course. Thinking "I am a lazy bum" renders a negative affective assessment of oneself (i.e., the subject *I*) and so does "I am unprepared." But to understand the full meaning of these affective assessments, we have to consider the words used and their relative qualitative impact. Although both extensions are negative, the "bum" meaning is in all likelihood more seriously negative than the "unprepared" meaning. At times I have referred to affective assessment as involving *meaningfulness* rather than *meaning*; the former refers to the direction and extent of preferential significance that a meaning takes on (liked–disliked, positive–negative, etc.) and the latter to the specific, dictionary meaning under evaluation (i.e., *I, vacation, bum, unprepared*) (Rychlak, 1966).

People do not always have well-defined reasons for why they may like or dislike items in their experience. They may be and frequently are unaware of the affective assessments they have rendered concerning certain things. The transcendence of affective assessment concerns the contents being thought about and not the process of affectively assessing per se, which rarely becomes a target for transcendent predication and therefore is overlooked (I will revisit this issue in Chapter 10). Affective evaluations are made spontaneously and hence appear to be automatic and even biologically determined. Of course, logical learning theory refuses to allow the

Bios to creep into the explanation at this point: People are simply innately capable of rendering evaluations, both intellectual and affective. It is the (introspectively conceived) human identity and not some (extraspectively conceived) biological mechanism that renders such evaluations.

Why do some people prefer the color red to blue or carrots to cauliflower? It is, of course, possible to seek reasons for such preferences in one's early experiences, but what of the newborn infant? Can the newly born frame such affective judgments *from birth*, or must we postulate instinctive forces making the initial decisions for them? Logical learning theory holds that, as an aspect of generic oppositionality in the innate predicational process, infants can render their own judgments of like–dislike from birth (or whenever cognition may be said to begin). We can think of this in terms of the Euler circles, so that a large circle labeled "liked" would target certain things, and outside this circle would then pattern other (disliked) things. Naturally, the reverse labeling could be used (i.e., disliked inside, liked outside). The main point to be captured here is the further role of oppositionality in human cognition. Affective-assessment effects have been demonstrated in the learning of young children as well as adults (see, e.g., Rychlak, 1975a; Rychlak, McKee, Schneider, & Abramson, 1971; Rychlak & Saluri, 1973; Rychlak & Tobin, 1971; Rychlak, Tuan, & Schneider, 1974).

One example that makes plain the predicational nature of affective assessment is that if people who are asked to learn something have a positive assessment of this task, or of themselves as individuals (self-assessment), they will learn liked items in the task (e.g., words, designs, pictures of paintings or faces, etc.) more readily than disliked items. It is also true that if they dislike the task situation, or have a negative opinion of themselves as individuals (self-assessment), they will be found learning disliked items either more readily than liked items or at an equal rate. Meanings extend affectively from situational and self predications (positive vs. negative) to what will be learned in the task at hand (for empirical support see Rychlak, Carlsen, & Dunning, 1974; Rychlak, Galster, & McFarland, 1972; Rychlak & Marceil, 1986; Rychlak, McKee, Schneider, & Abramson, 1971). There is clearly a precedent-sequacious line of affective meaning-extension that occurs in thinking and memory that is reflected in a person's learning style. In light of this, it is interesting to note that we have found high school and college students coming from the lower socioeconomic levels relying more on affective assessment in their learning efforts than middle-class students (Rychlak, 1975b; Rychlak, Hewitt, & Hewitt, 1973).

Affection is assumed to be an ongoing evaluation that manifests a delimiting oppositionality of mental imagery resulting in the first cognitive discriminations being drawn by the infant (via like vs. dislike). Logical learning theory differs from traditional learning theories in that it accepts an affective judgment of the sort "I like carrots" as sufficient for the explanation of why the person is seen reaching for this vegetable instead of cauliflower. This preferential judgment is clearly a final-cause phenomenon, and such causal accounts do not have to be reduced to underlying material or efficient causes (supposedly shaping these preferences) before they are fully explained.

Note that because LLT addresses the *Logos*, and emotions as physical reactions are rooted in the *Bios*, the theory maintains a clear distinction between feelings emanating from the physiological realm of experience and the naming of such feelings as emotions (i.e., giving meaning to the feeling). Even though the same physical equipment is "firing off" a complex sensation, whether this will be judged by the person as merely excitement or actual fear can well depend on the predicating context—the life circumstance that the person is engaging. If anticipating a friendly tennis match, the sensation can be felt positively as general excitement. If confronting an unfriendly court appearance, it can be felt negatively as anxiety or fear. The affective assessment of the *same* neuronal firing pattern can be diametrically opposite, depending on the total context of meaning under predication by the person concerned with the situation at hand.

Can the person be indifferent toward some item of experience and to that extent refrain from making an affective assessment of it altogether? The person may say "I have no opinion about opera one way or the other." Logical learning theory does not reject this possibility of negating the very process of rendering an affective assessment. However, as a practical matter, this failure to assess affectively seems to occur rarely. What is probably meant by indifference concerning an activity like opera is that it is not framed by clear understanding-intentions (i.e., is an unknown realm of experience). In most cases, however, when things have no appeal one way or the other, the indifference per se suggests a mildly negative assessment.

PSYCHIC CONSCIOUSNESS VERSUS UNCONSCIOUSNESS

Now that we have surveyed some of the basic concepts of LLT, I would like to turn to a consideration of the interpretation of psychic consciousness that follows from this account. As noted at the close of Chapter 1, this phrase "psychic consciousness" refers to both conscious and unconscious experience. It is not possible to explain the one without explaining the other. I will draw on the predicational model to explain what both of these psychic manifestations involve and how they must necessarily engage each other.

Basic Issues

Logical learning theory draws on four points to explain consciousness:

1. Psychic consciousness is a further elaboration of the predicational process. (The word "psychic" signifies that we are speaking of the mental and not the biophysical, thereby confining our analysis to the *Logos* ground.)
2. The content-meanings in the predicate location of this process are more important to an understanding of consciousness than are the contents in the target location. Psychic consciousness and unconsciousness are to be understood as contrasting ways in which predicating meanings are employed by the person.
3. Psychic consciousness and unconsciousness continually interfuse in ongoing cognition.
4. There are good and bad forms of *both* psychic consciousness and unconsciousness. (I use "good" and "bad" not to render judgments about what should or should not take place, but merely as a descriptive elaboration that is difficult if not impossible to avoid. I am not suggesting or implying any prescriptions or proscriptions of a right or wrong nature.)

Considered in light of the thematic in Chapter 1, the LLT view of consciousness draws from the *awareness* interpretation: To the extent that a person is aware of content-meanings outside of the larger Euler circle in the predicational process (see Figures 2 and 3), a *psychic consciousness* is taking place in ongoing reasoning. The essence of consciousness is thus recognizing that things could be (predicated) other than they are now. On the other hand, to the extent that a person who is *not* aware of—or is negating (avoiding, "repressing," etc.)—certain meanings in the broader realm outside the predicating circle, *psychic unconsciousness* is taking place. The reasons why a person may engage in relatively greater consciousness or unconsciousness in any given instance depend on the meaningful contents being intentionally processed in the predicational context. These meanings can be considered good or bad, helpful or harmful, no matter whether they occur in consciousness or unconsciousness. Obviously, affective assessment also has a profound influence on the dynamics of psychic consciousness and unconsciousness.

An example of *good* psychic consciousness occurs when Robert is sailing his boat, enjoying the marvelous afternoon of sunshine, yet is cognizant of his location relative to the distant shoreline and sensitive to a cloud or two on the horizon. The predicating context is something like "a beautiful day for sailing," but Robert has not forgotten that things can change rapidly on the ocean. A *good* form of psychic unconsciousness occurs when Lindsey is playing her piano one day. She is unusually facile today, and is so caught up in the flawless performance of the beautiful musical score that she feels "one" with the instrument. Lindsey has "lost" herself in aesthetic fulfillment and is oblivious to the insistent ringing of a doorbell. The realm of her predication narrows accordingly, for to consider an alternative framework for what is now occurring would be to derail the perfection underway.

A *bad* form of psychic consciousness occurs when Mark, pressed by his business interests, has taken on more than he can manage. He grumbles about "juggling too many balls in the air," is continually answering telephone calls, sometimes carrying on two conversations at once over separate lines. Even so, he always has his "ear to the ground," open to all of the financial possibilities. He also wants very much to further his son's Little League baseball activities and seizes the opportunity to coach the team. He is narrowly getting by; despite his good front he has a nagging urge to "run and hide." Mark's life predications of wanting to be a successful businessman *and* father have obviously lost their focus, and he is now being torn by certain alternatives that he should probably be ignoring.

A *bad* form of psychic unconsciousness occurs when Sally finds it impossible to make a decision (what to buy, whom to invite to a party, etc.) unless she first goes through a "lucky" ritual. She has to take the time of day (say, 2 PM) when the decision arises (a protopoint!) and multiply it by the day of the month (say, the 16th of June). An even-number total signifies "go ahead and decide" and an odd number signifies "wait a while before deciding." For especially important decisions she also has to take the minutes or seconds into consideration. This ritual is proving increasingly disruptive and fatiguing. Why does she do this? She does not know. All Sally knows is that if she tries to make a decision without doing it she is gripped by anxiety that something terrible will happen. The predication which got this pattern of behavior underway has long since "gone underground."

Searle (1992) described what he refers to as the "overflow" of conscious states: "the immediate content [of consciousness] tends to spill over, to connect with other thoughts that in a sense were part of the content but in a sense were not" (p. 137). This overflow metaphor is compatible with the LLT view of consciousness as what we will now term *transpredication*. The prefix "trans" comes from the Latin meaning across, over, or on the other side of things. Understood in terms of the predication model (see Figures 2 and 3) this would suggest that in a state of consciousness the content-meaning framed as a predication is not limited to the target. There is some sense of implied meanings outside of—or, in opposition to—the predicated meaning, as when Robert keeps a wary eye on the possibility of a storm even though the day is beautiful, or Mark is continually alive to other business possibilities despite the fact that he is already engaged in many (targeted) transactions.

Sometimes predications just do not admit to meanings outside of their range of convenience (there is no transpredication involved). We can see this occurring in the very beginnings of thought (we will return to this point more than once; see especially Chapter 10). For thought to proceed, a framing predication fixing the meanings to be affirmed and extended has to be logically in place—which is why there are protopoints to consider in any line of thought.

The protopoint fixes thought in a given context of meaning. In a practical sense this can be something like deciding "*Now* is the time to clean out that over-stuffed closet." There comes a point when the meanings in thought align in this way, to generate a "new" idea (understanding intention) or "suggest" some kind of overt activity (action-intention). The closet is affirmed "right now" as crammed with junk. Certainty or realism is not at issue here. A neighbor, viewing the same closet, may say: "Well, it's not so bad, you should see *my* closet."

A more abstract kind of protopoint can be found in Plato's (1952b) famous realm of the "first" principles (p. 387), in which perfect idea-forms existed but could not be experienced directly by the human mind. Although imperfectly realized in lived reality, these forms nevertheless function as predicating meanings (categories) casting their shadow-meanings onto human reality to influence what can be known. All basic assumptions work this way. A fixed and silent (albeit imperfect) meaning must be affirmed for stable thinking to proceed. As Whyte (1960) expressed it so well,

> Reason can never know the hidden assumptions which restrict its momentary reasoning; no rational system—logical, mathematical, or scientific—can ever be used to define its own boundaries. For that the implicit assumptions must be made explicit in terms of a wider vision of possibilities. (p. 40)

Whyte touches on the same point that Gödel's famous mathematical theorems address (Nagel & Newman, 1958). Gödel demonstrated that in order for a system like elementary arithmetic to be explained or proven internally consistent it must be subsumed by a more comprehensive formulation (p. 6). In LLT terms, this broader system transcends and thereby predicates the narrower, targeted system. To then account for this broader predicating system demands an even more abstract system predicating it, and so on, ad infinitum. We are, of course, considering this matter of framing systems by increasingly abstract systems from an extraspective perspective. If we can recast this model introspectively, whereby the person must don predicating glasses in top-down fashion, it follows that psychic consciousness has its limits. The originating realm of meaning—the ultimate predication—exerts an influence that cannot be escaped. In philosophical discourse, these ultimate predicates are termed *universals*. Universals are abstract starting points that might be targeted for reflexive philosophical analysis, but they nevertheless function in this very analysis. In the main, such assumptive frameworks have a silent influence on thought. Hence, they function unconsciously. It is impossible to think or discourse without having such assumptive influences taking place. I will return to this point in later chapters (see Chapters 4, 8, and 10).

Logical learning theory employs the term *unipredication* to capture the insularity of unconscious processing. The prefix "uni" derives from the Latin meaning single, or tending to oneness. A unified predicate is not open to the alternative possibilities beyond its boundaries (i.e., beyond the encircling line defining the wider Euler circles of Figures 2 and 3). We might even say that oppositionality is itself negated so that a kind of unipolar form of "absolutist" reasoning takes place—a characteristic of unconscious reasoning that I will be detailing in later chapters.

It is possible for one end of this psychic dimension of conscious—unconscious to so occupy a person's outlook that the other end will be relatively diminished. Lindsey's commitment to her music may become such a fascination that it actually detracts from other conscious possibilities. But this immersion in a good form of unconsciousness does not trouble her. Even though she may be considered a loner, possibly slightly eccentric, the benefits of her unipredication far outweigh its drawbacks. And Mark's hectic immersion in consciousness undoubtedly keeps him from the peace of mind he would receive from time spent in meditation. Of course, having heard about meditation, he would also like to give it a chance if he can find the time.

Some Pertinent Details

There are some details to be considered at this point concerning the LLT interpretation of consciousness and unconsciousness. First of all, it should be clear that reflexive thought is limited to the former and cannot occur in the latter. That is, in order for a reflexive thought to occur it must be possible for the thinker to transcend or move outside of the predication (large Euler circle) under affirmation and put questions to himself or herself. Transpredication is therefore essential to reflexivity. And since unipredication is the case in psychic unconsciousness it follows that there is not the same reflexive, "rational" facility open to this form of reasoning that there is to consciousness. It takes transpredication to examine the contents of unipredication, as when a philosopher attempts to delineate and specify the nature of universals. Most "dynamic" clinical interpretations assume that the unconscious is more intelligent or at least more clever than the conscious. The LLT interpretation could well cast doubt on this assumption, but I want to reserve judgment in hopes of demonstrating later why this view of the unconscious as a realm of mind with deep secrets, clever strategies, and so on, has been adopted in the first place (see Chapters 4, 8, and 10).

As I continually refer to "the" psychic conscious or unconscious it may appear that a reification is taking place. It should be understood that in no way am I thinking of an independently existing "thing" by referring to these concepts in this manner. Tradition would allow me to speak of "levels" of greater or lesser consciousness, but I do not find this usage particularly helpful. It can even prove misleading because it implies that there is some kind of layering making it impossible for the person to move from consciousness to unconsciousness (or vice versa) within the same mental level. I think this promotes views like the one that people cannot be both conscious and asleep at the same time, because sleep also involves moving across a limen of wakefulness. We may have good reason to question this view when we take up altered states of consciousness in Chapter 8.

Another significant detail has to do with the role of memory in consciousness. Recall that I noted in Chapter 1 how frequently it is assumed that a forgotten idea must therefore be unconscious, since it can be recalled and thus "made conscious." It is true, as we shall see in Chapter 4, that unconscious ideas are frequently difficult to integrate with the rest of the mind so that they take on the quality of a forgotten meaning. But this is only an appearance. Logical learning theory does not consider a forgotten idea to have necessarily been an unconscious idea. True *forgetting* occurs when we are unable to frame a predication in which the target to be recalled is lent the relevant and properly organized meaning. The relevance of a meaning has to do with the person's concerns at the time.

Scott wants to call a friend on the telephone. What is her number? He struggles to "retrieve" the number, which means he tries to capture or reframe the predicating context when he first put it to memory. This can be difficult because the number has not itself been enriched by a stable, already known predication. He has memorized "Susanna's number is 538-7932." Since meaning extends predominantly from the number "to" the image of Susanna, Scott is in the position of having to come up with a predication instead of a target (see Rychlak, Stilson, & Rychlak, 1993). But because meanings extend from predicates to targets, this makes the task difficult. Scott needs a predicating meaning which targets the phone number per se. Here is where memory schemes help (e.g., Lorayne & Lucas, 1974). They provide the person with a ready-made predicating context within which items to be remembered can be targeted. I will consider such mnemonic strategies in Chapter 3.

One could argue that the very process of predication favors the development of unipredication. Since the basic alignment of the predication process is from the broader context of meaning to the less comprehensive, targeted meaning, there seems to be a logical thrust to narrow, specify, and limit this meaning-extension for any one act of predication. This is not always positive, for as the specificity increases the meaning clarifies, but memory is now heavily dependent on the slim thread of a singular (unipolar) frame of reference (i.e., a unipredicate). Meanings also extend most readily to the least well-understood or completely unknown aspects of experience (termed the *principle of meaning-extension* in LLT; Rychlak, 1994, pp. 51–53). We tend to attempt explanations for what we do not know first, setting aside those things that we have some, albeit poorly grasped hunches about for later consideration. The logical weight or impact of predication is reflected in *affirmation*. Affirmations are rendered at the protopoint, where the person conveys "this is that" or "this is not that" to initiate a line of thought. In traditional logic an affirmation is viewed as the opposite of a negation, so that asserting "this is not that" would fail to qualify as an affirmation (i.e., it would be a negation). Logical learning theory does not follow this traditional usage. In LLT, the concept of affirmation captures the active, precedent-sequacious processing of meanings in terms of predicate-target relations even though this relation may be that of negation. In telosponsivity, the person is said to affirm a premise (encompassing a predication) at the protopoint—or *not*. A negation is also possible at any time. John is affirmed as reliable even as the person affirming this is fully aware that subsequent experience with John may reverse this opinion.

In pairing contents according to delimiting oppositionality one of the members of this pair tends to be more salient than the other. Thus, in the pairings of heavy–light, cautious–impulsive, and sweet–sour, the first member of a pair has a relevance that the second usually cannot achieve. I say "usually" because it is possible to give the less salient member more importance by altering the context under which the pairing is made in the first place. Let us recognize that a context—a wider realm of meaning— is by definition a predicating meaning. Such context changes occur through bringing even more abstract predicating meanings to bear on what is under consideration. For example, when the predicating context of a discussion is merely "weight" then an estimation of something that is "heavy" is more relevant than something "light." But if we were to think of a predicating context in which "light" would be the most desired alternative, we could shift the salience accordingly. Assume we are now considering (i.e., predicating the context of) seasoning a very delicate sauce. Too much seasoning would be detrimental, so now the contextual emphasis called for a "light" herbal treatment. In this case the salience would shift from "heavy" to "light." There is a quality of thesis–antithesis to be seen in all such delimiting opposites—a further manifestation of dialectical reasoning (Rychlak & Barnard, 1993). The *thesis* captures the initiating context of meaning under affirmation (weight, seasoning sauces, etc.) and the *antithesis* then fills in the less relevant (negating) side (Chapter 7 goes into such matters in detail).

I should also mention the vastly important role that affective assessment plays in delimiting word pairings like this. People know the affective quality of a predicating word-content before they have learned or remembered this actual word (Ulasevich, 1991). It is highly probable that a more salient word for a given context—whether judging weights or cooking sauces—is going to be given a positive affective assessment, and its counterpart will be given a negative assessment. We often "feel" our way affectively in thought even before we have selected or learned the words to be used in expressing what we intend to say. Not infrequently, we select the wrong word meaning but the right affective meaningfulness in an effort to say what we mean. We recall the name of a charming new acquaintance as Nadine, our favorite teacher's name, when actually it is Mandy.

All such facts lead to the very important question of whether the meaning-extensions of predication are "in" the meanings of the word-contents or "in" the treatment given to them by the predicational process. Logical learning theory holds that word-contents in the predicational process are instrumentalities that have been adopted and formalized for general use in a sociocultural context (see Chapter 9). The sociocultural realm per se does not create the meanings that individuals express through use of such linguistic word-contents. The meaning of words is expressed intentionally by the person who so intends. The very same words (contents) can be used either in the target or the predicate location of the predicational process. Word meanings can be used analogically and metaphorically. The meaning conveyed will vary accordingly, which further establishes that it is not being carried by these word-contents. It is the selection and patterning of words by the predicational process that matters.

Thus, we can say anything we like in framing a predication, joining unusual or even nonsensical word relations (akin to the jumbling kaleidoscope discussed above). We might say "An ant is an elephant." This seemingly meaningless statement can be elaborated by a reasoner, who may place it within a broader (predicating) context of "At the insect level, an ant is an elephant" as indeed we find upon observing ants lugging huge (relative to their size) chunks of material about. Reversing the sentence, we can say "An elephant is an ant," and draw out meanings concerning the fact that looked at in the wider scheme of things, both organisms have similar needs, relatively comparable life-sustaining tasks to perform, and are but fleeting impressions in the sands of time. The encompassing breadth of the word (ant or elephant) in the predicational process is *not* carried by the word.

This is not to deny that some words are more pregnant with meaning than others, or that levels of abstractness are irrelevant to predication. An abstract word meaning is doubtless easier to use as a predicate in a sentence than is a concrete word. For example, the sentence "A pebble can be a fantasy" is easier to make sense of than "A fantasy can be a pebble." But both of these statements do convey meaning, and they do so thanks to the predicational process. So, the encompassing nature of predication (verb usage) is not dependent on the word-contents being processed, even though certain word combinations in this process make for a more meaningful expression than do others.

I referred to the *nonconscious* in Chapter 1 as something other than either consciousness or unconsciousness, relating more to plants than anything else. But this concept has also been defined as "knowledge and mental processes that are not currently in consciousness. That is, we are not subjectively aware of them at the moment . . ." (Farthing, 1992, p. 16). This definition is unacceptable to LLT for it would seem to include what we have been calling unconscious contents as well as forgetting. Because LLT bases its interpretation of psychic consciousness on how contents are predicated, it follows that a nonconscious process would not involve predication. There are doubtless many processes in the *Bios* (and *Physikos*) that influence types of consciousness other than the psychic variety that we are presently analyzing. A malfunction in some bodily organ might detract from a person's capacity to be alert on any day. If the person does not predicate her or his physical problem—try to account for a slump in alertness today—then it should be termed a nonconscious influence. Actually, all of the physically silent processes taking place in the body are nonconscious in this sense. We are rarely aware of our blood circulation or rate of breathing.

Self-Consciousness and Agency

I noted in Chapter 1 that identity conceptions are invariably wound into concepts of self and self-understanding (see Chapter 6). Mary Whiton Calkins (1863–1930) captured this inevitability when she observed that

> one never has consciousness, the sleepiest or most inchoate, which does not involve an experience qualitatively similar to that later consciousness which every one agrees to call self-consciousness. This simplest self-consciousness is not a reflective distinction of self from environment, though it may later be replaced by such reflective consciousness. But anything less than self-consciousness would not be consciousness at all: to be conscious is to be conscious of a conscious self. (1906, pp. 67–68)

There are problems with this concept of a self because it seems to suggest the existence of a *homunculus*, a little person within the personality system that makes decisions and frames intentions. Yet, only a mechanistic system, in which there is no intentionality built in from the outset, calls for a homunculus. Thus, if we follow John Watson's advice to consider the person an organic machine, ready to run, we will have to sneak in a "driver" (intender, decider, chooser, etc.) of this machine—that is, assuming that we want it to model what people do. Logical learning theory does not require such a little person to do the driving because the predicational process turns the *entire person* into a homunculus: a telosponder rather than a mechanical responder, mediator, or outputter.

In LLT, the concept of *self* refers to the predications (contents) relating to personal identity as framed telosponsively (process). The human organism—the *person*—is innately telosponsive, but in time can (a) reflexively target an introspective viewpoint as an "I, me, my, mine" lending it meaning on the basis of predications drawn from personal experience, as well as the opinions and impressions of others ("I am smart"); (b) become increasingly conscious of doing so ("I know myself better now"); and (c) intentionally seek to improve on the advantages gained from the use of further premises in which the "I, me" serves as a self-enhancing predicate ("That is mine") or in which the identity is targeted for enhancement ("I can be even better"). Of course, it is always possible to negate any one or all of these points. People can be self-destructive for several different reasons.

There are two major concepts wound into the LLT interpretation of selfhood: intentionality and identity. The basis of *intentionality* is found in psychic consciousness per se. That is, in transpredicating the person necessarily knows that things could be otherwise than what they now are—they could be different, opposite, better, worse, and so forth. Knowing this, an obvious logical inference is that something might be done to take circumstances in a direction leading toward one end and consequently avoiding another (i.e., frame an action-intention). The telosponder can do something to alter the environment. Whether it is the infant reaching for a rattle or an adult submitting an application for a job, certain movements can be carried out to attain these respective ends. As for the self-destructive intentions, people can frame unreasonable goals that set them up for failure again and again, resulting in a chronically negative self-image. The concept of a self-fulfilling prophecy is not without merit in such circumstances. I have already noted that understanding-intentions presage and grow into action-intentions. In time, the telosponder acquires the experience suggesting that there is also an *identity* involved in this process.

It is in naming this identity that self-predication is born. The process of predication has been in place from the outset of life. As life proceeds, significant others (parents, relatives, teachers, etc.) in the sociocultural environment instruct the child in the use of words like *I*, *me*, and *self*, but it is in the introspective awareness of a *sameness* taking place across the hours and days of life that self-consciousness is grasped and put into words. The telosponder finds that she or he is the same person over time, has the same desires, feelings, interests, physical characteristics in the mirror, and name called out by others. Note the further role of tautology here, helping to frame a personal identity from one life circumstance to the next.

Children's self-predications are doubtless facilitated when they begin recognizing themselves (e.g., as in a mirror), which seems to begin at about 18 months of age (Lewis & Brooks, 1974). The precise age here is not as important as appreciating that self-consciousness is a content of the predication process. The child comes to recognize a continuity in his or her behavior, as well as an ongoing capacity to reflexively self-examine via transpredications. The child also sees that he or she can affect the course of events, and that still other events might have "gone otherwise" had the child acted to change things. Life can be influenced, leading to a sense of self-direction in the person who exerts such influence successfully.

Indeed, what stamps the human organism as fundamentally different from lower organisms is this capacity to influence its circumstances by way of repredicating what will exist or take place. This ability to influence our life circumstances is what LLT means by *free will*. A more technical term for such personal influence on events is *agency*. Logical learning theory defines agency as the capacity that an organism has to behave or believe in conformance with, in contradiction to, or without regard for what is perceived to be environmental or biological determinants. Thanks to transpredication, Shawn does not have to accept the convictions of others. He can readily reason to the opposite of what his doctor tells him and refuse to follow diagnostic recommendations. There is a risk here, of course, for if the doctor is correct poor Shawn may suffer physically or even die. According to LLT, *free will* may be defined as this capacity to frame the predication for the sake of which behavior will be intentionally carried out.

The "freedom" here comes before an affirmation is rendered in the telosponsive act. The "will" occurs after the predication has been affirmed, which is what is meant by *psychic determinism* in behavior. This predication need not always be well reasoned. People can behave impulsively "as immediate circumstances dictate" or "just for the hell of it." Habits can be formed, of course. But, thanks to the oppositionality of human reasoning, there is always the free-will possibility of behaving differently, all circumstances remaining the same. The implication here is that in order for a freely willing intelligence to function there must be psychic consciousness: that is, an awareness of potential alternatives. This is an interesting point that must be kept in mind as we forage through the various topics of this volume. I will eventually look more deeply into theories of free will (Chapter 6) and even come to a more sophisticated position on the possibility of unconscious free will (see Chapter 10). But there is much preparatory ground to cover first.

The final point I will mention in this chapter has to do with the *unconscious* versus the *unintended*. Just as there are nonconscious aspects of human behavior, there are behavioral actions carried out without intention. Sometimes this lack of intentionality is a chance event, as when we accidentally spill a glass of water on the table as we are reaching for the salt. There is no unconscious intention to create this accident, although it might be possible to make this case if we knew more about the people seated at the table. Freud loved to find the hidden meaning of such seemingly innocuous misactions (see Chapter 4).

Sometimes an unintended outcome arises from an intention that has gone awry. While lecturing, the professor spontaneously thinks of an example to prove the point under consideration. Unfortunately, her choice of words offends a student in the class because it can be understood to reflect negatively on a minority group. It was not the professor's intention to address minority issues. So far as her intentions are concerned these tangential issues are *aconscious*—of no relevance to her personal consciousness whatsoever. The meanings emerging in the classroom are entirely in the student's realm of consciousness, interpretations made suggesting that the professor is harboring an unconscious intention to demean the minority group in question. Although this is always a possibility, of course, we can say in this instance that it is definitely not true. It would take an extensive psychoanalysis to settle the issue in any case. But the point of importance here is that unintended occurrences like this, which involve the student's (possibly equally prejudicial) predications as well as the professor's, are *not necessarily* unconscious. They may be entirely unintentional, just as the spilling of the water glass was unintentional. According to LLT, it is possible to have unintended outcomes of both conscious and unconscious predications. We can only know the intentionality of any act *with certainty* if we are privy to the (introspectively framed) predication(s) being meaningfully extended by those involved.

CONCLUDING COMMENT

Logical learning theory significantly alters traditional explanations of human cognition and behavior (refer to the Glossary for definitions of the major LLT concepts). The view of psychic consciousness that follows from the precepts of LLT is also considerably different from the predominant mediational explanations of today. To assess what is psychically conscious or unconscious we must think about human reasoning as relational, and even as dimensional. One manifestation of consciousness reaches widely beyond the framing meanings under predication to interlace with other possibilities in the *Logos* realm of patterns, and the other narrows to a rigid focus that restricts the possible influence of alternatives on thought. This bipolarity of wide–narrow is another manifestation of the oppositionality that LLT finds so central to human reasoning. These contrasting features of predication will have to make sense as we go on to consider several topics relating to consciousness. I begin this broader survey—widening our personal psychic consciousness on this topic—in Chapter 3, where I take up historical developments that laid the groundwork for the LLT formulations introduced in the present chapter.

3

THE CONCEPT OF PSYCHIC
CONSCIOUSNESS ACROSS THE AGES

There is more to be understood from the presentation of LLT in Chapter 2 than simply the interpretation of psychic consciousness that it affords us. That is, in order to make this interpretation it was necessary to rethink and revise the very human image that academic or scientific psychology has drawn on for over a century. In effect, we exercised our consciousness by going beyond the strictures of tradition to predicate human behavior teleologically rather than mechanically. We now have the theoretical tools to go forward in our study of consciousness. But the additional lesson to be learned here is that how we view this remarkable phenomenon—indeed, whether we acknowledge it at all—depends upon our self-understanding. The same can be said of this phenomenon in Western history. That is, how people have thought about themselves over the ages has been the key to what it means to be conscious or unconscious.

Certain precedent opinions and attitudes had to exist before the notion of consciousness could be framed. For example, a concept of identity or selfhood seems a necessary prerequisite. And why would this identity take an interest in its psychic consciousness in the first place? What of reflexivity in thought? And when the identity first turns back to examine things consciously, what motivates such self-examination? In the present chapter I trace the idea of consciousness across the ages in Western history to demonstrate that not until an independent, morally acceptable sense of selfhood arose could thinkers begin taking personal (or individual) consciousness seriously. With the rise of this self-consciousness in post-medieval times there was a parallel rise in artistic expression and scientific investigation. Mechanical inventions and measurements, particularly as employed in natural science, challenged and eventually dismissed the concept of consciousness. This dismissal had great significance for the human image that was to be fashioned in the rise of psychology and related social sciences.

I should emphasize that our glance across history involves differences in content over time and does *not* concern the nature of the process per se. Human beings have always reasoned according to a predicational process just as they have always ingested food thanks to a digestive process. The predicational process was not begun after the words signifying consciousness were first coined by some sociocultural collective—anymore than digestion began after food names were thus coined. I do not want to be understood as saying that consciousness as process is a mere cultural artifact, a terminological phrasing that has been itself shaped over the centuries as a linguistic content by yet another (e.g., *Socius*) process. In Chapter 9, I will take up social-constructionist theories that actually do view consciousness as a cultural artifact.

RELIGIO-MORAL BEGINNINGS: NEGATIVE SELFHOOD

The concept of consciousness begins in religious formulations. Speaking from a Jungian perspective, Popović (1991) has noted concerning the archetypal Garden of Eden myth: "With his [and her] first mouthful in Paradise [woman and] man *succeeded*, by tasting of the fruit of the tree of good and evil, *in becoming conscious*" (p. 115; italics added). This capacity to understand good *and* evil as the many among one dimension of moral oppositionality beautifully symbolizes the birth of transpredication. What is more, the resulting guilt arising from the negation of a godly prohibition thrusts self-identity onto Adam and Eve. These individuals are now responsible for what transpired and they must pay the penalty for their sinful self-expression. The resultant sense of self is decidedly negative. The self is pictured as weak, succumbing to temptation and falling short of the demands placed upon it. Psychic consciousness was therefore initially tied to self-denigration. Indeed, Engelberg (1972) has noted that the words *consciousness* and *conscience* are etymologically related: "The two words were close relatives, consciousness evolving from conscience as the latter became increasingly associated with good or bad, that is, with moral definitions" (pp. 11–12).

When contemplating one's responsibility in a life event, sinful or otherwise, the matter of a reflexive thinking process necessarily arises. I have already suggested that the human being has always had a predicational process taking place in thought—although it may not have been given emphasis at any one period of history. I take this human cognitive process to be fundamentally reflexive. But in order for psychic consciousness as a concept to be developed further in the history of ideas we would surely have to see an emphasis being given to introspective examination, which in turn calls for a recognition of self-reflexive thinking. Snell (1953) correctly observed that the discovery of the human intellect "exists by the grace of man's [and woman's] cognizance of himself [and herself]" (p. vi).

Most scholars attribute this early display of reflexive thinking to St. Augustine (354–430). In his *Confessions* Augustine (1961) uses his reflexive intelligence to explore the weaknesses of a self that can only win eternity through total submission to the grace of God. Conscience is heavily wound into the resulting consciousness. Taylor (1989) has shown how Augustine shifts our attention from the Graecian belief in an external order to the inward examination of a disorganized self (soul) needing such ordering (pp. 111, 121). The Platonic adage to be ruled by reason called for such an extraspectively conceived ordering: "Thus the good life for us is to be ruled by reason not just as the vision of correct order in our souls but also and more fundamentally as the vision of the good order of the whole" (p. 122).

Augustine (1961) draws us inward, to an introspective examination of his disordered inner self—a "house divided against itself" (p. 170). In elaborating on this division, Augustine blames himself for his evil ways (p. 34), appreciates that God has given him the gift of selfhood (p. 40), distrusts his personal reasoning capacity (p. 117), and even denies his personal will in favor of God's will, interpreted now as *grace* (p. 181). The extent of actual consciousness here is open to question, as when Augustine concludes that "For even what I know about myself I only know because your [God's] light shines upon me; and what I do not know about myself I shall continue not to know until I see you face to face and *my dusk is noonday*" (p. 211; italics in original). There is a delimiting of consciousness here, a studied (good form of) unconsciousness being suggested. The "inner self" was soon to be equated with the "soul" (p. 212).

At this period of history, to have placed oneself "above" God, in the sense of achieving one's salvation on the basis of personal achievements or capacities would be considered Pelagianism. Pelagius (circa 360–420) was excommunicated for preaching in a humanistic vein: for example, he suggested that "I do not obey God, I agree with him. I follow him because of my own conviction, not because I have to" (Heer, 1962, p. 37). The matter of free will was obviously involved here. Pelagius was trying to put more responsibility on the individual's shoulders. A freely choosing self must consciously decide whether to predicate things "this or that" way, including the claims of religious dogma. Depending on one's viewpoint this could involve a bad form of psychic consciousness. Augustine (1961), who struggled to learn that faith was fundamental to belief (p. 117), found that the only conscious decision a Christian need make was whether to accede to God's will. Once this accession was made, a good form of psychic unconsciousness was in place. The negative selfhood of humanity was corrected through the benefits of divine grace.

The Arabic scholars, Avicenna (980–1037) and Averroës (1126–1198) introduced the concept of *cogitation* as a kind of reflexive thinking (Carruthers, 1990, p. 53). Earlier Latin scholars had referred to a *cogitativa*, a sort of conscious but yet prerational mental activity such as knowing instinctively what to do in situations. The Arabian modification put more awareness into the concept, laying the groundwork for later thinkers like Spinoza (1632–1677) who used *cogitatio* to mean the faculty of reflexive thought. Averroës also stressed the importance of imagination and memory in thinking. Reflexivity thus was to become a recognized aspect of cognition, and as the means by which transpredications can arise it is surely an essential aspect of psychic consciousness (see Locke vs. Kant on reflexivity in Chapter 1).

RENAISSANCE AND BEYOND: POSITIVE SELFHOOD

As it ended in a complete dependence on the deity, Augustine's inward self-exploration did not encourage the autonomy of selfhood. The religiously devout person would, in effect, practice positive unconsciousness by limiting himself or herself to dogmatic instructions, inspired by divine grace. Even so, the emphasis Augustine placed on will as a power to confer or withhold assent to this grace did eventually effect a modest Pelagian influence on medieval thinkers. Initially, this emphasis on will and willpower was understood completely within a religious context. As Brown (1987) has observed: "Medieval men thought of one another . . . not as personalities with deep inner drives and tensions, but as moral characters whose virtues and vices were apparent in their speech and actions" (p. 34). The self concept retained its negative connotation through the 15th century (Rosenthal, 1984, p. 9). But over the two following centuries there was a gradual shift to a more positive attitude toward this concept.

Respect for all of humanity was on the rise, and this value was not advanced solely amongst the intelligentsia. There were significant peasant uprisings throughout the 11th century, and for several centuries to follow there were associations of peasants, all calling for "the natural equality" of human beings (Heer, 1962, p. 62). Christian values were penetrating basically pagan societies, and with this infusion came a rising appreciation for a selfhood that had to assume *individual* (free-will) responsibility for its actions. Indeed, the leading historian of the Italian Renaissance, Jacob Burckhardt (1818–1897), once observed that 15th-century Italy began "to swarm with individuality" (Rosenthal, 1984, p. 13). The political attitudes and efforts of the nobility to break away from the dominion of the Pope promoted individualism in this century (Heer, 1962, p. 188). The psychological change taking place here was from selfhood construed as a kind of indiscriminate *soul*, submitting to the deity's intentions, to selfhood as a unique identity—referred to eventually as *subjectivity* (Rosenthal, 1984, p. 13). To achieve such subjective identity requires transpredication, the capacity to view things unlike anyone else and to behave for the sake of unique—often "higher"—ends. The Renaissance period is virtually synonymous with the broadening of one's own (subjective) psychic consciousness in this manner. Whyte (1960) has noted that by the 17th century, the meaning of *conscious* had dropped its Latin derivative of "to know with . . . another" and become "to know in oneself, alone" (p. 38).

There was also a dark side to the developing optimism of the early Renaissance. I refer here to the world as depicted by Jean de Meung (around 1277) in his encyclopedic work *Roman de la Rose*. Heer (1962) found a "somber vision" of the world prompting this book, which claimed that "the universe was a mechanism, like a watch. Man's life was determined by iron necessity and fate [was] dependent upon the stars and the laws of nature . . . [for] there is neither freedom nor personal individuality" (p. 147). This schism between individual selfhood and universal mechanism was to become a major concern of the post-Renaissance philosophies. The philosopher who is usually credited with first separating and then interacting mind (psychic consciousness) with body (physical mechanism) is René Descartes (1596–1650). Straus (1958) believes that this eminent French thinker had finally distinguished between the religious and the purely psychic understanding of consciousness, as follows: "The word *conscientia* with the connotation of 'conscience' is a classical term; the use of the word *conscientia* with the connotation of 'consciousness' begins with Descartes. The Cartesian consciousness is a worldless, bodyless, incorporeal thinking substance" (p. 141). Descartes's use of "systematic doubt" as a method for finding truth also contrasts with Augustinian introspection on the question of negative versus positive selfhood. Taylor (1989) summed up this contrast:

> For Augustine, the path inward was only a step on the way upward. Something similar remains in Descartes, who also proves the existence of God starting from the self-understanding of the thinking agent. But the spirit has been altered in a subtle but important way. Following Augustine's path, the thinker comes to sense more and more his lack of self-sufficiency, comes to see more and more that God acts within him. In contrast, for Descartes the whole point of the reflexive turn is

to achieve a quite self-sufficient certainty. What I get in the cogito, and in each successive step in the chain of clear and distinct perceptions, is just this kind of certainty, which I can generate for myself by following the right method. (p. 156)

This self-generated certainty is what I meant by the Pelagian influence of Augustinian introspection on post-medieval thinkers. This search for certainty dominates philosophy as the 17th century unfolds, lending its growing influence to the rise of scientific experimentation that Roger Bacon (circa 1220–1292) had extolled centuries earlier (Heer, 1962, p. 135). How do we know we have certain truth? What method of proof can establish such certainty? *Truth* is by definition not to be questioned. In our terms, truth is a unipredication concerning some item of interest. One does not transpredicate true facts. Truth is truth, period. Descartes believed that "clear and distinct" ideas were the foundations of such truth. His rational method was consistent with a teleological image of human behavior. But the irony is that as this increasing self-confidence was manifested, in which the self could generate and scientifically test its "clear and distinct" ideas, there was a concurrent and equivalent limitation being placed on teleological description thanks to the growing mechanization of nature that this very science promoted. Positive selfhood promoted a confident scientific method consistent with, and eventually limited to, the efficient causation of mechanism—a point I will elaborate on at the close of this chapter.

There is a theory-versus-method issue involved here as well because using a Cartesian standard like "clear and distinct" ideas is relying on a coherence view of truth, involving what I termed in Chapter 1 a procedural form of evidence. Is Descartes's rational–cognitive test of plausibility sufficient grounds on which to believe in something with certainty? For self-belief, for subjective conviction, it is surely enough. But what of the more objective form of truth which transcends subjectivity to hold across the board? In this case we look for a correspondence measure of truth, relying on validating evidence. The danger here is that we might confuse our method of obtaining proof with the theory under test.

The contrast of a machine-like world of natural laws and the choices of a freely willing self was to haunt the human image from the 17th century onward. How are we to understand the latter in terms of the former? We have still not solved this riddle in psychology, although we continue trying to do so. I next turn to an examination of the influence that mechanism had on the understanding of psychic consciousness.

THE MECHANICAL INTRUSION

Descartes suggested that the mechanical body and the psychic mind interacted through the pineal gland of the brain. Taylor (1989) referred to this suggestion as a *disengagement* (p. 162), for once he had shifted from self-reflexive examination of direct experience to a physical gland that conveyed the sensations of this experience mechanically, Descartes had separated (disengaged) himself from directing things as a willful self (p 163). The internal experience of something like holding to a conviction is lost to such external formulations of glands secreting their substances to effect mechanical changes for the self. In our terms, Taylor is here pin-pointing a shift from first-person (introspective) to third-person (extra-spective) understanding and description. An introspective theoretical ex-perience cannot be captured through extraspective terminology because the latter invariably calls on material and efficient causation whereas the for-mer demands formal and final causation. As philosophy was to develop, the British influence became increasingly important. This line of thought followed John Locke, who totally disengaged himself as an "observer" from the "object" under study (Taylor, 1989, p. 164). Underlying this Lockean disengagement was a view of the universe as mechanical: that is, moved solely by an independent realm of efficient causation. There are many ways in which to analyze the roots of the mechanistic worldview propounded in the 17th century. We will limit our consideration to three major sources of influence bearing on selfhood and psychic consciousness.

Time

The flow of efficient causation, which was presumed to be moving linearly across time, was central to the development of what was to become Newtonian science over the 17th and 18th centuries. In fact, Isaac Newton (1642–1727) held that there was a flow of *absolute time* taking place—someplace—and against which variations in rate of change, speed of mo-tion, and so on, could be calculated. He believed that this stream of time "was independent of man [and woman]; it flowed by itself" (Fraser, 1987, p. 42). Newton's need for such a concept was primarily mathematical. That is, with the assumption of absolute time it was possible for Newton to formulate scientific laws that could be expressed in equations. The time factor was a "constant" in such equations, lacking precise definition but filling an essential role (p. 41). Such constancy could be used as an anchor point against which variations in rate of motion could then be measured. Immanuel Kant early recognized the predicational nature of time, noting that this idea is an assumption we humans make because it is required for our minds to work properly and not because it has an independent exis-tence all its own (p. 42).

Einstein later dropped the notion of absolute time in his theory of relativity. Imagine two celestial bodies observed to be closing in on and then moving right past each other in space. There are no reference di-mensions (like other bodies) framing or predicating this event—just sheer void as a spatial background. What can we say in answer to questions like which body is moving and at what speed? Without a predicating context our task would be difficult and ultimately the answers given would be arbitrary—that is, relative to "where" we anchored our measurements (e.g., on the basis of yet a third body acting as a reference point). One or the other of our two bodies could therefore be said to be moving while the other was considered stationary. Or, both bodies could be assumed to be moving (relative to the third). The speed at which one or the other body moved would be similarly determined by our anchoring selections. The matter of time's passage is obviously up to us here in how we wish to conceptualize things—a transpredicational act if ever there was one. It is therefore not surprising to find a modern astrophysicist like Stephen Hawking (1988) saying that "time is imaginary and indistinguishable from directions in space" (p. 135).

How is it that human beings find it difficult to think about the concept of time as an imaginary assumption? Sometimes we are totally unaware of time's passage, as it flies by at an astonishing rate. On other occasions, time drags on at a snail's pace. Such contrasts surely imply that a meaning-endowing predication is playing a role in our experience of this "thing" called time. There seems to be something about our human nature that leads us to reify time. As teleological organisms we are fundamentally oriented to the future—both in the immediate and longer term sense. We can and do telospond to the "past," but the basic sense we have of life is as always extending from "now" to the "next" event (occurrence, happening, etc.). This future orientation strongly suggests that something is passing. We call this something *time*.

The logic seems to be: "Life goes on, so time must pass." Furthermore, a sense of selfhood is doubtless suggested by the fact that we can deny our future. As Fraser (1987) has observed, "Many animal species prepare for the future, but unlike humans, they cannot *not* prepare" (p. 8; italics in original). Animals are instinctively prompted to behave in a state of constant unconsciousness—albeit of a good variety because it is adaptive. But as we humans are highly oppositional reasoners, we find it possible to break free of any such life-directing promptings, including negating life altogether if we have a (sound or unsound) reason for doing so. Suicide might be termed a way of holding one's personal time constant "forever."

Although there have been many different conceptions of time's progression (see Fraser, 1987, p. 64; Slife, 1993, pp. 14–15), the predominant view—especially in the West—has been that of a linear passage. One of the major influences on such linearity was the steady advance of a mechanistically framed Newtonian science, to which I have alluded and will return to later in this chapter. Mechanistic accounts are the very opposite of teleological accounts, for they do not employ final causation (Reese, 1980, p. 345). They are founded on a regularity of linear motion taking place over what can be viewed as fixed and measurable units of time's passage.

Time measurement has an interesting history. Initially, it was measured via the changing angles cast by the shadows of vertical structures like trees and even people over the course of a "day." This measurable unit of time was, of course, dependent on the earth's rotation in relation to the sun. In fact, we might want to see in this patterned relation between the sun and earth *the* fundamental definition of time's passage. Note that we would be relying here on a formal-cause circularity and not on an efficient-cause linearity. The Egyptians were apparently the first people to perfect a sundial, although some people think the Chinese preceded them. The earliest devices keeping time without using the sun as a referent were water clocks, in which it was assumed that water moved through an orifice at a constant rate (Fraser, 1987, p. 49). Sand clocks relied on a similar assumption concerning the rate of sand's motion before mechanical pulleys, gears, and pendulums were introduced. Deciding when a single day took place in the course of the sun–earth relation has varied. Most primitive groups took sunrise to be the beginning of a day. But the ancient Egyptians counted a day from midnight to midnight, as modern societies do (p. 47). In traditional Judaic culture, a day began at sunset. Teutonic tribes counted nights instead of days. As with our celestial bodies in space, how days, nights, hours, and so on, are measured is pretty much up to the predicating intentions of those who devise the measurements.

A mechanical measuring device that had immense influence on the daily lives of pre- and post-Renaissance city dwellers was the town clock:

> The mechanical clock seized the imagination of our ancestors. Something of a civic pride which earlier had extended itself to cathedral building was now directed to the construction of astronomical clocks of outstanding intricacy and elaboration. No European community felt able to hold up its head unless in its midst the planets wheeled in cycles and epicycles, while angels trumpeted, cocks crew, and apostles, kings and prophets marched and countermarched at the booming of the hour. (White, 1962, p. 124)

With the emphasis on time by way of such marvelous mechanisms, the medieval individual could now "clock" his or her daily routine according to a precise, linear unit. If time flowed and could be broken up in this manner then the individual qua self enacting things under the timing of such units could also break up, arrange, align, and carry out an efficient day's activities. Such achievements strengthen the concept of selfhood as an agency that accomplishes projected goals, falls into routine habits, and so on. I am reminded here of Kant's famous afternoon walk, carried out with such daily precision that his fellow citizens used to set their time pieces as he passed by (Russell, 1959, p. 238).

Such commitment to the ordering of linear time facilitated certain transpredications. The time-conscious individual is capable of looking to some changing development or alternative taking place in the next hour, minute, or second. In the style of Dickens' Mr. Micawber, he or she can be eternally waiting for something to turn up. Of course, carried to the extreme, such time involvements can go in the other direction and result in a psychic consciousness typified by the unipredications of compulsivity and obsessiveness. Mumford (1934) notes that in the 19th century, when cheap watches were finally produced, people began increasingly to live according to the dictates of time rather than their spontaneous inclinations (p. 17). For example, they ate during the noon hour whether hungry or not. This may have begun as a helpful unipredication, a desire to reduce life's uncertainties through systematization. But one can be paralyzed by rigidity if the goal becomes systematization for systematization's sake.

Time is also related to memory, an aspect of cognition having relevance for consciousness. Carruthers (1990) has suggested that there have been two models of memory in Western history: "memory as a set of waxed tablets upon which material is inscribed; and memory as a storehouse or inventory" (p. 14). Recall from Figure 1 that the mediation model relies on a tabula rasa assumption of blank sheets or waxed tablets, onto which the external world inscribes its mediating influences. The focus here is entirely on the receptive wax, which passively receives what is inscribed. The meaningful patterning of this inscription originates outside the mediation process so there is no need to explain how these patterned impressions are created. We are, in effect, dealing in mere signals and not meaningful symbols (see Chapter 10). As mediation modelers, our job is limited to explaining how these signal-patterns are input "ready formed" and then come to determine the course of mediation.

In contrast, a predication modeler (see Figure 2), to whom meaning is paramount, considers the selective intentions of the creator of the meaningful pattern found inscribed on the wax. The assumption is that what has been inscribed could have been patterned otherwise all circumstances remaining the same. Indeed, a negating or contradicting pattern of meaning could just as easily have been impressed except for the decision of the person using the stylus to imprint the wax. Aristotle was the first thinker to raise this active–passive, or creative–instrumental issue. As for the storehouse conception, Aristotle appreciated that what is put away or what is retrieved depends on the intentions of the "user" of the storehouse. As a teleologist, he grasped that there was a difference between intentionally trying to retrieve something from memory and having it simply pop into mind.

Thus, assume that a mental storehouse is to be tapped for one specific memory. How do we go about digging it out for present use? Aristotle (1952c) distinguished between *recollection*, an active effort to remember something from the past, and *association*, a passive form of remembering. Such automatic associations of one mental item with another were seen as occurring in a rote fashion, with passive alignments that did not require an intentional effort on the part of the thinker (pp. 412–413). As Carruthers (1990) notes concerning Aristotle's views on association: "Rote repetition, since it is not 'found out' by any heuristic scheme, is not considered recollection or true memory *(memoria)*" (p. 20). Recollection requires an active effort on the part of the thinker. Thus, Aristotle (1952b) asks "Why does one thing attach [relate] to some other?" and then answers: "We are inquiring . . . why something is predicable of something . . . . the inquiry is about the predication of one thing of another" (p. 565). Carruthers (1990) emphasizes that "For Aristotle, recollection is the active, intellectual process, distinct from the passive receiving nature of memory" (p. 62).

So there are two points in the sequence of memory where an active formulation might take place: at the initial organization of memory and then subsequently, at a later time when the effort to remember is made. This means that what goes in the storehouse may not be an exact copy of what is supposed to go in. And, what comes out need not be an exact copy of what went in. In both ancient times and the Middle Ages it was therefore the goal of scholars to train the memory "at both ends" of this process. Of the two, the initial organization, the heuristic framing of a memory was seen as the more important side (Carruthers, 1990, p. 61). But it is also true that these two were the opposite sides of the same coin. If we use an effective heuristic when an item is put into the storehouse we can also use this heuristic to draw out (recollect) the item at a later time.

A popular mnemonic was the *method of loci*, in which the person would use a predicating context of some imagined or real setting, like a building with many spaced columns, a street scene, or a pathway through a garden. This well-known predicating context was then extended to pattern items targeted for memory. For example, things to be retained in memory were "placed" (via imagery) at familiar locations (loci) along these columnar spaces, streets, or garden pathways. A grocery list might require that, as we walk through our familiar garden, we put the bread at the gate, the vegetables at the rose bush, the milk at the pool, and so on. Upon entering the grocery store we merely retrace our mental steps through the garden and "pick up" these items in mind as we also purchase them in actuality (p. 93).

Aristotle (1952d) had proposed the following four aids to recollection based on how he believed that ideas in the mind were initially organized: *similarity, contiguity, frequency,* and *contrariety* (p. 693). We remember things more readily because they are similar to other things (e.g., two animals with beaks), or they are contiguous in time (e.g., thunder follows lightning), or because we are very familiar with them (e.g., we have admired interesting architecture for years). All of these factors enter into how our memories are organized—that is, predicated—initially. But note that, in singling out contrariety (e.g., tall people are opposed to short people), Aristotle is essentially supporting the claim that the predicational process involves a generic oppositionality. I will have more to say about Aristotle's recognition of oppositionality in reasoning when I take up his contrast between dialectical and demonstrative reasoning strategies in Chapter 7.

Movable Type

A historic development that significantly influenced concepts of self-hood, individualism, and consciousness was the writing and especially the publishing and distribution of books. Johann Gutenberg (circa 1398–1468) invented the machine that made movable type possible (circa 1438–1439). The widely cited book by Marshall McLuhan (1962) entitled *The Gutenberg Galaxy* provides a context for considering this topic. McLuhan has several interlacing themes wound into his analysis, and there is no need to cover all of them. But there is relevant material here that can take us from our consideration of time to the discussion of natural science that follows.

The earliest forms of writing were pictorial. Pictographs were eventually reduced to formal symbols that stood for the production and recording of speech sounds: the *phonetic alphabet*. Note that a pictorial system is essentially a matching procedure, a kind of tautological identity drawn between the item pictured and its independent existence in reality. If the phonetic alphabet had not been devised, the Gutenberg revolution would never have taken place (McLuhan, 1962, p. 54). According to McLuhan, with the advent of the phonetic alphabet and movable type, Western civilization moved from an oral to a visual culture. McLuhan also holds that with the rise of the electronic media (telegraph, radio, and television) we are beginning to revert to an oral culture once again (pp. 91–92).

From about the 11th century, there was a growing interest, aided by the invention of eyeglasses, in the reading of books (Carruthers, 1990, pp. 156–159). Even so, before 1500 few books were assembled in editions larger than 1,000 (handwritten) copies. People in antiquity and the Middle Ages read aloud, often in an effort to put the text to memory (p. 11). Thanks to the eloquence of Cicero (106–43 BC), a growing interest in oratory developed. A talented orator was thought to have wisdom. But this wisdom was not attributed to the orator per se. That is, in line with the modest role for selfhood during this period of history, an orator was seen as expounding an intellectual tradition rather than expressing a personal or individual point of view. Books of this period might not even list the name of their authors; sometimes the scribe was given instead of the author (McLuhan, 1962, p. 160).

In 1500 no one knew how to market the books that were mass-produced through movable type. Books had always been circulated in a used or second-hand market, like other works of art (McLuhan, 1962, pp. 159–160). In time, the importance of print as a commodity was realized and an industry formed around the mass production of books (p. 153). Such mass production became a model for many different aspects of modern culture (p. 250). In other words, McLuhan uses the printing and distribution process as a metaphor for all of culture, speaking of a print culture, typographic culture, and mechanical culture as essentially the same thing. To explain the influence of this media-generated milieu on the consciousness of a culture's participants, McLuhan contrasts a print (i.e., visual) with an oral (phonetic) culture:

> A child in any Western milieu is surrounded by an abstract explicit visual technology of uniform time and uniform continuous space in which "cause" is efficient and sequential, and things move and happen on single planes and in successive order. But the African child lives in the implicit magical world of the resonant oral word. He encounters not efficient causes but formal causes of configurational field such as any non-literate society cultivates. (p. 28)

Modern society has indeed been fashioned with the understanding that all causation is exclusively efficient (mechanical) causation. I want to close this chapter with a discussion of this fact, although I will be tracing its origin to something in addition to the linearity of movable print. That is, I will trace the modern restriction of causation to the efficient by way of the rise of natural science.

McLuhan was quite interested in showing the influence of print on science. He believed that just as scientists must be constantly aware of the influence that their instruments have on their senses, so too do we require a study of the ways that ideas are shaped by the various media. We want to avoid being unconsciously biased by the media's limitations (p. 42). Printing is not only itself a mechanical enterprise (p. 153), but "with the Gutenberg technology we move into the age of the take-off of the machine" (p. 189). McLuhan concludes that with this increasing mechanization there is a concurrent decline in the ability to appreciate the total pattern, the field, the "'formal causality,' both in our inner and external lives" (p. 155).

Language is metaphorical. It enables the thinker to translate experience from one mode into another. "Money" is one such linguistic metaphor because it stores skill and labor, and translates one skill into another (McLuhan, 1962, p. 13). We can frame life in terms of such value exchanges, economic maneuverings, and the like. Language encourages transpredications to take place. We can break the bonds of routine habits in many ways, but at least one of them is to begin thinking about our circumstances analogically or metaphorically—taking from "this" in order to capture "that." The narrowing of psychic consciousness that occurs in a mechanical world works against such metaphorical creativity, favoring rather a specialist's world. Specialists do not have to know very much about things beyond their predicating expertise. They are cautious about speculating "out of bounds." Specialization is thus a useful uniprediction, but it also has certain drawbacks.

David Riesman distinguished between an inner- and an other-directed form of human consciousness. This distinction has to do with the basis for affirming predications that would guide or direct one's life. What is common to other-directed people is "that their contemporaries are the source of direction" including not only those whom they actually know or interact with, but various images as presented in the mass media (Riesman, Glazer, & Denney, 1953, p. 37). For inner-directed people, on the other hand, the source of direction in behavior "is implanted early in life by the elders and directed toward generalized but nonetheless inescapably destined goals" (p. 30). Riesman's thesis was that other-directedness was increasingly evident among the upper-middle class of the larger cities in the United States at mid-20th-century (p. 34). McLuhan (1962) argued that inner-directedness, which is the sort of consciousness that individualism is based on, was not possible until there was a "fixed point of view" (p. 39) taking place. He felt this preliminary was necessary because "a stable, consistent character is one with an unwavering outlook, an almost hypnotized visual stance, as it were" (p. 39).

In the scribal reproduction of books this point of view was not apparent, the visual "slant" on what was being conveyed could not so readily be broken off from the audile–tactile process (p. 72). There is a certain impersonalism conveyed in a mass-produced book that is lacking in the "in touch" mode of the scribe. The scribe conveyed a tradition "through" this more personalized effort that gave a different predicating meaning to the content being read than the visual "looking at" of the printed materials:

> As the literal or 'the letter' later became identified with light *on* rather than light *through* the text, there was also the equivalent stress on 'point of view' or the *fixed* position of the reader: 'from where I am sitting.' Such a visual stress was quite impossible before print stepped up the visual intensity of the written page to the point of entire uniformity and repeatability. (McLuhan, 1962, p. 138; italics in original)

Note that when we take into consideration "from where I am sitting" we of necessity shift the predications under consideration from an extraspective (third person) to an introspective (first person) perspective. There is a recognition here that how "I" see things, how "I" predicate what is taking place has relevance to the understanding of what a communication or message means. When intellectual traditions were being uncritically copied and thus sent "to" the reader by the scribe, instead of having the reader frame them from where he or she was sitting, the introspective understanding of messages was minimized. But this growing recognition of the introspective viewpoint changes things dramatically. The possibility and extent of an introspectively framed viewpoint has continued to make itself known in the intellectual history of Western civilization, and is vitally important today. There is a continuing debate over whether and how much a person can actually frame a unique point of view (see Chapter 9).

A common alternative to the individual point-of-view position is to say that the collective provides this for the person:

> To a large extent, behavior is shaped and modified by the socially defined situations in which people find themselves. While there remains much individual variation within a given situation, there is also a larger consistency in the patterned variations most people exhibit as they move from one type of situation to another. (Meyrowitz, 1985, p. 27)

The social order (*Socius*) here plays the role that the intellectual tradition played in medieval times, defining for the person what is to be assumed, believed, and carried out. There is the same diminution of selfhood in such modern formulations as was typical of the pre-Renaissance world.

McLuhan (1962) appreciated that there is always a role for individualism within social organizations, and he at least mentions oppositionality in this context: "Print created national uniformity and government centralism, but also individualism and opposition to government as such" (p. 282). As noted in Chapter 2, LLT would suggest that the capacity to counter governmental (as with all group) pressures stems from the human being's oppositional (dialectical) reasoning capacities. Printing one point of view—reflecting the predication of certain events—*always* implies some form of opposite position (via contradiction, contrariety, negation, or contrast regarding this predication). I will return to this question of the collective's influence on the individual (and vice versa) at several points in this volume (see especially Chapter 9).

Elaborating on post-Renaissance individualism, McLuhan (1962) noted that through its capacity to engage one or more points of view, print *decollectivizes*: "Print is the technology of individualism" (p. 192); "Print intensified the tendency to individualism as all historians have testified" (p. 213; see also White, 1962, who made the same point). Many forgotten and unknown writers of ages gone by were now brought into prominence (McLuhan, p. 245). Print served as a virtual public address system, amplifying the individual voice that was soon popularized in Elizabethan drama (p. 237). The portability of books facilitated such amplification (p. 248).

This new print culture obviously created a period of burgeoning transpredication, hence increasing psychic consciousness on all fronts of visual or observable knowledge. The Renaissance had initiated this sense of a growing consciousness which continued on into what has been termed the Ages of Reason (17th century) and Enlightenment (18th century). Even so, there was a limitation placed on the broadening of consciousness in other sensory modalities: "Paradoxically, . . . the first age of print introduced the first age of the unconscious. Since print allowed only a narrow segment of [visual] sense to dominate the other [auditory, tactile] senses, the refugees had to discover another home for themselves" (p. 292). There is much to know in the widening of psychic consciousness that a print culture is prone to overlook. Dramatically summarizing this point, McLuhan says: "The unconscious is a direct creation of print technology, the ever-mounting slag-heap of rejected awareness" (p. 293).

This formulation meets our interpretation of unconsciousness. To the extent that a culture does indeed focus on one point of view—in this case, the visual—and thereby overlooks alternatives reaching beyond the restricted range of predication made possible, we would be justified in saying that it promoted the hypertrophy of psychic unconsciousness. That is, any implications being suggested but not admitted to awareness would be tossed on the slag-heap of missed opportunities to widen consciousness. This treatment shares certain features with Carl G. Jung's interpretation of unconsciousness that I will take up in Chapter 4. The Romantic Age has sometimes been said to have encouraged an interest in the unconscious as a reaction against the Enlightenment (see, e.g., Taylor, 1989, p. 413), ofttimes expressed today in terms of the emotional versus the physical sides of experience. McLuhan (1962) says essentially the same thing: "Our fascination with all phases of the unconscious, personal and collective, as with all modes of primitive awareness, began in the eighteenth century with the first violent revulsion against print culture and mechanical industry" (pp. 42–43).

Scientific Experimentation

McLuhan traces the take-off of the machine age and natural science to the Gutenberg revolution. There is surely validity to this claim. But we cannot overlook the fact that Roger Bacon was calling for experimentation in the 13th century, long before movable type was invented. Experimentation involves setting up a sequence of events so that by first manipulating what was to be called the *independent variable* we could subsequently observe its effect on the *dependent variable*. If we turn up the heat we can measure both the increasing temperature (independent variable) and the effect this has on a pot of water, ice, or lead pellets (dependent variable). Even though this experimental sequence obeys a formal-cause, logical patterning, experimenters gave it an efficient-cause interpretation as a cause–effect taking place across time (as in the heat's impact on liquids or solids). The experimentalists therefore helped reify the concept of linear time (see above), which they presumed they were observing flow past them. Such experimentally observed efficient-cause sequences were even measurable and reproducible. This pre-Gutenberg call to science was to help magnify the importance of mechanical explanations for all things. There was also an important religious theme tying into the emergence of mechanical explanation in science.

For centuries, Aristotle's four causes were used collectively to frame explanations. Final-cause usage was common in science up to the 16th century when a combination of historical events was to do away with telic explanation. One such event was Galileo's notorious clash with the churchmen of the Inquisition. The churchmen, relying on biblical accounts stemming from a deity teleology, deemed the solar system *geocentric* whereas Galileo's empirical studies using the telescope supported a *heliocentric* explanation of the solar system. His house arrest and (insincere) recantation heralded the beginning of the rejection of final-cause description in science.

But an even more important event that led to the dropping of final-cause description in favor of efficient-cause (mechanistic) description in science was Francis Bacon's (1561–1626) vigorous assault on Aristotle. Bacon argued that it was bad scientific explanation to say, as Aristotle had said, that leaves on trees are "for the sake of" protecting the fruit, or that skeletal bones are frames "for the sake of" holding up the fleshy parts of the body. The *Baconian Criticism* held that final-cause phraseology added nothing to the basic description of what we can empirically see when we observe trees or human bodies (Bacon, 1952, p. 45). Such phraseology was simply irrelevant to an understanding of these natural objects. Bacon did not reject the use of final causation in areas of knowledge where it was relevant, such as in ethics, aesthetics, and metaphysics. Such value-laden endeavors call for final-cause analysis. But he saw no reason for empirical scientists to add such unobserved preferences into what they actually see taking place "over there," in ongoing reality. He was trying to take what McLuhan later called the "point of view" out of physical science. Ideally, science should shun excessive interpretation—the scientist's valued explanation—and deal strictly with the extraspectively observed "facts." For Bacon, the facts speak for themselves: scientific knowledge is apodictic.

If we take away final causation, what is left for a science to employ in its theoretical formulations? Quite obviously, what remains is material and especially efficient causation, with a secondary role for formal causation in referring to lawful patternings like the space orbits of the planets and so forth. From this time (17th century) onward the word *natural* as modifier of *science* or *evolution* meant "without final-causation." Bacon's critique was the opening salvo in what was to become the philosophy of British empiricism and the Newtonian brand of science that it promoted.

Isaac Newton was an uncompromising realist who drew a distinction between mathematical truths (in the mind) and physical truths (in the physical reality of the universe) and contended that there was no such thing as a priori certainty. He combined mathematics (a formal-cause discipline) and experimentation (an efficient-cause discipline) in a new way. Whereas Galileo viewed experiment as something he did when, for example, his mathematical efforts (intellect) led to two alternative outcomes and one had to be eliminated by experimental evidence, for Newton experimentation was the means by which a scientist clocked or mapped the precise lawfulness of what was then conceptualized as a mathematical universe (Burtt, 1955, p. 215).

Newton's universe was most assuredly a perfectly running machine. Laws of precision and exactitude existed independent of the scientist's point of view, so that for any event taking place before one's eyes there is a discoverable antecedent event (efficiently) causing it to take place. Though Newton relied on mathematics to frame his laws and predict their influence, it did not occur to him that the formal causation involved in mathematics could be a contributing factor to what he was empirically "observing." Newton and his followers succeeded in making a worldview or metaphysic out of a method of experimentation (p. 243). Bronowski (1958) further clarified this reification and elevation of efficient causation into natural lawfulness. He notes that scientists used the machine paradigm quite differently between the time of Leonardo da Vinci (1452–1519) and Newton: "when da Vinci wanted an effect, he willed, he planned the means to make it happen: that was the purpose of his machines. But the machines of Newton (and he was a gifted experimenter) are means not for doing but for observing. He saw an effect, and he looked for a cause" (p. 25).

And because all machines rely exclusively on efficient causation, it naturally followed that the causes Newton found were always of the efficient variety. Hence, the world became a grand machine. McLuhan warned about this confusion between the theory and the method used to prove that theory. Following Newton, 18th-century scientists elaborated the machine model and looked for mathematical certainty in all things. The pushes and pulls of basic, immutable laws, probably few in number and mathematically related to one another, were to be found in the world of reality, not postulated in the world of thought. The Age of Rationalism was giving way to the Age of Enlightenment. A hard determinism, resting on efficient-causation, gripped the empirical sciences. Such hard determinism reached its most eloquent expression in the famous remark of Laplace (1749–1827), "that a superhuman intelligence acquainted with the position and motion of the atoms at any moment could predict the whole course of future events" (Burtt, 1955, p. 96). The natural clock of linear time was wound; it would run its eternal and inflexible course.

Scientific and intellectual culture modified this mechanistic and completely deterministic attitude in the late 19th and early 20th centuries, as reflected in the writings of Hertz, Poincaré, and Duhem (Cassirer, 1950, Chapter V). As I noted earlier in this chapter, the Newtonian dream of tracing events in uniformly measured steps of efficient causation (i.e., via absolute time) has long since been abandoned in modern science. Units of measurement vary, depending on the location of an observer in a field (i.e., the observer's predicating context). It is even possible to think of familiar efficient-cause movements like passing through past, present, and future time as existing all at once, as a mosaic pattern (formal cause) with distinctive features known by these names (de Broglie, 1949). What one experiences as past, present, and future depends on the slice of space–time within which an observer frames the predicate assumptions about that which is being observed. Ernst Mach (1838–1916) showed how Newton's calculations rested on what are ultimately arbitrary assumptions, so that more than one mathematical system can explain the same empirically observed reality (Bradley, 1971, p. 83).

All such talk of the scientist influencing the course of empirical measurement is in line with the enhancement of selfhood that we saw taking place following the Renaissance period. Although he believed in the existence of a reality independent of its measuring instruments, Einstein also appreciated the role that the scientist qua predicator played in framing this reality. Citing Kant as his precedent, Einstein said that there are concepts "which play a dominating role in our thinking, and which nevertheless, cannot be deduced by means of a logical process from the empirically given" (Holton, 1973, p. 279). Prigogine and Stengers (1984) have suggested that the fact that relativity is founded on a constraint applying only to physically localized observers, to beings who can be in only one place at a time and not everywhere at once, gives Einsteinian physics a "human quality" (p. 218).

This human quality is diametrically opposed to the mechanism of Newtonian physics. What is the essence of a human quality? Surely it is the formal and final cause nature of any process under consideration. Pattern and organization enter into every corner of knowledge, observed or rationally induced and deduced. The formal has replaced the efficient as the most important of the four Aristotelian causes. This centrality was never more apparent than at the subatomic level of experimentation. It was becoming clear to the physicists early in this century that they could not hope to "picture" the world through mechanisms of the sort that Newtonianism had proposed, such as *ether* (Cassirer, 1950, p. 110). Subatomic particles are not "things" in the palpable sense of a material cause; nor do their motions follow linear time. Subatomic particles make jerky movements, jumping across units of uniform, linear measurement. Indeed, efficient causality breaks down completely in the realm of the subatomic, where physicists are prone to speak of particles as "complex structures" (Bohm, 1957, p. 33) that change in patterned organization without discernible efficient-cause sequences intervening.

Thus, when an electron changes orbits (or shells) around the nucleus of an atom, there is no way in principle to observe the electron moving from one orbit (shell) to the next in efficient-cause fashion. All we can observe is the changing pattern of what Niels Bohr called a given *stationary state* of the atom from one organization to the next (1934, p. 108). The passage of time is not a factor in such quantum leaps from one pattern to another, for they occur instantaneously. Each of these states or patterns must be considered an individual process, with its unique probabilities of occurrence; the change from one stationary state to another is not and never will be amenable to "detailed description" (p. 109).

One of the more dramatic examples of subatomic patterning occurs in demonstrations of Bell's theorem (Davies & Brown, 1986), which states that when two subatomic particles are emitted in reverse directions and the properties of one of them are measured, the properties of the other will be found to be correlated or linked to the first when it too is measured. Even if the distance between the two particles is that of light-years, the patterned relationship will hold. Such findings suggest that physical events occurring at subatomic levels have relevance for the broader reaches of the everyday world as well (Stapp, 1975). Although it has been common for advocates of a more Newtonian view of human beings to suggest that subatomic theories have little or no relevance for our macroscopic experience (see Dennett, 1984, p. 67, for an example of this attitude), the drift of speculation in physics today seems clearly to be that there are direct theoretical links between the findings at the subatomic level and the actions of human beings (see, e.g., Bohm, 1987). The linking tie here is that of formal causation—the influence of a wide-ranging pattern on the elements within its province.

I might note in passing that this form of theorizing is still extraspective, and is not what LLT advances in referring to the predication process of moving introspectively from broader (field-like) realms to narrower targets in meaning-extension. Even so, these findings suggest a fascinating question: Are these extraspectively framed theories of fields necessarily capturing a free-standing "reality" or might they be products of the physicist's (introspectively conceived) predicational process? Modern physicists—as all natural scientists—are at least open to the possibility that their basic thinking processes influence the theories that they come up with.

That is, finding that formal causation may be the most basic of all our four causes is not limited to subatomic physics. Chemistry (Prigogine & Stengers, 1984, pp. 136–137), biology (Sheldrake, 1988, p. xix), and mathematics (Gleick, 1988, p. 55) have all received important new concepts that are based exclusively on formal-cause meanings. Efficient causation has been jettisoned here entirely. There is a change taking place in the role of the modern scientist, who no longer traces smaller and smaller elements in hopes of getting to that basic substrate at which the blind forces of efficient causation supposedly whip up such elements into patterned Newtonian regularities.

Scientists today are beginning to suspect that there may *first* be (precedent) patterns or orders in nature and only secondarily does the motion of events come about as a reflection of this preexisting organization. As we noted in Chapter 2, the conceptual participation of the scientist's intellect with nature apparently supplies some of this order (Zukav, 1979, p. 29). Could it be that we are seeing here the two sides of the *Logos*, a combining of introspective with extraspective patternings? I admit this is a bit heady, but not as foolish a question to ask as it once was (see Bohm, 1987). As Prigogine and Stengers (1984) sum things up: "Out of the dialogue with nature initiated by classical [Newtonian] science, with its view of nature as an automaton [mechanism], has grown a quite different view in which the activity of questioning nature is part of its intrinsic activity" (p. 301). In short, the questions we ask of nature determine what we will learn about nature. Questions rely on assumptions, and the meanings at play here are clearly the province of the predicational process. Idealism has returned from its cold Newtonian grave to haunt the materialistic realists of today's science.

CONCLUDING COMMENT

Although people have always had the appropriate mental process enabling them to reason reflexively, our historical review suggests that it was not until the leading thinkers in Western civilization began framing a more positive view (mental content) of selfhood that this capacity was released. Consciousness benefitted immensely. This is an important lesson about human nature. The power of belief and its derivative convictions should never be underestimated. Such convictions act as precedent meanings, predicating what can possibly be carried out if human purpose is put to the task. There was a time when running a mile in less than four minutes seemed an impossible predication to frame. But once it was actually achieved, a sudden repredication occurred and numerous athletes fairly rapidly began to attain this formerly miraculous goal.

Nature seems to have provided us with a logical process in which we can either limit our interests to hone in on a narrow range of meaning and grasp it intensely, or back off to widen our expanse by leaping across formerly limiting boundaries. When there was little confidence placed in selfhood there was little motivation to do much leaping. As a result, the individual could not appreciate that he or she held a point of view concerning life, much less that it could be otherwise, *all circumstances remaining the same*. The image of a *Renaissance person* was to change this limiting cognizance. New meanings were generated, and as this enlightenment proceeded, the inevitable need to fix on evidence limiting what could be held forth as "the truth" arose.

The experimental method of science was one manifestation of this need to keep the "jumping across" predicating boundaries in some kind of check. Bacon's efforts were aimed at limiting excesses by taking humanistic predications out of science. A machine-like "natural" world is the quickest way to achieve this limitation because the free play of a reflexively open, teleological course of reasoning is what allows ideas to run wild in the first place. But the subsequent Einsteinian insights put humanity back into the center of the scientific equation, where it has continued playing a major role. Formal causation, which can interlace with each of the other three causal meanings, has replaced efficient causation as *the* important explanatory principle in the Aristotelian array.

But I am now speaking of modern developments. Much of what is thought of as consciousness and unconsciousness was forged into textbooks at the turn of the 20th century by the ground-breaking work of psychoanalytical investigators like Freud and Jung while they were still under the dominant influence of Newtonian science.

4

PSYCHOANALYZING PSYCHIC CONSCIOUSNESS

So far, I have been presenting *psychic consciousness* as essentially a dimension of meaning-extension bounded by unipredication at one end and transpredication at the other. But there is much more to be said here. As we do have a dimension, and not an either–or dichotomy, various degrees of such meaning-extension are possible. We might even be conscious about certain meanings and unconscious about others at the same time. Some unconscious things are on the tip of our tongue and others are totally beyond our general sense of awareness. We can also see this dimension reflected in fleeting ideas as well as the more protracted lines of thought. As Reggie sits with eyes half-closed on the subway train heading home after a hard day's work, many ideas float past his awareness. He notices some things. He seems occasionally to drift into sleep, but he is not certain. Every time a specific idea that he does not care to think about comes before his "mind's eye" he quickly changes the subject of his floating reveries. Why does this disliked idea come up again and again? How can something that is put out of mind come back? Are these maverick ideas conscious or unconscious?

As with anything relating to the mental, such questions are challenging. We human beings surely have certain innate biological capacities enabling us to do things like walk, talk, and think. But Reggie's questions concerning the sorts of things we think about—or, try to avoid thinking about—are especially tough to answer in *Bios* or *Physikos* terms. They invite us to consider the reasons, the motivating intentions, the wishful ends that our thought has put into play. This kind of analysis is better suited to a *Logos* formulation, where the crucial issue invariably points to something teleological. Francis Bacon would not blame us for seeking such final-cause explanations when it comes to understanding human thought. If we are lucky enough to find answers to Reggie's questions, we could add significantly to this understanding.

The field of investigation that has made the greatest effort to explain the intentional and defensive aspects of psychic consciousness is surely psychoanalysis. Sigmund Freud and Carl G. Jung provided the basics of this style of explanation, and therefore we will want to look into their work. But there were precedent thinkers from whom Freud and Jung drew, and we will consider two of the most important: Pierre Janet and Josef Breuer. Volumes could be devoted to other precedents, of course, but this would not add significantly to the main point I want to bring out in this chapter. We begin with Janet, move on to Breuer, and then take up Freud and Jung together so that these two "fathers" of psychoanalysis can be compared and contrasted. The chapter closes with a discussion of all four theorists from the perspective that we adopted in Chapter 2.

PIERRE JANET: DISSOCIATION (FIXED IDEA)

Janet (1859–1947) studied under Jean Charcot (1825–1893), professor of pathological anatomy in the medical faculty of Paris and founder of the neurological clinic at the Salpêtrière Hospital. He specialized in the study of hysteria using hypnotism. This kind of patient might have become blind or unable to walk even though there was no discernible physical cause bringing this condition about. Charcot proved that these symptoms could be removed while a patient was under the *suggestions* of the hypnotist. There seemed to be a separation of the personality across wakeful activity and the sleep-like trance of a hypnotic state. Freud spent a year studying at the Salpêtrière and was fascinated by Charcot's clinical demonstrations in which the lame were made to walk and the blind to see. According to Janet (1929/1965): "Charcot used to say that hysteria is an entirely psychic malady" (p. 322). Wittels (1924) suggested that Freud learned from Charcot that "ideas can induce bodily changes" (p. 29). The *Logos* versus *Bios* involvements here are obvious.

The challenge arises when we try to define just what "psychic" means, and what kind of explanation will satisfy the scientific community in this regard. By the latter half of the 19th century Newtonianism had swept through every nook and cranny of the scientific edifice. An explanation was not considered to be complete until it had traced the material–efficient-cause trail back down to its atomic origins—usually identified in the genetic history of the person, the species (homo sapiens), or combinations thereof. The *Bios* held sway in these medical-model explanations. Physical reductionism has yet to give up its hegemony in medical circles. Even today, the medico scientific community is likely to view *Logos* explanations as half-baked speculations. And things were a lot worse in the 1880s!

We can therefore understand the dilemma faced by the physicians of that era, who were trained to think in Newtonian terms but faced a startling new dynamic when their hypnotized patients shed symptoms on command (we will look more deeply into the phenomenon of hypnotism in Chapter 8). Janet's frank discussions on this matter are enlightening. He was a sophisticated theoretician who realized that the physiological definitions of the medical profession are frequently nothing more than "mere translations of the psychological ideas" held by their patients (Janet, 1929/1965, p. 323). But Janet also defended traditional medical knowledge and was reluctant to give in to psychology completely, as Freud seemed more willing to do.

Although Janet is sometimes cited as the author of the concept of a *fixed idea* in explaining hysterical symptoms (e.g., see Watson & Evans, 1991, p. 529), he credits Charcot with this authorship (Janet, 1929/1965, p. 233). Janet (1924) defined fixed ideas as "erroneous but fixed beliefs, developed by a psychic mechanism analogous to that of suggestion" (p. 257). The hysterical disease "consists essentially in an idea of which the patient is perfectly conscious" (Janet, 1929/1965, p. 233) even though it is clearly fantastic, erroneous, or unsupported by medical diagnosis. For example, a male patient "thinks" that a carriage wheel has passed over his legs and therefore he cannot walk: "It is not necessary that the carriage wheel should really have passed over the patient; it is enough if he has the [fixed] idea that the wheel passed over his legs" (p. 324).

Now, if the person is enacting this fixed idea (e.g., "My legs have been run over so I cannot walk"), on what basis is this a psychological rather than a strictly physical event? We can understand and explain the fixed idea as a stimulus–input that is being modified by mediators into a response–output (see Figure 1). Because this is taking place in the realm of learned signals (inputs and outputs), we might want to call this a psychological rather than a physical event. Physical events are not affected by learned mediators like this; they work automatically no matter what signaling is going on. A leg that is physically able to walk should engage in walking. But this man thinks he cannot walk on a perfectly healthy leg, so he does not walk. Under hypnosis he is told that his leg is all right, so he walks. There is a split in consciousness here—Janet (1929/1965, pp.

331–332) called it a *dissociation*—between what one side will enact and the other will not. But what are we really investigating, the fixed idea as a mediating *content* or the *process* that automatically carries it along? I think it is clear that we are emphasizing the mediating content and raising no questions about the process per se. The process is presumed to be mediational.

This distinction between the process and its content was generally overlooked by the French physicians, so that if something in the patient's thoughts (cognitions, etc.) influenced the purely mechanical (non-telic) sequence of mediation it was considered to have a psychological component. These were not the same kind of "dynamic" psychological components that Freud was later to propose—truly psychic strategies such as projection, reaction formation, sublimation, and so on—none of which were easily brought into the mediational assumptions of the medical model.

Janet reveals this reliance on what I would call a physically based mediational model in two ways. First, he suggests that people who are vulnerable to hysteria are biologically more sensitive to things; they take ideas more seriously and react more emotionally than others. Their ideas "seem to penetrate more deeply into the organism, and to bring about motor and visceral modifications [easily]" (p. 325). This intellectual and physiological sensitivity is what makes these people suggestible and emotional in comparison to the general population. Suggestion is "a too-powerful idea acting on the body in an abnormal manner" (p. 326). Second, Janet is quick to mention hereditary predisposition as a contributing factor in this trend to suggestibility and emotionality (p. 333). This explanatory strategy does not strike me as fundamentally psychological.

In fact, Janet liked to point out that not every hysterical loss can be easily tied to a fixed idea. Sometimes the doctor must notify the patient that he or she has a malady, like an unnoticed (unconscious?) loss of vision in only one eye (p. 327). Some fixed ideas occur without being tied to the symptom manifested, as a woman who was suffering from somnambulism but who also had the false idea that her mother was dead (p. 328). Though fixed ideas are not always perfectly aligned to the symptom picture, there does always seem to be an absentmindedness and a "retraction of the field of consciousness" occurring in hysteria (p. 331). The personality of the patient seems to be losing its synthesis. Here is Janet's summary definition of hysteria:

> Hysteria is a form of mental depression characterized by the retraction of the field of personal consciousness and a tendency to the dissociation and emancipation of the systems of ideas and functions that constitute personality. (p. 332, italics in original)

Note that the major emphasis here is clearly on the *dissociation* of mental contents under processing. Janet feels no need to take up the question of mental processing per se, because the medical model and its Newtonian foundations are already presumed. Janet, as any well-prepared physician of his day, knew how to frame a "proper" scientific explanation. But the problem remained that the conventional theoretical conceptions did not easily subsume the manifestations of the hysterical disorder. Even so, Janet goes on to give what is still a fundamentally biological rendering of hysteria. He says that it begins, as all other neuroses, with "a depression, *an exhaustion of the higher functions of the* [brain's] *encephalon* (p. 333; italics in original). Due to this exhaustion there is a lowering of "nervous strength" and then "consciousness, which is no longer able to perform too complex operations, gives up some of them" (p. 334). The result is "a localization of the mental insufficiency" (p. 335) in some specific loss like the immobility of a limb, inability to remember certain things, blindness, or the stubborn acceptance of a fixed idea. In all such cases, "the conscious will of the subject had no longer any control" (Janet, 1924, p. 40).

Janet was not pleased with the work of Breuer and Freud, from which psychoanalysis was spawned. He complained that Freud took Janet's clinical insights and after renaming his working theoretical speculations, "transformed a clinical observation and a therapeutic treatment with a definite and limited field of use into an enormous system of medical philosophy" (pp. 41–42). There is no doubt that Freud captured the imagination of the fledgling psychiatric field, but I am not sure that Janet understood why he was so successful. Freud succeeded because he expanded the investigation to include the psychic *process* as well as its various contents. Freud plunged into the question of how the psyche actually worked to bring about the various manifestations or contents of maladjustment.

JOSEF BREUER: HYPNOID STATE

Josef Breuer (1842–1925) was an older, established neurologist who had a successful practice in Vienna. Breuer befriended Freud and helped him to begin the practice of neurology in Vienna following the latter's completion of his Parisian studies at the Salpêtrière Hospital. Although they were to develop different interpretations of hysteria, the two men collaborated on a volume concerning this disorder, with Breuer taking senior authorship (Breuer & Freud, 1893–1895/1955). Breuer had worked with the celebrated patient, Anna O. (a pseudonym), who suffered from several different symptoms of hysteria. The chief or core symptom was an immobilized right arm. After Breuer had placed her under a light hypnosis, Anna recalled—indeed, relived—the onset of her illness.

Her mother was out of the house and the servants were dismissed for the evening. Anna was left with the responsibility of looking after her father, who was terminally ill. She eased herself into a chair near his bed with great trepidation. Suffering from fatigue and prone to what she called *absences* (momentary blackouts), Anna seems to have had what Breuer called a *waking dream* (p. 38). She "saw" a black snake coming from the wall next to her father's bed, ready to bite him. Anna tried to fend the snake off, moving her right arm from the back of her chair where it had been resting. Apparently it had become slightly numb due to the lack of proper blood circulation, for when she tried to move it, she could not. Glancing at her hand, Anna was horrified to see that her fingers had turned into snakes with her fingernails appearing to be like death's heads. This hallucination dissipated but Anna's right arm continued to be immobilized.

Though she was unable to scream out the terror she felt at the time, Anna *did* do so belatedly, under hypnosis, and this emotional release led to an improvement in her condition. After several such emotional relivings of the past, her arm returned to normal mobility. Breuer and Freud were to call this mental reliving of a situation out of the past an *abreaction* (abnormal–belated reaction). The physical expression of the emotion was termed a *catharsis* (cleansing, clearing-out). This abreactive–cathartic procedure formed the initial model for Freud's therapy. However, the explanation of why it was that a hysterical disorder developed in the first place found our collaborators taking separate paths.

Freud opted for what he termed a *defence hysteria*, in which he routinely found unconscious wishes of a sexual nature at play in the patient's psyche. This explanation was basically and genuinely psychological in that wishes are intentions, to be understood as final causes and not mechanical-efficient causes. Breuer, on the other hand, although he recognized that sexual longing was one among many psychological involvements in hysteria, decided to remain more faithful to the traditional medical model. He therefore proposed that hysteria was due to an innate biological propensity that certain people have to form a *hypnoid state* of mind. This is, of course, an exclusively material- efficient-cause formulation of things.

Breuer believed that even if a patient had developed hysterical symptoms due to sexual concerns, a hypnoid state would still be underwriting this abnormal outcome (pp. 216, 235). These states of mind bore a striking similarity to hypnosis:

> The basis and *sine qua non* of hysteria is the existence of hypnoid states. These hypnoid states share with one another and with hypnosis, however much they may differ in other respects, one common feature: the ideas which emerge in them are very intense but are cut off from associative communication with the rest of the content of consciousness. (p. 12)

These cut-off ideas are thus denied the normal wearing-away process that occurs thanks to their coming into contact with, and evaluation by, the many other ideas at play in the mind (p. 11).

The role of emotion in such cut-off ideas is apparent; indeed, Breuer called them "affectively coloured ideas" (p. 218). Thus, Anna was unable to say to herself something plausible like "Look, that black-snake business was just a dream you had while you were so tense at father's bedside. Your arm had 'fallen asleep' on the back of the chair, and as a part of your dream you saw those silly death's heads. Dreaming is not reality. Forget it!" This salutory working-over of a frightening event through self-reflexive examination was not possible because the cut-off part was not in contact with the rest of the mind.

It is not difficult to see why Janet may have felt that his German colleagues were plagiarists. Breuer's theoretical analysis in particular reads like a rephrasing of Janet's views. Instead of "dissociation," Breuer speaks of the "splitting of psychical activity" (p. 221) or "splitting of consciousness" (p. 231). He does tip his hat to Janet on occasion (e.g., p. 227). But he is also critical of Janet's suggestion that there is always a mental exhaustion or congenital mental weakness that disposes people to hysteria (p. 231). Sometimes people with hysteria are exceedingly efficient individuals, so much so that they habitually carry on more than one train of thought at the same time (p. 233). The emotional impact from reading a book or viewing a drama can also stay with the individual who is prone to hypnoid states, spilling over into ongoing life events where they are not relevant. Such emotional moods, which color unfolding life events, cannot be put aside (p. 233). They function under their own weight.

Breuer also points to the dynamic that I think everyone who writes about consciousness also brings up at one time or another: that is, the ability our mind has to be "elsewhere" as we mechanically carry out some (even complex) task (p. 233). The most popular example used nowadays is that of driving an automobile. At first, in learning to drive, we are quite concerned with getting everything organized—starting the engine, checking the location, pulling into traffic, managing the brake, shifting the gears, judging distances, and so on. After some time all of these actions are carried out smoothly as we move through traffic while thinking about where we are heading, what we have to do later in the day, or listening to a discussion on the radio. Sometimes, after we reach our destination we are unable to recall much about the drive itself. We just got in the car at point A and showed up in due time at point B. The rest is a mystery.

This would seem to be an example of Claparède's law, which holds that "the more smoothly we use a relation in action, the less conscious we are of it; we become aware of what we are doing in proportion to the difficulty we experience in adapting to a situation" (Vygotsky, 1986, p. 163). Hence, the smoother our driving actions become, the less conscious we are of their occurrence. According to Breuer, the person suffering from a hypnoid state of mind is frequently in this amnesic condition. Things happen, goals are met, but there is no recollection of what transpired

(Breuer & Freud, 1893–1895/1955, p. 216). Breuer referred to such un-recalled ideas as being *unconscious*: The unconscious, split-off mind in hysteria is pre-eminently suggestible on account of the poverty and incompleteness of its ideational content. But the suggestibility of the conscious mind, too, in some hysterical patients seems to be founded on this. They are excitable from their innate disposition; in them, fresh ideas are very vivid. In contrast to this, their intellectual activity proper, their associative function, is reduced, because only a part of their psychical energy is at the disposal of their waking thought, owing to a splitting-off of an "unconscious" (p. 239).

This account is similar to Janet's, except that Breuer is not attributing the hysterical patient's suggestibility to an exhaustion of higher brain functions. His thesis is that due to the splitting of the mind there is a poverty of ideational content, of the knowledge that might have accrued had the person brought a reasonably integrated psyche into play. This is a somewhat more psychological treatment than Janet's. Breuer also points to the role of the process in all of this. Even so, relying ultimately as he did on innate disposition, Breuer failed to innovate. Freud and Jung devised more creative theories.

SIGMUND FREUD AND CARL G. JUNG: THE REPRESSED WISH AND THE NEUROTIC COMPLEX

Since there is both agreement and disagreement in the outlooks of Freud and Jung concerning the psyche it helps to present their views jointly. I will first review their basic agreements on several points relating to the conscious and unconscious, and then take up their disagreements under a separate heading.

Points of Agreement on the Psyche

Process and Content in the Psyche

What is so remarkable about psychoanalysis is that its proponents are willing to depart from explanations relying exclusively on the medical model. Not that Freud or Jung dismissed efficient-cause explanations altogether. Especially when we consider libido (see below), we will find them using mechanistic explanations to give their fundamentally teleological theorizing the sound of scientific authenticity. But Freud was willing to consider the dynamics of mental abnormality from the point of view of the person living it (i.e., introspectively), departing thereby from the standard medical-model approach. He humanized the clinical picture. Doubtless this openness to introspective theoretical formulations stemmed from the fact that Freud began psychoanalysis in large measure through self-analysis. The meanings deviously symbolized or openly confronted in his dreams and fantasies established that the psyche was something other than—or at least more than—a biological mechanism. What exactly *was* it, and *how* should he describe it as working?

We find Freud and Jung using conscious(ness) and unconscious(ness) to signify both a process and a content of that process. This process-content shift occurs regularly and abruptly in their writings. On the one hand, Freud may define unconsciousness as "psychical processes which behave actively but nevertheless do not reach the consciousness of the person concerned" (1906/1959b, p. 47). He often refers to the unconscious as a "system" (e.g., 1900/1953, p. 568). But on the other hand, he can say: "In the *Ucs.* [unconscious] there are only contents, cathected with greater or lesser strength" (1915/1957b, p. 186; italics in original). Certain contents produced in the unconscious called *derivatives* sometimes cross over to consciousness by way of an intermediate psychic region—changing their appearance in the form of dream symbols (pp. 190, 194). Notorious examples are the symbolizing of genitals into elongated objects (penis) or pockets (vagina; p. 232). The intermediate system of the psyche, the *preconscious* (or *foreconscious*), is located between the two other systems and retains latent ideas that can be brought to mind with intentional effort (like forgotten telephone numbers, addresses, or names) (1911/1958, p. 262). But we never pull up things from the unconscious like this.

Freud's basic conception of the psyche is thus a three-tiered process that produces and retains certain contents. Although we are fleetingly aware of conscious contents, and can willfully recall contents from the preconscious, we have no direct basis on which to speak of the unconscious: "we call a psychical process unconscious whose existence we are obliged to assume—for some such reason as that we infer it from its effects—but of which we know nothing" (1932/1964b, p. 70). We know that there is an unconscious process because it sends its contents—what it creates or produces—into consciousness. Consciousness has no part in forming this content, which expresses wishes outside of awareness (1915/1957b, p. 194).

Jung also views the psyche as a process: "The psyche is just . . . a self-regulating system" (1953b, p. 60). This process produces imagined contents: "Every psychic process is an image and an 'imagining,' otherwise no consciousness could exist and the occurrence would lack phenomenality. Imagination itself is a psychic process" (1958, p. 544). Jung believed that the contents of the psyche were essentially images (1960b, p. 325). Consistent with Freud, he suggests that the contents produced in the psyche may or may not cross over from one location to another: "The unconscious contains all those psychic events which do not possess sufficient intensity of functioning to cross the threshold dividing the conscious from the unconscious" (1960a, p. 203).

Consciousness Is Less Important Than Unconsciousness

One is struck by the light treatment of consciousness in psychoanalysis. Freud defined consciousness as "a sense organ for the apprehension of psychical qualities" (1900/1953, p. 574). Consciousness therefore has to do with immediate awareness, which is continually changing (1911/1958, p. 260). Consciousness per se is not essential to cognition, because the unconscious can carry on the "*most complicated achievements of thought*" without it (1900/1953, p. 593; italics in original). At birth, unconscious thinking is the natural state for everyone; indeed, throughout life "every psychical act begins as an unconscious one" (1911/1958, p. 264). As the psyche develops into its three-tiered arrangement, a *censor* located in the preconscious keeps certain ideas from entering consciousness (1915/1957b, p. 173). Freud tended to equate consciousness with perception: "What consciousness yields consists essentially of perceptions of excitations coming from the external world and of feelings of pleasure and unpleasure which can only arise from within the mental apparatus" (1920–1921/1955b, p. 24). Because consciousness cannot retain the memory traces of these perceptions it has little to do with organizing the dynamics of memory (pp. 24–25).

Jung distinguished between personal and collective aspects of the psyche, but for the present I will confine my comments to personal consciousness. Jung's definition of consciousness is quite similar to Freud's: "Consciousness is primarily an organ of orientation in a world of outer and inner facts" (1960b, p. 123). It is something like perception (1958, p. 550). Jung asks: "How does consciousness arise in the first place? . . . when the child recognizes someone or something—when [she or] he 'knows' a person or a thing—then we feel that the child has consciousness" (1960b, p. 390). Knowing involves perceiving differences between things; indeed, "without awareness of differences [there would be] no consciousness at all" (1967, p. 197). As with Freud, Jung held that thinking begins in the unconscious and is then carried forward into consciousness as the child perceives the complexity of differences in a widening experience.

Both Freud and Jung spoke of the unconscious as taking up a larger piece of psychic territory than the conscious. Freud cautions that although every mental content that is repressed is unconscious, the reverse is not true. The unconscious can think on its own and does not rely exclusively on what consciousness sends its way (1915/1957b, p. 166). Thus, in referring to his memory, Freud once observed, "I extend my conscious memory by invoking my unconscious memory, which is in any case far more extensive" (1901/1960b, p. 136). Freud once spoke metaphorically of the unconscious as a "large" entrance hall and the conscious as a "narrower" drawing room (1916/1963, p. 295). Jung presents the psyche as a kind of region in which various contents (complexes) take up their residence. He was fond of using an island metaphor to contrast the spatial distribution of psychic regions: "the conscious rises out of the unconscious like an island newly risen from the sea" (1954a, p. 52). He also spoke of separate islands issuing from below the sea to form a "continuous land mass of consciousness" (p. 190). Psychoanalysts increasingly pictured the psyche as a region (including spatial "levels"). This development plays an important role in the interpretation of unconscious free will from a psychoanalytical perspective (see Chapter 10).

The Psyche Is Intentional

We come now to a point that is controversial as it applies to Freud but not Jung. There are those who believe that Freud was a mechanistic, reductionistic theoretician in the style of medical modeling (see, e.g., Sulloway, 1979). I have argued, to the contrary, that what is distinctive about Freudian dynamics cannot be found in biological theorizing (see especially, Cameron & Rychlak, 1985, pp. 123–134). Freud did not speak of the psyche as teleological in so many words; however, there are several examples where he characterized the psyche as purposive. A concept he used widely was that of the *wish*. Whether we think of this as a process of longing (wanting, desiring), or the content (i.e., end, goal, target) that is longed for (wanted, desired), this word bears a clearly teleological meaning. Freud was basically a teleologist. Here is a fine example of his definition of repression, in which the telic aspect of a persistent wish seeks its end even in the face of secondary thinking having the opposite purpose in view:

> Among . . . wishful impulses derived from infancy, which can neither be destroyed nor inhibited, there are some whose fulfilment would be a contradiction of the purposive ideas of secondary thinking. The fulfilment of these wishes would no longer generate an affect of pleasure but of unpleasure; and *it is precisely this transformation of affect which constitutes the essense of what we term "repression."* (1900/1953, p. 604; italics in original)

In commenting on the dissociation that takes place in hysteria, Freud observed that one essential condition must be fulfilled: "an idea must be *intentionally repressed from consciousness* and excluded from associative modification" (Breuer & Freud, 1893–1895/1955, p. 116; italics in original). There is a *censor* or censoring agency that sees to such things. He told of a case in which a patient held a repressed death-wish against his brother-in-law. The patient brought this repressed wish into consciousness during analysis and the symptoms it prompted were removed through the insight achieved. Even so, a nagging remnant of the death-wish remained. Fortunately, the patient was able to suppress intentionally this weakened version and suffered no pathological consequences (1920–1921/1955b, p. 185). It is often said today that a *suppression* is a conscious move to keep something out of mind whereas a *repression* is automatic and not susceptible to conscious control. I think it is correct to say that each of these psychic manifestations borrows from a teleological capacity to direct thought intentionally.

Jung did not have a central role for repression in his theory. At one point he suggested—in most unFreudian fashion—that repression "is a voluntary act of which one cannot help being conscious" (1956, p. 58). When he contrasted suppression and repression, Jung brought in a morality theme:

> Suppression amounts to a conscious moral choice, but repression is a rather immoral 'penchant' for getting rid of disagreeable decisions. Suppression may cause worry, conflict and suffering, but it never causes a neurosis. Neurosis is always a substitute for legitimate suffering. (1958, p. 75)

Jung's commitment to teleology is complete, as when he states that "There are no 'purposeless' psychic processes; that is to say, it is a hypothesis of the greatest heuristic value that the psyche is essentially purposive and directed" (1956, p. 58). Or again, when he states "What I would call the psyche proper extends to all functions which can be brought under the influence of a will. Pure instinctuality allows no consciousness to be conjectured and needs none" (1960b, p. 183).

Freud's concept of the wish gets at only half of what it takes to complete a teleological line of behavior: the *motive* to pursue or merely fantasize some desired end (e.g., sexual object). This motivation encompasses the "reason" for the sake of which an intention is carried out (formal or final causation). But intentions can come into conflict, so it is important for a telic organism to evaluate and select certain ends rather than others. Here is where the unconscious falls short. It is not an effective evaluating process; indeed, it avoids the responsibility of choosing. Freud admitted that the unconscious was a system "whose activity knows no other aim than the fulfilment of wishes and which has at its command no other forces than wishful impulses" (1900/1953, p. 568). But a wish that is unconscious can be and frequently is in contradiction of yet another wish. This can occur because of the peculiar nature of unconsciousness, which at its nucleus "consists of wishful impulses. These instinctual impulses are co-ordinate with one another, exist side by side without being influenced by one another, and are exempt from mutual contradiction" (1915/1957b, p. 186). We shall see in the next section how oppositionality plays a core role in explaining how such contradictory manifestations arise in the psyche.

In time, Freud was to revise his concept of the censor and arrive at the now famous tripartite division of the psyche into *id*, *ego*, and *super-ego* (1923/1961a, pp. 24, 36). These distinctive identities or homunculi become residents of the psyche, living within or across the three levels (or regions) of mind. The id took up residence exclusively in the unconscious, and thus is typified as reasoning exclusively in the manner of this region—that is, selfishly, immune to contradictions, enacting hostile intentions, and above all seeking immediate need-gratification (pleasure principle). Although the super-ego stretches its identity across all three levels of the psyche, it is rigidly committed to the values of the sociocultural milieu within which it took conscious form. Thanks to these unyielding commitments, the super-ego can be as cruel and one-sided in its righteousness as the id is in its pleasure seeking (1923/1961a, p. 54). It is the ego's lot to effect compromises in the psyche, to somehow satisfy both the hedonism of the id and the asceticism of the super-ego. These negotiations are conducted within the unconscious sphere of the psyche. But there is yet a third party to consider in this effort at compromise.

Because the ego also stretches across the three levels of the psyche it has ongoing contact with the same external reality from which the super-ego received its dictatorial value system. Freud actually referred to the "three tyrannical masters" of the ego as "the external world, the super-ego, and the id" (1932/1964b, p. 77). The super-ego takes in rigidly framed dictates without a capacity to examine them reflexively. The ego must engage in such reflexive examination as well as in reality-testing to evaluate the possibilities and suggest alternatives that can compromise the intentions of the id and super-ego. Thanks to its reality-testing and compromising outlook, the ego manages to hold the personality together lest it self-destruct.

Jung also had his identities strategizing and balancing off perceived differences in the psyche, pictured now as conscious and unconscious regions. Within these regions collections of psychic contents formed into *complexes*, a general term Jung used to describe the fact that the images of certain psychic contents coalesced into identifiable unities around an emotional core (1957, p. 97). A complex is thus an identifiable collection of attitudes or behaviors, like the *ego* for example. As with Freudian theory, these complex-figures essentially served as homunculi in describing the activities of the personality. Consciousness was the primary residence of the ego complex (1959, p. 283) and in the unconscious another complex, an *alter-ego* or *shadow*, took up residence (1953b, p. 65). In the example I used for Figure 2, when John as a young person began to be on time, to keep his promises, and so forth, he was building a complex of contents into an ego that others eventually characterized as being reliable. But he also had an unreliable side: a lazy streak and a tendency to make excuses for not carrying out plans or missing deadlines. John frequently denied these proclivities as he exerted effort to behave in the opposite direction. But such unreliable psychic inclinations did not simply evaporate. They formed into John's shadow complex (alter-ego), his darker side, as potential behavioral alternatives.

John is sometimes closer to behaving like his shadow than his ego, but never in public. When he confronts people socially he manifests yet another complex: his *persona* or *mask*, a social facade that we all learn to "wear" from dealing with others socially. The mask is actually defined by our group—we are taught how to behave interpersonally—so there is a collective consciousness balancing off the collective unconscious aspects of the psyche (1953b, p. 155). If John's reliability were entirely a manifestation of his mask he would be a phony and in time would undoubtedly be exposed as such. But he, like the rest of us, is a mixture of sincere ego efforts to behave correctly (reliably) and a desire to be seen by others in a certain (usually but not always) positive light.

Jung also has a concept of the *self*, which may or may not be fashioned in any one personality (1958, p. 82). The self is formed when the many sides of the personality are balanced off so that the person is no longer one-sidedly misled to believe that the psyche is limited to consciousness. This balancing of consciousness with unconsciousness usually occurs in the so-called "individuation" stage of a Jungian analysis (1954b, pp. 70–74). The self is actually a kind of grand transpredicator, in which all viewpoints and proclivities of the psyche are known by the person. The person whose self has been formed no longer needs to wear masks, and will stop projecting onto others shortcomings that he or she is tempted to enact via a personal shadow complex.

Psyche Is Oppositional

It is important for Jung to balance off the psyche at some point because he assigned great importance to the role of oppositionality in thought. As he said, "The structure of the psyche is so contradictory or contrapuntal that one can scarcely make any psychological assertion or general statement without having immediately to state its opposite" (1954b, p. 77)—a fact that will not be lost on Derrida in framing deconstructionism (see Chapter 9). Jung held that the way in which such oppositionality is manifested is *across* the regions or levels of the psyche. That is, the unconscious is involved with meanings that are opposite to those meanings embraced and enacted within consciousness. This enables the unconscious to compensate one-sided emphases being placed on things in consciousness. As Jung phrased it, "In normal people the principal function of the unconscious is to effect a compensation and to produce a balance. All extreme conscious tendencies are softened and toned down through a counter-impulse in the unconscious" (1960a, pp. 205–206).

If consciousness goes too far out of balance, and fails to admit a responsibility for—or even a fascination with—the weaker or darker side of the psyche, the result can be disastrous (p. 206). A "new" complex can then form at the unconscious level. This is the *neurotic complex*, which assimilates all of the ignored and unadmitted feeling-toned beliefs and attitudes, and breaks through to the region of consciousness where it prompts actions in diametric opposition to the person's customary way of behaving (1954a, p. 153). These one-sided beliefs and attitudes are intractable. They embrace a position that is not open to alternatives. I began this book with an example of this neurotic complex, when a female voice broke through to challenge Jung's understanding of what he was doing during his self-analysis (see first paragraph of Chapter 1).

There is now a totally different—an opposite—slant on life to deal with, represented by this smaller identity (neurotic complex) making itself known as a representative of unconsciousness *within* consciousness. The ego is under attack by attitudes and inclinations that are entirely foreign, reminding us of a Janetian dissociation. The key here is to understand that for too long these totally rejected and ignored psychic contents have been shunted from consciousness as if they had never existed, never been fascinating, never been attractive to the person concerned. So Jung had to carry out an extensive debate with his dissociated neurotic complex, who spoke initially with the voice of a female therapy patient, arguing until such time as he had completely demolished the views of this formidable opponent. Jung literally argued the neurotic complex to pieces.

The basic oppositionality here is between conscious and unconscious levels rather than within each psychic region (as Freud eventually had it). It is only when opposites confront each other in consciousness that trouble arises. The same holds true for Freud, who was not so outspoken about the oppositional nature of the psyche but who nevertheless did have this same contrapuntal emphasis in his formulation. Although Freud held that unconscious thought could achieve anything that conscious thought could, he also said that "the laws of unconscious activity differ widely from those of the conscious" (1911/1958, p. 266). He meant by this that although consciousness must struggle to resolve its contradictions, in the unconscious we find "no negation, no doubt, no degrees of certainty" (1915/1957b, p. 186). Nor is the unconscious concerned with time. Freud states specifically that the unconscious process is timeless. No account of reality is taken by the unconscious whatsoever (p. 187). Living according to a reality principle is the ego's problem, and it must solve conflicts arising in consciousness. So long as everything remained unconscious, the person could have her or his cake and eat it too. Unconsciousness—or, in time, the id—saw nothing illogical here. As Freud beautifully summed things up,

> Urges with contrary aims exist side by side in the unconscious without any need arising for an adjustment between them. Either they have no

influence whatever on each other, or, if they have, no decision is reached, but a compromise comes about which is nonsensical since it embraces mutually incompatible details. With this is connected the fact that contraries are not kept apart but treated as though they were identical, so that in the manifest dream [of a person] any element may also have the meaning of its opposite. (1939/1964a, p. 169)

Consciousness–Unconsciousness and Conscience

Because the unconscious region is either prone to be one-sided (Jung) or incapable of judging good–bad or right–wrong (Freud), it is up to the conscious region to arrive at such ethico-moral decisions. In Freudian theory, the source of conscience is the "social anxiety" (1915/1957b, p. 280) experienced by individuals when they transgress mandates laid down by the group. There is an inherited aspect to this anxiety stemming from the Oedipal complex (pp. 332–333), but the essential meaning of conscience is that of keeping certain psychic contents repressed—pushed out of consciousness by a "scrupulous conscientiousness" (1913/1955c, p. 68). It is the super-ego that now acts as this censoring agency, and, as already noted, it takes its authority from the external mores of the society (1929/1961b, p. 128). Here is a fine summary of Freud's final view of the super-ego:

> The super-ego is an agency which has been inferred by us, and conscience is a function which we ascribe, among other functions, to that agency. This function consists in keeping a watch over the actions and intentions of the ego and judging them, in exercising a censorship. The sense of guilt, the harshness of the super-ego, is thus the same thing as the severity of the conscience. . . . We ought not to speak of a conscience until a super-ego is demonstrably present. As to a sense of guilt, we must admit that it is in existence before the super-ego, and therefore before conscience, too. At that time it is the immediate expression of fear of the external authority, a recognition of the tension between the ego and the authority. (p. 136)

The actual sense of guilt is inherited, stemming from remorse over the Oedipal patricide. Indeed, the super-ego is characterized as "the heir of the Oedipus complex" (1923/1961a, p. 36). Because the super-ego and ego extend over all three regions of the psyche they can confront the id at the unconscious level. However, as I noted above, like the id, the super-ego holds to its views unyieldingly; it is not about to make the effort to understand the id's equally rigid point of view. Indeed, as we have seen, it is the ego's job to negotiate compromises between the id and the super-ego at this level. But we cannot say that this negotiation is entirely unconscious because it relies crucially on the ego's grasp of the demands of reality, which takes place in consciousness. The id must also be allowed its hedonistic gratifications, compromised somehow by the super-ego's ethico-moral demands. As the identity "in the middle," the ego is hard pressed to work things out to the satisfaction of its three masters.

Jung reverses this direction in his analysis of complex-formation. Instead of the ego working out its compromises in the unconscious, he has it struggling to confront the neurotic complex within the conscious region of the psyche. The neurotic complex makes itself known consciously, and if the ego does not defuse (depotentiate) the one-sided views of the neurotic complex, the psyche can fall victim to these oppositional ideas and the person's customary behavioral pattern can flip-flop. John, of Figure 2, might suddenly becomes horrendously unreliable! If Jung accepted the neurotic complex's suggestion that what he was doing was "art," he might have taken a totally different route in his professional development—from a scientist of the mind to a creative author or painter. Fortunately, the ego has a good grasp of right and wrong on which to found its countering arguments to the one-sidedness of the neurotic complex (1964, p. 447). This evaluative capacity is also the source of a personal conscience (p. 439). Jung defined this concept as follows: "Conscience is a psychic reaction which one can call *moral* because it always appears when the conscious mind leaves the path of custom, of the *mores*, or suddenly recollects it" (p. 453; italics in original).

Points of Disagreement on the Psyche

Collective Psyche

The first point of disagreement is not a major issue separating our two thinkers. As I noted earlier, Jung had both a collective and a personal side to the psyche. The collective conscious was represented by the mask (persona) that people wear in social relations (1953b, p. 155). As socialized beings we imitate certain acceptable behaviors, put on our "good face" in public, and so on. But a far more important role played by the collective unconscious is as the source of the archetypes. The *archetypes* are not inherited ideas per se, but rather represent a "functional disposition to produce the same, or very similar, ideas" (1956, p. 102). These ideas reflect universal themes that all humans confront, such as entering into relations with the opposite sex, or sensing the existence of a deity. Certain symbols taken from the culture of the group enable an expression of the archetypal meaning under consideration. Thus, one culture may symbolize the deity archetype as a king, another as the sun, yet another as a volcano, and so on (1953a, p. 14). The specific idea-symbols change but the deity theme is "objective" because it applies universally to all human beings regardless of their cultural identification (1953b, pp. 269–270).

Jung calls the unconscious the "mother" of consciousness because the latter psychic sphere "grows out of" the former (1959, p. 281). It is interesting to see Jung also using the familiar island metaphor to describe the relationship between the collective and personal consciousness: "Just as the sea stretches its broad tongues between the continents and laps them round like islands, so our original [collective] unconsciousness presses round our individual consciousness" (1964, p. 138). I added the word collective in brackets here because this is what Jung meant by "original." The first human beings lived in tribes and did not think for themselves as individuals. They viewed themselves as an aspect of the totality of nature, and were thus essentially participating in—and only in—collective thought (1953b, p. 204). Later, thanks to the evolution of oppositional thought in which differences could be distinguished, a psyche with personal consciousness developed. The capacity to see differences broadened personal awareness and broke the human free from the rigid conservatism of the collective unconscious (1967, p. 12).

Although Freud failed to distinguish between collective and personal aspects of the psyche it is not exactly correct to say that he flatly disagreed with Jung on this issue. In a letter to Jung dated 13 August 1908, Freud said the following: "One thing and another have turned my thoughts to mythology and I am beginning to suspect that myth and neurosis have a common core" (McGuire, 1974, p. 169). Later that year, on November 11th, Freud was "delighted" to learn that Jung was going into mythology, and that he might come to agree that "in all likelihood mythology centers on the same nuclear complex as the neuroses" (p. 260). Of course, Freud had the Oedipal myth in mind here and could not foresee the lengths to which Jung would go in bringing the psyche into close relationship with all manner of mythologizing. In his postscript to the notorious Schreber case, published in 1912, Freud said that "Jung had excellent grounds for his assertion that the mythopoeic forces of mankind are not extinct, but that to this very day they give rise in the neuroses to the same psychical products as in the remotest past ages" (1911/1958, p. 82). Finally, in 1915 Freud had this to say about the unconscious:

> The content of the Ucs. [unconscious] may be compared with an aboriginal population in the mind. If inherited mental formations exist in the human being—something analogous to instinct in animals— these constitute the nucleus of the Ucs. Later there is added to them what is discarded during childhood development as unserviceable; and this need not differ in its nature from what is inherited. A sharp and final division between the content of the two systems does not, as a rule, take place till puberty. (1915/1957b, p. 195; italics in original)

Given that Freud was initially drawn to the idea and was supportive of Jung's efforts, it is probably wrong to say that this issue of collective factors in the psyche was a major point of disagreement. But to have added yet another region to his three-tiered model of the psyche did not seem worth it to Freud. Possibly, had they not parted ways so bitterly (McGuire, 1974, p. 488), Freud and Jung might have worked out a middle-ground position on this matter—although considering the severe rift brought on by the question of libido (see below) it seems highly unlikely that any meeting of the minds was possible.

Unconscious Emotions

As psychotherapists, Jung and Freud were deeply involved with their client's emotions. But precisely how the emotions engaged psychic matters differed for the two theorists. The concept of emotion draws from the *Bios* grounding. Freud actually poked fun at colleagues who were constantly seeking to find psychic differences in biological reductionism, as in equating psychologists trying to locate "the bacillus or protozoon of hysteria" with the religiously devout who are waiting for the messiah (McGuire, 1974, pp. 115–116). Although he had at one point in his career speculated on a schizophrenic toxin, Jung (1960a, pp. 36–37) was also critical of colleagues who tried to fit everything psychic into a "physiological and biological straitjacket" (McGuire, 1974, p. 374). Nevertheless, Freud was more concerned than Jung to keep the *Logos* realm of explanation separate from the *Bios* in his analysis of the psyche. Nowhere is this clearer than in his conclusion that, technically speaking, there are no such things as unconscious emotions.

Freud was careful to distinguish between bodily processes, such as the instincts, and strictly psychic processes. In referring to the antithetical or oppositional nature of consciousness and unconsciousness, which are *Logos* conceptions, Freud is careful not to mix a *Bios* formulation like the instincts into the account:

> I am in fact of the opinion that the antithesis of conscious and unconscious is not applicable to [bodily] instincts. An instinct can never become an object of consciousness—only the idea that represents the instinct can. Even in the unconscious, moreover, an instinct cannot be represented otherwise than by an idea. If the instinct did not attach itself to an idea or manifest itself as an affective [emotional] state, we could know nothing about it. When we nevertheless speak of an unconscious instinctual impulse or of a repressed instinctual impulse, the looseness of phraseology is a harmless one. We can only mean an instinctual impulse the ideational representative of which is unconscious, for nothing else comes into consideration. (1915/1957b, p. 177)

Instincts can be attached to ideas or emotions, and this is how they make themselves psychically known. But is an emotion to be found in the same psychic sphere as an idea? Unfortunately, too many interpreters of

Freud have equated the concept of libido with emotion, while in fact we have a difference of *Logos* (libido) vs. *Bios* (emotion) groundings taking place here. We will be taking up libido in the next section. For now I want to emphasize that Freud was careful *not* to mix somatically generated emotions into the psyche (where libido was to be found). He followed a dualistic assumption in which the two sides were technically distinguished even though they could be united linguistically, as follows:

> Strictly speaking ... and although no fault can be found with the linguistic usage, *there are no unconscious affects* [i.e., emotions; italics added] as there are unconscious ideas. But there may very well be in the system Ucs. [unconscious] affective structures which, like others, become conscious. The whole difference arises from the fact that ideas are cathexes [of libido]—basically of memory-traces—whilst affects and emotions correspond to processes of discharge, the final manifestations of which are perceived as feelings. (1915/1957b, p. 178, italics in original)

Cathexis is a mental filling-up (occupying) of the image of some desired object (such as a sexual object) with libido. *Libido* is a purely psychic energy. In saying that ideas are cathexes, Freud is making it clear that ideas are compounds of libidinal energy, occupying the images of desired objects and thereby orienting the psychic process to attain these conceptualized ends. We also see in the above quote that Freud thought of emotion as a physical discharge, the actual bodily feeling that a person experiences. Libido is consigned to the development of ideas in this theory, not to the physical discharge per se. Hence, *libido is not a drive!* A psychic energy like libido has its role to play in the strictly ideational understanding of ongoing experience and the directive alignment of any behavior that follows. This teleological line of theorizing is inconsistent with those who wish to see Freud as a "biologist of the mind" (i.e., Sulloway, 1979).

In his doctoral dissertation of 1902 Jung (1963) undertook an explanation of so-called occult phenomena, as when mediums call up the loved ones of others from the grave and speak "for" them during a seance (pp. 106–107). He demonstrated how mediums who appear to be speaking for a deceased loved one are in fact forming an emotionally charged automatism in their psyche—a split-off identity that functions under its own weight just like the hysteric's fixed idea. He referred to this autonomous identity as a feeling-toned complex or a feeling-toned train of thought (p. 97). Freud would have it that the ideas pertaining to some emotional episode would be "in the psyche," but the feelings per se are discharges "in the soma."

Jung's need to have *Bios* conceptions mixed into his *Logos* conceptions begins in his interpretation of the archetype. The archetype was defined as the *"instinct's perception of itself"* (1960b, p. 136; italics in original). Just as instincts are certain behaviors performed by all people (e.g., to suck at birth), so too the archetypes are certain experiences encountered by all people in the descent of humanity (e.g., to sense a divine presence or influence; p. 135). Archetypes are readily assimilated into complexes. As instinctive reactions, emotions also mix into the psyche during the formation of complexes. Indeed, the very life of a complex depends on the emotions at its core because when this feeling extinguishes so too does the complex (1960a, p. 43). The person who loses a feeling for the divine (God archetype employed) loses what is active in the life of faith. He or she might recall the principles of the faith and possibly even go on attending church services as a sort of spiritual zombie.

Because Jung so often discussed complexes that were formed around emotional upsets (1960b, p. 98), it is easy to gain the impression that every complex in the psyche is harmful. Actually, the complex-formation process is simply one of the major ways in which the psyche expresses itself, and a complex can have either a positive or a negative role in the total personality (p. 101). The shadow is a complex and so is the ego and its mask. Even the self, if it is individuated in a given personality, is a complex of psychic contents. But the neurotic complex is the one that tends to fascinate us because of the interesting dynamics that it brings about in the personality. People with such complexes change before our eyes. Optimists become pessimistic, the shy become forward, and the cautious begin taking risks. These people are awake and alert. But are they conscious?

Libido

Freud and Jung were theorizing during an era when the Lockean precepts of Newtonianism were still very much in vogue. Jung had a better grasp of where science was going than Freud, but he nevertheless accepted the traditional medical-model demand that Freud tried to meet, which was to name some kind of force or energy that moved psychic events along. Freud and Jung may have deplored the mindless reductionism of their colleagues, but they did not escape the bias so endemic to natural science that an explanation is not really an explanation until someone has stipulated the source of an energy that supposedly makes things happen in efficient-cause fashion. Teleological formulations, resting as they do on (formal- and final-cause) intentions do not take the explanation down to such thrusting forces.

So, if Freud wanted to say that the person's unconscious influenced behavior in one direction rather than another, it was not enough to say the choice depended on certain meanings in relation to an end. The medical-model colleague did not accept the statement that a person simply evaluated a desirable sexual object positively and then actively strategized to achieve ultimate satisfaction in copulation with this object. Better to say that the neurons of the brain that imaged the sexual object were filled with (i.e., cathected by) some kind of energy. And the energy is what directed the behavior of the person, not an intention. Freud had learned how to conceptualize behavior in terms of efficient causation during his medical training, even though his only effort to write a natural-science form of psychology—the ill-fated *Project for a Scientific Psychology* (1892/ 1966, pp. 283–343)—proved a total flop. In time, he began to meet the requirements of his colleagues to discuss his cases in terms of an energy, and the word he selected to describe this force was *libido*.

I have already pointed out that Freud did not use libido in his final theory as a physical energy. Its sphere of influence was the psyche, and he referred to it over the years variously as *"psychical desire"* (1894/1962, p. 107; italics in original), "sexual desire" (1910/1957a, p. 101), "erotic tendencies" (1917/1955a, p. 139), and "the motive force of sexual life" (1932/ 1964b, p. 131). That he was uncertain about just how this energy was employed in the psyche there can be no doubt. He admitted that it could not be quantitatively measured (1920–1921/1955b, p. 90). In fact, the energy is usually described instrumentally—for example, as being sent into the images of desirable (loved, lusted, etc.) objects by the id. Such cathexes can be opposed by the ego and superego's anticathexes (1900/1953, p. 605). This is another way of speaking about repression, or the keeping-out of unacceptable impulses from consciousness (such as seeking sexual union with a cross-sexed parent). Freud referred to repression as the corner-stone of psychoanalysis (1915/1957b, p. 16). And here we have a perfect example of how Freud is able to explain the dynamics of behavior in either an energic or a nonenergic way. He can refer to the meanings of the Oedipal theme—murder and incest—in one breath and switch to the pseudo-energic language of cathexes and anticathexes (repressions) in another.

Jung was just as willing to frame his theoretical commentary in terms of libido as was Freud, and initially he used the concept in the standard Freudian way. But then, fairly rapidly, he decided that for it to be useful he would have to change the meaning of libido significantly. Jung was more openly and knowingly a teleologist than Freud. He understood that they were employing teleological conceptions to explain the dynamics of the psyche. As this change in his understanding of libido took place Jung was falling increasingly out of favor with Freud. To completely explain their breakup would take us far afield, but in a nutshell, as played out in their letters over the period of roughly 1906 to 1913 (McGuire, 1974), Jung felt that Freud was trying to keep his originality and independence reined in. Jung did not wish to be the docile son, mouthing only what the father allowed to be said. But even as this personal drama unfolded, there were significant points being made concerning the nature and role of libido in the psyche. In December of 1909, Jung wrote to Freud: "I should like to pump you sometime for a definition of libido. So far I haven't come up with anything satisfactory" (p. 270). A few weeks later Freud answered that he saw nothing wrong with the definition of libido as an analogy to "hunger" but now "in the sexual context" (p. 277). About a year later, Jung defended the theory of libido against attacks being made on it by Alfred Adler (1870–1937), another former colleague who was gradually leaving the fold (McGuire, pp. 382–383). In February of 1911, Jung spoke proudly of how he insisted on his students "learning to understand dreams in terms of the dynamics of libido" (p. 392). Jung began to elaborate on the concept in the next few months, suggesting that libido is concerned with symbol formation (p. 408), that it has implications for the field of the occult (p. 421), and that the signs of the zodiac are actually "libido symbols" (p. 427). Freud was strangely silent, but in November of 1911, he lent what appears to be ambivalent support to Jung's paper on symbols of the libido (p. 459).

The first signs of a serious rift show up in a letter from Freud to Jung dated November 30, 1911. Freud wondered what Jung meant when he referred to an "extension of the concept of libido," and went on to say that a misunderstanding seemed to have been developing between them (McGuire, p. 469). He then rejected Jung's suggestion that "libido is identical with any kind of desire" and cautioned in no uncertain terms that libido is the power behind the sexual instinct (p. 469). Jung replied in a fortnight that he could not see how the loss of reality in a disorder like dementia praecox (i.e., schizophrenia) can be due to repression of a sexual hunger (p. 471). He also told Freud that he had put his many ideas on libido into the chapter of a book and that, as he now viewed things, the concept goes beyond mere sexual hunger. The misunderstanding soon heated up. In January of 1912 Freud wrote to say that Jung was trying to demonstrate the existence of innate ideas, and this effort led far beyond the original limits of psychoanalysis (p. 480). Freud added that he did not think analysis should follow this path.

In a February 1912 letter Freud needled Jung a bit about the use of libido in their respective lives. He jokingly bragged about his capacity to turn off "my excess libido" at will (McGuire, p. 488). In April of 1912 Freud said that he was eagerly looking forward to Jung's second paper on libido, particularly in light of the "Declaration of Independence" (p. 500) going on: that is, the effort being made by Jung to free himself of Freud's dominance. One month later Freud attempted to delineate the problem he had with Jung's use of libido, and he did so by drawing a parallel to Adler's insurgent modifications of psychoanalysis then taking place:

He [Adler] said: the incest libido is "arranged"; i.e., the neurotic has no desire at all for his mother, but wants to provide himself with a motive for scaring himself away from his libido; he therefore pretends to himself that his libido is so enormous that it does not even spare his mother. Now this still strikes me as fanciful, based on utter incomprehension of the unconscious. In the light of your hints [concerning the revision of libido], I have no doubt that your derivation of the incestuous libido will be different. But there is a certain resemblance. (p. 507)

This is a fascinating comment, revealing that Freud was critical of Adler's attempt to reduce the role of libido in the personality to an arranged instrumentality—a purposeful strategy to scare oneself away from libido—rather than reflective of a true Oedipal desire. He feared that Jung was about to reduce drastically—if not drop—the sexual thesis just as Adler had done. He was correct in this fear, of course. Jung was now off and on his own. In a letter dated November 11, 1912, he informed Freud that he had "won over many people who until now had been put off by the problem of sexuality in neurosis" and added for Freud's benefit the following: "I regret it very much if you think that the modifications in question [i.e., concerning libido] have been prompted solely by resistances to you" (McGuire, 1974, p. 515). In January of 1913 they broke off contact (pp. 539–540). Again, the dispute over libido was not *the* reason for the breakup. There were many themes in the disintegration of this complicated relationship, including ambition, competition, dominance, rebellion, and even darker themes that do not interest us here. But there is also an extremely important point to be made concerning the split.

Freud and Jung were struggling to make sense of the psyche. They compromised with the Newtonian climate of their time. There was no language of teleology to use so they were forced to analogize from blind, physical energies to energies of the mind, which somehow entered into intentional lines of thought and behavior. Jung drifted gradually but consistently to the view that there was more to psychic motivation than just the sexual. Because he continued to garner his share of therapeutic cures with this alternative view, he gained the confidence to say things like, "Libido is intended simply as a name for the energy which manifests itself in the life-process and is perceived subjectively as conation and desire" (1961, p. 125). He equated libido with many other telic formulations such as Schopenhauer's *Will* and Bergson's "*élan vital*" (1960b, p. 30; 1964, p. 147). Freud was committed to his Promethean insight concerning the role of sexuality in human affairs, and he was therefore of the opinion that Adler and Jung were merely giving in to defensively motivated cultural pressures. This was a compromise that Freud could not make. He insisted that psychoanalysts who followed him avoid the temptation to employ euphemistic language in hopes of gaining an easy acceptance.

A PREDICATIONAL ANALYSIS OF THE PSYCHOANALYTICAL PSYCHE

In this final section of the chapter, I consider the psychoanalytical account of the psyche and its levels of consciousness from the LLT point of view.

Psychoanalysis Employs a Predicational Process

The rich metaphors of the unconscious as the wider realm of meaning, a sea surrounding the narrower island of consciousness, and so on, imply that Freud and Jung followed an unacknowledged predicational line of theorizing. Figure 4 illustrates this explanatory line even more clearly by capturing what turns out to be a common *content model* used by the theorists of this chapter.

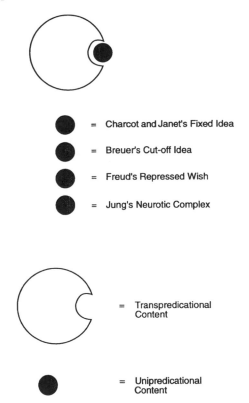

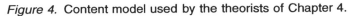

Figure 4. Content model used by the theorists of Chapter 4.

At the top of Figure 4 is a depiction of this content model in which a larger area is separated from a smaller, darkened area. Nothing is labeled in this model for it can refer to all four of our theoreticians, who are listed in the middle of Figure 4. Reading down this array we can see that the Charcot–Janet fixed idea (darkened circle), which has been dissociated from the rest of the psychic contents (larger area), is readily captured. Next we have Breuer's cut-off idea as the darkened circle, to which, due to the hypnoid state, the other contents of consciousness have denied a working-over. We then have Freud's repressed wish, which the other contents of consciousness pushed off from admission or recognition. Finally, the Jungian neurotic complex that, although popping into the conscious realm, is not "of" consciousness and thus expresses views in stark contrast to the ego-content. At the bottom of Figure 4 the two aspects of the content model are labeled: The larger area represents *transpredicational content* and the smaller (darkened circle) area represents *unipredicational content*.

I should emphasize that Figure 4 does not depict the predicational process in toto, but is limited to the contents per se. The circles of Figure 4 should not be confused with the Euler circles of Figure 2, which depict the complete predicational process. The large area of Figure 4 is *not* the predicate and the smaller (darkened) circle the target. The smaller circle is a separated section of the larger circle, and both of these figures represent contents (ideas, images, etc.) in the psyche.

It is undoubtedly easy to think of the mind in spatial terms by analogizing to our personal experience, so that when awake and moving about we consider ourselves to be in one region of consciousness, and when in bed asleep, in another region. Now that we have these regions established, the next step would seem to be that we populate them. Here again, we analogize to ourselves as walking around, taking identities and placing little actors (homunculi) like I, me, not-me, self, ego, id, mask, superego, or shadow in the psyche. The distinction between process and content is now thoroughly blurred. We must always remember that the psychic regions—conscious, unconscious, preconscious—were proposed initially as reflecting a *common* process that created various contents within and between them. The psychic regions were not places to house yet other processes. We shall see in later chapters (especially 10) how Freud and Jung both fell into the habit of referring to consciousness as involving different spatial regions or levels.

What about the homunculi? Are they contents in the mind, cooked up by the processes of consciousness and unconsciousness—or, are they entirely different processes doing their own thinking? Here is where the descriptive effort begins falling apart. We have to take our stand as to what is a process of thought and then explain things in terms of how this process produces or employs its contents. My suggestion is that the theoreticians of this chapter relied basically on a predicational (*Logos*) process even though they introduced quasi-mechanical (*Physikos, Bios*) conceptions like libido to clothe their views in appropriate Newtonian attire. We readily overlook this confounding of logical and mechanical conceptions because it is so easy to slip back and forth between an extraspective and an intro-spective description of things. The dissociated or cut-off idea functioning in a hysteric's psyche should be understood from an introspective perspec-tive. The person thinks "I'm blind" and literally stops seeing. This idea (content) is not like a piece of furniture, transported (by a process) from the living room to the bedroom. It has a meaning. Something is being intended here, and we cannot see intentions like we see furniture being moved about (material or efficient causes). Intentions (formal or final causes) are understood introspectively, from the view of the person framing the intention.

The unipredicational content could be more vast than depicted in the smaller darkened circle, of course, but I am stressing that whereas transpredicational contents can be shared or partially influenced by other predications in psychic consciousness, the unipredicational content is locked within its relatively narrower framework of meaning. The split-off idea is a "loner," unable to further its real meaning in the company of others. The hysterically afflicted cannot talk or think themselves out of their symptoms, which have no basis in biological fact. I want to capture this singularity of meaning-extension in using only one darkened circle whereas there could be many split-off ideas, each independent of the other.

A unipredicated idea-meaning under affirmation and extension is not seeking alternatives. Unipredication can occur in either a *proactive* or a *reactive* sense. A proactive unipredication occurs when the meaning under affirmation is perfectly acceptable to the meaningful understanding of psy-chic consciousness (the transpredicational content of Figure 4). However, there is some reason for keeping the unipredicated meaning clear of the rest of consciousness just now, such as its singular fascination, the necessity of avoiding distractions for the time being, the fact that it is not easily rationalized by the other predicating meanings of mind at present, and so forth. Often a positive affective assessment is involved in such proactive unipredications. This is the kind of unipredication I was getting at in Chapter 2 in speaking of a "good" kind of unconscious experience, as when one becomes "lost" in playing a piano or deeply absorbed in a religious experience. But sometimes we also have to narrow our attention to a dis-liked task that must nevertheless be accomplished (like filling out tax forms).

On the other hand, a unipredication can be reactive, in which case the reason for its isolation in the psyche is because the broader realm of transpredicated (hence conscious) meanings will not readily "join hands" with it. Negative affective assessment invariably plays a major role in the reactive logical maneuver (i.e., conscious thoughts avoid affirming what is greatly disliked; see Rychlak, 1994, pp. 206–208). This is the kind of unipredication I was getting at in Chapter 2 in speaking of a "bad" kind of unconscious experience. Here is where we would place Freudian repression. The unacceptable meaning being formulated—for example, an urge to kill a parent—simply cannot relate to or share other predications that are targeting both the parent and the self-image (i.e., predications targeting the self). Parents are caretakers, loved ones, authorities, and not candidates for murder by their children. The person has also predicated his or her *self* with meanings contradictory to *murderer*. The affectively acceptable meanings concerning the parent and the self allow for transpredicational relatedness—in other words, form into what we call consciousness. But the affectively unacceptable meanings are isolated or repressed from consciousness (reactive unipredication). In this state of isolation they cannot be joined, worked over, or communicated with through transpredication. So, they do not go away, but remain as unconscious mental content.

Oppositionality Is Present But Not Known in Unconsciousness

The writings of Freud and Jung teach that, although oppositionality is fundamental to the organization and processing of the psyche, its role in the unconscious realm per se is nil. As noted above, Freud stressed the inability of the unconscious aspect of mind to negate its content meanings, much less to grasp contradictions between them (1915/1957b, p. 186). Conflicting affections are also found in the unconscious (e.g., being attracted and repulsed by the same sexual object). The lack of oppositionality in unconsciousness is also suggested by Jung's concept of the one-sidedness that develops across the levels of conscious-unconscious. Jung observed that, "As a rule, unconscious phenomena manifest themselves in fairly chaotic and unsystematic form" (1959, p. 276). Looked at strictly from the viewpoint of the unconscious, Jung is suggesting that opposition is really apposition (the state of being side-by-side). Thus, a woman might have the unconscious belief that her mother loves her and also hates her. Whereas consciously this woman would puzzle over such a contradiction, unconsciously it would have no more significance than the fact that her mother is both a Christian and a socialist.

It is only when we consciously look into our unconscious (via dreams, etc.) that we actually perceive contradictions existing side by side, including those that are in direct negation of what we believe consciously. As LLT claims, psychic consciousness arises because of transpredication—which in turn is what we mean by awareness. Hence, in consciousness we are continually employing oppositionality and can also recognize its important role in an unconscious line of thought. We dream of our old family home. The place does not look like our old home, but we know in the dream that it is nevertheless. The negation and contradiction stemming from oppositional reasoning that is involved in this unconscious episode is accepted as natural. Actually, both Freud and Jung viewed the unconscious as reflecting the very origins of thought in the evolutionary sense (see Chapter 5). Consciousness presumably emerged out of this original form of cognition.

In one sense, oppositionality is not actually in nature independent of our reasoning capacities. When we say that the north pole is opposite to the south pole what we are actually doing is talking about our own predicational capacity to organize (pattern) knowledge. In actuality, the north and south poles "in nature" are side by side (i.e., apposite) but there is a great distance between them. Another way of expressing this is that extraspective theorizing, which is what "natural" science has always employed (see Chapter 3), does not require oppositionality in its material- and efficient-cause formulations. Oppositionality confounds extraspective formulations whereas it is extremely helpful to the introspective formulation.

Repression is one such introspective formulation making good use of oppositionality. Freud did not believe that it was present from the very outset of life. Repression, Freud said, "cannot arise until a sharp cleavage has occurred between conscious and unconscious mental activity—that *the essence of repression lies simply in turning something away, and keeping it at a distance, from the conscious*" (1915/1957b, p. 147; italics in original). Whether he intended this or not, Freud's introduction of the three homunculi—id, ego, and superego—allowed for a modicum of oppositionality within the unconscious realm: These three identities could confront each other while representing conflicting intentions and arrive thereby at some kind of compromise to be carried out in overt behavior. But the basic clash of oppositionality continued to be between the conscious and the unconscious attitudes, beliefs, biases, and so on. The main thrust was to keep unacceptable ideas (wishes) out of consciousness.

Jung had the unconscious represented in consciousness by the neurotic complex (called the *anima* in a man), which confronted and attempted to convert the ego to its point of view. In this case the ego works out the inconsistencies and contradictions through active argumentation. Rather than reaching a compromise one side or the other must prevail (hopefully the ego, which represents consciousness). The neurotic complex can teach the ego important things, but eventually it must be depowerized or depotentiated (1967, p. 38). If it is not, consciousness will be dominated by the one-sided contents rising from the unconscious. As we have seen in Jung's encounter with his neurotic complex, this depotentiation is no easy matter: If a complex is personified (i.e., takes on a human form including speech) it can be a threat to the autonomy of the ego. This takes us into a unique characteristic of unconscious meaning-extension: It is always universalistic.

Why the Unconscious Seems So Wise

Thanks in part to psychoanalysis we are prone to think of the unconscious as having more knowledge, a broader perspective, and a deeper insight than consciousness. A hidden secret can disguise its true purpose in dream symbols and thereby get its intentions expressed in a most clever manner. Post-hypnotic suggestions planted by the hypnotist are automatically enacted following the unconscious trance state. In cases of multiple personality disorder, the secondary (unconscious) personality may know more about the primary (conscious) personality than vice versa (see Chapter 8). The cards all seem to be stacked in favor of the unconscious on such occasions.

What Freud and Jung had to say about the unconscious is reminiscent of Plato's views on the nature of thought. Plato, in line with Socrates, held that human beings had descended from a Golden Age in which they had actually known a great deal more than they do today. There was a possibility of recovering such long-forgotten knowledge through an exploration of one's thoughts, employing dialectical questions and answers to move from concrete reality to the abstract levels of what we have already alluded to as universals, but in this context are termed "first principles" (Plato, 1952b, p. 387). The Socratic theory of ideas held that there were two spheres of intelligible experience: the sphere of things as sensed in immediate experience (the realm of *becoming*); and the sphere of unchanging absolutes or universals embodied in highly abstract ideas (the realm of *being*). Only in the latter sphere could the unblemished truth be found.

In effect, universals or first principles predicate their targets to lend them meaning. A major first principle was that of *form*. All objects in experience have some kind of form, and to know any object well is to know its form. Because we do not see perfect forms in our lived realm of becoming we do not see perfect truths. A "perfect" white horse does not exist in the realm of becoming or, as we may now term it, in our "lived reality." Our reality is full of forms—images that capture, however imperfectly, what we know. Images in the realm of becoming are like shadows cast upon the wall of a cave. We see the shadow of the perfect white horse, but never the universal form that is the source of the shadow. We therefore live in a world of shadows. It takes a Socratic dialogue to ascend to the realm of being and come thereby to grasp the perfect, unchallengeable certainty of a universal idea that exists there. All else in life—in becoming—is a mere copy, a shadow on the wall, an approximation of the truth.

What has all of this to do with the unconscious? Well, there are two parallels to be drawn between the psychoanalytical treatment of the unconscious and this early Socratic–Platonic doctrine of potential knowledge in the psyche. The first has to do with the fact that mythological themes can reflect something basic to the psychic structure, as in the Jungian collective unconscious with its universal archetypes (1966, p. 80). Freud also touched on this possibility of a mental heritage, as when in discussing the universal Oedipal conflict he referred to the "unconscious understanding ... of all the customs, ceremonies, and dogmas left behind by the original relation to the father" (1913/1955c, p. 159). He was referring to the primal father here, who was, according to his theory, eventually slain by the male offspring who had been banished from the primal horde.

The second parallel is more subtle, but all the more exciting because of its tremendous implications. Although it may appear paradoxical at first, *absolute truth is always unipredicational and hence essentially unconscious.* This is why absolutes are not themselves easily predicated. They can only be grasped through hard work, relying in large measure on self-reflexive study of highly abstract, transcendent thought. Once "found" at some ultimate protopoint, such universals capture our intellectual commitment as unassailable truths and give no ground. Descartes's *cogito* was taken in this universal sense, as a first step in the pursuit of knowledge that could not be denied. The same kind of process occurs in religious submission. Think of the Ten Commandments. As the presumed assertions of a deity, the Ten Commandments are not open to transpredicational revision. People who read the Bible in a fundamentalist sense are not looking for alternative formulations. They believe they have found a universal font of truth, and consequently are often labeled literal, rigid, unreasonable, even unconscious—all terms that can be applied to unipredication (see Chapter 10).

Telosponsive meaning-extensions from the unconscious are always of this universalistic stripe, no matter how mundane their content may be. Why is this true? Because the unconscious, which processes in unipredications, cannot extend meanings from a position of what is called *doubt.* To experience doubt, the line of reasoning must be capable of transcendence. But transcendence is itself dependent on transpredication, on reaching outside of the framing meaning as depicted in Figure 3. Because of this unique feature, any meaning-extensions (ideas, assertions, viewpoints, etc.) originating in the unconscious come across like universal pronouncements delivered in *ex cathedra* fashion. That is, they seem to be infallibly true. If the meaning being expressed conveys something that the person does not want to admit or has dissociated or repressed as unacceptable, then an impression is formed that the unconscious is somehow more knowledgeable about what is going on in the personality than is the conscious. Indeed, such reactively unipredicated contents can make consciousness appear defensively stupid compared with the presumed wisdom of the unconscious (see Chapter 8).

This commanding aura of the universal expression gives unconscious claims a kind of integrity that consciousness lacks because of its capacity to see alternatives, thereby raising self-reflexive doubts and self-criticism (or guilt). The charges made by the unconscious meaning-extensions—whether accurate or inaccurate—are *never* expressed tentatively. There is no transcending soul-searching in the unipredicational assertions of the unconscious. Even when its claims are wrong it seems to be conveying unquestionable truths, not open to emotional or intellectual countering until the psychotherapist assists consciousness to carry out a counter-attack. Then, with luck and perseverence so-called insight may develop as the person comes to frame a predicating context that can properly target the previously unacceptable content.

CONCLUDING COMMENT

The predicational process postulated by LLT stands up very well in an analysis of the psychoanalytical views of conscious and unconscious thought. The going gets a bit tough as we try to keep our process and content distinction clearly in mind. There is also the difficult question of just how thought is directed. Meaning and its affective quality must always be taken into consideration here. But thinking (as well as overt behavior) implies that there is an identity carrying such activity forward. Logical learning theory refers to a *self*, but this is strictly as a self-predication (also termed a self-image). There is no reification, no homunculus involved here (see Chapter 2). People take on self-predications during maturation as they learn about themselves both intrapersonally and interpersonally (Rychlak, 1994, p. 273). But this does not mean that LLT has shifted the thinking (predicational) process from a *person* to a *self*. There is only one *thinker* who frames an identity (self-predication) based on a lifetime of experience. In LLT we embody the predicational process in the person. The person is the processor, introspectively framing the self as content.

For example, a woman can frame several points of view about herself, some conscious and some unconscious. These views might even conflict, one with another. She believes herself to be intelligent and stupid, well-directed and scatterbrained, interesting and dull, and so on. Personality theorists find it necessary at this point to fashion several different identities, homunculi, or sub-personalities doing such conflicting thinking *for* the woman. Logical learning theory does not find this necessary, for all this amounts to is a lumping together of self-predications. In LLT the assumption is made that people routinely frame inconsistent predications—of the self and otherwise. Of course, seriously contradictory self-predications ladened with affective qualities may result in maladjustment. But it is not necessary to invent internal homunculi to understand such dynamics of personality.

Many references to the unconscious suggest a universalistic form of meaning-extension. People who say "I just had a great idea pop into mind from my unconscious!" are experiencing a more positive form of the same type of ex cathedra pronouncement as the person who "hears" self-demeaning voices during a psychotic illness. Psychologists have referred to the *hothouse effect* of unconscious experience, in which an idea set aside earlier continues to bloom until it comes through to consciousness totally solved. Jules Henri Poincaré (1854–1912), the great French mathematician, told of an instance like this when he set aside a vexing problem with Fuschian functions and took a brief bus tour to get his mind off things: "Having reached Coutances, we entered an omnibus to go some place or other. At the moment when I put my foot on the step the idea came to me, without anything in my former [conscious] thoughts seeming to have paved the way for it, that the transformations I had used to define the Fuschian functions were identical with those of non-Euclidean geometry" (Ghiselin, 1952, p. 37). His vexing problem was solved.

The positive outcome of things falling into place (formal causation) at an unexpected moment does not have to be explained as the result of energic forces moving the mind about in mechanical fashion. Nor do we have to postulate little people working on the mathematical problem while the conscious mind is enjoying a holiday. The patterned solution has always "been there" in the *Logos* for recognition. It just required that some of the transpredicating possibilities that doubtless flooded Poincaré's efforts to solve the problem had to be cleared away. He might have erased such distractions another way, by intentionally narrowing his consciousness and focusing on the problem with merely a few or even no possibilities under consideration whatsoever, in the style of a focused meditation (see Chapter 8). The vacation period gave such unipredication an opportunity to take place—and so the solution "popped into mind," to his great satisfaction. Such proactive unipredications are always cause for celebration when they bear fruit.

Not so with reactive unipredications, in which case the person is haunted by guilty self-recriminations that can expand through their own hothouse effect into something wretched, on the order of a mildly scary dream escalating into a terrifying nightmare. The unconscious at this point is experienced as a different identity altogether, an unrelenting, bullying force from within. What is being forced to consciousness, of course, is the logical extension of meaning that has been framed unipredicationally in reaction to a strongly negative affective assessment by conscious thought. The person has affirmed an unacceptable attitude that "Everyone hates me" or "I am no good" and, although striving to repress the implications here, must confront this meaning as it is repeatedly "shouted" outward from the deeper recesses of psychic unconsciousness. It does not matter that the assertion is untrue. The evaluation has been rendered in the mode of a universal and now is expressed accordingly, with all of the certainty and confidence that universals reflect.

We do not need to use energic metaphors to capture such logical pressure. The weight of logic is unyielding. A meaning that has been framed *must* be expressed, considered, understood, and then either carried forward in subsequent adaptation or rejected as meaningless, irrelevant, or forgettable. But when unexpressed, hence unexamined (via transpredication), the only option appears to be that this unipredication, like Poincaré's more happy experience, pops into cognizance to express an unwanted albeit universal "truth." That is, the fearful intention being expressed unconsciously is delivered in that universalistic, confident and demanding sense. Psychic consciousness is thus under seige by a "deep truth" from within, which makes unconsciousness appear more knowledgeable than it probably is. Janet's patient has his unconscious say "I have been run over by a wheel and cannot walk," so in obedience to this deep truth he does not walk.

5

THE EVOLUTIONARY CONNECTION

The eminent psychological theoretician and researcher O. Hobart Mowrer (1961) once observed that American psychology has been "profoundly and pervasively" influenced by the theory of organic evolution, adding that, "Mind, rather than being something to be studied in its own right, has been conceived as 'an organ of adaptation,' an appendage of the body instrumental to the achievement of bodily ends" (p. 15). Evolutionary and archaeological speculations about consciousness in mental events continue to abound in psychology, usually tied to the most recent findings and attendant theories in brain research. In this chapter, I will review a few of the more prominent speculations of this type. We begin with Darwin, and then move on to four somewhat different but widely discussed evolutionary theorists: Roger W. Sperry, George M. Edelman, Robert Ornstein, and Julian Jaynes. I hope to show that the *Logos* interpretation of psychic consciousness I espouse is broadly consistent with these organic explanations, and that it adds to our understanding in a way that these formulations do not. In this effort, I am not trying to mix *Logos* and *Bios* concepts together but rather show how the former account can independently complement the latter (Rychlak, 1993).

CHARLES DARWIN

Charles Darwin (1809–1882) had a special genius that enabled him to assemble broadly empirical observations into a coherent whole, and then to clarify things by using certain theoretical concepts that were not necessarily unique to him. Concepts frequently identified with Darwinian evolutionary theory include the *struggle for existence* (Darwin, 1952b, pp. 32–33), the *survival of the fittest*, and *natural selection* (p. 32). Herbert Spencer (1820–1903) had suggested the "survival" thesis earlier, and even natural selection had been bandied about previously, albeit in a different sense than Darwin gave it (Gruber, 1974, pp. 104–105). Initially, natural selection was understood as a conservative force in nature, selecting out certain alternatives so that a stability in organismic structure was assured from one generation to the next. Darwin saw that natural selection could be a two-edged sword, cutting out maladaptive variants, but at the same time assuring that organisms better adapted to the environment—hence, being the "fittest"—would survive and through their progeny actually change the course of organic evolution.

The interpretation of natural selection as a force for change rather than stability was to take over the entire meaning of this concept. This takeover becomes especially important if one appreciates that Darwinism has been used extensively to explain the behavior of individuals. Gruber, the compiler of Newton's unpublished notes, has observed that "Darwin was not especially interested in drawing a direct analogy between evolution of species and individual psychological development" (p. 226). Darwin preferred to think of individual adaptation as due more to learning and intelligence than to an independent process of natural selection (p. 227); he was not the advocate for mechanistic psychology that some have made him out to be (p. 14). Even so, the behaviorist B. F. Skinner (1974) rationalized his learning theory on something like Darwinian natural selection (see p. xii). The individual organism emits behavior and the "natural" environment then selects whether or not this will be contingently rewarded, interpreted now as shaping (molding, changing, etc.) rather than stabilizing behavior.

It is in regard to such changing behaviors in an individual that consciousness becomes an issue. If learning means adapting to the environment in some unique (new, creative, etc.) way other than through an instinctively fixed (stable, routine, etc.) manner, then this selective adaptation can readily be thought of as purposive or intentional. Darwin was not in favor of free will as an explanation of human learning. Sounding much like Skinner later would, he stated in his unpublished notes that "From *contingencies* a man's character may change—because motive power changes with organization" (Gruber, 1974, p. 389; italics in original). People are deluded into believing they have a free will because they can seldom analyze the motives that are the real (efficient) cause of their behavior (p. 389).

Darwin also wrestled with the matter of whether human behavior has a spiritual or otherwise nonmaterial mental component, eventually deciding that he could not support such formulations. He concluded that "the mind is [a] function of the body" (p. 217). Having considered a career in the ministry at one point, he was only too familiar with the ethico-moral possibilities in evolutionary change. In The Descent of Man (1952a), Darwin pondered the ironic fact that advanced societies do everything possible to assist the survival of their weakest members—such as building asylums for the mentally retarded, vaccinating the general population, and instituting poor-laws (p. 323). This would at first blush seem to be going against natural selection. As a counter to this criticism, he suggested that societies that reflect such altruism are likely to be more cohesive and therefore successful in competition with other societies that are less caring of their members (p. 322). Also, the poorest specimens of a social group are probably not as likely to marry and thereby procreate (pp. 323–324).

As for consciousness per se, I find Darwin using the term in two different ways: one informal, the other formal. Informally, while he analyzed a human characteristic like blushing, he referred to the fact that one can become conscious that others see one's complexion changing to a reddish hue (Darwin, 1989, p. 253). This usage would fall under the awareness theme that we discussed in Chapter 1. Darwin suggests that children at a very early age do not blush because they lack the self-consciousness that generally accompanies this emotional reaction (p. 257).

But more formally and technically, Darwin considered consciousness to be the effect of "sufficient perfection of organization" of a bodily structure (Gruber, 1974, p. 215). In this sense, a physical structure that is adaptive to the environment permits the organism to survive, and this adaptive quality even conveys a seeming purposivity to the action taking place. Many plants have such an excellent facility for adaptation that we are moved to assign them consciousness—as when the sunflower follows the course of the sun throughout the day. Lower animals and especially humans have obvious structural utilities like eyes and limbs to improve their daily adaptation to the environment. Darwin's protégé, George Romanes (1848–1894), later suggested that "consciousness evolved gradually, making its first rudimentary appearance in the coelenterates (e.g., jellyfish, coral)" (p. 233). The evolutionist therefore held that as we move up the animal kingdom, from lower to higher organisms, the improvement in structural organization is prima facie evidence of increasing consciousness.

Darwin did not describe precisely how new bodily structures came about to influence conscious adaptation. He knew that his position demanded a theory of genetics that would explain how variations in structure occurred. But this genetic formulation, which the work of Gregor Mendel

(1822–1884) later provided, still did not explain why evolution took place. Natural selection answers questions that hereditary variation in structure cannot. Darwin stood firmly on the non-telic formulations of his theory. He did not, as Alfred Russel Wallace (1823–1913), a codiscoverer of Darwinian-like evolutionary theory, suggest that in the higher levels of evolution the human being possesses intellectual and moral faculties that originate in the "unseen universe of Spirit" (Gruber, 1974, p. 31). Darwin never referred to a Creator in his published writings (p. 58). Although at times ambivalent on the subject, he did accept Lamarckian views on the likely inheritance of acquired characteristics—that is, changes in physical structure of organisms during their lifetime (as in building up muscles through exercise) are transmitted to their offspring via heredity (pp. 106, 192).

This matter of how variations in structure came about genetically, and how they were then transmitted, led to difficulties for Darwin. He occasionally referred to the "creation" of new structures—an unfortunate choice of words due to the obvious religious connotations. In fact, in a letter to his close friend, Joseph Hooker, Darwin confessed that he had given in to public opinion when he elected to speak of an evolutionary creation—by which he really meant something that had "'appeared' by some wholly unknown process" (p. 209). In time, this kind of appearance was to be called an emergence. *Emergent developments* were those remarkable, unexpected changes that took place as in moving from a lower to a higher organization. The term today means a nonreductive occurrence: a leap from a less organized to a more complex patterning. What emerges cannot therefore be explained by reducing it to a lower-level—that is, a supposedly better-understood organization "below" it in the course of evolution. Emergents can, of course, be mere chance occurrences, a leap up from some lower to a higher structure that facilitates the survival of a species. As we shall see, the concept of emergence is useful in modern theories of evolution. Whether it actually explains anything is another matter. Some critics feel that it is a descriptive and not an explanatory term, a mere statement of what takes place.

We are left with the question under consideration in this chapter: How well does our psychic interpretation of consciousness complement the Darwinian interpretation of consciousness as the adaptive organization of bodily structure? I believe there are reflections of unipredication and transpredication in what Darwin discusses as consciousness. A major concept of his is that of the *instinct*, which he defines as "memory transmitted without consciousness" (Gruber, 1974, p. 191). *Habits* are also behavioral patterns lacking in consciousness. It is only after many successive generations of a species have adopted a certain habitual pattern that it becomes an instinct. Due to the subtlety of such adaptations, the illusions of free will, purpose, and choice arise. Looked at from the perspective of this volume, Darwin would be said to be explaining the gradual acquisition and transmission of unipredicated actions (increasingly routinized habits into instincts, etc.).

But transpredications are also apparent in Darwin's theorizing. For example, he discusses the possibility of a "double consciousness" (p. 281), in which two quite separate trains of thought are going on at the same time. This doubling does not occur in a habitual train of thought, where one idea calls up another in lock-step fashion. Being cognizant of engaging in two separate thoughts at the same time is transpredicational by definition. Darwin's explanation of unconsciousness stressed the transformation of conscious behavioral patterns into the habitual, which is quite consistent with our analysis of the narrowing of consciousness from trans- to unipredication (p. 233). Dreaming presents Darwin with a perfect example of unconsciousness: "The dream's vividness can be explained by the fact that it is a single train of ideas, whereas waking thought involves many parallel trains and the effort of relating them to each other" (pp. 321–322). Trans- and unipredication are strongly indicated here; indeed, this interpretation of the dream could have been made by the psychoanalysts of Chapter 4. Clearly, there is support in Darwinian theory for the interpretation of psychic consciousness that we are pursuing. Let us turn next to some more recent evolutionists to see if this support for LLT continues.

ROGER W. SPERRY

Roger Sperry (1914–1994), a Nobel laureate, achieved his major reputation from his pioneering work in "split-brain" research and therapy (Meyers & Sperry, 1953; Sperry, 1961, 1985). However, he also proposed a *two-way causation model* (Sperry, 1993, p. 880) that stressed the role of consciousness in brain function; it is this aspect of his work that I would like to discuss. Sperry's model draws from the evolutionary concept of emergence: "It is characteristic of emergent properties that they are notably novel and often amazingly and inexplicably different from the components of which they are built" (1993, p. 880). This statement is consistent with what Darwin believed about creative or emergent events in evolution.

Sperry's theory follows generally on the Darwinian idea that consciousness is found in the growing adaptability of a species' bodily structure to its environment. But he adds a significant point that greatly elaborates the nature of such adaptation. When Darwin claimed that consciousness depends on increasing organization, he relied on the traditional Aristotelian causes, excepting the final. The concept of selection places great emphasis on formal causation, construed extraspectively as patterns taking shape "over there." An animal or a plant that is observed expanding its adaptation to the environment—albeit unintentionally—has an ever greater chance for survival. Of course, if this adaptation becomes highly specific to the environment there is a risk. The more specifically detailed this matching of organism and environment, the greater the chances are for a collapse in adjustment when the environment changes either permanently or temporarily. Human beings are among the most adaptable organisms in nature, and hence it would seem that there may be more to the story of consciousness than Darwin's adaptation thesis provides. Here is where Sperry offered a *mentalistic* alternative.

Sperry made two major points regarding consciousness. First, he suggested that mental states are "dynamic emergent properties of brain activity" (Sperry, 1993, p. 879). The bodily structure that is perfecting its organization through evolutionary advance is therefore the brain. To speak of mental states does not require that we introduce a Cartesian dualism into our theory (p. 880). Sperry insisted that he was a monist in theoretical formulation because he conceived of a lower *physical* organization of the brain laying the groundwork for a higher *physical* organization to emerge. There is no jump from physical to mental in this emergence. Sperry's second point takes care of the mentalistic features of this higher brain organization, for he added that there is a "top–down causal control" (Sperry, 1992, p. 266) in the more highly organized physical structure of the brain.

Sperry called for a basic revision in the concept of causality. He argued that the whole is not only different and more than the sum of its parts, but the whole "also causally determines the fate of the parts, without interfering with the physical or chemical laws for the subentities at their own level" (Cousins, 1985, p. 46). Evolutionary concepts have encouraged us to think of causation in a bottom–up way—from the parts to the total. What Sperry now asks us to appreciate is that once the whole has emerged as a higher organization, it lends direction to the parts of which it is constituted. Once this higher organization has emerged in the brain, the "firing orders [of the cerebral cortex] come from a higher command" (p. 48). There is a world of diverse causal forces existing within the human cranium: Forces within forces geometrically extend their influence from a dynamic totality in which physical parts like molecules get hauled and pushed around by the spatially larger configurational forces of the entire physical brain (p. 47). Although Sperry believed that he had introduced a new causal concept, this theoretical analysis would be dealt with in Aristotelian terms by referring to a kind of shift from efficient causation (bottom–up) to formal or final causation (top–down).

It is this unique top–down patterning that constitutes subjective consciousness: "Top–down control of the parts by the emergent whole is . . . a core concept [of this theory]; it legitimizes consciousness and the subjective for science" (Sperry, 1992, p. 267). Consciousness in this sense becomes an integral part of the brain process itself: "Consciousness is put to work and given a use and a reason for having been evolved" (p. 263).

Bottom–up causation is *micro* whereas top-down (conscious) direction is manifested in the *macro* world of everyday experience (p. 268). Sperry (1993) drew the line at relying on the mechanisms of quantum physics (see Chapter 3), because he felt that such subatomic conceptions did not explain things in the macroscopic world very well (p. 880). Sperry did not explicate unconsciousness clearly: "The same reasoning by which conscious mental states become causal applies as well to unconscious mental states" (Sperry, 1992, p. 271). One would think that at least the nonconscious aspects of physical behavior originate in the bottom–up processes of the physical body, as organic evolution had initially postulated.

Sperry (1992) considered himself a mentalist (p. 261). He surely reads like a teleologist when he writes that "Subjective agency may thus be viewed as a special instance of downward control, a special case of emergent causality in the reciprocal up–down paradigm for causal control" (Sperry, 1993, p. 882). We are also told that the "circuit properties" of the whole brain may "undergo radical and widespread changes with just the flick of a cerebral facilitory 'set'" (Cousins, 1985, p. 48). Such changes of set are involved when we experience a shift in attention, a turn of thought, a changed feeling, or even a new insight. Sperry (1976) tells us that such sudden changes provide a rationale for the belief in free will (p. 15).

We must not forget that additional information routinely flows upward—in bottom–up fashion—to the holistic organization of the brain. There is a reciprocal interaction going on between lower and higher, but Sperry was always careful to add that "The lower level forces . . . are enveloped, overwhelmed and overpowered by the higher" (Cousins, 1985, p. 80). In time, he was to refer to this action across levels as the *principle of downward causation*, adding that "Under the mentalist view, traditional reductionist interpretations emphasizing control from below upward are replaced by revised concepts that emphasize control from above downward" (p. 158).

Sperry has most assuredly built on the emergence concept, and his interpretation of consciousness is much richer and closer than Darwin's to what we are considering in this volume. If we think of the person as changing "set" in order to shift attention or modify a point of view, it certainly has the ring of formal or final causation—in which an agent can introspectively select the grounding assumption for the sake of which he or she will then be determined. This would be a genuine teleology, where the set is the "that, for the sake of which" a first-person point of view is being framed or an action is being carried out. This strikes me as predicational theorizing at its best. And yet, I have decided misgivings about the Sperry treatment because it remains extraspective. Teleologies written in the third person just do not seem to capture true psychic consciousness. They tend to stay away from oppositional conceptions.

When Sperry refers to a two-way causation (bottom–up versus top–

down), I fear he merely doubles the efficient-cause determination taking place, then lends greater weight to the unilinear course of influence emanating from the whole rather than its parts. There seems to be no clear connection between the patterning of this wholeness and the directedness of behavior. How are these behavioral directions brought about? Sperry refers to the change in a brain state caused by the "flick" of a facilitatory set. This metaphorical allusion to flicking a set (point of view, assumption, etc.) is too close to efficient causation for comfort. There is a nagging mediational theme in here that I feel Sperry was surely trying, without complete success, to move beyond.

The basic problem here is a lack of proper theoretical terminology to frame explanations. Although I see intimations of an agreement with the LLT position on psychic consciousness, basic terminological differences always intrude. Thus, when Sperry reaches to the whole as more influential than the parts, I think that he is describing the role of predication in thought. From years of studying people with various physical brain disorders, he had concluded that the bits and pieces of the brain simply do not "add up" to self-direction for the individual concerned. This Lockean, constitutive assumption is just not working when it comes to explaining human thought and behavior. He required a Kantian conceptual formulation from the more abstract, hence broader reaches of thought, to capture things appropriately. He characterized this revision in theorizing as moving from a bottom–up to a top–down form of causation; but, as already suggested, I would argue that he is shifting from the building-block notions of efficient causation (bottom–up) to the patternings of formal causation (top–down).

Sperry's talk of flicking cerebral sets around to change the person's line of understanding and behavior is an obvious transferal of *Logos* meanings (i.e., transpredications) into *Bios* meanings (i.e., brain circuits). He wanted to remain a *Bios* monist. Supporters of LLT want to be *Logos* monists. As I argued in Chapter 1, there is no reason why this multiplicity of theorizing cannot be complementary. But the problem Sperry's explanation does not come close to solving is this: How are we to think of the process going on in the top–down organization that flicks from one set to another? This is another way of considering the directedness of thought and behavior. Is the brain a planner, chooser, and decider of what takes place or merely an instrumentality of what takes place in thought and action? Do we not require a homunculus predicator to decide "for" the instrumental brain whether "this" or "that" set should be flicked-on in the circuitry of the physical brain? There are a lot of unanswered questions like this in Sperry's formal treatment, but I am pleased that we can see intimations of LLT conceptions in his general outlook. It is just impossible to capture *Logos* theories in *Bios* terms. At best we must simply complement one with the other (Rychlak, 1993).

GEORGE M. EDELMAN

Edelman, a Nobel laureate, has for many years been using modified evolutionary theory to explain brain organization and function. He believes that both emergence and natural selection are at work patterning nerve cells within the brains of individuals, referring to this use of evolutionary concepts in individual biological development as *neural Darwinism*. We thus can speak of the *natural selection* of animal species, which vary in their capacity for adaptation to the external environment; and we can also speak of *neuronal group selection* in the internal environment of a single animal (Edelman, 1987, p. 9). The latter theory holds that at birth the specific cerebral neuronal cells to be activated are not yet patterned, so there is a kind of conflict or "struggle for activation" among them before this organization is selected.

As Mountcastle's (1975) work helped establish, the basic organization of nerve cells in the brain is modular. The modules contain up to 10,000 nerve cells locked together by mutual synaptic connections in a mind-boggling organization of zigs and zags that fire in patterns. Each of these modules takes electrical power from its neighbor if given the chance to be activated. Eccles (1977) once opined, "We think the nervous system always works by conflict—in this case by conflicts between each module and the adjacent modules" (p. 234). Edelman (1987) fashioned his theory on such findings, suggesting that in seeking adaptation to the external environment, certain emergent neuronal groupings in synaptic contact with others facilitate adaptation whereas other groupings do not (pp. 17–18). The adaptive emergent neural synaptic patterns are selected for retention in the organization of the particular (subjective) brain under development, and those that are nonadaptive are selected out. He referred to this latter mechanism as a *somatic selective system* (p. 329). Edelman wrote that

> The major experimental tasks set by the theory of neuronal group selection are to discover the developmental origins of variability, the rules governing synaptic populations in degenerate neural networks, and the temporal and physical constraints of reentry, all within the context of the larger evolutionary constraints upon the behavior and form of a given species. (1987, p. 19)

The concept of *reentry* refers to a kind of parallel processing of brain cells, in which sensory inputs (e.g., sounds, images, etc.) connect into a patterned map or signal. This is a dynamic process in which there is a constant circulation of these symbols, interrelating without a fixed program directing them. From among this changing pool certain symbols are selected in, others selected out.

Edelman (1992) is as convinced as Sperry was that consciousness is intentional (pp. 67, 112). The lower-versus-higher strategy of explanation that seems endemic to developmental theorists is prominent in Edelman's interpretation of consciousness. He tells us that there are two levels of consciousness—a *primary* state in which the organism is aware of things in the world by experiencing images of them, and a *higher-order* state in which there is "the recognition by a thinking subject of his or her own acts or affections" (p. 112). In higher-order consciousness, the individual is also "conscious of being conscious" (p. 112), which suggests a capacity for transcendence and self-reflexivity. Primary consciousness is more bound to the present, lacks concepts of self, past, or future, and is beyond description at its own level. Thus, "beings with primary consciousness alone cannot construct theories of consciousness" (p. 116). Edelman lays great stress on the emergence of reentrant circuits in the course of the brain's evolution; these circuits enable an organism to link perceptual events into an ongoing sequence (p. 119).

Perception is extremely important to the development of higher-order consciousness, where images of scenes are received and categorized. *Categorization* is a process allowing "the individual to correlate properties in the world and thus to go beyond the immediate or given stimulus. To be of adaptive value, categorization must entail generalization, or the ability on the basis of a few stimuli to respond or recognize a much larger range of stimuli" (Edelman, 1987, p. 245). Primary consciousness is a kind of limited, "remembered present" where images and scenes are perceived as immediately sensed (Edelman, 1992, p. 120). But in higher-order consciousness, which emerges from primary consciousness (p. 124), there is a capacity to see a continuity in ongoing experience. Categorization is carried on in the cortex of the brain, which Edelman calls a *correlator*. So, the brain categorizes, which means it correlates the properties of several images in a certain way so as to facilitate higher-order consciousness, freeing it from exclusive dominance by immediate experience (p. 149). The higher-order consciousness of the brain thus can discern (correlate) similarities and differences in events as they take place sequentially over time.

Edelman (1992) argues that, although language is vital to the development of higher-order consciousness, the infant must already have some capacity to engage meanings (semantics) even before language syntax is acquired. He then suggests that infants have innate conceptual categories that enable them to build a syntax (pp. 129–130). Although language is tied to a community, it is also highly personal. The learning of a *self* takes place interpersonally in primary consciousness, which in turn demands that the individual name and intend things (p. 136). This amounts to the development of attention, which is not the same thing as consciousness, but is rather the lending of a directional component to behavior. Attention "focuses our mind on its objects and obliterates or attenuates surrounding 'irrelevancies'" (p. 141). Attention is central to conscious learning. However, it is also possible to learn without attention, in which case we can speak of an unconscious performance (p. 142). Unconscious behaviors are those that can become conscious, but some aspects of brain and behavioral functioning remain nonconscious and therefore can never reach even primary consciousness (p. 143). How did consciousness arise? Edelman answers:

> My first premise is that consciousness appeared as a result of natural selection. The mind depends on consciousness for its existence and functioning. A related notion is that consciousness is efficacious, enhancing fitness in certain environments. Consciousness arises from a special set of relationships between perception, concept formation, and memory. These psychological functions depend on categorization mechanisms in the brain. In addition, memory is influenced by evolutionarily established value systems and by homeostatic control systems characteristic of each species. (p. 149)

With the onset of language, concepts of self and of past and future events also emerge (p. 150). All of this enhances consciousness, which is central to the advancement of society and science alike. Selfhood is not merely "the individuality that emerges from genetics . . . but the personal individuality that emerges from developmental and social interactions" (p. 167). Language is an important aspect of categorization, which takes place on the basis of the values that the self takes on (p. 163). Memory is also an important factor contributing to consciousness. Memory emerged thanks to a "reentrant [brain] circuit linking value-category memory to classification" (p. 207). This gave continuity to life and allowed for the further emergence of higher-order consciousness. Memory underlies meaning (p. 207). The self relies on remembered meanings to give consciousness a sense of continuity from out of the past and a directedness toward the intended future.

The emphasis Edelman places on selection through adaptation is remarkably similar to traditional learning-theory explanations in psychology. Traditional drive-reduction theorists like Clark Hull would say that learning occurs when a stimulus–response sequence is reinforced thanks to a drive reduction. A hungry rat (high drive state) dashes about the layout of a maze in random activity until it comes upon the goal box where it finds something to eat and satisfies its hunger (drive-reduction). On subsequent trials in the maze this dashing about gradually reduces to a smooth sequence of leaving the starting box and reaching the goal box increasingly rapidly. Hull (1952) called this steady improvement *learning*. Edelman would appear to be describing the same sequence and calling it *neuronal group selection*. Hull thinks about the total pattern of learning manifested by the rat, and Edelman thinks about the rat's brain, where perceptions of experience are being recorded in primary consciousness as modified by the somatic selective process. Edelman might also want to call the overt maze-running a form of natural (as opposed to neural) selection, contending as he does that there is always such a duality in the selective processes.

I have no argument with this double-edged explanation of external and internal adaptations. Both Hull and Edelman could be correct without contradiction, as indeed their theories are both extraspective, efficiently causal, and mediational in style. But given this similarity it is also interesting to note that they take opposite positions on the relevance of consciousness. Hull thought this concept unnecessary in explaining the behavior of not only rats, but human beings as well. He thereby followed the antiteleological attitude of the founder of behaviorism, John Watson (1913). What Edelman calls intentionality and conscious directedness from past to future, Hull would consider a sequence of behavioral responses controlled by both current and past (i.e., mediated) stimuli.

Intentionality for Hull was merely an anticipatory goal response, as when the rat begins to salivate and move its jaws as it draws closer to the (previously located) food-laden goal box, even before it has taken this food into its mouth. This looks superficially as if the rat is expecting or intending to eat, but the truth is that efficiently caused responses can begin even before the goal is reached (Hull, 1952, chapter 5). The same holds for the person who, with an image of the forthcoming feast in mind, arranges the knife and fork in close proximity to the plate before dinner is served. There is no expectancy or intention being manifested in such anticipatory goal responding. No formal or final causation can be found in this extraspective formulation of behavior. Only efficiently caused responding is occurring.

I find Edelman using *emerge* and *emergence* in the way that a psychologist would use the words *learn* and *learning*. What is curious about this is that, whereas important psychological theorists like Skinner relied on Darwinian conceptions because they rescued them from speaking of intentionality and purpose in behavior, Edelman is drawn to the same formulations as a theorist trying to revive such teleological formulations. For example, Skinner's (1974) notion of an *operant response* held that organisms gave forth (emitted) certain actions without any purpose, having no particular intention in mind, and then the environment shaped these behaviors into continuing habits through contingent reinforcement. The bird pecks at the bark of various trees, operantly emitting these pecking responses until it punctures a certain type of bark and stumbles onto a lode of nutritional insects. We now observe the pecking behavior increasing and seeming to occur in a selective manner, as if the bird were purposively choosing one kind of tree bark (similar to the initial type) over another. But, as with the Hullian explanation of the rat in the maze, no such intentionality is taking place.

An unintended pecking response that was emitted to operate on the environment is being contingently reinforced, thereby shaping the bird's subsequent behavior. A *contingency* is a state of affairs following an emitted response that makes this response more likely to occur in the future—to "reproduce" itself, so to speak. Looked at in evolutionary terms, this is not unlike natural selection. As Darwinians, we might replace "emit" with "emerge" and describe a series of events in which a species of bird that has a strong beak emerged one generation and is then able to break through thicker tree barks than a species with a weaker beak. Hence, the strong-beak species is rewarded (reinforced) by sustaining life when the insects are more difficult to locate because they are burrowed deeper into the tree limbs. The contingent "reinforcement" of natural selection is life itself.

The theoretical development here is identical for Darwin and Skinner. Skinner (1971) was fully aware of the parallel, for as he noted while discussing operant conditioning, "The environment not only prods or lashes, it *selects*. Its role is similar to that in natural selection, though on a very different time scale, and it was overlooked for the same reason" (p. 18; italics in original). As Sperry considered top–down causation to be something new in scientific description, Skinner (1974) also viewed selection as a unique form of causation: "Darwin simply discovered the role of selection, a kind of causality very different from the push–pull mechanisms of science up to that time" (p. 36). Actually, Skinner's operant conditioning is not a new form of causality for it is readily subsumed by the meaning of efficient causation.

The selecting environment for Skinner is not in the somatic realm, as it is for Edelman. Skinner was drawn to the *Socius* rather than the *Bios*, feeling that psychologists were missing their opportunity for a unique role in the sciences by continually tying behavior down to biological mechanisms. He held that "Consciousness is a social product" (Skinner, 1971, p. 192). The "individual is born of society" (Skinner, 1974, p. 149), and consciousness is naturally selected for its utility to the group. Much of so-called consciousness arises when the organism in a group is contingently reinforced for using language expressing the view that people can behave autonomously (Skinner, 1971, p. 19). Here is how Skinner might rebut the claim that psychic consciousness involves personal awareness: "A person becomes conscious . . . when a verbal community arranges contingencies under which he not only sees an object but sees that he is seeing it. In this special sense, consciousness or awareness is a social product" (Skinner, 1974, p. 220). Presumably the person cannot become aware of this manipulation by the verbal community. Consciousness is itself a shaped outcome of linguistic expression, or what Skinner called *verbal behavior*.

Strictly speaking, verbal behavior does not evolve but "it is the verbal environment that evolves" (Skinner, 1987, p. 75). The course of linguistic expression is shaped by natural selection on the basis of the utility of certain verbal signs (words, expressions, etc.) rather than others. Verbal usage, which is suggestive of reflexive thought, is selected in this way because it furthers survival by refining and improving the behavioral adaptations of community members (e.g., through critical verbal examination of what is taking place, etc.). The source of control on the individual here is *not* a transcending human capacity to predicate, as LLT contends. Human beings are not now nor will they ever become "originating centers of control" (Skinner, 1957, p. 460). Hence, there is no point in speaking of anything like an introspectively conceived, psychic consciousness.

Despite these parallels with traditional learning theories, I think that Edelman, like Sperry, has made a sincere effort to capture what I am calling psychic consciousness. There is a reaching here for the final-cause meaning, but unfortunately this meaning does not lend itself to the biological conceptions to which Edelman is committed. Final causation makes sense in the *Logos* but not in the *Bios*, a misfit in terminology that has been the continuing stumbling block to solving the mind–body riddle in psychology. In light of this fact, how well do the *Logos* concepts of LLT, which suggest psychic consciousness, stand up in terms of Edelman's arguments? I think we see the same kind of indications that we did with Sperry's theory. Edelman is trying to explain what I am also striving to explain.

A psychic consciousness would, of course, involve the higher-order form of consciousness that Edelman postulates. He stresses the importance of categorization in moving from a lower to a higher level. He tells us that people have a need as observers "to carve up their world into categories of things" (Edelman, 1992, p. 11). We might now remind ourselves that the term *category* stems from the Greek word *katēgorein*, which means "to predicate" one item of meaning by another (see Chapter 2). Unlike LLT, Edelman does not see this predicating activity as a uniquely *Logos* process. Edelman's categorizing process is some kind of grouping or gathering together of items that share certain features *after the fact of their occurrence*. This is like tossing various items that match up in some way (e.g., anything that is found to be square) into the same bag. Something else creates (orders, organizes, etc.) the potential category (in this case, squareness) and then the brain embodies the patterned meaning so organized by selecting the proper symbol-producing neurons to mediate this grouping. Values can also influence a grouping. For example, we may group people who "embrace our attitudes" versus those who "oppose our attitudes."

From the LLT point of view, there is no *psychological* point in speaking about what exists independently of a construing individual's predication of events. To say that potential categorizations like "people who share our views versus those who oppose them" exist whether we frame this fact or not is simply to say that this truism is being framed by a third party. Looked at from the psychological (introspective) perspective, someone has to make this claim or *it* will not exist. According to LLT, nothing exists psychologically or phenomenally unless there is a conceptualizing intelligence making it so (which is not to deny the existence of noumenal reality). Hence, to understand human thought we must understand the predicational process. It is this process that generates or creates the meaning that Edelman (1992) finds embodied in the neuronal organization of the brain (p. 161). Predication is not grouping by matching, it is actively conceptualizing what can and will be known in terms of both what "is" and "is not" relevant. The brain stuff is an instrumentality here, a necessary but not sufficient aspect of the embodiment known as human reasoning.

Edelman's human is not born tabula rasa, as most mediational modeling contends. The newborn infant has innate categories available to get the brain organization underway, particularly in regard to language learning (Edelman, 1992, pp. 129–130). Transpredication is implied in Edelman's treatment of higher-order consciousness in which, as noted above, transcendence and self-reflexivity are made possible (p. 112). As with Sperry, there is not much treatment of unconsciousness. Edelman does refer to certain unconscious elements that can compete with attention (p. 143). His interpretation of repression stresses the evolutionary advantage achieved when the person would *not* recategorize things "that threaten the efficacy of [the person's] self-concepts" (p. 145). All of this is described in terms of circuitry making certain memories possible or not. There is no formal recognition of oppositionality in this theory, but Edelman's handling of categorizing could probably be seen in this light, as when he speaks of the categorization of "familiar and nonfamiliar events" (p. 118). I believe, however, that he is thinking here in binary terms that, as we shall learn in Chapter 7, are appositional rather than genuinely oppositional. Even so, I think it is fair to conclude that we see intimations of LLT's introspective concepts in Edelman's extraspective formulations.

ROBERT ORNSTEIN

Evolutionary theorist Robert Ornstein can be seen as forming a bridge to the computer or information-processing theorists of Chapter 7. That is, unlike Sperry or Edelman, Ornstein (1991) agrees that "mind can be thought to be similar to a computer: it operates in binary, it processes information, has input and output, serial and parallel ports, random and fixed connections" (p. 19). Of course, Ornstein adds, this does *not* mean that mind is *only* a computer (p. 19). The mind "evolved to adapt to the world" (p. 39). Like Edelman, Ornstein believes in neuronal selection. In fact, he speaks of three types of selection: natural, neural, and conscious. Natural selection is strictly biological, in which the organism adapts to the environment unconsciously (p. 77). As higher organisms evolved, neural selection was made possible exactly as Edelman presented it. Finally, however, as Darwin appreciated, conscious selection began taking place (e.g., animal husbandry, the human rights of weaker members of a society, etc.). Ornstein believes that, thanks to conscious selection, it is possible for human beings to develop the ability to select those aspects of mind that improve their adjustment potentials (p. 273).

Ornstein describes the rich complexities of the brain, including the excessive number of cells in its columnar organization, its organization into numerous and even disparate neural networks, the role of chemicals in processing signals, and the fact that different experiences can lead to subjectively unique brain organizations from person to person. All brains are not alike. Some are organized more emotionally than others. Indeed, Ornstein claims that "Emotional reactions have a different neural network than conscious, reasoned responses" (p. 80). This difference between emotional and conscious behavior stems from the fact that over the evolutionary succession, these two sides to human behavior were "laid down in separate eras" (p. 80). It is in the early years of the individual's life that most of the neuronal selection takes place, so that "individuals have different brains because of their early experiences" (p. 126). Here is a summary of Ornstein's basic position:

> The human brain, coming into the world with a vast oversupply of nerve circuits, wires up differently with different early experiences. It is a contest among the neurons like that of evolution itself; hence the name, neural Darwinism. Selection here is offered by the local environment, so to specialize our very general mind. The great brain gets developed differently so that each individual has a better chance to match her or his specific small world. (p. 130)

Ornstein sometimes uses the term *nonconscious* to describe doing things like performing in a sport, making music, or even just thinking deeply (p. 141). These are actions carried on without consciousness, strictly by the brain's physical organization of networks. At other times he will refer to such habitual performances as being unconscious. He recognizes that it is possible to negate such automatic actions: "An unconscious decision center may decide to initiate an action, then there is a period of time during which the conscious self can choose to stop the action" (p. 147). Ornstein made this suggestion on the basis of the work of Libet (1985), who demonstrated that even though a *readiness potential* may be picked up in the nerve tracts of the brain's cortex a half-second before some action that it is signaling occurs, this action can be negated before it is enacted. A person may have the inclination to move a wrist or flex a finger. Electrical equipment mapping the cortex picks up this inclination as a readiness potential one-half second before we see the person actually moving the wrist or flexing a finger. But every person that Libet tested could and did on occasion stop enacting such an inclination. So the cortex does not automatically signal the necessary carrying-out of movements. It is signaling a possibility, but not an ironclad eventuality. The person has an alternative brain capacity to stop the motor action in its tracks (or in its *tracts*).

Libet is willing to see this negation as an action of will. Interestingly, Ornstein has also carried out some experiments to demonstrate that people can switch from use of their right to their left hemispheres in mentally rotating objects. Ornstein (1991) concluded that "People can use their hemispheres differently in problem solving at will" (p. 137). Now, if the brain is similar to a computer, as Ornstein suggests, we can ask "Can a computer negate what it is being electrically stimulated 'to do' at will?" A computer theorist might point out that computers can be programmed to negate. But are programs actual machines, or strictly the mediated "software" contents directing the machine? Can the computer as a "hardware" machine process negate *any* program put to it, including the one directing it to negate? I will hold off discussion of such issues for Chapter 7, where we will take them up in detail.

Continuing in this programming vein, Ornstein speaks of the brain as containing "many small unconscious minds, each with its own program" (p. 147). The computer theorists described in Chapter 7 make similar claims of separate processing sources. Of what, then, does the mind consist? Ornstein answers that "neural networks merely gather and transform various forms of energy" (p. 176). And, "mind [or minds] thus evolved to select signals from the world" (p. 180). Our brain is constructed, in large measure, on assumptions that have been selected in the past (p. 189). The various minds in our brain do not always communicate with one another (p. 205). Here is where conscious experience enters. Consciousness is divided, spread out on different levels and the "trick in managing the mind is to bring the automatic reactions into consciousness" (p. 225). Ornstein's basic definition of consciousness is as follows:

> Consciousness is a word with many meanings, including being awake, being aware of what is going on around us or of what we are doing or of ourselves. Being conscious is being aware of being aware. It is one step removed from the raw experience of seeing, smelling, acting, moving, and reacting. (pp. 225–226)

We do not have to be conscious all of the time. Consciousness enters later in the ongoing sequence of brain activity. It is usually a weak force, easily overridden by environmental circumstances, habitual mechanisms, the influence of other people, and so on. Consciousness can be a potent force, however, and it comes into play "when deliberate, rather than automatic, control or intervention is needed" (p. 227). Ornstein speaks of waking consciousness as gradually building a model of the world on the basis of past experience, but also including our expectations, hopes, and other cognitive processes. He also discusses Pierre Janet's work (see Chapter 4), and agrees that consciousness can be split into two or more sections (p. 228). Consciousness is said to be more flexible than unconsciousness. Ornstein refers to subconscious awareness, meaning by this that "we can be aware of something without being conscious of it" (p. 231). For example, we can be aroused from sleep by hearing our name, whereas we would not awaken if someone else's name were mentioned.

Ornstein gives the general impression that consciousness is rather inconsequential in most people's lives. He says we never really "make up our minds," for they have been made up long ago by the various selective brain processes going on (p. 238). The oneness we sense in consciousness is an illusion. Actually, we have these many differing minds that can be called into play, accounting for why we tend to be so inconsistent. Fortunately, we can improve our conscious control by self-observation: "The development of consciousness lies not far away in a bedazzled or dazed mystic trance, but in conscious selection" (p. 273). Conscious selection allows us to take evolution into our own hands by selecting those parts of the mind we find most useful (p. 273). Conscious intuition is a faculty to select the right part of the mind for the job to be done. This capacity to comprehend instantly and to direct the mental system is the often unrealized aim of "conscious development" (p. 275).

One could readily feel that something is left out of Ornstein's account—namely, the homunculus who intuitively selects the right part of mind to get the job done. In LLT, the aim is to frame things as if we were capturing the cognitive activities of precisely this homunculus—which, indeed, turns out to be nothing less than the person himself or herself. Ornstein's homunculus seems to be what he calls the self, defined as "the commanding, controlling mental operating system," of the brain that is more closely tied to the emotional than the conscious-reasoning circuitry (p. 153). Because there are many minds, and such things as "unconscious decision center[s]" (p. 147) in the brain, this self—as consciousness per se—would seem to be battered about by the many sides of brain functioning.

Ornstein discusses all of those significant points that *Logos* theorizing finds of interest, but in my opinion his *Bios* formulations fail to provide satisfactory psychological explanations. As already suggested above, I think this is true because these formulations are founded on processes that are unsuited to the study of meaning; and consciousness—at least, psychic consciousness—does not make much sense outside of meaning. I was particularly interested in Ornstein's analysis of negation, where it seems to me that oppositionality was sorely missed. He touches on transpredication in referring to the deliberate, non-automatic nature of consciousness, and on unipredication in agreeing with Janet on the splits in consciousness that we have schematized in Figure 4. Ornstein also appreciates the importance that self-observation plays in realigning the contributions that consciousness can make to ongoing human behavior. His definition of consciousness as including "being aware of being aware" is what we have been calling self-reflexivity. But, of course, without the capacity to transcend through oppositional reasoning, Ornstein's treatment is unable to clarify just how this reflexive dynamic takes place. We move next to a widely discussed, highly controversial theory of consciousness that combines evolutionary, archaeological, and historical speculations.

JULIAN JAYNES

Julian Jaynes (1976) has put forward a most intriguing account of the origins of consciousness. He proposes that at one time, early in the evolution of human organisms, the brain was divided into two parts, an executive part (right hemisphere) called a god, and a follower part (left hemisphere) called a man (or woman; p. 84). Neither of these parts was conscious. This *bicameral* mental organization resulted in a pattern of behavior that was very much like the efficient-cause, stimulus–response actions of behaviorism. As totally unconscious beings, people were not responsible for their behaviors—neither to be blamed for bad actions nor given credit for good actions. The individual with a bicameral brain was ordered about like a slave by a hallucinated voice (or voices), not unlike what we see today in the behavior of people suffering from schizophrenia (p. 93). Each person had his or her own god, which was not a fantasy of some (e.g., spiritual) entity but an actual (material) structure in the evolving nervous system. The god was thus not a content but an actual physical process. Drawing on the stores of previous experience the god structure "transmuted this experience into articulated speech which then 'told' the [woman or] man what to do" (pp. 202–203). This took place before there was a written language.

The rise of consciousness was greatly influenced by two considerations: *language*, and *social control*. Actually, these considerations are related because language has great social-control value. Initially, the language of people was involved with only one brain hemisphere (the left) in order to leave the other free for the language of the gods (pp. 103–104). Jaynes suggests that "The gods . . . were amalgams of admonitory experience, made up of meldings of whatever commands had been given the individual" (p. 106). This sounds more like a content than a process, but in any case, with the rise of a more complex language, there was an increasing role being played by the commands of certain human beings rather than exclusively the gods. If the recognizable voice of a human being rather than a god were hallucinated, the experience became a social interaction (p. 137). Jaynes now relies on a *Socius* formulation to suggest that civilization was beginning to exert control on individuals through the growth of language. Hence, left- and right-hemisphere conflicts were inevitable, particularly because many of the problems that arose in the social context were reaching beyond the strictly *Bios* experiences of the evolving physical organism.

A new form of evolution was taking place creating new problems and tensions in the interpersonal rather than the biological realm.

The earliest users of language did not have a grasp of selfhood. There was no self-reflexivity in mind. These early speech users were therefore unable to grasp themselves as behaving in relation to others. They were "signal-bound" (p. 140). The voices, now both godly and human, continued to direct and solve problems for the still unconscious person. The hallucinated human voices were those of important superiors like kings, whose commands were conveyed by other authorities in the society as well as parents. Stress is what brought on these hallucinatory incidents. The more stress in life the greater the chances for hallucinations to occur. Problems causing the stress were dealt with through admonitions or encouragements. Thus, a worker carrying out a difficult task in the fields might hallucinate the "voice of the vizier over him admonishing him in some way" (p. 190). There was no awareness (i.e., psychic consciousness) here that such admonitions were recollections. The voices heard were current and real.

The bicameral mind was fragile. Its major weakness was that it could not deal with complexity and contradiction. Conflict resolution proved very difficult. Another way of putting this is that the bicameral mind was binary (see Chapter 7). There was no capacity to say that both sides in an either–or dispute might be correct in some way: It was one side or the other, period. As Jaynes expressed it, neither gods, kings, or viziers are likely "to command individuals into acts of compromise" (p. 207). Note that this characterization nicely aligns with the ex cathedra nature of unconscious pronouncements discussed in Chapter 4. As language developed, and especially its recording in writing (dating from circa 2500 BC; p. 228), the auditory authority of the bicameral mind eroded significantly until the social structure on which it was founded collapsed entirely:

> The input to the divine hallucinatory aspect of the bicameral mind was auditory. It used cortical areas more closely connected to the auditory parts of the brain. And once the word of god was silent, written on dumb clay tablets or incised into speechless stone, the god's commands or the king's directives could be turned to or avoided by one's own efforts in a way that auditory hallucinations never could be. The word of a god had *a controllable location* rather than an ubiquitous power with immediate obedience. (p. 208; italics in original)

According to Jaynes, consciousness first occurred in Mesopotamia toward the end of the second millennium BC, during a chaotic period of mass migration and invasions of peoples from every corner of the known world (pp. 209, 246). The voices of the gods became less adequate and were eventually suppressed during this period of social chaos, where every group seemed to have its own godly answers to contradict those of its neighbors. But even with this suppression of voices the need for certainty and personal direction was not forsaken. Indeed, quite the opposite took place. With the rise of language the person was given certain descriptive terms in the Skinnerian sense of shaping. Out of such reactions from parents and others in the social context each person fashioned a so-called *analog-self* or *analog-I* (pp. 62, 65). The resultant subjective identity enabled the individual to frame a narrative account of his or her behavior, including the outcome of personal actions.

This conscious evaluation of personal behavior was, in effect, a sense of morality (p. 286). As Jaynes expressed it, "Consciousness and morality are a single development. For without gods, morality based on a consciousness of the consequences of action must tell men what to do" (p. 286). Jaynes characterizes religion as "the lost bicamerality" (p. 297) of a people who had become subjectively conscious. From the 9th to the 5th century BC there was to be a progressive decline in bicamerality and a concomitant gain in subjectivity. Even so, as outlined in Chapter 3, selfhood was not highly prized for centuries in the AD world.

So, to speak of the collapse of bicamerality is to speak of the concomitant rise of consciousness and the conflict in alternatives that it engendered. But is this rise in consciousness an emergent evolution of the process of thought, or merely the contents that thought carries along as linguistic mediators (words and statements)? Consciousness is a process rather than a substantial object or repository of some type. Jaynes notes that it works by forming a so-called analog space within which an analog identity moves about and behaves metaphorically (p. 65). In order to understand this definition of consciousness, we will next turn to an analysis of what Jaynes means by metaphor and analog, contrasting his usage with that of LLT.

First, however, I would like to emphasize that Jaynes is obviously dealing with the same notion of consciousness and unconsciousness that is under study in this volume. The bicameral mind, founded on a *Bios* split into two brain chambers, is unipredicational in nature. The bicameral person is directed by an unconsciousness that speaks in ex cathedra fashion. It is in this unipolarity of meaning expression that the bicameral mind finds its ultimate collapse, for when confronted with alternative formulations it lacks the capacity to transcend, self-reflexively examine its universalistic assertions, and thereby make corrective adaptations. A new kind of stress (social chaos) brings on this need for self-examination, sophisticated defensiveness, and possible repredication, but the voices of old are unable to meet such needs because they cannot transpredicate—which is to say they are not conscious.

Jaynes also agrees with our finding in Chapter 3 that initially there was no distinction drawn between conscience and consciousness. In calling religion the lost bicamerality of a subjectively conscious people,

Jaynes implies that the first moves to consciousness apparently *had* to be conscience-oriented because the non-bicameral human was trying to re-experience the authoritative directedness of the lost voices. Religious myths, rituals, commandments, and so forth, all bespeak the need to recapture the unipolarity of a universalistic claim on reality (as well as spirituality). Living a life of grace, in which the deity directs all, is consciously to decide upon recapturing the certainty of the earlier unconsciousness.

The disagreements between Jaynes and the views of the present volume stem from his essentially extraspective account. He begins his analysis on a point that I found to be encouragingly similar to LLT: All languages make great use of the metaphor (p. 48), as when we might say that "A clock has a face" or "a needle has an eye." He calls the predicate word of such sentences (face, eye) a *metaphier* and the subject word (clock, needle) a *metaphrand* (p. 48). There is a mathematical allusion here in that the metaphier is thought of as operating on the metaphrand to increase its volume of meaning (akin to the multiplier operating on the multiplicand).

In LLT terms the metaphier and metaphrand would be termed the predicate and target respectively, with the assumption that the former extends its meaning to the latter in precedent-sequacious fashion. As an introspective formulation, LLT would have us think about the face and eye concepts as a context-providing pair of spectacles through which we would construe the clock and needle, lending them meaning predicationally. The face and eye would be the larger Euler circle (see Figures 2 and 3), which would be brought to bear on the smaller circles within its circumference labeled clock and needle. But Jaynes does not think of predication in this manner. He has the metaphier and metaphrand conceptions associated together in the standing language structure, and even enlarged upon by secondary words called *paraphiers* and *paraphrands*, which greatly increase the associated matrix of meaning (pp. 56–57).

An even more telling difference between LLT and the Jaynesian position is his treatment of an analog. As noted in Chapter 2, LLT interprets an analogy as a partial tautology in which only a portion of the predicate meaning is extended to the target; that is, there is always a disanalogous aspect to any analogy. Analogies approximate as they are only partially identical relations between the precedent predicate and the target to which this meaning is sequaciously extended. Jaynes, on the other hand, defines an analog as a special kind of model. It is not a predicating model, as LLT would have it. Rather, "an analog is at every point generated by the thing it is an analog of" (p. 54). Jaynes gives a map as an example of an analog. A map is generated by the geographical region it is supposed to represent. Jaynes sees the actual physical terrain as a metaphier and the map as a metaphrand in the sense that "the relation between an analog map and its land is a metaphor" (p. 54). Logical learning theory would view this relation of map to its land as a match—a tautology—rather than as an analogy. The (formal-cause) pattern of these two items is identical. Analogies are never 100% matched identities.

On the basis of this interpretation of the analogy, Jaynes views personal identity as something taken in: a map of external circumstances as defined by language to create an analog-self or an analog-I (p. 286). In LLT terms, Jaynes is resorting to a mediational model in which efficiently caused linguistic determinants are at work shaping the person's understanding. Indeed, Jaynes extends this analog notion as follows: "Subjective conscious mind is an analog of what is called the real world. It is built up with a vocabulary or lexical field whose terms are all metaphors or analogs of behavior in the physical world" (p. 55). It is difficult for me to decide what process is at work here, for Jaynes goes on to say that the subjective conscious mind is an "operator" (on the side of a metaphier?) and is "intimately bound up with volition and decision" (p. 55). Yet an analog such as a map or the belief in a self is not a process but a content brought about by some kind of process. I believe that Jaynes's process is predication, but he fails to capture decision making or volition in this process.

Ultimately, these more teleological considerations in human behavior are the result of social contact and conflict. Thus when Jaynes says that "consciousness is the work of lexical metaphor" (p. 58) we wonder whether he means the process whereby metaphorical reasoning is made possible, or the contents that are produced by this process. He has referred to consciousness as the metaphrand in some cases and the metaphier in others (p. 59). He adds that consciousness is not a repository but is rather an operation (p. 65). But then he goes on to situate his outlook in the tradition of British empiricism:

> Conscious mind is a spatial analog of the world and mental acts are analogs of bodily acts. Consciousness operates only on objectively observable things. Or, to say it another way with echoes of John Locke, there is nothing in consciousness that is not an analog of something that was in behavior first. (p. 66)

This clearly implies a mediational model, in which the observable or behavioral item is prefigured externally and then brought in to the conscious (mediating) process as an analog-match, akin to the map and its terrain. Jaynes has apparently confounded process and content in his interpretation of consciousness.

CONCLUDING COMMENT

Every time I read an analysis of consciousness in terms of the physical brain and its evolution, I wonder if it actually bears on the question of the initiation and direction of thought or behavior. I recall in particular the insightful discussion of Wilder Penfield (1975) on this subject. Penfield gained prominence in the field of brain study as early as 1933, the year he discovered the remarkable effects to be found in behavior and speech when the cortex of the brain is electrically stimulated. Even so, after decades of conducting such cortical stimulations Penfield concluded that they did *not* in any way control the mind. For example, he tells of how, when a patient has the parietal region of the cortex stimulated and consequently moves his right hand, "he does not say 'I wanted to move it.' He may, however, reach over with the left hand and oppose his action" (p. 77).

In another instance, Penfield caused a patient to move his hand by electrical stimulation of the motor cortex, only to be told by the patient, "I didn't do that. You did" (p. 76). Vocalizations receive the same reactions: when made to say something by stimulation of their speech center, patients routinely comment afterward, "I didn't make that sound. You [Penfield] pulled it out of me" (p. 76). From such clinical experience Penfield was moved to say, "The mind of the patient was as independent of the reflex action [i.e., brain stimulation] as was the mind of the surgeon who listened and strove to understand. Thus, my argument favors independence of mind-action [from brain-action]" (p. 55).

It is surely not a contradiction of the empirical findings on brain structure and function to suggest that we are totally in the realm of instrumentality at this point. We need the brain to think like we need legs to run or dance. But brain action per se cannot direct what we will think about anymore than our legs can determine where we will run or the tune to which we will dance. To say that mechanical brain stimulation captures the basic thought process is not consistent with empirical findings like those of Penfield or Libet. These electrical discharges seem more like instrumental pathways and signals than they do executive decision makers. Now, I do not want to make the mistake of trying to explain such *Bios* formulations on my *Logos* grounds, but it seems fair to say that in speaking of consciousness as transpredicational, we do not contradict the empirical literature in brain research. People do seem to retain a distance between their own phenomenal identities (uniquely affirmed predications) and the purely mechanical activity that may be influencing their bodily action in some way (moving, itching, vocalizing, etc.). Must we continually seek an explanation of the phenomenal in biological terms on the assumption that this is the only worthwhile avenue to understanding?

It seems that the course of explanation often goes in the other direction. Rather than explaining the psychological by reducing it to the physical, I think many researchers use their informal knowledge of psychic consciousness and then frame their formal brain research in physical terms. There have been examples in this chapter of teleological concepts like self-reflexivity or intentionality that are at the heart of our understanding from the outset, even though it is then made to appear that brain studies are discovering or suggesting such entirely "mechanical" brain functions. I suspect that if we did not have this informal knowledge predicating our formal studies we would make little sense of many of the findings in brain research. This gambit of using introspectively meaningful aspects of psychic consciousness to rationalize formal organic speculations is what encourages me to pursue a singularly *Logos* explanation. I know that if this effort proves instructive it will find its way—analogically if nothing else—into the biophysical literature.

6

THE TELIC TRIUNE:
CONSCIOUSNESS, SELF,
AND FREE WILL

The concepts of *self* and *free will* or *agency* invariably wind their way into any analysis of psychic consciousness. The inevitability of this combination prompts me to refer to it as the "telic triune." Sometimes terms other than self or free will are used, but the reason for the triune taking shape is not hard to discern. For example, Franz Brentano's insistence that intentionality is fundamental to consciousness resulted in his student, Edmund Husserl (1859–1938), claiming that consciousness is always a *"consciousness-of,"* or a *"pure reference-to"* (Needleman, 1963, p. 5, italics in original). Consciousness is not merely a physical state, but is rather a "going-out-to-something" or a "what is intended" (p. 5). Such active phraseology suggests that there is an identity, a being or a self who is bringing conscious thoughts to bear intentionally or purposively. It is then plausible to suggest that this active identity is free to select or choose what will be thought about, enacted, negated, and otherwise directed.

Can people really direct their actions one way rather than another, as we suggested in Chapter 2? Once a line of intentional action has been carried out can we confidently believe that, given identical circumstances, it is possible to have behaved in any other way than the one enacted? If the answers here are in the affirmative, then free will is possible.

If they are in the negative, then free will is an illusion. Psychologists have been known to argue in favor of attributing free will to people even though they believe such agency to be an illusion (e.g., Immergluck, 1964; Lefcourt, 1973). A natural-selection rationale is advanced, suggesting that the stability and viability of a society is enhanced if people think that they are responsible for their personal behavior even though they are not.

I think we can push the Brentanoan thesis back some 1,500 years and argue that initially it was conscience that provided the basis for saying that intentionality is central to behavior. An organism that behaves intentionally must necessarily have a conscience, because it can always transpredicate to judge its ongoing behavior and see that things could have been framed otherwise, all circumstances remaining the same. The framing could have been less selfish or sinful, more considerate of others, and so on. Jaynes (1976) contended that such alternative reasoning was not possible until after the bicameral period. The human capacity to evaluate actions resulted in both a sense of the inadequacy of selfhood and the religiously motivated intention to turn the responsibility of self-direction over to a deity. Jaynes would suggest that the motive here was to reengage the god-like voices of bicamerality. In a more conventional sense, we can see how the concept of grace reflects this human desire to let the perfection of a deity direct things, to forego the frequently challenging and confusing demands of decision making (free will) in favor of the authoritative, morally certain path laid out by the deity. Note that even in this case, the moral way was initially freely selected by the person. As explained in Chapter 2, the "freedom" here occurs in the initial decision to accept the grace of a deity. The "will" then flows from the commands (dictates, examples, etc.) of the deity, as reflected in the religious dogma.

No psychologist in history devoted more personal and professional effort to a consideration of the telic triune than William James (1842–1910), whom we will be taking up in this chapter. He was not, in my opinion, successful in clarifying the constituents of this triune, particularly because in time he was to assign a fading role for consciousness in human behavior. Why then should we devote a chapter to James? First, James's metaphor of the "stream of consciousness" is so widely cited in discussions of this topic that it would seem a major oversight to give his views only brief mention. Second, James's analysis of the various manifestations of selfhood is equally popular and frames the field for many scholars. Finally, although he did not solve the riddle of free will in his psychological efforts, James did take this matter seriously. He never dismissed human agency from consideration, as so many of his colleagues were to do in the rise of rigorous academic psychology. Indeed, he wrestled with the questions of religious faith and belief his entire life (see James, 1958).

The present chapter contains a review of James's theorizing as a sort of prototype example of the intricacies of the telic triune. Along the way,

I will present the standard explanations of free will and James's preferred account of such human agency. I will show how, though he initially spoke of consciousness as an active stream, James's final interpretation did not assign a Brentanoan conceptualizing role to it. I will offer various LLT interpretations as we cover the topics of this chapter. It is my hope that by contrasting LLT with Jamesian theorizing, I can put into bold relief the challenging and problematic issues that arise if an effort is made to capture the human being as a telic organism. It is important to understand why, for example, James came to believe that free will would never be captured psychologically. I disagree with this conclusion and would like to demonstrate via LLT conceptions that it is incorrect. Furthermore, I believe it is instructive to see how two lines of theoretical development, each aimed at elucidating the essentials of the telic triune, may agree at certain points along the way and yet arrive at conflicting positions in the final stand.

JAMES IN PERSONAL SEARCH OF FREE WILL

William James is probably more honored than understood by psychologists today. Throughout his life he was heavily involved with the problems of uniting religion and spirituality with science. He seemed temperamentally best suited to the *Logos* sphere of knowledge, yet devoted a major share of his academic life propounding a *Bios* view of the physiological underpinnings of psychology. Though he pushed himself to support British philosophers like Locke, Berkeley, Hume, and the Mills, he could not accept the materialism, associationism, and mechanistic determinism that this school of thought advanced. He tried to bring psychology into the scientific mold by promoting laboratory work in which he was personally disinterested. In the closing years of his life, James seemed only too pleased to shift from psychology to philosophy. He had a cyclothymic temperament, with mood swings resulting in some prolonged periods of depression during early adulthood. He also had life-long neurasthenic problems like chronic exhaustion, insomnia, eye fatigue, lower back pain, and digestive disturbances. Despite these problems, he managed to highlight the core issues of human behavior in his classic work, *The Principles of Psychology* (James, 1890/1952).

James received his MD in the spring of 1869, and by the fall of that year he had slumped into a moderate depression that lasted for the next two years. Apparently, there were both career and religious concerns troubling him. He struggled with the concept of predestination as embraced in his beloved father's Calvinism. As a countermeasure to this rigid determinism, James studied the French philosopher, Charles Bernard Renouvier (1815–1903), who championed free will. James's biographer, Ralph Barton Perry (1948), said that Renouvier "was the greatest individual influence on the development of James's thought" (p. 153). By April 30, 1870, James had found some reassurance in his studies, for he recorded in his diary on that date the following:

> I think that yesterday was a crisis in my life. I finished the first part of Renouvier's second *Essais* and see no reason why his definition of free will [i.e.,] "the sustaining of a thought *because I choose to* when I might have other thoughts"—need be the definition of an illusion. At any rate, I will assume for the present . . . that it is no illusion. My first act of free will shall be to believe in free will. (H. James Jr., 1920, p. 147; italics in original)

Renouvier was a Kantian idealist who believed that only phenomena (appearances) have real existence, and then only through a logical relation to other phenomena. He rejected mechanistic interpretations of behavior, stressing the inner person as opposed to outer determinants. He also held it reasonable to believe in a finite deity. James did not accept Renouvier's idealism, but he was deeply impressed by the latter's freewill formulation. In fact, we find James using this identical phrasing—of beginning a freewill study by freely affirming belief in free will—decades later in his formal writings (e.g., see James, 1890/1952, p. 661).

If we were standing behind James as he wrote in his diary we might think of this event introspectively, from his unique point of view. He is recording what he as a person (an "I") chooses to believe. Generic oppositionality might be suggested in the fact that he can believe or not believe in something *at will*. As symbolically depicted in Figure 3, he could step out of the broader Euler circle predicating a current belief to entertain some (negating, contradicting, etc.) alternative. Of course, James does not take up such process considerations in his simple statement of belief. What he does here is consider free will as a belief-content within an as yet unidentified process. This is a crucial point, for what the theoretician accepts as a process must necessarily direct her or his understanding of a freewill action.

And here is where James came up against a problem that has divided psychologists since the inception of their field. He set out to write the *Principles* on the assumption that he could trace the physiological basis of psychological actions. This meant that James's process would be that of efficient-cause motion rather than formal- or final-cause intention. Furthermore, this *Bios* effort moved his explanations to the extraspective perspective. From the LLT point of view, James had effectively removed himself from any chance of capturing what Renouvier is talking about. Renouvier's Kantian process is in the *Logos*, where it requires an introspectively framed predication to make sense of the idealism suggested. James had confounded the process of free will with the belief-content that free will is a plausible concept. Believing in free will is, of course, a good beginning. But the next step would seem to be the belief in a process capable of making freely willed actions happen without losing such agency to underlying biological mechanisms.

The British philosophy that James embraced supported his reductive efforts, but it also frustrated him when he turned to what personally interested him the most—that is, the teleological side of human action. He never did unite the freewill suggestions of Renouvier with the reductionism of his biological theoretical efforts, and in time would be forced to conclude, "My own belief is that the question of free-will is insoluble on strictly psychologic grounds" (James, 1890/1952, p. 822). This conclusion is certainly correct if we are to limit psychology to *Bios* groundings, but a theory like LLT is positioned on the *Logos* and is therefore not tied down by material and efficient causation. James adopted a style of theorizing that accommodates his emphasis on biophysiological underpinnings as primary in human action, with secondary actions to follow.

JAMES'S SECOND-EVENT ARGUMENT

In trying to explain how the psychological realm is rooted in the physico-biological, James found it useful to develop what I have termed a *second-event argument*. He used this argument primarily to explain how the biophysiological origins of action eventually result in learned behaviors, but we see this style of thought in nonbiological analyses as well. The fundamental argument holds that because behavior derives from physical actions like adapting the eye to light, or moving the arm to reach for something, the *very first* actions made by an organism must have been built into its biological and physiological structures. Thus, the very first time such actions occurred they were purely reflexive or instinctive. We are considering things now exclusively in light of material and efficient causation, described from the extraspective perspective. The first time a motion takes place the organism can have no expectations about what will or could possibly take place. First actions like looking, stretching, or grasping simply "happen."

Organisms can have no a priori idea of a movement because, as James said, "Before the idea [of movement] can be generated, the movement must have occurred in a blind, unexpected way, and left its idea behind" (1890/1952, p. 827). As Locke would have it, the blind action etches its occurrence on the tabula rasa (mind). Memory then changes the circumstances of a behavioral action. Once these actions have occurred *as a first event*, it becomes possible for such actions to be known, recalled, adapted, and delayed *as a second event* in ongoing behavior. Having initially grasped and held a rattle reflexively, the infant can subsequently recall this experience to reach for and grasp other things. James also explained the functioning of sensation in this second-event manner. Thus, he observed that *"pure sensations can only be realized in the earliest days of life"* (p. 456; italics in original). Following this initial spontaneous experience, one's grasp of a sensation becomes colored by memories of these now past events, plus the associated contexts within which they had previously occurred. Whether or not James meant it to be, his theorizing in the second-event manner is highly suggestive of a mediation model (see Chapter 2). This is surely how he is interpreted by the majority of psychologists today.

In an LLT account, the role of consciousness would be introduced at this point. A purely reflexive occurrence popping into awareness suggests a unipredication insofar as the infant grasps that something—"this" movement or sensation—is taking place. The suggestion for the LLT advocate would be that the infant could transpredicate through generic oppositionality and opt to carry out or not to carry out some activity, such as break off gazing at an object that had held attention previously. Affective assessments would also be rendered to support the direction that an infant's interest would take. In other words, a rudimentary choice would become possible. As for sensation, given our analysis in Chapter 4, even certain sensations could be repressed, denied, or dissociated from psychic awareness so that further unipredications would also be possible. Naturally, the complexity of such psychic dynamics would be quite limited in infants and very young children, but the capacity to employ cognitive oppositionality begins with birth. We do not find this oppositional emphasis in the Jamesian treatment, of course, because he is formulating things in the British empiricist tradition.

The second-event argument is apparent in James's well-known interpretation of the emotions, although in this case, he did not focus on the changes that an organism with a memory can impose on the spontaneous physical experience. The so-called *James-Lange theory of emotions* holds that bodily changes reflexively occur first, and then the changing feelings that an organism senses *is* the emotion. Thus, James says, "we feel sorry because we cry, angry because we strike, afraid because we tremble, and not that we cry, strike, or tremble, because we are sorry, angry, or fearful as the case may be" (p. 743). James was pointing here to the purely physical changes as a second event rather than the cognitive factors that trail such physical actions in memory. This theory of emotions suggests that we see the bear in the woods, run without thinking (i.e., reflexively), and then subsequently experience fear in our rapid heartbeat, quivering jaw, heavy breathing, and muscular tensions as we pound along with all our might.

Here again, the consciousness James suggested as a second event is unipredicational. In LLT we would probably want to put more emphasis on transpredication at some point. For example, the hunter might be seeing yet another bear, reflexively fleeing once again, but as he runs away a second time he transpredicates the responses of his nervous system (heavy breathing, perspiration, rapid heartbeat, etc.) to interpret them as shame and not fear. Or, one might want to say that the hunter feels both fear and shame. But it is in the predicating context of the specific behavior that "an" emotion must be "felt," not solely in the activity going on at the biological level. Furthermore, our timorous hunter would undoubtedly be rendering negative affective assessments of his cowardly behavior. Such assessments are not second events. Affections are first events, lending a meaning to what is taking place from the unique vantage point of the individual concerned. Affections are usually unipredicational (see Chapter 10).

The final Jamesian second-event argument I will mention is from his philosophical theory of *Pragmatism* (James, 1907/1943). Even though he did not accept the idealism of Renouvier, James did appreciate that our ideas influence our understanding of reality. As we perceive a set of empirical circumstances, we frame ideas about what is taking place, what probably happened previously, and what is likely to occur from now on. We then act on these ideas, and, depending on how well they frame our understanding of what is taking place, or predict what is about to take place next, we can judge them to be practical (pragmatic) or not (pp. 202–203). James spoke of this second-event evaluation of our ideas as reflecting their *cash-value*. Ideas either pay off with ongoing understanding (knowledge, etc.) or they do not. The cash-value of an idea is determined by how much of a difference it makes in our lives. This is not a copy of reality but rather a framing of reality.

In fact, two people may frame the same set of circumstances differently, yet find their conflicting ideas each paying off by providing an acceptable understanding of what happened. Both saw the same accident take place, but confidently assign the fault to different parties in the unfortunate event. What is important here is that the meanings of the ideas in question successfully order the ongoing cognition of the person involved. Ideas have to coalesce with one another, so that one body of already established true beliefs can intermingle or align with a newly acquired belief purporting to be true. When ideas fail to order or coalesce like this, they lose cash-value and are discarded. Our ideas should organize and predict accurately—be reality oriented—if we hope to carry on a rational existence with our neighbors. But occasionally we can, with perfect confidence, deny the reality that others believe in, and live according to our unique understanding of things. It all depends on the second-event evaluation—the cash-value payoff—how long ideas framing our understanding can be profitably used. It should be obvious that LLT would be in considerable agreement with Jamesian pragmatism, which basically draws on the human capacity to predicate. Note that James has now left the *Bios* and is theorizing exclusively in the *Logos*.

THE JAMESIAN CONSCIOUSNESS: FROM EMPHASIS AND SELECTION TO KNOWING

There are two different treatments of consciousness in James's writings: his extensive analysis of consciousness throughout the *Principles* (James, 1890/1952, see especially chapter IX) and a paper entitled "Does consciousness exist?" published some 14 or 15 years later (James, 1904/1967). The term consciousness also appears in most of his analyses of such mental functions as reasoning, attention, choice, perception of reality, and will. If free will was but a belief-content in James's personal ruminations on the topic, is it possible that we can find a process of consciousness that will account for how such contents are produced? And is this process then also reflective of free will?

As we have already noted, Renouvier described conscious thinking as an active, conceptualizing process that was underway from the very outset of life. The Kantian phenomenal realm frames ongoing experience a priori, as a first event, lending experience its very meaning. But in his psychological writings, James did not view thought as actively conceptualizing (in LLT terms, as predicating) in this manner. He saw it coming into play as a second event, surmising that if thought issues from physical processing in the brain, then just as with other experiences like motions or sensations, the brain's ideational actions would have to begin reflexively. After the reflexive ideation occurred, second-event thinking would come into play to sort out matters. James (1890/1952) therefore concluded that, rather than active conceptualization (a first event) "emphasis and selection seem to be the essence of the human mind" (a second event) [p. 670]. As an aspect of mind, consciousness functions the same way:

> The mind is at every stage a theatre of simultaneous possibilities. Consciousness consists in the comparison of these with each other, the selection of some, and the suppression of the rest by the reinforcing and inhibiting agency of attention. (p. 187)

Attention is the "taking possession by the mind" (p. 261) by one of several possible trains of thought. The precise process under consideration is still not clear, although the definition suggests a mediationism. James's hope of redefining psychological concepts in physiological terms forced him into such theorizing, where initially material-efficient causation brought on experience in first-event fashion, and then the more psychological aspects like (psychic) consciousness could mediate things. However, even the psychological conceptions were given a physiological coloring so that the formal or final causation that James seemed also to appreciate did not quite take hold in his total formulation.

For example, James (1890/1952) tried to unite the mind–body aspects of his theorizing by embracing the so-called *ideo-motor theory of action* (p.

790). This theory held that before we carry out an action, an idea of this act must occur in mind. Ideo-motor action is a sequence in which movement occurs upon the mere thought of it. If such ideas are not carried out it is "because other ideas simultaneously present rob them of their impulsive power" (p. 792). Here is where a willed movement can take place. "A willed movement is a movement preceded by an idea of itself" (p. 827). We hurriedly pore over the menu, decide on the fried chicken, and wave to the waiter. Of course, even this willful idea is a memory of a previous movement that "occurred in a blind, unexpected way, and left its idea behind" (p. 827). We actually began waving reflexively as infants in the crib. As the sequence of behavior unfolds, we can (as a second event) compare, emphasize, suppress, and select one course of ideation over another through a so-called *fiat of the will*. Maybe waving at waiters is not a good idea—perhaps a bit gauche! What's the hurry anyway?

So, ideas keep occurring to us, presumably fed by past experience, and we can select alternatives through a fiat of the will. Recall from the LLT presentation of telosponsivity in Chapter 2 that an affirmation is freely made before some course of action is chosen, and then from this point forward a willful course of behavior is carried out—bringing *free* and *will* together as aspects of a common process. This affirmation would seem to be similar to a fiat, except that in the Jamesian account there is no concocting an opposite to the idea emanating from past experience. The fiat merely keeps a selected idea "steadily before the mind until it *fills* the mind" (James, 1890/1952, p. 817; italics in original). Once filled, we enact the idea. A "filling-up" is a material-cause metaphor, of course, reflecting the typical Jamesian effort to explain psychological action in physiological terms. Such willful filling of the mind is said to be tantamount to consent.

Once mentally filled we have consented to carry out the idea in overt behavior. The key second-event concept here is attention, which must occur for the filling to take place. Unattended ideas cannot fill the mind. Attention is said to be fundamental to both the will (p. 274) and choice (p. 275), and James literally equated it with volition (p. 291). I am still not clear on precisely how this attentive taking possession of the mind occurs. There seems to be some kind of capacity to process thoughts available to the person that is neither input from experience nor exclusively physiological. Once again, the LLT advocate would suggest that it is impossible to convey accurately such a *Logos* process in *Bios* terms.

James invented the metaphor of consciousness as a *stream* of water flowing along as a dynamic totality. He actually subsumed three referents under this famous metaphor: "*the stream of thought, of consciousness, or of subjective life*" (James, 1890/1952, p. 155; italics in original). Conscious thought flows along, offering possibilities for consideration by attention, which can then willfully block off a portion of the flow and hold its meaning before the mind for a time. Of course, the stream of thought or consciousness always reflects what sensation sends its way, so that the person does not select the initiating point of attention (i.e., what in LLT is termed the protopoint of affirmation). It is the external object impinging on the sensory apparatus that has the capacity to draw attention in typical first-to-second-event fashion. We first see the door leading out of the room. It draws our attention. We can then willfully attend to this object, having its idea fill up our mind (emphasizing it), and then via the ideo-motor action find our way out. This emphasis is choice (p. 275) and the action taken in leaving the room reflects volition (p. 291).

Here James closely paralleled the concept of thought with that of consciousness, for either of these functions are said to emphasize, suppress, or select certain elements within the stream. Unconsciousness is not brought in here at all. But what of the reference to a "subjective life" in the stream? This refers to the selfhood aspect of the triune. As we have seen previously (in Chapters 1 and 2), theorists find it necessary to describe choosing or acting voluntarily in terms of an identity "doing" these things, using the stream to initiate action, and so on. I noted in Chapter 2 that at such times a homunculus is likely to be relied on to explain how conscious thought is directed. Thus, in mechanistic accounts we find concepts like cognitive maps, confirmatory reactions, expectancies, decision centers, or executive functions brought in to do the telic work of a homunculus when needed. Homunculi are also found in psychoanalytical formulations, such as the ego, id, and superego (see Chapter 4). The aim of LLT is to explain the process employed by this "little" person because this is the very same process employed by the "big" person. In LLT, the person *is* the homunculus.

Although consciousness does have occasional discontinuities and sudden shifts via the voluntary choices being made, there is always a sense of continuity or wholeness in this stream. James proposed that the natural name for this wholeness of consciousness is "*myself, I, or me*" (1890/1952, p. 155; italics in original). Enter the agent of our triune. James opined, "The universal conscious fact is not 'feelings and thoughts exist,' but 'I think' and 'I feel.' No psychology, at any rate, can question the *existence* of personal selves" (p. 147, italics in original).

It is possible to speak of thought and even consciousness in an extraspective manner. But when a "personal self" is introduced, the account begins to take on an introspective slant. This is what we see James doing. It is this back-and-forth switching, from the extraspective material- and efficient-cause explanations of physiology to the introspective formal- and final-cause explanations of a psychological self that sometimes confuses James's interpreters. A subjective life is lived by a self who can make use of emphasis, selection, and suppression in thought or consciousness to render individual choices. The behaviorists who followed James and relied on mediation models did not think of the person as an individual. Watson's

(1924) famous allusion to the person as an organic machine "ready to run" (p. 216; see Chapter 1) captures the image of an assembly line of robots, totally lacking self-determined individuality (which is why they require the homunculus to steer them about).

As we saw in Chapter 5, the non-telic, efficient-cause style of explanation pictures the person as an effect and never a cause. Unfortunately, the Jamesian second event formulation furthered this style of theorizing for it made the person qua agent a kind of afterthought in the course of behavioral generation. This is not what James intended, of course. He was thinking strictly of the biophysiological origins of behavior and not of sociocultural causes uniformly shaping all people alike, as in Skinner's (1948) *Walden Two*. James was an uncompromising defender of individuality, which is a variant way of expressing subjective choice. It is ironic that he should further mechanistic mediationism, but his choice of theoretical terminology grounded in the *Bios* foreshadowed this eventuality.

In a paper appearing late in his career, James questioned whether consciousness exists (James, 1904/1967). Here he specifically noted that consciousness is a process and not a content. Consciousness does not exist as a material substance, but is most assuredly a "function" (p. 3). What is this function? That of *knowing*: "'Consciousness' is supposed necessary to explain the fact that things not only are, but get reported, are known" (p. 4). Consciousness is a timeless process, although it is witness to the happenings that take place in time. James next affirmed that consciousness involves awareness (see the thematic of Chapter 1): Consciousness is a process of knowing in which "*awareness of content* takes place" (p. 6; italics in original). Even if we become aware of our selves, this self-knowledge is an example of consciousness (p. 7).

Instead of referring to process versus content as we have been doing, James drew essentially the same distinction in terms of consciousness versus content. Consciousness is a process that holds certain contents. He rejected a material-cause interpretation of this process, preferring to think of it as a formal-cause process. In a nutshell, James is dissuading us from reifying consciousness:

> Consciousness connotes a kind of external relation, and does not denote a special stuff or way of being. *The peculiarity of our experiences, that they not only are, but are known, which their "conscious" quality is invoked to explain, is better explained by their relations—these relations themselves being experiences—to one another.* (James, 1904/1967, p. 25; italics in original)

The relation of greatest importance to consciousness is the one between knower and known. We know the "pure experience" of a pen by its function—the fact that it holds ink, has a certain shape and physical heft, obeys the guidance of our hand, and so on (James, 1904/1967, p. 23). This knowledge is what it means to be conscious of the pen. James's treatment here leaves us wondering whether knowledge is always a second event, a mere continuation of the logic of reception, or can it also frame alternatives as a first event, capturing thereby the active mind that Brentano and Husserl (Needleman, 1963) were pursuing in their phenomenology? In knowing that the pen *does* write do we also know that it *does not* write—that it is a pipe cleaner, an item of jewelry, a tapping instrument, and so on? Or must we have each of these alternatives presented to our consciousness as first events (inputs, etc.) before such awareness takes hold as second events?

JAMES AND CONSCIOUSNESS OF SELF

In the *Principles*, at the close of Chapter IX on the stream of thought, James (1890/1952) stated that we all split up the universe into halves—the me and not-me (p. 187). This oppositionally based claim led him in Chapter X to consider the consciousness of self. Consistent with his interpretation of consciousness as knowing, James analyzed the various ways in which we know our selves. His emphasis was totally on the content that identifies what selfhood means—its constituent feelings and actions. The LLT advocate would have no quarrel with this strategy, although precisely how this predicational pie would be sliced might differ from one theoretician to the next.

The broadest sense of selfhood for James is the *me*, or *empirical self*. This is the basic me (versus the not-me), and includes all those items that a person is conscious of calling his or her own—such as the knowledge of having a personal body and mind, various possessions, marital partner, offspring, level of education, ancestors, friends, occupation or career, and so on (p. 188).

Another way to think about this array of self-knowledge is as a *material self*, which takes form at the innermost level of our physical being. Certain bodily parts seem more intimately self-like than others (p. 188). For example, the head is closer to the person's "me" than a foot. One's clothes come next in this physical sphere, followed by family members—blood relatives, marital partner, and so forth. Then comes material wealth, or any products of one's physical labor.

The *social self* is yet another way to think of one's self, stemming from the reactions that others have to us (p. 189). Strictly speaking, a person has as many social selves as there are individuals who recognize him or her. These individuals carry an image of us with them, and each image may differ although they are all social selves. Reputation, honor, fame, notoriety, and so forth, all capture this social aspect of the self.

There is also a *spiritual self* to consider, an "inner, or subjective being"

(p. 191) that encompasses our psychic faculties and dispositions. Such psychic aspects of selfhood are the most enduring and intimate part of the self for they encompass most centrally who we are, our moral sensibilities, conscience, and indomitable will (p. 191). It is this aspect of the self that "presides over the perception of sensations, and by giving or withholding its assent it influences the movements they tend to arouse. . . . It is the source of effort and attention, and the place from which appear to emanate the fiats of the will" (p. 192). It would seem that the spiritual self is an aspect of the process that directs thought, a process that might possibly go beyond purely biophysical functioning (a lurking homunculus?). But James did not allow for such speculations.

True to his biophysical mission, he instead suggested that for the most part the spiritual self relies on bodily processes *taking place within the head*" (James, 1890/1952, p. 193, italics in original). For example, mental effort seems tied to the opening and closing of the glottis, contracting the jaw muscles, and furrowing the brows. James apparently drew these conclusions on the basis of his personal introspections, and although he did not mean to limit thought to such considerations, he did find that "these cephalic motions are the portions of my innermost activity of which I am *most distinctly aware*" (p. 194; italics in original). There were also other obscure feelings during mental activity, intimations of a process going on in connection with the spiritual self, but whether this is a distinctive mental process or simply a sense of "fainter physiological processes" remained an unanswered question for James (p. 197). He went on to analyze various self-feelings such as complacency, dissatisfaction, and the seeking of advantage. He noted that we all have several empirical selves that we would like to manifest so as to broaden our attractiveness and influence (p. 199). We would like to be the expert athlete and scholar combined, but this is rarely possible. There is an empirical reality that we must admit to, or take advantage of. We must make choices about our selves and develop our potentials accordingly, which is why some of us spend more time on the sports field than at the library or vice versa (p. 200). James also discussed the self-esteem that can issue from success, and how we learn to subordinate our lower to our higher selves. The spiritual self is at the top of a hierarchy of selves (p. 203). We all feel a love of self, for this is our evolutionary heritage:

> All minds must have come, by the way of the survival of the fittest, if by no directer path, to take an intense interest in the bodies to which they are yoked, altogether apart from any interest in the pure Ego which they also possess. (p. 208)

The *pure ego* is a "pure principle of personal identity" (p. 213) that enters the person's awareness as a sense of sameness, the knowledge that "*I am the same self that I was yesterday*" (p. 214; italics in original). This identity factor is extremely important in the "'stream' of subjective consciousness" (p. 216). An awareness of personal identity is exactly like other perceptions we make concerning the sameness of phenomena. We repeatedly see the same object in our experience and come to know about it by associating the perceived identities over occasions. One cloud or tree looks pretty much like another. Our selves look pretty much alike from day to day as well.

The major thrust of James's explanation of the self or selves is the enumeration of content meanings rather than process meanings. His self concept is not really a homunculus, driving the organic machine around. The various manifestations of the self appear to be learned over the course of life. But James did not offer a theory of learning on the basis of physiological structures. James suggested that something of the sort takes place, but he did not find helpful—indeed, he did not favor—the quasi-engineering explanations of learning that might have explained away free will. It remained for the behaviorists who followed him to bring in such mechanistic accounts. As we have seen, although he doubted that free will could be explained psychologically, James *did* want to view people as having this capacity. We next turn to some theories of free will to locate James more technically along this array.

JAMES'S CONCEPTION OF FREE WILL

There are two fundamental definitions of free will that capture what most people mean by this concept, one of which encourages an extraspective analysis and the other an introspective analysis. From a more extraspective perspective, we might say that a person has free will if he or she could have behaved differently in a situation *"all circumstances remaining the same"* (O'Connor, 1971, p. 82; italics in original). We can think of this definition introspectively, but I believe that it encourages an extraspective analysis because it directs our attention to the circumstances per se without highlighting the fact that it is the individual actor in a situation who must frame what a *circumstance* is or is not in the first place. A more decidedly introspective definition of free will is to say that a person is free who can select the grounds for the sake of which he or she is to be determined (i.e., the individual is self-determined). This is the definition we employ in LLT (see Chapter 2), and it clearly brings the person into the circumstances as the one laying down or accepting the circumstantial assumptions, restrictions, mandates, and so on, that determine her or his behavior.

Recall that the word *determine* has Latin roots meaning to set a limit on something (see Chapter 1). As applied to behavior, the limitations are usually thought of as alternatives that might be carried out in the course of events but are prevented from taking place. All four of our causes can be seen to exert determinations on behavior. Flesh and bone as material causes of the body are limited in the amount of physical abuse that they can sustain. Efficient causes direct our instrumental actions, as when we reach for the salt and not the pepper, or modulate our vocal apparatus to express only "this" and never "that" point of view. Formal-cause determinism is found in the mathematical schemes we use, where "one plus one" pattern their values into nothing but "two," or in the fact that we can pick out our friend's distinctive physiognomy in a crowd. Our willful efforts to attain a challenging goal, like a college degree or a job promotion reflect final-cause determinations. Nothing is allowed to divert the aspirations of the person who is truly determined to achieve these goals and therefore will accept no alternatives.

There have been numerous efforts to explain free will or human agency in the traditions of Newtonian science—that is, *without* formal or final causation. One such favorite is to say that free will is nothing but the statistical unpredictability that we come up against when psychologists study behavior (Boneau, 1974, p. 308). Just as weather forecasts are not always correct, so too a certain amount of error encumbers predictions made about the likelihood of this or that behavior taking place. Free will in this view becomes the error variance of a prediction drawn from some measurement (e.g., a test score). Psychologists who take this position are thinking about things in an extraspective manner. They believe that if all factors could be measured reliably, the predictions of a person's future behavior would be "lawfully" perfect, and there would be no need to speak of free will. The underlying efficient causation that supposedly brings such lawfulness about is 100% accurate in its determinate action. This explanation confounds a *theory* of agency with a *method* of measurement.

Free will is *not* always unpredictability because it frequently refers to a freely affirmed but fixed target: "I want that and only that!" The specific and highly predictable end is willfully aimed for, although it may be difficult to reach or even prove unattainable. We can and do fail. Reaching for the doorknob in order to leave a room is readily attained. "Reaching" for a desired weight loss, or the termination of a smoking habit, may not be so readily attained. As encompassed in our introspective definition of free will, the freedom aspect has to do with the psychological capacity to set freely the grounds—in this case, the aims—for the sake of which one is subsequently limited in behavior (i.e., determined). A highly predictable course of action may therefore reflect free will, as in the zealot's continuing efforts to convert the world to his or her way of thinking, or the scientist's unwavering commitment to finding a solution to some problem. Both zealot and scientist are free to select and, hence, affirm the initial grounding beliefs and hopes that send them on their unyielding course. Freedom comes first, determinism follows.

An explanation one finds in the behavioristic literature is that the concept of free will merely represents the number of mediating alternatives open to an efficiently caused organism. The more mediated alternatives available in the mechanical process of behavior, the greater is the *illusion* of free will (Skinner, 1974, p. 168). A person who has been taught many different ways in which to behave is freer than a person who has been given only limited shaping (see Bandura, 1986, p. 42). This is like claiming that a dog trained to do five tricks has more free will than a dog trained to do only two tricks. The theorizing here is limited to the contents of an extraspectively conceived mechanistic process of antecedents that signal and otherwise push consequents along. This mediational process has no capacity to determine the grounds for the sake of which events take place. I have found that theorists of this persuasion are prone to confuse sociopolitical freedom with agency. For example, if a society affords many freedoms to its members, they are thought to have more agency than citizens in a repressive society. But freedom per se is not what free will is about. Even a prisoner in solitary confinement has the same free will he or she enjoyed before internment (see Chapter 10 for an example like this drawn from the life of Gandhi).

From a strictly psychological point of view, it makes no difference whether people have many or few alternatives open to them. Taking liberties away does not affect the psychological process underwriting agency. The challenge is to explain how a teleological process works and not to conduct an inventory of the number of contents being carried along by a mediational process. When Skinner (1948, 1961) designed the cultural milieu of *Walden Two* along efficient-cause lines, he thought he could build the illusion of free will into a society by increasing the number of predetermined alternatives made available to people. Yet psychological freedom is not founded on the number of alternatives open to the behaving organism, but rather on the capacity to *negate* those alternatives that may present themselves—whether this amounts to 1 or 100. Such negations stem from the capacity to reason oppositionally, as LLT suggests.

An interesting variation on the mediational-model explanation is the claim by some psychologists that free will refers to "when" mediating influences actually come into play on the passing time dimension. For example, suppose that as a youth a person has learned to "goof off" on the job and then later in life is urged by fellow workers to meet a deadline. If the goofing off continues despite such pressure from coworkers, then this worker's behavior may appear to derive from a freely willed decision to ignore or negate such current interpersonal pressures. In actuality, the worker is merely carrying forward—through mediating influences—the shaping accomplished in years gone by. Thus, if we knew the reinforcement history we could see that there is no such agency taking place. It is all a matter of earlier shapings mediating later shapings in linear, efficient-cause fashion (see Hebb, 1974, p. 75, for a view of this type). The worker is not capable of such negation if initially shaped to goof off, of course. Such initial, spontaneous negation would require generic oppositionality in the reasoning process, something that is not included in behavioristic and cognitive theorizing.

James's interpretation of free will followed the British philosophical line. We can trace this interpretation to John Locke, who began his speculations with a material efficient cause notion of an *uneasiness* in the tissues of the body that motivated willful action (Locke, 1690/1952, p. 193). We are made uneasy by hunger and thirst, and are impelled thereby to eat and drink. But because the will is a mental action it does not have to be carried out immediately. We can hang-fire, so to speak, and suspend the acts of eating and drinking for a time assuming that we have a reason to do so. This capacity to defer action led Locke to state that "This seems to me the source of all liberty; in this seems to consist that which is (as I think improperly) called *free-will*" (p. 190; italics in original). During this suspended course of action the human being can look over things from several angles and evaluate the benefit or harm, good or evil of what it is that he or she is about to do. Things that bring pleasure are good, and those that result in pain are bad. We can even project this goodness or badness into the future, comparing a present satisfaction with a later one. The overweight person confronting an ice-cream parlor is in this situation. Summing it up, Locke concludes, "Liberty, it is plain, consists in a power to do, or not to do; to do or forbear doing, *as we will*" (p. 193; italics in original).

The problem here, as axiologists have noted (see, e.g., Rickaby, 1906, p. vii), is that Locke did not clarify the process by which the mind hesitates or suspends action to consider alternative contents. That is, why do we sometimes *not* suspend action but behave quite spontaneously and even impulsively in the handling of our uneasinesses? Occasionally the overweight person shrugs and enters the ice-cream parlor; at other times, the parlor is bypassed. There is a missing feature of the mental process in Locke's account, and I think we know what it is: In restricting themselves to the linearity of efficient-cause determinism, the British philosophers could not really capture self-reflexivity. They had no way of conceptualizing a mental action intrinsically turning back on itself to concoct alternative grounds for the sake of which behavior would then be redirected. Lockean alternatives are always seen "out there," in the externally shaping circumstances, rather than "in here" as the frameworks lending meaning and relative merit to these circumstances at the outset.

Locke once discussed a man who, when told how much better it is to be rich than poor, did not choose to work his way out of poverty—presumably because he felt no uneasiness (motivation) to change things (p. 90). Locke concluded from this that mental choice follows motivation on the basis of the assumption that choice is a unipredicated impulsion to behave one way rather than another. But it is just as easy to conclude the reverse, that a decision following transpredicational analysis can determine the level of motivation. That is, why could this man not examine all the pros and cons of his economic circumstances as he frames them and then choose a lower level of wealth as a satisfactory life goal (telos)? His family and friends may have been living at this poverty level for generations. Having made this freewill decision following transpredicational analysis, the man is not then made uneasy by having less than other people. In this reading of the facts, motivation follows choice.

Even though it does not quite capture the full process, the hanging-fire view of free will has been widely adopted in psychology. Rollo May (1977) once characterized free will as delaying the flow of stimulus to response in a succession of events. Once again, the process accomplishing this delay is not spelled out. For James, free will was another second event in which something comes before the mind initially and then is held in place secondarily for a time.

We can outline James's theory as follows. Will is the fixing of attention on some object toward which motion is to be expended in hopes of attaining it. A willed movement is always preceded by an idea of itself, and a consent (mental filling) to let its implications come about. The effort of attention is crucial in willful action, relating particularly to the things that we are capable of doing. If we lack the power to achieve some end by way of voluntary motions this is a wish. And free will comes down to a more sustained fixing of attention; as James expressed it, ". . . the operation of free effort, if it existed, could only be to hold some one ideal object, or part of an object, a little longer or a little more intensely before the mind" (James, 1890/1952, p. 825). The object would be presented to sensory input, and the attention would allow for a second-event delay "before the mind." The controversy over free will, James suggested, "relates solely to the amount of effort of attention or consent that we can at any time put forth" (p. 822). There is no oppositionality in this formulation, no real explanation for how self-reflexivity comes about—although James did believe that human beings enjoyed this capacity for "self-consciousness or reflexive knowledge" (p. 685).

James also said that a freely willing person would act as if his or her beliefs were real, thereby bringing them about in overt behavior—much as the cheerful mood is willfully brought about by thinking happy thoughts. His pragmatic philosophy is suggested in this observation. Beliefs become overt truths thanks to their willful execution by the believer. Pragmatically considered, free will signifies that there are novelties in the world, with the attendant "right to expect that in its deepest elements as well as in its surface phenomena, the future may not identically repeat and imitate the past" (James, 1907/1943, p. 84). He went on to refer to free will as a cosmological theory of promise, "Just like the Absolute, God, Spirit or

Design" (p. 84). He even suggested that the freewill concept would be unnecessary if the world were "perfect from the start" (p. 84).

James was obviously thinking here of free will as many religionists do—as a force bringing about improvements and the higher, perfect, "good" side of things (including human behavior). Free will swings into play if something observed empirically (first event) can be improved (second event). If no improvement is called for, no free will is called for. In LLT there is no effort to tie free will exclusively to the higher ends of life. People can and do freely opt for evil alternatives. Saint or sinner, it is all the same process. As with his initial vow to believe in Renouvier's position, James here placed free will on the side of content rather than process.

JAMES AND OPPOSITIONALITY IN THE LOGOS

I have suggested in this chapter that James failed to present us with a suitable process to establish the *Logos* implications of his views. He seems to have presumed that because there are *Bios* processes like instincts and reflexes that produce sensations or actions as first events (i.e., automatically), second events like attention, emphasis, and choice must be extensions of these initiating processes. The processes of the *Bios* are studied in such fields as medicine, biology, chemistry, and physiology. James apparently did not believe that it was his responsibility as a psychologist to specify the nature of a *Logos* process that might be functioning independently of such *Bios* processes—particularly because it was his aim to explain the former in terms of the latter. However, as a philosopher, he subsequently analyzed thinking from a nonphysiological, pragmatic perspective, and in this case there *was* a process introduced and analyzed of a purely *Logos* (logical) nature (James, 1907/1943). James was no longer bothered by the mediationism of biological structures, and so we find him turning to a predicational process in his philosophy of pragmatism.

Logical learning theory finds a rationale for free will in the capacity to contradict or negate mental contents (see Chapter 2). We follow the introspective formulation of free will here to say that the person who can affirm the predication for the sake of which his or her behavior will be carried forward is an agent. The agent always has a capacity to step outside of the predicating meaning under extension (the larger Euler circle of Figure 2). Agents can *do* or *not do* what is framed for action. They can *believe* or *not believe* what is framed as knowledge. They can behave or believe in these opposite or alternative ways because this is how the predicational process works.

It is true that to affirm *this* predicating assumption rather than *that* predicating assumption, the individual may occasionally be seen delaying for a period of time. Action is under deliberation. Choice is being contemplated, and it can be timed. But this delay in time does not constitute free will. It is the capacity to transpredicate and see several possibilities before affirming just one that is the essence of free will. Unfortunately, James did not accept that it is possible for a reasoner to frame beliefs in opposition to what may currently be under predication. As a loyal British empiricist he wanted to find some other belief to which the original must give way. He therefore said, "We never disbelieve anything except for the reason that we believe something else which contradicts the first thing. Disbelief is thus an incidental complication to belief, and need not be considered by itself" (James, 1890/1952, p. 636).

James went on to say that the opposite of belief is doubt and inquiry rather than disbelief (p. 636). He did not view oppositionality as an intrinsic second event—a process enabling belief and disbelief to occur at the same time—in the way that LLT does. As we noted in Chapter 3, the capacity to process thoughts oppositionally has been referred to historically as *dialectical* reasoning (I will return to this in greater depth in Chapter 7). A first-event thought on this model would be termed a *thesis*, and its directly implied second event an *antithesis*. The latter thought is always opposite to and hence contradicts the former thought's meaning. Dialectical reasoning was dismissed by British empiricism, where it was assumed that every meaning in mind stood independent of its contradiction. Because James followed the British philosophy of empiricism he was not going to suggest that there may be an innate capacity for the mind to generate alternatives free of such empirical input. Disbelief was therefore not fundamental to the processing of ideas. It takes an entirely different contradictory idea forming in mind to bring about disbelief.

In the continental philosophies of Kant (1788/1952) and Hegel (1821/1952b), such contradictions were believed to occur entirely within the mental process of thesis–antithesis (usually but not necessarily followed by a *synthesis* of these contradictory meanings). In this instance each and every belief *immediately* implies its contrary, contradiction, or negation. This is the formulation that we have embraced in LLT, as when we noted that to believe "John is reliable" we immediately grasped the implied meaning of "John is not reliable" as an aspect of the targeted John. This negation issues from an even broader realm of meaning extending to the target than the larger, predicating circle of Figure 2. Belief and disbelief are thus intrinsically related (oppositionally) within a single idea. In opting to affirm that John is reliable, we are taking a position "for" one end of such a reliable–unreliable dimension of meaning—or at least in this direction. This position-taking is a reflection of the *same process* that, in another context, would be more readily called an act of free will (e.g., choosing *to do* or *not to do* something).

Told that "A is right and good," the oppositionally reasoning individual *immediately* understands the possible implication that "*non-*A is right and good," exactly as Figures 2 and 3 depict. Of course, this contradiction would probably be rejected in a flash as an erroneous idea. Experiences of this nature are fleeting and always subtle. We fail to notice when reasoning or acting that we are *taking a position*, and are actually free to affirm things one way or the other, setting the grounds for the sake of which we will then be determined as our thinking and behavior proceeds. But James (1890/1952) argued that a changing conception like moving A to the non-A side of the ledger would arise only from new acts of attention, new situations, and not from some "endogenous" (intrinsic) capacity to reason from what is to what is not the case (p. 304). In contrast, LLT holds that generic oppositionality enables such contradictions to arise within any one act of attention.

Consciousness becomes less relevant to Jamesian psychology because of this tendency to emphasize what is given or *known* empirically rather than what might be generated as alternatives through generically oppositional reasoning. Consciousness on this view is not much involved in the transpredicating effort of perceiving what is not now the case but "might be" knowable. Consciousness deals with what is empirically presented. James specifically rejected dialectically framed philosophies like Hegel's in preference to the unipolarities of the British. Nor did he do much with the concept of the unconscious, which is easily opposed to consciousness. James did acknowledge that in making inferences "we are commonly unconscious that we are inferring at all" (p. 665). He took an interest in the writings of Freud but was not convinced of this approach by any means. James said that in some people consciousness can split into two parts that coexist but ignore each other. However, rather than being antagonistic (oppositional) these halves are "*complementary*" (p. 135; italics in original). Actually, by the turn of the 20th century, James was pretty much removed from psychology and working more as a philosopher. In these later writings we find greater agreement with LLT.

JAMES ON PREDICATION IN THE LOGOS

I do not want to give the impression that there are no allusions to predicational theorizing in the *Principles*. James's interpretation of mental association is a case in point. The British philosophers viewed the association of ideas in efficient-cause terms, suggesting that the more often we are confronted with two items contiguously in time, the more likely it is that we will form an automatic association between them. We always purchase popcorn at the movies, so eating popcorn anyplace else reminds us of the movies. The behaviorists extended this associationistic or connectionistic model to explain every aspect of learning and memory. Behavior (qua "mind") was all a matter of hooking-up one item to another by way of such frequency and contiguity considerations.

James, on the other hand, embraced "*association by similarity*" (p. 678, italics in original), by which he meant a capacity that humans have to find identities within a sea of differences. This abstracting of similarities makes higher thought possible and is what most clearly differentiates the human from lower organisms (p. 686). That is, by seeing identities and partial identities in things, the human being can reason analogically (partial identity)—capitalizing on knowledge in one sphere to extend to another (pp. 678, 688). Knowing how to roller skate can facilitate learning how to ice skate. This treatment of analogical reasoning is highly consistent with LLT. Note that it has *nothing* to do with innate biological processes like instincts or reflexes. We are in a *Logos* realm of explanation at this point, relying on a predicational model to make our case.

In his more philosophical writings, James employed a "mother-sea" metaphor: "there is a continuum of cosmic consciousness, against which our individuality builds but accidental fences, and into which our several minds plunge us into a mother-sea or reservoir" (Perry, 1948, p. 206). This wider-to-narrower intimation of a sea of consciousness from which we take individuality is definitely predicational in nature. Recall that Jung used a similar sea metaphor in his analysis of the relation of consciousness to unconsciousness (see Chapter 4). Although James once said "I am intensely an individualist" (p. 262), it is also true that he believed that the consciousness of one person is continuous with a "wider self" (p. 261) through which supporting and saving experiences arise. This too is suggestive of predication. Indeed, James "construed experience as a larger area *within* which the boundaries of consciousness and self can be defined" (p. 278; italics in original).

Pragmatism also employs a predicational model. James (1907/1943) spoke of the "pragmatic method" but he meant by this a logical process of meaning extension from a predicate to its target. The pragmatic method involves the testing of ideas by tracing their "respective practical consequences" (p. 42) or "cash-value" (p. 46). If two ideas result in the same consequences they mean "practically the same thing, and all dispute [over their presumed difference] is idle" (p. 42). What should not be overlooked in this treatment is that any idea being formulated consists of an affirmed predication extending to its target. The target can exist in reality or be purely an abstraction. Identical cash-values for two "different" ideas signify that here is a distinction in meaningful terminology without a difference in targeted referent. One philosopher's "X" is another philosopher's "Y." James did not discuss the precedent-sequacious extension of predicated meanings under affirmation "to" what they signify referentially. But such an analysis of his writings is possible and if undertaken it is clearly supportive of the tenets of LLT.

The cash-value of ideas also involves their truth value, especially for the individual holding to them. An idea that is supported by ongoing experience is one that will be retained as true or "a truth." It is therefore not surprising that pragmatism is also interpreted by some as a "*theory of truth*" (James, 1907/1943, p. 47, italics in original). Of course, the sense of truth here may be quite personal and might not stand the test of scientific evidence. James's pragmatism is empirical, but it is not exactly positivistic. The proof that James required of an idea was not of the same type as the proof demanded by science—with operational definitions and clear predictions to an independent criterion. In the positivistic mode, if one cannot show how to put ideas to test in this scientific sense, they are said to be meaningless (Ayer, 1946, p. 35).

But James found a way for beliefs that were difficult or even impossible to prove scientifically to have meaning. For example, he specifically noted that pragmatism has no a priori prejudices against theology: "*If theological ideas prove to have a value for concrete life, they will be true, for pragmatism, in the sense of being good for so much. For how much more they are true, will depend entirely on their relations to the other truths that also have to be acknowledged*" (James, 1907/1943, p. 57; italics in original). As for the proof of conceptions like God, James felt they lie primarily "in inner personal experiences" (p. 78). He was not about to dismiss such individually held beliefs as meaningless on the basis of some positivist assumption. Religious beliefs are among the most significant affirmations made from the dawn of human existence, and therefore have proven their cash-value beyond doubt. James favored a pluralistic approach to knowledge, which included ideas about such ineluctible matters of existence.

COMPARISONS AND DISSATISFACTIONS

Our survey of Jamesian thought has highlighted certain similarities and differences with LLT on the telic triune. Both positions view consciousness as a process, and the self as a content (self-image, self-definition, etc.) within this process. Recall from Chapter 2 that in LLT the self refers to the predications that people have about themselves, growing out of interactions with others as well as reflexive awareness over a lifetime. The word *self* can also be used technically by a psychologist to describe the repeated behavioral style of others under her or his observation. This is, in effect, what James does in distinguishing between the various self categories (empirical self, material self, etc.). I believe it is also true that not everyone thinks about his or her self per se. Some people are, in effect, "selfless." These might be individualists who merely do what is before them and rarely engage in self-reflexive examination, or they might be highly oriented to influence by others so they literally lose themselves in the group (see Chapter 9 for further analysis along this line).

An important difference between the Jamesian view and LLT arises concerning the nature of free will. Logical learning theory understands free will as a process. Free will is a natural outgrowth of transpredication, founded on the capacity to interpret "fixed" circumstances from an opposing perspective and thereby to act for the sake of this freely affirmed alternative. James, on the other hand, emphasized free will as a content, a Renouvierian commitment or a cognitive recognition of the fact that experience is far from perfect. Though at times he referred to free will as a force, it was always in conjunction with this effort to make things better. When James finally concluded that the question of free will was incapable of being solved on strictly psychological grounds, I think he was absolutely correct because—and only because—he had limited psychology to *Bios* considerations. Such concepts meshed with British philosophy, but they left James no opportunity to say how it is possible to behave differently, all circumstances remaining the same. He tried to explain free will in a Lockean vein, as holding up the biological processing, keeping the mind from filling up with one idea by opposing it with another idea (or ideas); but he was never satisfied with this explanation. His theory of pragmatic thinking gives us a better indication of where free will might enter, although he still avoided a basic role for oppositionality.

Note that the LLT interpretation of free will puts it in the realm of consciousness. To act freely is to alter or redefine by negation (contradiction, etc.) the promptings of either biological or environmental pressures. Such denial could occur unconsciously, of course, but then we would find it difficult to speak of it as reflecting free will. This would suggest a Janetian dissociation (see Chapter 4). There is a more involved issue here concerning the possibility of unconscious free will, but I will put this off until Chapter 10. For now, it is sufficient to note that free will is intrinsically tied to consciousness because it involves framing alternatives via transpredication. As discussed in Chapter 2, the exercise of free will can be harmful or helpful. Resisting sound suggestions from a financial advisor or a physician can lead to unfortunate outcomes. At other times, when people stand up against group pressures on principle, we are likely to admire their self-motivated strength of character (see Chapter 9).

CONCLUDING COMMENT

James has proven to be a most enigmatic "father" of American psychology (as he has been called). He was a spiritualist who favored biological reductionism, an empiricist who accepted meanings unamenable to empirical proof, a staunch defender of science who could not bring himself to enter the "brass instruments" laboratory of his time, and who ended his days more a philosopher than a psychologist. He was, of course, struggling for much of his career with the impossible task of uniting mind with body. I think in large part due to his commitment to British philosophy—where one is drawn empirically to what is palpably *there* rather than what is *not there*—he found little need to assign an active role to unconsciousness. And, in fact, his earlier emphasis on consciousness as a selective agency duplicated what he had to say about the role of attention in such mental activities as will, choice, and volition.

Later, his suggestion that consciousness is a process of knowing or awareness was limited to contents provided by experience and not concocted through an actively oppositional directedness of the thought process. As an empiricist he had to find some point in the environment from which first-event influences issued, and this bias made it inevitable that he would find consciousness to be a passive second event where emphasis, selection, and then knowing, was its major role in the psyche. There was not a great deal of compatibility with LLT in James's early psychological writings. His avowed commitment to the *Bios* took him out of the *Logos* context in which LLT seeks its explanations.

Fortunately, once we turn to James's later, more philosophical endeavors, the parallels with LLT are more apparent. The concepts of predication, precedent-sequacious meaning-extension, analogy (via partial tautology), and even affective assessment are all reflected in Jamesian pragmatism. As he moves away from the biophysiological realm, his writings take on a more decidedly introspective tone. We find ourselves thinking along with the person who has ideas and projects them into ongoing experience to see if they have cash-value. Even if we might disagree with the merits of these ideas, so long as a person finds meaning in them he or she has every right to cash in on their personal relevance. Logical learning theory is completely supportive of this side of Jamesian theorizing.

7

COMPUTERS AND CONSCIOUSNESS

The social sciences have been involved for some time in a "cognitive" revolution in which the machine continues to be a metaphor for the human being. Of course, the machine now under consideration is a computer rather than a telephone switchboard as it used to be. But the emphasis placed on cognition in this revolution has engendered even greater interest in consciousness than before. One could say that the mechanists of yesteryear were ignoring the problem of consciousness altogether. However, now the wheel has turned and we find some interesting explanations in the computing literature on just what computers and consciousness have in common. In the present chapter, we begin with a review of four historic developments that dramatically altered the conception of a machine, take up major computer theories in both academic psychology and the artificial intelligence community, and then offer an LLT interpretation of what computing machines have to do with psychic consciousness.

CAN A MACHINE THINK?

There was a time when, even in scientific circles, the question of artificial intelligence would probably have been considered ridiculous. The received view of that era followed a Cartesian separation of body from mind, with the former said to be *extended* in space and the latter *unextended*. Mind did the thinking and the body was a biological machine. This distinction suggested that the material- and efficient-causes of the *Bios* did not lead to the same explanations as the formal- and final-causes of the *Logos*. Machines were rigid structures, working in a pulley-and-gear fashion that could not accommodate the maneuverings of active thought. However, in the mid-20th century a new kind of machine-processing was being perfected—one that would not only significantly affect how modern life would be lived but also make its claims on the human image. I am, of course, referring to the computing machine. The first practical digital computer was built in 1944 by H. H. Aiken (Dreyfus, 1979, p. 71). In addition to the advancements in materials and technology that the new machinery required, I believe that there were four major theoretical developments at about mid-century that made the opening question to this chapter increasingly plausible.

The first development stemmed from what has to be one of the most important Master's degrees in history. In his Master's thesis, Claude Shannon (1938) equated an electronic switch that is either *on* or *off* with a flow of information, respectively signifying *true* or *false*. The word-meanings *on*, *off*, *true*, *false* merely describe the process and therefore are not contents within this process. From a strictly engineering point of view, there is no meaning-content being conveyed by the electrical (information) processing (see Shannon & Weaver, 1962, p. 99). Any meaning that this process might carry along as a content would involve a signal system that could be correlated with its purely engineering function (e.g., symbolic representations of a "software" program correlated to the processing of the electrical "hardware"). As we noted in Chapter 2, Shannon makes it clear that the "semantic [i.e., meaningfulness] aspects of communications are irrelevant to the engineering problem" (p. 3). The engineering problem focuses on the electrical *signals* of the process per se, and not on some correlating *symbol* system being mediated as a content in this process (see Chapter 10 for further discussion of signs vs. symbols).

The basic unit of information in the electrical signaling process of a computer is the *bit*, short for binary digit. This refers to the amount of information required to select one electrical impulse or signal from two equally probable alternatives (regardless of the meaning-content under processing). A bit involves halving the total complex of signals available in the binary sense of "either–or." Thus, if there were four equally probable alternatives open to a course of electrical signaling, it would require two bits of information to decide on a singular course of action. One bit would reduce the four alternatives to two, and another would select one of the two remaining possibilities. Electrical information processing is therefore a matter of reducing electrical impulses by ("either–or") halves (Shannon & Weaver, 1962, pp. 3, 99).

McCulloch and Pitts (1943) then went beyond Shannon to place meaningfulness at the center of an ancillary form of information processing. McCulloch and Pitts first suggested that the all-or-none firing properties of nerve cells could be construed in the binary fashion of Shannon's electronic switching. An active or firing neuron was *on* and an inactive neuron was *off*. Neurons were the acknowledged instrumentalities of communication in the central nervous system. McCulloch and Pitts tried to map the binary logic of machine processing onto the structure of the central nervous system, and thereby initiated the neural network form of theorizing that has become so popular in modern psychology. Once psychologists realized that meaningful contents could be correlated with electrical signals, *cognitive information processing* was born. Henceforth, an effort would be made to explain the behavior and cognition of living organisms on the basis of the computer model. The upshot is that we now have two uses for the concept of *information*—one referring to a process that has no meaning function and a second that refers to the meaningful content being processed (as in human reasoning). It is easy to confound these two.

The second important historic development occurred when Rosenblueth, Wiener, and Bigelow (1943) employed the *feedback* conception to explain human agency. Norbert Wiener (1954) is the significant person here, having founded what he called the field of *cybernetics* somewhat earlier. This term has Greek roots meaning "steersman," so the field of cybernetics has something to do with directing a course of events—like the processing of a machine. Such control of a machine process is accomplished through input, output, and feedback in the flow of information. The unique thing about cybernetics is that it provided the means for a machine robot or missile to guide itself over a course of action. Cybernetics defines *input* as any event external to the machine that modifies its actions. *Output* is any change produced in the surroundings by the machine.

Feedback is of two types: *positive* and *negative*. Positive feedback is a fraction of the output from the machine returning as input (Rosenblueth et al., 1943, p. 19). Speaking anthropomorphically, we might say that the machine "tells itself" what it is now doing as some action is being carried out. A machine may thus move to the left (output) and tell itself that it is "moving to the left" at the same time through positive feedback. On the other hand, feedback can be negative if the machine is being directed by the margin of error obtaining between its actions and a specific goal it has been programmed to reach (p. 19). In this case, again anthropomorphically expressed, a machine drifting off its designated course can measure and "inform" itself of this fact through negative feedback, bringing about mechanical adaptations that correct for this error to put it back on course.

For example, if a spacecraft is aimed at a certain target, it will continually monitor its position relative to this target by bouncing signals off of it. As the spacecraft strays off course this negative feedback—the difference between a target's location and where the spacecraft is now heading—will be duly recorded and adjustments made in its rocket firings to correct its course. As it does so, positive feedback is used to signal that these correcting adjustments are actually being made (output). Rosenblueth et al. took this self-controlling, guidance feature of cybernetics as a rationale for *purpose* in the mediating mechanism of the machine. Purposeless machines could not be interpreted as directed to a goal, but purposeful machines adjust through negative feedback to attain a goal—"to a final condition in which the behaving object reaches a definite correlation in time or in space with respect to another object or event" (p. 18). The conclusion is then reached that "teleological behavior thus becomes synonymous with behavior controlled by negative feedback . . ." (p. 24).

Here is a confounding of process with content. That is, a machine relying on negative feedback is in the process mode. It does not "have" a goal in the sense of framing its own intention. The machine's information processing is without meaning. It cannot negate the goal it is processing. Even in the case of an executive program permitting a robot to "select" its own target there would be a delimited range within which this process would be permitted to occur (e.g., the robot could not "decide" to negate the executive program upon its initial submission or intentionally shut it down for extraneous reasons at any point following activation). The meanings of interest to the programmer of the robot would set the limits of the "creative" processing that might take place. Even so, cybernetics lent great support to those scientists who advocated describing living organisms in machine terms. Wiener (1954) spoke for these advocates when he said that "the physical functioning of the living individual and the operation of some of the newer communication machines are precisely parallel . . ." (p. 26).

The third significant development occurred in 1950 when the young genius, Alan Turing, proposed what he then called an "imitation game" to test whether a machine could be said to "think" or was "conscious" (Turing, 1950). The game was played with a man (A) and a woman (B) located in one room, and an interrogator (C) located in another room. In the original game, players communicated between rooms through use of a linotype machine; in reenactments today a computer is used. The object of the game is for C to determine which of the other two players is the man and which is the woman. Thus, C asks A and B various questions in making the determination about their respective sexes. For example, C might ask A "How long is your hair?" Presumably, a woman's hair would tend to be longer than a man's (especially in the 1940s–1950s). However, if A were the man, A could tell lies to deceive C, claiming to have long hair, done

in large curls, and continue doing so even though B complains with justification that A is using deceit and that she is really the woman. But then,
from C's perspective, B could be the man doing the lying. The essence of
the Turing test is what happens if a machine takes the part of A. Could a
program be written so that the interrogator would have no awareness of
the fact that A is a machine replying, misleading, and following through
on questions just as the actual human being would?

The Turing test has been given a broader interpretation today, so that
this original scenario need not be enacted. Any kind of program that mis-
leads an observer into believing that an interaction with another human
being is taking place is now considered to have passed a Turing test (Gardner, 1985, p. 17). Such a program has presumably simulated the cognitions
of an actual, living person. A veritable field of *simulation* (i.e., "having the
external characteristics of") was soon established, in which program writers
tried their hand at all manner of such pretenses. In their classic work on
human problem solving, Newell and Simon (1972) thought of themselves
as studying the "simulation of cognitive processes" (Simon, 1985, p. 7).
Simon literally equated artificial simulations of this nature with the work
of psychology, suggesting that "psychology is a science of the artificial" (p.
89). Another historic work, *Plans and the Structure of Behavior* by Miller,
Galanter, and Pribram (1960) also showed psychologists how to adapt the
language of AI to explanations of human behavior.

Note that simulations occur as contents being processed by the machine. The "intelligence" of artificial intelligence is therefore not found in
the electrical machine-process but in the creativity of the program writer's
content-meanings that are under processing. It is not unheard of today for
program writers to feel slighted because so many people believe that the
machine process is thinking-up "on the spot" all of the uniquely truthful
and untruthful replies during Turing tests. Joseph Weizenbaum (1976) was
shocked to find that people became emotionally involved with his ELIZA
program, which simulated an interaction with a Rogerian therapist, calling
such involvements a "reckless anthropomorphization of the computer" (p.
205). There is surely intelligence reflected in such remarkably creative programs, but it is *not* artificial; it comes from the program writer's real-life
ability (for an in-depth analysis of program writing, see Rychlak, 1991,
Chapter 3).

The fourth and final mid-century development I would cite as relevant to our opening question is that of *recursion*. Kurt Gödel had apparently
suggested this concept as a way of making absolutely precise the notion of
defining a mathematical function in terms of other more elementary functions (Hodges, 1983, p. 133). Turing did some work on this concept as
well. In the AI literature we find recursion discussed in the context of
"levels of processing" and "repetition of function." As Boden (1977) has
defined it,

A recursive structure is one with an essentially hierarchical character, that can be naturally described at several levels of detail. And a recursive procedure is one that can refer to and operate on itself, so that it can be 'nested' within itself to an indefinite number of hierarchical levels. (p. 372)

Thus, an algorithmic rule of some sort can be repeatedly used in a program at both higher and lower levels of complexity. An *algorithm* is a rule or set of rules enabling the solution of some task (e.g., a formula for calculating the mean value of a distribution of test scores). This solution would be called an "effective procedure." The algorithm is essentially a pattern—a formal cause, shall we say—which is moved along as a content by the efficient causation of the machine's electricity. Because this pattern can be used at both specific and broad-ranging levels of analysis, an algorithm makes *iteration* (repetition) possible. For example, suppose we wrote the following algorithmic rule into a program for the computer: "If the first number in a series of numbers is larger than the second, add the first to the second; if the first number is smaller than the second, subtract the first from the second." In carrying out this effective procedure the numbers processed might be low in value (3, 4, 8, 6, etc.) or high in value (1023, 1384, 1575, 1126, etc.). This is an iteration of the *same* effective procedure taking place with different values of the content processed. Note that our algorithmic rule is written in binary fashion (high–low), making use of bits of information in the machine-processing sense to determine the course of processing in an either–or manner.

I should mention at this point that not every computer theorist would consider an algorithm to be a content in a process. For example, if we find the brain carrying out patterns of neuronal firing that can be put into an algorithmic formula, are we not directly tracing or gauging a process? Some linguists believe that rules of syntax are not learned (contents) but represent an innate process for organizing language (Searle, 1992, p. 153). There are many processes carried out in the physical body with algorithmic regularity. From this perspective, an algorithmic rule is identical with the process it traces. In reply to such claims, and without attacking the realism on which they rest, I would suggest that to capture and record the patterned regularities of scientific observation, a symbol system of some type must be employed. The symbols of this system, which may represent an observed algorithmic regularity, are then processed as contents aimed at further explaining what has been observed. It is this cognitive processing aspect of the total picture that the LLT advocate is trying to understand. In this chapter, the aim is to understand certain human thinkers who have framed machine-theories of consciousness. To accomplish this aim it is necessary to speak of algorithmic symbolization as a content within some kind of cognitive process. There can be different theoretical formulations of the process that convey or create "the same" algorithm. We should not confuse the explanatory task with the observed regularities that are being explained. Algorithms are an aspect of the explanatory task even though they also measure the observed data, or, in the case of computers, direct the effective procedures.

The capacity to break down problems into more manageable units, solving a smaller unit before combining it into a larger complex, suggests a parallel to the human reasoner who breaks down a complex problem into lower-level solutions before tackling the whole. Minsky (1986) coined a recursion principle as follows: "*When a problem splits into smaller parts, then unless one can apply the mind's full power to each subjob, one's intellect will get dispersed and leave less cleverness for each new task*" (p. 161; italics in original). Minsky notes that the mind does not "shatter" as it tackles the parts of problems: "We can imagine how to pack a jewelry box without forgetting where it will fit into a suitcase" (p. 161). This is a metaphorical allusion to the recursive *nesting* of one item (jewelry box) into another (suitcase), as we might nest one idea or problem solution within another. Recursion and iteration obviously share the same machine-processing capacity.

The four developments we have now reviewed surely convince us that the hardware process of a computer, assisted by its programmed software, is something new under the sun. Here is a machine that can analyze problems, breaking them down into manageable units that can be nested for a time and then brought back to achieve an overall solution. This machine has a self-directing feature enabling it to attain goals and adapt to changing circumstances along the way. It can take on the appearance of human intelligence, simulating discourse through use of language. Considering all of these remarkable achievements it is no longer foolish to ask: Can machines think? And if they can think, a further question would seem to follow: Are machines conscious? Before answering these questions from the perspective of LLT, I would like to present a few of the views that one finds in the psychological and AI literature on these matters.

TYPICAL VIEWS ON COMPUTER CONSCIOUSNESS

Computer Theorizing in Academic Psychology

At mid-20th century, psychologists in leading universities were almost exclusively behavioristic in theoretical persuasion. The founder of behaviorism, John Watson, was unequivocal concerning his attitude toward consciousness. In his famous behaviorist "manifesto," Watson (1913) asserted that "One can assume either the presence or the absence of consciousness anywhere in the phylogenetic scale without affecting the problems of behavior by one jot or one tittle" (p. 161).

Behaviorism took the high road of Newtonian tough-minded science, eschewing all teleological suggestions in its strictly empirical approach. The theoretical stance here was enthusiastically extraspective, framing behavior as if it were exclusively "over there," where it could be put to measurement, controlled, and then predicted according to the efficiently caused "natural laws" that supposedly propelled it along. The philosophy of science here was realistic (or materialistic), untroubled by suggestions that scientific observers might significantly influence their accounts due to the (formal-cause) predications being affirmed in their theories at the outset. Here was a free-standing reality before them, ready for mapping, so naturally they wanted to get on with it. The concept of behavior that resulted was efficiently causal, supplemented by material causation (as in bodily drives). Formal-cause patterns of behavior (e.g., habits) were merely outcomes shaped by the underlying laws and never the cause of human action. True to its Newtonian pedigree, behaviorism completely dismissed the possibility of any final-cause influence on behavior.

Although they realized that there was something taking place inside the brain, at mid-20th century the behaviorists—prompted in large measure by the views of Skinner—no longer believed they had to explain the specifics of this "inside the organism" process. One did not need to look inside the "black box" in order to study its behavioral patterns. But with the cognitive revolution of the 1950s all of this changed. Now, instead of simply controlling and predicting in the empirical study of learning, computer technology made it possible to speculate on the inner workings of the black box—such as neural networks, short- and long-term memory stores, retrieval capabilities, and so forth.

The problem of consciousness never need arise for an electrical engineer like Shannon. But when psychologists began attributing his form of information processing to the brain, affixing a symbol system to the mechanical flow of neuronal electricity, issues arose concerning a possible role for consciousness that could no longer be ignored. First of all, it just seemed more reasonable to discuss consciousness in light of a cognitive (inside) rather than a behavioral (outside) process. More importantly, it was found through empirical research that the cognizing person was aware of certain mental processes but totally unaware of others (e.g., Bowers, 1984). This implied a conscious versus unconscious difference in the very nature of processing.

What, then, do we find computer-oriented psychologists saying about machine consciousness? I would say that the predominant schematic usage is some form of awareness (see Chapter 1), frequently with the emphasis placed on stimulus input. In behavioristic theory, stimuli are the efficiently caused thrusts that make things happen, including the responsiveness of consciousness. The feedback concept is also quite important, because a machine that can adapt to change is more plausibly described as acting consciously than one that cannot. In almost all cases, awareness is said to arise thanks to an electrical *activation* of the elements in memory.

For example, the (electrical) energy derived from two stimuli activating a memory *representation* (copy, image, etc.) that has been previously stored makes it more likely that this "memory" will enter consciousness than if only one stimulus were prompting such retrieval (Anderson, 1983, pp. 28–29). Doubling the prompt facilitates the recall. This form of explanation takes its rationale from the hardware rather than from the meanings encompassed in the symbols of the software. Meanings (contents) are present, but they get pushed into application by the thrust of electrical energy rather than by their meaningful significance to the person concerned. The presumption is that what the person would consider significant is that which would generate the greatest electrical force in the first place.

An interesting dispute arose concerning the nature of consciousness in perception. On the one hand, it has been suggested that consciousness occurs when there is a good *match* between current input and some memory schematic mediating ongoing perception (Marcel, 1983). We are conscious when today's perception of the layout of our new apartment matches yesterday's perception of this room arrangement. It has been shown empirically that this habituation or redundancy phenomenon takes place in hearing, olfaction, taste, and touch (Baars, 1988, p. 190). On the other hand, it has also been suggested that when such matches are too perfect they become habituated and *lose* consciousness thanks to their redundancy (Berlyne, 1960). We carry out routine tasks while "a million miles away," moving about the apartment without actually perceiving the distinctive adjustments we are making to the room locations and furniture placements.

To further complicate matters, consciousness is decidedly heightened if what we routinely anticipate happening does not occur—as when the bathroom door in our new apartment suddenly becomes difficult to close. All unexpected occurrences such as novelty, surprise, or confusion raise our level of consciousness—and, paradoxically, this is a *mismatch* of what has been perceived earlier with what now confronts us. Note that when we speak of expectation we are referring more to meanings than to the activating power of a machine process. Information processing here is not merely electrical. It has to do with the extension of meanings in the correlated symbol system. Consistent with this stress on expectation, some psychologists think of consciousness as arising when the organism must correct a problem—or better yet, continually prepare for such eventualities through trouble-shooting efforts beforehand (Mandler, 1984).

A searchlight metaphor has been invoked to explain consciousness (Crick, 1984). This suggests that conscious experience is like a spotlight playing over the elements of the nervous system, bringing them selectively into awareness. The issue of importance here is whether we are to think of this spotlight as a mechanical energizer of thoughts, which would take us back to activation, or as a frame of reference lending organization to the meanings entering consciousness—like Plato's realm of Being throwing its forms onto the realm of Becoming (see Chapter 4; also, Baars, 1988, p. 31). This is never a question of matching because the former realm predicates the latter. Indeed, Plato (1952c) was apparently the first philosopher to define predication (pp. 554, 569). Computer modelers must fall back on the activation thesis at this point or be forced to invoke a homunculus to aim the searchlight onto items in memory selected for retrieval. Activation levels, however, can be said to be shaped by past experience in the typical frequency–contiguity form of explanation utilized by behaviorism.

Computer Theorizing in the AI Community

The field of artificial intelligence (AI) was organized in the period between 1955–1960, although it has mathematical and engineering precedents trailing back to the 19th century (for historical overviews see Gardner, 1985; Newell & Simon, 1972). I have selected three important figures who have written on the nature of consciousness from an AI perspective: Douglas R. Hofstadter (1980), Marvin Minsky (1986), and Daniel C. Dennett (1991). Minsky is lauded as one of the founding fathers of AI, and Dennett is sort of its court philosopher. I will bring out the views of consciousness offered by these leading AI advocates during a critical analysis of their theoretical assumptions and strategies.

The first thing to notice about AI theorizing is that it retains an extraspective theoretical perspective. Dennett (1991) is most outspoken on this point, insisting that a theory of mental events must be "constructed from the third-person point of view, since *all* science is constructed from that perspective" (p. 71; italics in original). Dennett sees first-person accounts as "subjective" in nature, hence lacking in the objectivity of true scientific knowledge (p. 125). Searle (1992) has criticized Dennett for this insistence on extraspection, which he feels ignores the person's actual, meaningful intentions (pp. 157–158). For example, a person's intention is to drink a glass of water, not a glass of H_2O. Things get even more removed from the person's meanings if we consider increasingly complex life intentions.

Third-person terminology has, of course, been the formal language of traditional Newtonian science. As discussed in Chapter 3, modern scientists have a growing appreciation for the contribution that their first-person viewpoint makes to the very phenomena they seek to explain (Holton, 1973, p. 246; Prigogine & Stengers, 1984, pp. 218, 224). Quantum physicists in particular are referred to today as *participators* rather than *observers* in the experimental context, so evident is it that they contribute meanings to what is being empirically and objectively observed (Zukav, 1979, p. 29). Hence, Dennett's claim that modern science avoids all forms of first-person theorizing must be rejected. We have to explain the scientist as human investigator (introspective theory) in order to explain the subject matter (extraspective theory) under investigation.

The next point to consider stems from the bifurcated logic that Shannon's engineering feat made possible. That is, no matter how the AI theorist fills in the details of the process under consideration, he or she will always begin things from a clear, either–or, binary unit—halving the material under consideration or sending the course of processing one way rather than another. This binary process is also framed in a bottom–up fashion, after the explanatory style of British empiricism. These AI theorists are making a fundamentally constitutive assumption concerning the nature of mind. Larger patterns in mind are made up of smaller patterns, which in turn reduce eventually to an either–or singularity. Minsky (1986) reduced the mind to singular "tiny machines" called *agents*, which connect with each other to form a "society of mind" through their patterned relations (p. 19). One has the impression he is thinking of each brain cell as an agent (p. 26). These agents direct such activities as grasping, balancing the body, satisfying thirst, and so on (p. 18).

Hofstadter (1980) relied on a levels-of-mind conception, in which there are neurons firing away at the bottom-most level, and at the very top there are hundreds of symbols ready to be triggered into action by the underlying neurons (p. 357). The symbols are therefore efficiently caused responses. And a "*thought* corresponds to a *trip*. The *towns* which are passed through represent the *symbols* which are excited [by the sensory input of the neurons]" (p. 377; italics in original). The symbols are therefore brought into systematic relationship, akin to Minsky's agents connecting with each other. Hofstadter does not speak of a society of mind, but at one point he does use the metaphor of an anthill (pp. 311–335) in which there is a kind of societal organization emerging from the mayhem of each ant, busily scurrying about to fulfill a specific task.

Dennett (1991) spent considerable time debunking the top–down formulations of Cartesian philosophy, in which thought was viewed as being initiated by a comprehensive formulation or picture of things—as if a scene were being enacted in a play. There is no such Cartesian theater in the brain (p. 107). Descartes's first-person studies (*Cogito ergo sum*) were "a treacherous incubator of errors" (p. 70). Dennett cast his lot with British empiricism, which holds that our "inner world is dependent on [external] sensory sources" (p. 55). The mind (i.e., brain) is a bottom–up structure, relying as Hofstadter has claimed on lower-level subprocesses that record the sensory inputs after being duly processed by what Dennett called a "Multiple Drafts" model of consciousness; thus, "information entering the nervous system is under continuous 'editorial revision'" (p. 111). For example, visual stimuli evoke certain trains of events in the brain:

At different times and different places, various "decisions" or "judgments" are made; more literally, parts of the brain are caused to go into states that discriminate different features, e.g., first mere onset of stimulus, then location, then shape, later color (in a different pathway), later still (apparent) motion, and eventually object recognition. These localized discriminative states transmit effects to other places, contributing to further discriminations, and so forth. (p. 134)

I think it is easy to see what is taking place here. Our three theorists are drawing on the computer as model for mind or brain, with its maze of wirings moving hither and yon in the overall hardware, activating (*on*) or deactivating (*off*) according to the bifurcated logic of bits, which partition the signals one way rather than another. Thus, Minsky (1986) tells us that *"each agent in our society, at each moment, is either in a 'quiet state' or an 'active state'"* (p. 85, italics in orginal). Hofstadter (1980) speaks of the bit as a magnetic switch which is in "either of two positions . . . 'up' and 'down,' or 'x' and 'o,' or 'I' and 'O'" (p. 288–289). The neuronal firing that triggers symbols would follow the same scenario, of course, although the symbols per se would not be simply "on" or "off" in this manner (p. 371). Symbols are more complicated than neurons; for example, they can express an illogical sequence of information even though the neuronal firing would not be erroneously activated (p. 575). Dennett (1991) discussed brain signals caused by things in the environment, noting that early in evolutionary history they "meant either 'scram' or 'go for it!'" (p. 178). Through natural selection, certain signals were wired into the brain on the basis of the environmental situations confronted and successfully mastered. A kind of survival of the best-wired connections resulted (p. 182). This reads very much like the neural-selection theories of Edelman and Ornstein (see Chapter 5). Indeed, all of our AI theorists rely on evolutionary concepts to support their case at one point or another.

Is there a reason why this common tendency exists among AI theorists to refer to a compendium of connecting neuronal hook-ups, zigging and zagging throughout a maze of connections that have supposedly been hardwired by natural selection into some kind of bottom–up system? I believe there is a maxim here stating that, in a system this complicated, the left hand does not—and need not—know what the right hand is doing. There is no Cartesian scenario, no predicating frame of reference directing mental events. Much of mind is totally automatic, or, as is often expressed, unconscious.

Thus, we find Minsky (1986) referring to his agents as carrying out mindless actions (p. 17) without knowing "anything at all" (p. 23). It is in this sometimes messy cross-connection of agents that the laws of thought evolve (pp. 17, 23). If a conflict occurs between agents, this matter is sent "upward to higher levels" (p. 32). The picture here is that of millions of agents blindly joining hands and, from the resulting pattern shaped by evolution, a society of mental lawfulness emerges. Thus, "each part of the mind exploits the rest, not knowing how the other parts work but only what they seem to do" (p. 169). Hofstadter (1980) noted that individual neurons in his hierarchy of mind need not "be intelligent beings on their own" (p. 315). Using the ant colony as an allegory for symbolic organization in the brain, he discussed the layers of organization to be seen emerging from the seemingly harried actions of individual ants:

> From an ant's-eye point of view, a signal has NO purpose. The typical ant in a signal is just meandering around the colony, in search of nothing in particular, until it finds that it feels like stopping. Its teammates usually agree, and at that moment the team unloads itself by crumbling apart, leaving just its members but none of its coherency. No planning is required, no looking ahead. . . . But from the COLONY'S point of view, the team has just responded to a message which was written in the language of the caste distribution. Now from this perspective, it looks very much like purposeful activity. . . . Colonies survive because their caste distribution has meaning, and that meaning is a holistic aspect, invisible on lower levels. (p. 321)

Hofstadter's *colony* is Minsky's *society*, and it is in the organizing patterns of these multiplex groupings that we find meanings generated sans purpose or intention—that is, final causation is decidedly *out*. There is only formal-cause organization forming into an extraspectively arrayed signal to which the individual participants are blind. This is like arranging for a group of 100 people seated in a football stadium to hold up cards that, taken together, spell out some word or produce a picture. Each individual holds up his or her card when signaled to do so without knowing what is being represented in the totality. Dennett (1991) captured the same notion of organization-producing-meaning when he spoke of the individual subprocesses of a computer as being stupid. As with our card holders, no part of a computer has to know what it is doing or why: "Nevertheless, the clever organization of these stupid mechanical processes yields a device that takes the place of a knowledgeable observer" (p. 91). Of course, in the actual patterning of computer information, it is the human programmer who determines the organization of such signaling. But if we focus exclusively on the physical brain qua computer (p. 149) the organization occurs via what I have referred to as survival of the best-wired. The organization that works is the organization that remains, even though it may be somewhat clumsy in design.

So now the AI theorists have tied up the brain and computer into a neat package in which thought goes on, thanks to the contribution of millions of little elements that summate into a pattern of efficient-cause influence. There is no real meaning here, but one can call the resultant pattern "meaning" if such terminology is being asked for by the non-AI community. Evolutionary themes are wrapped into this package as well. Computers also "compute" and there is much dispute over just how correct it is to describe the brain as also "working" according to such a mathematical process—which strikes the LLT advocate as mixing what is fundamentally a *Logos* grounding (mathematics) with a *Bios* grounding (neuronal firing, etc.). Even so, according to a computer model of the brain, the patterned organization that we have been referring to can presumably be captured by an algorithm. Roger Penrose (1994) has been the most outspoken critic of such computational explanations of brain functioning. He stresses that mathematics is more than mere computation, for it requires an *understanding* that the computer lacks (p. 48). I will have more to say on this matter of understanding in the final section of this chapter.

Minsky (1986) frankly admitted that he uses the word *consciousness* "mainly for the myth that human minds are 'self-aware' in the sense of perceiving what happens inside themselves" (p. 327). His view is that consciousness never captures what takes place in immediate mental activity, but only reflects a little of the recent past. We know from studies of human learning that people have a short-term memory that dissipates its contents if they are not soon rehearsed. If we do not repeat a newly heard telephone number several times it is likely to slip from our memory. Consciousness is limited to this short-term memory. Minsky says that remembering is essentially *matching* today with yesterday, like seeing the same thing over again (p. 89). To become aware of everything going on in the brain at the moment would leave no room for ongoing thought (p. 290). So, in the society of mind, consciousness comes down to having a record of what has transpired. The smallest agencies have no such memory, and hence no awareness (p. 290).

The human's language-agency helps promote memory, for it is an important part of thought (although not the whole of it; p. 197). Minsky holds that those functions, carried on by agents, that do not make it into memory are unconscious (p. 153). The agents handle most of our behavioral actions without consciousness as it is. Minsky does not rely on his recursion principle to explain consciousness, but instead limits recursion to an analysis of how we can solve problems through breaking them down by "using the same agency over and over again" (p. 161).

Hofstadter (1980), on the other hand, made considerable use of recursion in his explanation of consciousness. He views recursion as "something being defined in terms of simpler versions of itself" (p. 152). This results in such *nestings* as stories inside stories, movies inside movies, or paintings inside paintings (p. 127). Now, to a Cartesian or any comparable predicational theorist, the story A framing a story B within it would seem to be of a wider compass, suggesting that there would be an aspect of the process utilized by A that would not be relevant to B. If we put this in mathematical terms, we might say that an algorithm covering B would not be capable of covering the broader realm of A. However, Hofstadter has already told us that recursions occur if something is defined via simpler versions of *itself*, so that he would now argue that the *same* algorithm could be used to cover both A and B—albeit the latter would be a simpler version of the former (in line with the example given earlier in this chapter). Suppose that we were to use the same mathematical system to balance our checkbook that we had used earlier to purchase groceries. The check-balancing A is a more complex version of the same mathematical system employed in the supermarket B—although now the grocery bill is included ("nested") with other expenses to be calculated against income.

Why is this formulation of recursion so important to Hofstadter? Because he is trying to meet a problem stemming from the two famous mathematical theorems of Kurt Gödel that I briefly mentioned in Chapter 2. The first of these establishes that in any *consistent* system powerful enough to produce simple arithmetic—which, of course, includes a computing machine—there are formulae that cannot be proved true by this system even though a human being can see that they are, in fact, true. In effect, this theorem states that it is impossible to achieve an axiomatic method in which endlessly true formulae about some area of inquiry will be generated (Nagel & Newman, 1958, p. 6). Gödel's second theorem, which is a corollary of the first, establishes that it is impossible for a consistent system to prove itself consistent. The unique thing about this theorem is that it is fundamentally self-reflexive, calling for an *introspective* examination of the system in question. As Lucas (1961) has observed,

> The essence of the Gödelian formula is that it is self-referring. It says that "This formula is unprovable-in-this-system." When carried over to a machine, the formula is specified in terms which depend on the particular machine in question. The machine is being asked a question about its own processes. We are asking it to be self-conscious, and say what things it can and cannot do. (p. 124)

Gödel's theorems support the notion that there is a wider realm of what Penrose would consider understanding (knowledge, etc.) that targets the formal system to explain its inconsistencies, but the formal system does not have access to this realm. The formal system is trapped within its assumptions and is unable to transcend its processes the way that a human can (see the discussion of universals in Chapter 10). Hofstadter (1980) has a hope that recursion can answer this difficulty. Thus, what appears to be a leap outside of the formal system (i.e., transcendence) is nothing more than the increasing level of complexity within which the very same algorithmic rules are recursively in operation. Building on the feedback concept, Hofstadter introduces the concept of a *strange loop* or *tangled hierarchy* that can move either up or down the levels of a system so that "we unexpectedly find ourselves right back where we started" (p. 10). Hofstadter believes that strange loops are "at the core of intelligence" (p. 27). They are also involved in language mediation, for "where language does create strange loops is when it talks about itself, whether directly or indirectly. Here, something *in* the system jumps out and acts *on* the system, as if it were [an emergent] *outside* the system" (p. 691; italics in original). Hofstadter is now prepared to define consciousness:

> My belief is that the explanation of "emergent" phenomena in our brains—for instance, ideas, hopes, images, analogies, and finally consciousness and free will—are based on a kind of Strange Loop, an interaction between levels in which the top level reaches back down towards the bottom level and influences it, while at the same time being itself determined by the bottom level. (p. 709)

This definition echoes Roger Sperry's ideas on emergent processes (see Chapter 5). An important ingredient of this interaction across levels is the "self" symbol or subsystem (p. 385). Personal identity arises from the special influence that the self has on other aspects of the cognitive network. But conscious awareness is not magical; rather, it is the "direct effect of the complex hardware and software" (p. 388). Reminding us now of Minsky, Hofstadter stresses that consciousness is a kind of "monitoring of brain activity by a subsystem [self] of the brain itself" (p. 388). Unfortunately, Hofstadter does not really solve the Gödelian requirement of a self that can reflexively examine its own processing to see and correct inconsistencies that the mathematical substrate is unable to rectify.

That is, recursion cannot account for the human mind's ability to rise above and beyond a systematic mathematical system and recognize an inconsistency that the system per se cannot identify. Here is a stupidity of the system as a whole to match the stupidities of the parts (such as Minsky's agents). Recursion is always within the system, an aspect of the very process known as "the system." A Gödelian perspective from outside or "above" the system is *not* a more complex version of this system as per Hofstadter's suggestion. A Gödelian perspective is the wider view of a different system, with additional assumptions targeting the lower level in typical predicational fashion.

Dennett (1991) relied heavily on an evolutionary rationale in describing the nature of consciousness. He suggests that initially behavior was unconscious because it lacked purpose. There was no teleology in the world (p. 173). But after millennia, simple replicators emerged to represent interests—a primary one of which was the interest in self-replication (p. 173). Enter now the importance of selective wiring: "The organisms with the good fortune to be better wired-up at birth tend to produce more surviving progeny, so good hard-wiring spreads through the population" (p. 182). Here is where the multiple-drafts also were selected out over many generations (p. 188). To this point, Dennett has been stressing the evolution of brain hardware, which is where both Minsky and Hofstadter had placed emphasis in their explanations of consciousness. But now Dennett shifts emphasis away from the hardware:

> Our brains are equipped at birth with few if any powers that were lacking in the brains of our ancestors 10,000 years ago. So the tremendous advance of *Homo sapiens* in the last 10,000 years must almost all be due to harnessing the plasticity of that brain in radically new ways—by creating something like *software* to enhance its underlying powers. (p. 190; italics in original)

The brain's hard-wiring at birth takes care of important "categories in life" like hunger and thirst, but other wiring must be organized through neural selection in early development (p. 192). Early language development helped also, because initially questions might have been asked of others but in time the developing organism actually answered its own question— giving birth to self-consciousness and then consciousness in general (p. 195). Now the interests prompted by evolution became reasons for doing things, and a sense of both proximal and distal anticipation was made possible (pp. 178–179). Exchange of ideas among people, and the teaching of one by another enhanced cultural transmission, which played an almost equal role in the rise of consciousness as natural selection (p. 203). A unit of cultural transmission is termed a *meme*, involving such things as ideas, tunes, catch-phrases, clothes, architectural forms, and so on (pp. 201–202).

Dennett focuses on the software by referring to a *virtual machine*: ". . . a virtual machine is a temporary set of highly structured regularities imposed on the underlying hardware by a *program*: a structured recipe of hundreds of thousands of instructions that give the hardware a huge, interlocking set of habits or dispositions-to-react" (p. 216; italics in original). The powers of the virtual machine greatly enhance the underlying powers of the organic hardware on which it runs, not the least of the reasons being that it conveys huge numbers of memes (past cultural knowledge). The software program is a grand mediator functioning in the brain (p. 140). And what, then, is consciousness? Dennett answers:

> I hereby declare that YES, my theory is a theory of consciousness. Anyone or anything that has such a virtual machine as its control system is conscious in the fullest sense, and is conscious *because* it has such a virtual machine. (p. 281; italics in original)

Dennett does not dismiss the role of recursion in consciousness. He describes the capacity for transcending ongoing thought as first-order ideas being thought about by second-order ideas, and so forth to even higher levels (pp. 306–307). There is no concern about jumping outside of the system here as there was in the work of Hofstadter. The "self" is created by attributions from others in the culture as well as recursive thoughts about oneself (pp. 423, 427). The virtual machine (program) directing the brain continues to evolve over the life span of the person concerned (p. 431). Dennett urges his reader to think of the brain as a computer of sorts: "By thinking of our brains as information-processing systems, we can gradually dispel the fog and pick our way across the great divide, discovering how it might be that our brains produce all the phenomena" (p. 433).

One cannot help wondering if brains in Dennett's scheme actually do produce their phenomena. After all, Dennett has assigned considerable responsibility to cultural transmission as well as individual learning to shape the virtual machine one way or another. Although shaped in bottom–up fashion, the virtual machine qua program comes to direct the brain's actions in top–down fashion (also reminiscent of Sperry's two-way causation; see Chapter 5). Dennett has not presented us with a theory of learning to complement natural selection as the source of such direction or shaping. Doubtless such a learning theory would draw from traditional behavioristic assumptions. In Chapter 5 we contrasted Skinner and Edelman along these lines. We could substitute Dennett for Edelman without significantly altering this contrast.

The LLT position on all of this is that the "selection" of natural selection need not always be as blind as it is made out to be—a fact that we found even Darwin recognizing (as in animal husbandry; see Chapter 5). Even if teleology "emerged" from purely mechanistic sources as Dennett contends, the resulting telic organism could then influence the course of evolution intentionally. This would seem to be especially true of neural Darwinism (i.e., survival of the best wiring in a single brain). The question arises of what kind of process is involved in this subsequent directing of evolution? Is it still a mediating *Bios* process or must we recognize the possible role of a predicating *Logos* process? The LLT answer here is obvious. We move next to an elaboration of the LLT view regarding computer thinking and consciousness.

Computer Thinking and Psychic Consciousness: The LLT Position

Critics of AI point out that whatever takes place in computer simulations of thinking is *not* what takes place in the brain. Thus, Searle (1990) argues that the brain does not simply mediate patterns framed by a program, but it actually "*causes* mental events by virtue of specific neurobiological processes" (p. 29; italics in original). Because the computer does not actually produce these neurobiological causes in its simulations of thought it is pointless to speak of a computer as actually paralleling the brain's functioning. Although I agree with this line of criticism I also believe that it would be instructive to ask what manner of "thinking" would be taking place if a computer were actually doing what a human being is presumed to be doing in the act of thinking.

I believe it is possible to answer this question by drawing on a long-standing distinction between two modes of reasoning that were first detailed by Aristotle, and showing how this important contrast relates to the Boolean logic that has been the basis of computer reasoning. In speaking of a comparison between human and computer reasoning I am *not* referring to a simulation. The Turing test is not involved here. What we are after is a way of contrasting the style of thought carried on by a computer with that of a human being—assuming that computers actually can think or reason.

The ancient Greeks were much taken with the role of oppositionality in the organizing and creation of knowledge, and no one was more influential on this score than Socrates (circa 470–399 BC), who had a means of instructive analysis often called the *dialectical method*. The Platonic (1952a, 1952b, 1952c) *Dialogues* document this method, in which Socrates would pose a question for his student, and then defend the point contradicting (i.e., in opposition to) the student's position. If the student chose A, Socrates defended *not-A*; if the student chose *not-A*, Socrates defended A. It was all the same to him, for Socrates did not think of himself as having knowledge uniquely stored in his mind that was not also present in his student's mind.

Socrates believed that every person descended from a Golden Age of gods and hero figures, who naturally knew more and could therefore pass such knowledge on to the lesser, human intellects who followed and made the proper effort. The remarkable implication of this view was that knowledge could be gained through dialectical discourse. Even though they might begin their exchange in error, the participants in a dialectical discourse could come to know its contradiction—truth—because all meanings were united through oppositionality. Knowledge was all of a piece, so it did not matter where the investigation began. As I noted in Chapter 3, the principle underlying this theory of knowledge was termed *one and many* or *many in one.*

Because Plato recorded these dialectical exchanges in writing—Socrates would never have done this!—it sometimes appears to a reader that Socrates is cleverly and subtly directing the conversation to a predetermined end. It is as if the dialogue followed a prearranged script. But this was precisely what Socrates was trying to avoid. His intention was to keep the conversation open, free to move in *any* direction imaginable, depending only on what would emerge in the free exchange of ideas. If a person employed dialectical questioning techniques in order to direct a conversation to some predetermined end, Socrates would have considered this an act of *sophistry* (i.e., insincere, often specious, but a deceptively manipulative line of discourse).

The spirit of dialectical discourse in the Socratic sense is ever-open to spontaneous alternatives and possibilities. Anything suggested in the exchange is to be given legitimate consideration, although a critical analysis to follow might establish its error, irrelevancy, and so forth. Actually, final answers are not always forthcoming in these exchanges. The real aim of Socrates was to get his students to think for themselves—to be critical, exact, and tenacious in pursuing any point under consideration. Such independence of thought could lead to questioning traditional beliefs and practices. Socrates was tried and convicted on such a charge of supposedly corrupting the minds of the young men of Athens. He accepted the sentence of death rather than escape, as he could readily have done.

In a true sense, the dialectical method is very creative, a way of formulating alternative ideas even though the meanings involved are not always completed or objectively certain. We might think of this as one mode of thought that we human reasoners can assume—looking at things from "this way or that," framing a position or continually keeping the alternatives open as possibilities for consideration. Aristotle had difficulty accepting dialectics as a suitable organon. Thus, when it came to what we now call science, he shifted emphasis from the speculative framing of knowledge to the extraction of knowledge in already framed ideas or, as he called them, premises. Aristotle introduced the syllogism, which I used in Chapter 2 to elaborate on certain LLT constructs. The major premise of a syllogism can be pictured very much like the Euler circles of Figure 2, depicting that "John is reliable." The traditional major premise used in examples of the syllogism is "All humans are mortal." In this case, "humans" would represent the darkened circle of Figure 2, framed by the larger circle of "mortality" or some such. The traditional minor premise would be "This is a human" and then the conclusion is reached: "This human is mortal." Aristotle drew a distinction in the way that we human reasoners arrive at our premises—especially our major premise, which frames meanings at the outset of a line of thought:

> Now reasoning is an argument in which, certain things being laid down [i.e., precedently], something other than these necessarily comes about [i.e., sequaciously] through them. (a) It is a "demonstration," when the premisses from which the reasoning starts are true and primary, or are such that our knowledge of them has originally come through premisses which are primary and true: (b) reasoning, on the other hand, is "dialectical," if it reasons from opinions that are generally accepted. (Aristotle, 1952f, p. 143)

By "generally accepted" opinions, Aristotle was referring to the fact that Socrates often sought knowledge in discourse with some individual who held a communal bias or opinion rather than the truth. It was inevitable that opinions would sneak into the discourse because of the very style of dialectical reasoning. Thus, whereas demonstrative premises framed one and only one of two contradictories—X is the case (and therefore *not-X* is not the case)—dialectical premises, said Aristotle, always depend on the adversary's choice between the two contradictories: "Which do you take to be the case, X or not-X? You say X? Fine, let us proceed; I will defend not-X"; but, just as likely, "You say not-X? Fine, let us proceed; I will defend X." Dialecticians were therefore not dealing with known, firm realities, but only with rhetorical considerations like attitudes, biases, preferences, and the like, either side of which they were prepared to support (Aristotle, 1952h, p. 573)

But this is still a worthy endeavor, for by dialectical examination we help clarify arguments that move knowledge along. Sophists may obfuscate and manipulate the direction of discourse through improper use of dialectic, but this is a moral issue having nothing to do with dialectical reasoning per se (Aristotle, 1952g, p. 595). Problems can arise, however, if the dialectician forgets that this mode of reasoning is not iron-clad as to truth value. Some dialecticians do not even care about checking their opinions with sensory experience where they can be put to empirical test:

> Lack of experience diminishes our power of taking a comprehensive view of the admitted facts. Hence those who dwell in intimate association with nature and its phenomena grow more and more able to formulate, as the foundations of their theories, principles such as to admit of a wide and coherent development: while those whom devotion to abstract discussions has rendered unobservant of the facts are too ready to dogmatize on the basis of a few observations. (Aristotle, 1952c, p. 411)

So, if we rely exclusively on opinion as we develop a line of belief, there is surely a possibility if not a certainty that we will be filling our account with considerable error. According to Aristotle's theory of knowledge, and in contradiction to Socrates, if one begins in error one cannot find truth. Only error can flow from error, in precedent-sequacious fashion. So it is essential on the Aristotelian view that any body of knowledge professing to be scientific frame its original premises in a *primary and true* fashion. Aristotle is considered the father of biology because he began the practice of studying organic life empirically and systematically. This act of publicly doing something in which others can participate (e.g., empirical study of living organisms) provided a groundwork for the various sciences and permitted them to exchange ideas in an objective manner. The Aristotelian innovation here was understood as moving from speculative opinion to observable certainty. In contrast to the one-and-many principle of dialectical reasoning, demonstrative reasoning is founded on the *principle of contradiction* (sometimes called the "law" of contradiction):

> It is impossible that contrary attributes should belong at the same time to the same subject . . . . and if an opinion which contradicts another is contrary to it, obviously it is impossible for the same man at the same time to believe the same thing to be and not to be . . . . we have

now posited that it is impossible for anything at the same time to be and not to be, and by this means have shown that this is the most indisputable of all principles. (Aristotle, 1952b, pp. 524–525)

Unlike dialectical reasoning, where alternatives are welcomed, in the demonstrative mode clarity and singularity are called for. A primary and true premise comes down to either some form of tautology (e.g., "All bachelors are unmarried individuals") or an empirically proven finding (e.g., "Silver is heavier than copper"). If we begin our line of reasoning from such premises we are likely to find truth. Truth is extracted from other truths, proven circumstances, extensions from the certainty of a clear definition, and so on. We should keep in mind that Aristotle was not classifying people as *either* dialectical *or* demonstrative reasoners. He believed that everyone reasoned *both* ways. Reasoning flows from affirmed meanings to other meanings and arrives in due course at a conclusion (an end, the telos, etc.). The way in which we initiate meanings in a line of thought —as framed by our major premises—determines whether we are reasoning in a dialectical or a demonstrative manner.

If we back off from the strictly philosophical implications of the Aristotelian analysis, I think it is fair to say that the LLT interpretation of consciousness can be seen to be depicted here. Demonstrative reasoning tends to the unipolar for it is not concerned with possible implications outside of the framing Euler circle of Figure 2. The person reasoning demonstratively asserts what is most certainly the case, and does not believe that there is a mere opinion guiding the meaning-extension. We might wish to challenge this conviction but the mind set of the person reasoning demonstratively is "this and only this is correct," and the line of reasoning (induction, deduction, etc.) proceeds accordingly. In contrast, the mind set of a person reasoning dialectically is transpredicational. To know the "pro" position of an attitudinal dimension is to know the "con" position, and vice versa. As already demonstrated in the Socratic strategy, the person can often argue either position equally well, even violating the law of contradiction by agreeing or disagreeing with *both* positions.

A question frequently asked at this point relates to the matter of habitual styles in reasoning. Would it be possible for any one individual to reason predominantly—or even totally—in either a dialectical or a demonstrative manner? Can the person as a sort of personality style develop in one or the other of these contrasting directions? There is nothing in the principles of LLT to deny this possibility. The only point to be made here is that even if a person might be seen reasoning predominantly in a dialectical or a demonstrative fashion, this does not mean that the contrasting manner of reasoning has been totally eclipsed or lost for all time. I have never observed a person reasoning totally (i.e., 100%) in either of these two directions for any length of time. It is quite another matter if we consider the "reasoning" manifested by a computer processing information.

It is generally acknowledged that computer processing relies fundamentally on Boolean algebra (Crevier, 1993, pp. 15–18; Gardner, 1985, p. 143). But what is not widely appreciated is that George Boole (1815–1864) framed his analysis entirely in terms of demonstrative reasoning. Boole (1854/1958) set out to further a "science of the mind" (p. 3) by showing that the laws of the "science of Algebra" (p. 6) are in agreement with the laws of logical reasoning. Boole claimed that his treatise applies to the "trains of propositions constituting the premises of demonstrative arguments" (p. 12). Now, a mathematician might use the phrase "demonstrative argument" without suggesting that he or she is opposing a dialectical argument. But there is a sense in which this is not true of Boole, whose genius extended to a mastery of Aristotelian philosophy, which he studied (and cited) in the original Greek. Furthermore, the closing chapter of his masterpiece—from which I am taking my analysis—offers convincing evidence that Boole was totally aware of the dialectical as well as the demonstrative mode of reasoning that we are now considering.

As the principle of contradiction is at the core of demonstrative reasoning, it would help my argument if we could find Boole establishing his approach on this principle. And so we can. Boole began by distinguishing a *Nothing* class from a *Universe* class, symbolized by the numbers 0 and 1 respectively. He selected this binary strategy for several reasons, one of which was his belief that

> Nothing and Universe are the two limits of class extension, for they are the limits of the possible interpretations of general names, none of which can relate to fewer individuals than are comprised in Nothing, or to more than are comprised in the Universe. (p. 47)

Another reason for the 1 and 0 division is that these are the only two numerical values that can be subjected to a basic law of Logic "whose expression is $x^2 = x$" (p. 47) or vice versa: $x = x^2$. Boole began his proof of the principle of contradiction from this base. Boole next stated that if x represents any class of objects, $1 - x$ will represent all those objects that are not comprehended in the class x. The "$1 - x$ class" is termed the complement (Edwards, 1967, p. 346). Boole (1854/1958) then went on to present an argument or proof for the principle of contradiction, on which his entire logico-algebraic approach rests—calling it "*the fundamental law of thought*" (p. 49; italics in original).

Relying on the algebraic laws of combination and transposition, Boole then followed a line of transformation to show that his basic law of Logic (*1*) encompasses the principle of contradiction, as expressed by equation 3:

1. $x = x^2$ Transforming formula *1* to
2. $x - x^2 = 0$ Transforming formula *2* to
3. $x(1 - x) = 0$.

To concretize this demonstration we must assign meaning to the symbols by quoting directly from Boole: "give to the symbol *x* the particular interpretation of *men*," and "then $1 - x$ will represent the class of 'not men'" (p. 49; italics in original). Hence, equation 3 combines (i.e., multiplies together rather than adds) two classes: the class whose members are at once *men* (*x*) and *not men* $(1 - x)$. But the outcome, as we can plainly see in the zero value resulting from this combination, is that no such combination exists. Boole therefore concluded that this equation (3) is the algebraic equivalent of the principle of contradiction: "*that a class whose members are at the same time men and not men does not exist. In other words, that it is impossible for the same individual to be at the same time a man and not a man*" (p. 49; italics in original). Equation 3 is also referred to as the "law of duality" (p. 51).

Boole (1854/1958) emphasized that both Aristotle (p. 49) and Leibnitz (p. 240) considered the principle of contradiction to be a fundamental axiom in philosophy and logic. He heartily agreed with this view (p. 240). The law of duality (equation 3) is what I have referred to in some of my previous writings as a Boolean *hard disjunction* (e.g., Rychlak, 1991, 1994). Reese (1980, p. 64) concurred that Boole did posit a hard disjunction (i.e., either *x* or *y* but not both), but that the subsequent development of Boolean algebra employed a soft disjunction as well (i.e., either *x* or *y* or both).

Oppositionality is a difficult concept for Boolean algebra because the opposite of *x* is placed in the complement $(1 - x)$. Yet, as the "many in one" principle of dialectical reasoning suggests, there seems to be something very special about opposite meanings. They have a dimensional relationship so that we cannot simply toss them into the complement as if they were totally other than their opposite meaning (see Rychlak, 1994, pp. 23–24). Knowing one end of the oppositional dimension demands that the other end be known as well. For example, consider Boole's distinction between the Universe and Nothing classes. To understand "everything" (Universe) we must ultimately understand "nothing" (and vice versa). These terms are *many* (i.e., two) sharing *one* dimension of meaning.

Did Boole recognize some such dialectical ramification in human thinking? He most certainly did: As I noted above, in the last chapter of his treatise he provided us with clear evidence that he was sensitive to the demonstrative versus dialectical modes of thought. To set the stage for this distinction, Boole (1854/1958) cautioned that the "mathematical laws of reasoning are, properly speaking, the laws of *right* reasoning only, and their actual transgression is a perpetually recurring phenomenon" (p. 408; italics in original). I think this admission is important because it acknowledges that just because a person is reasoning demonstratively under the phenomenal assumption that her or his premises are primary and true does not actually make them so. Secondly, and more important for present purposes, this recognition of a realm of *right* reasoning implies that there is another realm to consider—that of *wrong* reasoning—if we hope to capture the full range of human thought. Here Boole turned to examples of such wrong reasoning by drawing on what can only be the dialectical tradition in philosophy (see Rychlak, 1981, chapter IX). He even gave this dialectical mode of thought equal status with the demonstrative mode:

> In equally intimate alliance with that law of thought which is expressed by an equation of the second degree, and which has been termed in this treatise the law of duality [i.e., equation (3)], stands the tendency of ancient thought to those forms of philosophical speculation which are known under the name of dualism [i.e., dialectic]. (Boole, 1854/1958, p. 412)

In giving examples of such philosophical speculation Boole cited Empedocles' opposing principles of strife and friendship; the antitheses of Pythagoras such as rest and motion, left and right, good and evil; the Platonic contrast of being and non-being; and the distinction of ego and non-ego advanced by Hegel (pp. 412–425). I put "dialectic" in brackets in the above quote because obviously, these theoretical formulations are not simply dual—pairing different meanings of any sort, like *happy* and *dominant*. In every case cited the duality is oppositional. That is, one member of each pairing (e.g., *good*) delimits its opposite number (i.e., *bad*), so that it is literally impossible to completely divorce the intrinsic meaning (one) from its parts (many). The law of duality qua principle of contradiction does not hold here.

Boole was willing to speculate on the role played by the two types of duality under consideration, whether the resulting pairings are a true reflection of reality or not. He suggested that there may be a "connexion between the two systems" (p. 417), the one resting upon the law of duality and the other on what I now term a dialectical oppositionality. He even hinted that possibly it was because of the central importance of the law of duality in the first place that such dialectical theories arose (p. 417). In any case, he ended his discourse with a balanced assessment of human thought, in which he stressed that although mathematics must be included in any consideration of how human knowledge is created, there are other factors to be taken into consideration as well:

> If the mind, in its capacity of formal reasoning, obeys, whether consciously or unconsciouly, mathematical laws, it claims through its other capacities of sentiment and action, through its perceptions of beauty and of moral fitness, through its deep springs of emotion and affection, to hold relation to a different order of things. (p. 423)

This brings us to the point of this section: What can we say about a computer's thinking and consciousness assuming that it were not merely simulating the *Logos* functioning of a human being but actually reproducing it? Put another way, if there were a homunculus somewhere in the bowels of the computer, what sort of humanoid reasoning would it be carrying out? I think it is clear from our analysis of Aristotle and Boole that the computer homunculus would be an *exclusively* demonstrative reasoner. This homunculus would not *ever* be capable of dialectical reasoning. Why do I say this? There are two essential features of demonstrative reasoning: (a) A strict bifurcation between any dualities framed in reasoning—as representing one meaning but not another at the same time (i.e., the principle of contradiction); and (b) a certainty that any conception affirmed in thought is not open to contradiction because of its "one-for-one" copying or matching of reality. As we have already noted, this conviction about the "facts" sent inward (input) need not be objectively true. But for the homunculus there is no doubting such input.

A machine homunculus reasoning in this manner would clearly be in the demonstrative mode. And, thanks to its inability to generate alternatives by way of oppositionality, it would be psychically unconscious. Minsky's (1986) agents who work busily along, carrying out their jobs oblivious to their fellow agents in the society of mind, can do so because they are always in the demonstrative mode. Agents take their inputs literally, constitutionally unable to reason from what "is" under processing to what "is not" but "might be" under processing. To reason in the latter, dialectical mode, the agents would have to violate the principle of contradiction.

Hofstadter's (1980) strange loops are "strange" because they are feedback loops that violate this principle—as when a figure in an Escher painting walks continually up flights of stairs only to return to the point of departure. How can this person be going "up" and "down" at the same time? This is impossible on demonstrative assumptions. It is the same for "jumping" outside of the system. Hofstadter wants to get his homunculus "out" because how can it be both inside and outside at the same time? The mechanistic model lacks the dialectical capacity to reason according to what "is" under predication and, at the same time, what "is not" under predication. Hofstadter must find a way to get his homunculus completely outside of the system so that it can gain extraspectively framed information not obtainable from the inside. Dialectical reasoning allows for such transcendent self-examination without having to leave the system—because the very nature of this system is different, allowing for transpredicational analysis of ongoing reasoning.

Dennett (1984, 1991) deals with reflexivity as if it were merely recursive repetition in which second-order ideas are thinking about first-order ideas. The cognitive stance here continues to be extraspective for at neither level is it possible for an idea to generate its opposite meaning. Self-identity occurs thanks to the shaping influences of the social environment, which are input as primary and true directives. Even the virtual machine—which represents consciousness—is subject to such shapings over a life span. Dennett makes reference to emergents in the evolution of mind, but one thing that does not emerge in his formulation is a dialectical reasoning capacity to parallel demonstrative reasoning. The need to remain in the *Bios* and *Physikos*, where mechanisms make great sense, seems to prevent theorists like Dennett or Edelman (1987, 1992) from postulating an emergent *Logos* capacity in human reason that could enable the person to oppose and even violate the law of contradiction "at will." One could argue that this capacity to find alternatives in events has evolutionary viability. Wisely used, it enables creative leaps and bounds to be made in the natural selection process—a "survival of the most flexible reasoner," shall we say.

It is difficult to pinpoint the actual source of reasoning in a computer today, thanks to a shift in emphasis from hardware to software in many quarters of AI. Recall that it was McCulloch and Pitts (1943) who mapped the machine's binary (or Boolean) logic onto the structure of the nervous system. This mapping encouraged AI advocates to parallel the hardware process with brain physiology. Because the brain is a material substance that presumably thinks, the original analogy to the computer had it that the hardware actually carried on the thinking, albeit under the mediating influence of the software instruction. The brain too has its mediating influences, known as ideas, somehow imprinted in its substance or carried by its electrical circuitry.

This scenario is not so clear at the present time. Thinking is now being tied more directly to the software than the hardware, as epitomized in Dennett's use of the virtual machine to explain consciousness. Minsky has suggested that today's machines "could be as smart as a person if we knew how to program them" (Crevier, 1993, p. 310). There are those in AI who believe that the software so influences the hardware that "the hardware, together with the program loaded into its memory, has become a new machine, one whose behaviour is specified more by the software than by the naked circuitry" (Hayes, Ford, & Adams-Webber, 1992, p. 251). Indeed, modern developments in computer design have raised questions about whether it is possible to actually distinguish hardware from software, leading to new terms like "firmware" (p. 251).

This brings up the matter of precisely where the principle of contradiction is functioning in the computer's ongoing demonstrative reasoning —at the level of the hardware, software, or both? I think every indication is that it is functioning in *both* spheres of computer processing. Shannon's (1938) original insight concerning the on–off switching of information in hardware processing unquestionably encompasses the principle of contradiction. Of course, we must keep in mind that such "information" processing in the hardware has nothing to do with meaning. Meaning turns our attention to the software. But here too, the binary drafting of such programs is also reflective of the principle of contradiction, where even meanings are presumed to obey Boole's law of duality. A typical statement of this presumption is as follows: "All the information that reaches us through our senses can be broken down into little pieces [i.e., bits] of 'yes' and 'no'" (Crevier, 1993, p. 281). Finally, the demonstratively reasoning executive program—even if it "writes" further programs, or "learns" its current program—always "assumes" its initiating executive instructions (or inputs) to be primary and true. It cannot transpredicate to put these executive instructions or imprintings into question. It is locked unconsciously into the course of its singular reasoning style.

CONCLUDING COMMENT

If we pretend that the computer is reasoning, or that some homunculus lurking within its machinery is reasoning, the form that this cognition takes is 100% demonstrative, obeying at every turn the principle of contradiction (or, Boole's law of duality). By limiting its predicational range through the halving of information via bits—including, for the sake of argument, the "meaning" of such information—the computer is also reasoning unconsciously. Computers are designed to avoid the use of potentially confounding transpredications. The resultant unconsciousness is what we have been calling a "good" form because it very accurately furthers the line of "reasoning" being propounded in the mechanical sequence. This is akin to what we called in Chapter 4 a proactive form of unconsciousness. But consciousness is anathema to the computer. Thus, not only are Minsky's agents ignorant of each other, but Dennett's Cartesian theater does not exist to pull all (presumed) meanings into a synthesizing totality (the one among many)—particularly those meanings that are intrinsically opposite to each other. Computer logic does not deal in such dialectical unities as "*both* on–off, true–false, or yes–no."

The question naturally arises as to whether it is possible to build a computer that reasons dialectically. Logical learning theory does *not* reject or ridicule this possibility, but merely points out that computers as currently conceived are not of this dialectical nature. On this very question, Crevier (1993) discusses the remarkable program written by Douglas Lenat entitled Automated Mathematician (AM), which was designed to "learn" through discovery. This program made use of frames and was instructed, among other things, to look for inversions in certain data. Although highly creative initially, in time AM was described as going "off the deep end into strange investigations about numbers that would be at the same time odd and even" (p. 180). Could it be that in so violating the principle of contradiction by reversing odd–even from "different" to "same" this program stumbled into reasoning dialectically even as it relied on demonstrative processing at the hardware level? No, I don't think so. But I would accept that it had accidentally *simulated* dialectical reasoning.

The capacity to think "off the deep end" is typical of human beings, who move from such strange transpredications as uniting the non-unitable to a creative innovation drawn from the depths of such unthinkable impossibilities. The trick is to have both dialectical (generative) and demonstrative (evaluative) capacities involved so that when strange notions pop into mind they can be rationally judged, refined, and then put to proper empirical test. We come back again to the grounds on which we are to explain thought. In LLT it is assumed that a *Logos* ground is being used, and that the process underlying the resultant *psychic* consciousness is predication. Could it be that the AI enthusiast is mixing *Physikos* and *Logos* grounds instead of seeing their complementary roles in the working of a computer?

We could readily describe a program writer as framing things predicationally (*Logos*), drafting then a series of precedent directions that are carried out not sequaciously—because meaning is not involved—but instrumentally by the machine (*Physikos*). The machine is mediating its inputs as information, but the pattern of binary firing that then directs the course of this processing has been created externally (as is true of all mediational processes). This external pattern has been created by an intelligence that reasons not only instrumentally but self-reflexively as well, setting alternatives in action that can end in silliness or creativity depending on the soundness of the initiating predications (i.e., whether the computer can make assumptions, hunches, guesses, etc.).

It is this latter capacity to reason free of unidirectional influence at every turn that we want to capture in LLT. People are not machines and we do human nature an injustice to assert that this is all they are. There is a marvelously creative, eccentric, eternally unusual side to people that should never be dismissed as mere hoax or an error term to be explained away in due course.

8

ALTERED STATES OF CONSCIOUSNESS

I would like to consider some intriguing topics that attract those who are interested in the nature of mind: *hypnosis, lucid dreaming, channeling,* and *meditation.* These are usually discussed under the general rubric of *altered states of consciousness.* Experts have vigorously debated each of these topics concerning what is occurring (if anything), the grounds on which to explain things, and the extent of possible self- or interpersonal deception taking place. I can hardly presume to offer a final explanation of such remarkable phenomena in this brief survey. However, we can surely judge how well an LLT analysis adapts to the essentials of these phenomena, and in this effort hopefully gain additional insights concerning psychic consciousness. We will also consider some typical academic research done on unconscious behavior with an eye to assessing the level of insight or intelligence that may be reflected therein.

Ludwig (1966) defined an altered state as any mental phenomenon that is recognized as "representing a sufficient deviation in subjective experience . . . from certain general norms . . . during alert, waking consciousness" (p. 225). This is a very broad definition, of course, but it does stress that a *significant* change in personal experience must occur for it to be considered an altered state. Such changes can be induced through either arousal or perceptual deprivation. Sometimes the attention level seems influenced in both directions at once. For example, experimental participants who are easily hypnotized have been found to have large amounts of brain (i.e., *theta*) waves that are typical of people both in a drowsy, hypnagogic state and also in an intensively attentive state (Schacter, 1977). Dittrich, von Arx, and Staub (1981) surveyed a number of participants in various types of altered-states experiments. Example participant comments found for typical altered states of consciousness were as follows:

1. *Thought Disruptions*: "I couldn't complete a thought." "My ideas became disconnected."
2. *Time Changes*: "I sensed past, present, and future as the same thing—a oneness."
3. *Loss of Control*: "It felt as though I no longer had a will of my own."
4. *Emotional Intensity*: "I had this real scared feeling but couldn't say what was scaring me."
5. *Body-Image Effects*: "It seemed as though I no longer had a body."
6. *Visual Distortions*: "I saw strange images and illusions." "It was like looking at a movie with these mixed-up scenes rolling by."
7. *Meaning Shifts*: "Everything took on a different, strange meaning for me."

HYPNOSIS

The first topic we cover in altered states of consciousness is hypnosis, an ancient phenomenon that still eludes complete understanding. In this section, we first explore the two major schools of thought concerning the nature of this phenomenon to see how well our predicational model stands up in this mix of views. We then extend our analysis to the fascinating manifestations to be found in the hypnotic realm known as the hidden observer and trance logic. Once again, our guiding theory of consciousness will be called on to subsume these seemingly mystifying aspects of the human psyche.

Two Historical Schools of Thought

Although hypnotic phenomena like demonic possessions, speaking in tongues, or laying on of hands, are as old as human history, the modern examination of hypnotism dates from claims made by the Austrian healer, Franz Anton Mesmer (1734–1815). Mesmer believed that he transmitted an *animal magnetism* from his body to his patients, who, while in a light trance state were "cured" of such maladies as chronic headache or backache as well as various emotional upsets. The ultimate source of this magnetism Mesmer took to be the stars, which somehow used his body as a mediating influence on the patients. Mesmer was eventually proven a charlatan, although practitioners retained his technique of inducing trances and termed it *mesmerism*. Several years later, a well-known Scottish physician named James Braid (1795–1860) replaced mesmerism with the term we now use: *hypnotism* (from the Greek *hypnos*, meaning "sleep"; Boring, 1950, pp. 124–128).

Braid found in his study of the hypnotic phenomenon that he could induce sleep by having the patients fix their stare at a bright, inanimate object (e.g., the notorious pocketwatch). He believed this fixation induced some kind of impression on the nervous centers of the body, but that there was no such thing as an animal magnetism involved. That is, anything physical taking place was entirely within the patient's biological processes and had nothing to do with the hypnotist's body (as Mesmer claimed). Hypnotism was a form of nervous sleep initiated by paralyzing the levator muscles of the eyelids during the visual fixation. However, as Boring (1950, p. 127) has noted, it is a short step from "visual fixation" to the "fixation of attention." A concept like *attention* is more mental than physical, and it is therefore not surprising that Braid began using the word *monoideasm* (i.e., the state or condition of devotion to one idea or thought) to characterize the hypnotic state.

Braid appreciated that the single idea that captured the hypnotized person's attention was always suggested by another person—namely, the hypnotist (Boring, 1950, p. 128)—who encouraged entrance into the trance state in the first place. Before long, "extremely suggestible" and "hypnosis prone" became synonymous. As for *suggestion*, it has been defined as a verbal or nonverbal communication from one person to another, with the aim of bringing about some variation in the ordinary behavior of the receiver of this communication (Weitzenhoffer, 1957, p. 25).

Nothing could be more symbolic of what was to take place in the field of hypnosis than the shift from visual fixation as a biological state to fixed attention as a psychological state. This difference underwrites conflicts in the explanation of hypnosis that have carried over to the present. The first manifestation of this difference took place when Pierre Janet and Jean Charcot (see Chapter 4) confronted Ambrose-August Liebeault (1823–1904) and Hippolyte-Marie Bernheim (1840–1919; Alexander & Selesnick, 1966, p. 172). Charcot and Janet practiced medicine at the acclaimed Salpêtrière hospital in Paris. Liebeault and Bernheim practiced at their less prestigious clinic in Nancy. The Parisians, influenced chiefly by Charcot, contended that hypnotizability was produced by some kind of as yet undetermined organic weakness of the nervous system—the same weakness that produced the abnormal condition known as hysteria. Extreme suggestibility was therefore seen as due to the underlying biological weakness of a hysteroid constitution. As we noted in Chapter 4, Janet vacillated on this issue but in the main supported his mentor's position.

Liebeault and Bernheim rejected this physicalistic interpretation of hypnosis in favor of a psychological explanation. They argued that almost anyone could be hypnotized as long as the person took on the mental attitude of cooperation with the hypnotist. At the Nancy clinic hundreds of patients were being helped each year with the sorts of problems that Mesmer had successfully dealt with a century earlier. History has proven Liebeault and Bernheim to be correct, of course; people who are not prone to hysteria can still be hypnotized. But, this does not mean that the core issue dividing Nancy from the Salpêtrière has been resolved. Indeed, one can easily demonstrate that the same fundamental theoretical differences remain.

Today, these differences underwrite what many experts consider to be the two major current schools of thought on the nature of hypnotism (e.g., see Farthing, 1992, p. 336). The older, traditional school holds that the altered state of consciousness is something actually taking place in the biophysical functioning of the human organism. Sometimes practitioners say this is due to an inborn *trait* that causes material changes in the physical functioning of the person when a trance state is induced. In recent decades, a contrasting school of thought has arisen contending that hypnotic phenomena are sociopsychological in nature and occur without the necessity of biological changes taking place in the hypnotized individual.

Hilgard (1992) is of the older tradition, referring to his approach as a form of *neodissociationism* in the style of Janet (1929/1965). Recall that the dissociation occurs if a fixed idea has split off from influence by the rest of the mind (see Chapter 4). Hilgard defines dissociation as "the splitting off of certain mental processes from the main body of consciousness with various degrees of autonomy" (1992, p. 69). He draws heavily on the modern cognitive conceptions that we surveyed in Chapter 7, such as input, output, information processing, and so on. Fundamental to neodissociationism is the assumption that information processing systems have the capacity for subsystems to function independently of each other (in the style of Minsky's agents; see Chapter 7).

The independently functioning subsystems are not totally lacking in organized direction, for Hilgard postulates a central control structure that he calls the "executive ego" (see Hilgard, 1973, p. 405; 1992, p. 92). This dominant control system can transfer some of its executive power over the subordinate systems to the hypnotist: "The central executive function now divides itself into two parts, representing the role of hypnotist and hypnotized" (Hilgard, 1992, p. 94). In fact, the executive can be split (dissociated) in this fashion without a hypnotist present. Empirical evidence has established that such self-hypnosis is possible, even if the person concerned has never been previously hypnotized (Ruch, 1975).

Hilgard is theorizing in the style of Charcot because he believes there is something going on inside the organic processes of the individual who is placed in a hypnotic trance. He postulated that this stems not from a weakness in the nervous system, but rather from some trait-like capacity to dissociate: As noted repeatedly by experts, not everyone can be hypnotized and even those who can enter the trance state vary in the "depth" of suggestibility to which they succumb (Woody, Bowers, & Oakman, 1992, p. 24). Trance states are always a matter of degree, and people can even record (via ratings) just how deeply they are experiencing a state of hypnosis (Farthing, 1992, p. 351).

It is this sort of self-knowledge that invites the other theory of hypnotism to take the field. Drawing on the early writings of Sarbin (1950; Sarbin & Coe, 1972) and Barber (1969), a spirited tradition of explanation has arisen that casts the hypnotic relationship in the same way that all social relations are believed to be formed and carried out. On this view, hypnosis is merely a *social interaction* in which one person responds to suggestions made by another concerning changes in perception, memory, and experience (Kihlstrom, 1985). Hypnotized persons enact roles, and those who are effective in *role taking* (Sarbin, 1950) are called "good" prospects for hypnotism, whereas poor enactors are called "bad" prospects. Hypnotic acts rely on intentional compliance (Wagstaff, 1981), and we can assess such willingness through brief pretests like suggesting that a person is gently swaying and then observing whether such motions actually begin taking place. The more readily the person accedes to such suggestions the better prospect she or he is for the full-blown trance state. Hypnotic behavior stems from the fact that

> People are continually involved in organizing sensory information into schemas or categories that can be used to guide actions. From this perspective, people use their implicit understandings to negotiate social situations. . . . From a socio-psychological perspective the term "hypnosis" does not refer to a state or condition of the person. Instead, it refers to the manner in which the historically rooted conceptions of hypnotic responding that are held by the participants in the context labeled "hypnosis" express themselves in reciprocal interaction. (Spanos & Coe, 1992, pp. 108–109)

I do not want to give the impression that the field of hypnosis breaks down into two completely opposed camps—the *state* versus the *sociopsychological* viewpoints. According to Kirsch and Lynn (1995), there is considerable overlap today so that although we do not yet have 100% agreement on the explanation of hypnosis, the "notion of warring camps is now outdated" (p. 847). Indeed, today "most hypnosis researchers agree that the impressive effects of hypnosis stem from social influence and personal abilities, not from a trancelike state of altered consciousness" (p. 849).

Turning to an analysis founded on LLT precepts, I think it is fair to say that from Braid's monoideasm through the debates of the French and down to the current views on hypnotism, we can see definite implications for predicational theorizing. In his discussion of the ancient oracles (see Chapter 5), Jaynes cited the "narrowing of consciousness" that took place in their self-induced trance states (1976, p. 386). Hilgard's neodissociation views repeat the fixed idea conception of Janet, which we have thoroughly discussed in Chapter 4. All such views are consistent with unipredication. The social-psychological position has it that people have learned how a hypnotized subject is "supposed" to behave, and therefore when agreeing to serve as a participant in such activity they willingly carry out these learned schemata to create a social interaction known as hypnotism. This formulation is also consistent with LLT (see Chapter 2), because schemata may readily serve as predications brought to bear intentionally to establish contexts of meaning and to fulfill the resultant expectations. Of course, we can also view schemata as mediators that have been input rather than as predications that have been affirmed.

In carrying out the social interaction known as hypnotism, a participant may pretend to be in a deeper trance than he or she is actually experiencing. There is an element of intentional pretense in all of this. Nonhypnotized controls have been shown to fake the hypnotic trance perfectly (Barber, Spanos, & Chaves, 1974), and many hypnotized individuals will admit in follow-up interviews that they really did not experience the suggestions made to them as strongly as they appeared to do while in their trance states (Spanos, 1986). According to LLT, such variations in performance would reflect the differences along a dimension of unipredication to transpredication.

Varying the "level" of hypnotic depth involves the question of just how completely a unipredication is being focused. A "deep" hypnosis would constitute a quite thorough dismissal of transpredicated alternatives, a commitment to the "primary and true" meaning of the hypnotist's instructions, thereby bringing on demonstrative reasoning (see Chapter 7). People intentionally vary in their willingness to relinquish consciousness in this fashion, which accounts for the individual differences in the "ability" to be hypnotized. Research has shown that only so-called highly hypnotizable people tend to report complete involuntariness in carrying out their hypnotic instructions (Bowers, Laurence, & Hart, 1988). Only those who have become so immersed in the suggested hypnotic role that they have actually "become" that role believe that they are behaving in a completely involuntary fashion (Dixon & Laurence, 1992, p. 29). The less readily hypnotizable individuals frequently recognize their willful contribution to the hypnotic induction (Woody, Bowers, & Oakman, 1992, p. 24).

Some of the coming together of the practitioners in hypnotism may stem from the fact that they all seem to be gravitating to the same theory of cognition, drawing on the typical mediation model. Thus, the critics of state (or trait) theories frequently rely on the computer language of cognitive psychology to say that schemata framing how a hypnotized person is to act are learned in the sociocultural milieu. Some have even begun terming their view a *social-cognitive theory of hypnosis* (e.g., Spanos, 1986). Interestingly, these non-state advocates are seen falling back on the same kind of systems explanation that Hilgard (1992) has used in his neodissociationistic accounts. Hilgard's executive ego could have learned (input) many different schemata in previous social contacts to be used as ongoing mediational aids. In agreeing to share control with the hypnotist, the relevant mediating schemata could be transferred from the executive ego to the hypnotist's influence. The upshot is that there is no longer a basic contradiction between the state and the sociopsychological theorizers to fight over.

Hidden Observers and Trance Logic

I want to take up two aspects of hypnosis whose origins and validity experts have challenged. Once again, I am not going to review the complete evidence or try to find *the* true account. I merely propose to generate ideas on the nature of psychic consciousness and unconsciousness to see how well they are accommodated by LLT. The first phenomenon has been termed the *hidden observer* by Hilgard, who discovered this aspect of hypnosis. Hilgard (1992, pp. 74–75) tells of discovering this dynamic one day when he had hypnotized a blind, male student who was an excellent participant and quite experienced in taking on the trance state. He gave this student the suggestion that, at the count of three, he would become completely deaf to all sounds. He also told the student that his hearing would be restored when the hypnotist placed his hand on the student's right shoulder. Hilgard conducted this hypnosis before a class of students, one of whom raised the question after the trance had been induced as to whether there might not be a part of the blind student's mind that continued to know what was taking place.

Hilgard then gave a further instruction to the blind student, suggesting that "there are parts of our nervous system that carry on activities that occur without awareness" (p. 75), and implying that this might be the case here. He then added, "Although you are hypnotically deaf, perhaps there is some part of you that is hearing my voice and processing the information. If there is, I should like the index finger of your right hand to rise as a sign that this is the case" (p. 75). To his great surprise, the index finger rose and the blind student asked that Hilgard bring him out of the trance state. He wanted to know why he felt his index finger on his right hand rising when he had been thinking about a statistical problem while under hypnosis. It was as if his psyche had dissociated once again, into the part that was hypnotized and another part that stayed in touch with the hypnotist quite independently of the initial instruction (to become deaf).

A typical experiment on hypnotic analgesia and the hidden observer might take place as follows (this experiment is modeled on Hilgard, Morgan, & Macdonald, 1975). At the beginning of this experiment, 20 highly hypnotizable participants immerse their right hand in a container of ice water for varying lengths of time up to 1 minute. This immersion results in a painful stimulation, of course, and the 20 participants are pretested by having them rate the pain they feel in performing this act. The hypnotist then puts them under hypnosis and gives an analgesia suggestion (to feel no pain) before repeating the immersion test a second time. The procedure involves placing the right hand into the ice water, removing it, and pressing a key that records the extent of pain felt. A second instruction asks that at the same time their right hand is recording the pain felt, their left hand record the extent of pain felt by a "hidden" part of their mind. An amnesia suggestion is also given so that participants make the key-pressing estimations outside of conscious awareness. In this experiment, 8 of the 20 participants show the hidden-observer effect, with the left-hand hidden-observer ratings substantially *higher* than the right-hand ratings at all points up to 1 minute. The hidden-observer rating is still slightly lower than the ratings made in the nonhypnotic state. There have been many such experiments conducted, some using other sensory systems (hearing, etc.).

One insight LLT brings to this type of suggestion is the possibility that the so-called hidden observer represents the "other side" of the predication encompassed in the hypnotic instruction. The hypnotized person is intentionally conforming to the predication of the hypnotist; but, this does not mean the "outside" of the predicating Euler circle (see Figures 2 and 3) has been relinquished in every instance. Told "You will feel no pain," some individuals violate the principle of contradiction here to both feel and not feel pain at the same time. Looked at in terms of demonstrative versus dialectical reasoning (see Chapter 7), it appears that the hypnotized person is trying to reason demonstratively. That is, the person willfully affirms the premise "Feel no pain" as "primary and true" when conveyed by the hypnotist.

Farthing (1992, p. 389) reported that on average no more than half of the highly hypnotizable individuals put through such experiments reflect the hidden-observer phenomenon. This would suggest that, just as not everyone can willfully commit to being hypnotized in the first place, not everyone can willfully commit 100% to the complete demonstrative affirmation required by the hypnotist's suggestion. Some people considered good bets for hypnotism are still unable to relinquish the more dialectical implications of reasoning that are open to them. This would be another indication of "depth" in hypnosis, for the person who has assumed demonstrative reasoning completely is by (LLT) definition unconscious—that is, in a totally unipredicational stance at that instant.

The second aspect of hypnotism I would like to consider has been named *trance logic* by its discoverer, Orne (1959). Trance logic is a form of thought that permits two mutually contradictory states of affairs to be represented simultaneously in awareness. In other words, it is a logic in violation of the principle of contradiction. Here is how we would observe trance logic in action. A person, let us call him Ronald, is hypnotized and seated on a chair flanked by two other empty chairs. A confederate of the hypnotist's, call him Joseph, enters and sits on the chair to the right of Ronald. The hypnotist invites Ronald (who is in a hypnotic trance) to open his eyes; he is then introduced to Joseph, with whom he carries on a brief discussion. The hypnotist then tells Ronald to close his eyes once again. At this point the hypnotist asks Joseph to change locations by moving to the chair on Ronald's left. Of course, no such relocation takes place.

The hypnotist then tells Ronald to open his eyes and resume the conversation with Joseph, whom according to what has been overheard is supposedly now seated at his left. He does this, carrying on a discussion with a hallucinated Joseph. After a few minutes Ronald is asked to look to his right and tell what he sees. He immediately says that he sees Joseph, and may do a "double take" by glancing to his left and back to the right. But oddly enough, Ronald is not greatly bothered by this state of affairs. The hypnotist now asks Ronald if he can explain why there are two Josephs. He shrugs, and mumbles something about a magic trick done with mirrors. Ronald is then informed that there is only one "real" Joseph present, and the second is hallucinated; the hypnotist challenges him to identify which Joseph really exists.

Now, according to an LLT analysis, if the hypnotist invites the person in a trance to solve a problem of this sort, the invitation is being made to move from demonstrative to dialectical reasoning. Relying on the former type of reasoning, the person may not yet view the hallucination as a problem. We have already noted that hypnosis narrows psychic consciousness, inducing the unconscious trance through a unipredication and highly literal carrying out of what the hypnotist suggests (commands, etc.). By asking Ronald to explain a contradiction the hypnotist is loosening the "primary and true" ground rule that has been in ascendance to this point. Once again, as with the hidden observer, if various people are asked to settle this matter we witness a range of ability to do so.

A fair number have little difficulty in this resolution because, after some careful looking, they find they can see a chair through a transparent Joseph at the left-hand location. Others find this identification difficult, even if the hypnotist permits them to go over and "touch" each Joseph. The occasional individual reasons that a hallucinated image should obey imagined instructions, and on this basis intends for each Joseph to raise a hand. Only the one on the left does so, and therefore this must be the hallucinated image. Logical learning theory would hold that this latter individual had transpredicated sufficiently to have achieved a level of psychic consciousness even though the initiating hypnotic state of unconsciousness was still active. The parallel here with the hidden observer is obvious.

Of course, before moving on to the next section I should once again point out that there are critics of these phenomena who offer explanations that do not erase the dynamics observed, but simply explain them differently. Thus, Spanos and Hewitt (1980) would say that motivated participants are led by the content of hidden-observer instructions to construe themselves as possessing hidden parts that feel pain differently. In other words, this phenomenon is merely a further extension of the hypnotist's suggestions (in LLT terms, predications). The hypnotized individual construes or makes up a scenario that he or she then enacts just as all such hypnotic relationships are enacted. For example, Spanos, Gwynn, and Stam (1983) presented empirical evidence that highly hypnotizable people rated hidden and overt pain as being of equal magnitude unless they were given explicit instructions informing them that one type of pain was supposed to be more intense than the other. Spanos (1986) has also made similar claims about trance logic being supposedly due to certain idiosyncrasies of hypnotic instructions. Once again, I am not interested in choosing sides here, particularly because LLT can subsume either view with only minor adjustments. Velmans (1991) has carefully reviewed this field and concluded that although controversy has not dissipated, there surely is sufficient evidence to support the validity of phenomena like those considered in the present section (p. 660).

CHANNELING, MULTIPLE PERSONALITY, AND FALSE MEMORIES

Some mental phenomena may be hypnotically induced and then apparently carry on a life of their own. Self-hypnosis is often implicated in these conditions for they can occur in solitary individuals who avoid contact with others. In *channeling*, a person supposedly transmits messages—verbally or in writing—from one or more disembodied "identities" who are communicating from sources outside of his or her personal realm of consciousness (Klimo, 1987, p. 4). In *multiple personality disorders*, apparently two or more identifiable personalities exist within the *same* person's mind, each of whom may become consciously dominant at one time or another (Sutcliffe & Jones, 1963).

Returning to a distinction drawn in Chapter 4, I now suggest that channeling is due to proactive uniprediction and multiple personality to reactive unipredication. The message that is sent through the *channeler* (i.e., the self-hypnotized person) by some "discarnate" identity who supposedly lived thousands of years ago is invariably positive. As the channeler falls into a trance-like state and begins to express the message of this ancient entity, we are in all probability going to hear messages of unity and love, as well as exhortations to help and serve others (Klimo, 1987, p. 215). As discussed in Chapter 4, these unconscious pronouncements are rendered proactively in the ex cathedra fashion so typical of what the person accepts as an absolute truth (as primary and true, "sent" by an all-knowing deity or a wise entity from eons past, etc.). The vocalizing identity—who is not "of" the channeler's identity but of a wider (universal) intelligence that transcends petty individuality—is in the position of virtually *having* to offer something positively unifying (with occasional caveats about possible future missteps along life's way). The generally positive nature of channeling has even led some experts to refer to it as an enabling rather than a disabling phenomenon (p. 231).

If we begin to focus meaning on the individual rather than the universal identity, a more negative unipredication takes place. Entities who express universalistic themes are often brought on through *age regression*: hypnotic regression continued down through life until the hypnotized individual is eventually moved out into a realm of prebirth, presumably connecting thereby with ancient identities or re-enlivening a previously lived personality. Along this regressive path it is not unusual for people to recall verifiable details of their early childhood (studies suggest that few people have recollections before ages three or four: see Howe & Courage, 1993; Kihlstrom & Harackiewicz, 1982). Now, in this case a more negative form of unipredication can take place in which the hypnotized person recalls something personally harmful—like being sexually molested by a family member when he or she was 5 years old, for example. The empirical literature has severely questioned the validity of such memories (Nash, 1987). It now appears that hypnotic efforts to facilitate memory increase the person's confidence in the truth of a memory without affecting its veracity—which often enough is nonexistent (Bowers, 1992). Orne (1979) has shown how a hypnotically induced *false memory* becomes the person's reality and is thereafter extremely difficult to correct.

Why are such memories of a negative variety brought into consciousness as if they were factual when they are not? Or, if they are factual, why are they recalled if they were long forgotten? To answer these questions, we must draw a distinction between forgetting and unipredicating. Once one frames a clear, well-organized predication, a meaning is created in the *Logos* of the individual concerned. It is doubtful that this meaning qua memory is *ever* forgotten. Freud, of course, brought our attention to the timelessness of the unconscious (1920–1921/1955b, p. 28) and the fact that mental concoctions like dream contents are never truly forgotten

(1900/1953, p. 521). In LLT terms, *forgetting* occurs if the individual is unable to frame a well-organized predication for some occurrence or item in experience that has actually been encountered (see Chapter 2). There is no existing content-meaning that can frame the observed experience. In other words, forgetting occurs at the point of initial meaning-creation (formal-cause patterning) if a predication should be framed but for some reason it is not. Forgetting is an act of omission, an unintended outcome. Unconsciousness is an act of commission, an intended outcome that occurs if such a (uni-)predication *is* actually framed, and then in some cases can become severely dissociated from the other meanings of the psyche (see Figure 4). This happens almost always in a reactive rather than a proactive manner.

Let us take as an example the case of childhood sexual abuse. It is entirely possible that some person, as a child, was unable to frame a suitable meaning for such an event as it actually took place in his or her early life. It was so unusual that, although it was visualized while occurring, and bits and pieces of meaning were framed, because the child lacked a psychic content patterning it coherently, the incident was forgotten. I am not now referring to extreme cases of abuse where there may indeed be remembered pain and terror, threats from the offending adult, and so forth. But if an adult is later returned to the abusive situation via hypnotic age regression, a suitable predication is framed as the visualization is enlivened by a now adult psychic organization in which sexual abuse is understood. This results in a memory taking place (Dixon & Laurence, 1992). I am obviously giving the benefit of the doubt here to the person recalling the sexual abuse. To have such late-born memories of forgotten incidents makes sense, particularly because it is a tragic fact that sexual abuse of children is more frequent than we had previously realized (Daro, 1988).

On the other hand, it is also possible that certain innocent displays of affection in the past by a family member or acquaintance (e.g., hugging and patting the child) could be framed from the perspective of adulthood as immoral acts of abuse, then recalled as having actually taken place (Nash, 1987). Affirming a fallacious predication is not all that difficult to accomplish, particularly if a bias exists toward finding such negative circumstances in the first place (Loftus, 1993). Meaning extends from predication to target, and a biasing extension is always possible. Whichever direction we take here, the point of importance is that LLT can aid in the analysis. We do not have to take a position on the validity of childhood abuse claims made by adults who come upon such memories during a hypnotic trance.

Turning to the multiple personality, it is clear now that we are dealing with a particularly threatening form of unipredication and *not* with forgetting. Psychologists have traditionally classified this disorder as one of the hysterias, and so we could reprise the discussion of Chapter 4 relating to

Janet's study of dissociation. The unipredication of this disorder is made plain in the fact that the various personalities possess conflicting (i.e., oppositional) values and behaviors. As in the classic case of *The Three Faces of Eve* (Thigpen & Cleckly, 1954), one personality was diametrically opposed in value orientation to the other. This was resolved in time by the emergence of yet a third personality. As the years slipped by, additional reports of such cases appeared in which many more than three personalities were claimed (e.g., Keyes, 1981; Ludwig, Brandsma, Wilbur, Bendfeldt, & Jameson, 1972; Schreiber, 1974). Allegedly dozens and even hundreds of personalities may exist in the same individual: This is apparently limited only by the range of self-predications that a person is willing to enact as a supposedly "different" personality.

At the turn of the 20th century some fairly common hysterical symptoms were called *tunnel vision* and *glove (or stocking) anesthesia*. In tunnel vision, the person's range of sight was limited, as if he or she were looking through a tube ("tunnel") so the periphery was lost. Glove or stocking anesthesia was a symptom in which the person could not feel anything on the hand or foot although the nerve roots leading from the spine through the arm and leg to the extremity were functioning properly. Feeling in the arm and leg was normal. Only the hand or foot lacked sensation. Thanks to the advance of knowledge about the nervous system, it became clear that such symptoms were biologically impossible. With the dissemination of such knowledge in the culture, tunnel vision and glove or stocking anesthesias diminished until they are quite rare today. It would appear that the sort of predication taken on by hysterical patients in the late 1800s was no longer appropriate over the course of the 20th century. But is it now possible that the reverse is taking place, and hysteria in the form of multiple-personality disorders is on the increase? And could the possible number of personalities to be housed within the same psyche also be rising? By endorsing the view of independent personalities "existing" within a single person's psyche, could it be that we therapists may actually be promoting such role-playing tendencies?

In support of this possibility, I would like to discuss the case of a "budding" multiple personality that I was called in on as consultant many years ago. The client was a 20-year-old woman who was attending college as was her boyfriend. This woman, let us call her Marty, had been reared in a southern rural, devoutly fundamentalist home atmosphere where drinking alcohol, smoking, and above all, premarital sex were considered extremely sinful. Throughout her formative years, Marty had subscribed to this value structure completely. It was therefore a serious problem for her when the boyfriend, let us call him Ted, began urging that their lovemaking culminate in sexual intercourse. Marty was in love with Ted and wanted to comply, but she had what might be considered today an "old-fashioned" but nevertheless serious conflict on her hands.

One night after they had had their by now routine argument over "what to do" and Ted had dropped Marty off at the dormitory, he was awakened in the early morning hours by a telephone call. It was from a woman who spoke to him most salaciously. The voice was throaty and the attitude was cynical. The language was laden with obscenities. But Ted also noted a slight southern accent, and he wondered about who this was and how the woman knew so much about him. The next morning he asked Marty about this incident, but she knew nothing of it. The phone calls continued and so did Marty's denials.

A roommate subsequently reported that she had been awakened when Marty got out of bed in the early morning hours, dressed up in what she described as "slutty" clothes, heaped on lipstick and other cosmetics, produced a pint of whiskey and poured a drink, lit a cigarette, and then dialed Ted from a phone located in the hallway. The roommate was aghast at what she then heard Marty say. Ted immediately contacted my colleague. Over the initial clinical interviews Marty gradually admitted that she sensed a "different person" within her. How else could she explain the clothes, whiskey, and cigarettes in her bureau drawer? At one point my colleague asked that this "other" person "come out" to talk, and when Marty began to squirm a bit as if in preparation to switch personalities, she was quickly discouraged from doing so. At this point I was brought into the case.

After considerable discussion, we decided that although we might now go on to encourage an interesting case of multiple personality to develop here, it would be more appropriate (and ethical) to head off this manifestation. Fortunately, both Ted and Marty proved to be willing therapy clients. We therefore pointed out to them the conflict that Marty faced, and that in dealing with it she felt she had to be "one way or the other" —a moral person or an immoral "slut." She had dissociated in the reactive manner first analyzed by Janet (see Chapter 4). One who is sexually loose is one who drinks, smokes, dresses seductively, and uses indecent language. This is what Ted seemed to want and this is what he was going to get! Doubtless this line of interpretation would be supported by the sociopsychological theory of hypnosis. But what must be clarified here is the fact that this "role" as enacted was unipredicated, not really open to meaningful integration with the rest of Marty's psyche.

Even before therapy was completed, Ted proposed to Marty. They were married shortly thereafter, and our follow-ups over the next few years established that they had no recurrence of the "other" personality. I think we see in this case clear evidence for a predicational model of human behavior that includes the role of oppositionality and affective assessment. Unlike the computing machines of Chapter 7, if there is a serious conflict demanding resolution human beings can behave in a most uncybernetic manner to write programs in direct conflict with their standard programs.

Marty was struggling through such a conflict, and she was about to deny the principle of contradiction underwriting Boolean algebra by becoming two people at once. We offered her a more reasonable alternative, and she affirmed our predication rather than continue on with her own. I do not think we did this through a kind of self-hypnotic suggestion, for our interpretation was not offered demonstratively. She was given every opportunity in the many therapy sessions to consider our interpretation from several angles—to transpredicate and then arrive at a position knowing that it could be otherwise. In short, she achieved insight or learned consciously and behaved in all respects teleologically (for the application of LLT principles to psychotherapy, see Rychlak, 1982).

LUCID DREAMING

Dreaming has been a source of fascination and mystery since the dawn of humanity. The ordinary dream occurs as a kind of hallucination during sleep where we relinquish control of our thoughts and scenarios develop that capture our interest in both positive and negative directions. Dreaming has been defined as "thinking in pictures," but dream-thoughts do not always conjure up pictorial imagery. Scientists have conducted considerable research on the physical correlates of the dream state. Two primary measures have been used: (a) electro-encephalogram (EEG) brain waves and (b) rapid eye movement (REM) or its lack (NREM). Both of these measures rely on electrodes that are pasted on the scalp (EEG) or the area around the eyes (REM); these electrodes then record slight electrical potentials from the brain and nervous tissues. *Beta* brain waves, which measure 13 or more cycles per second, occur when we are awake and focusing attention in active thought. Sleep begins in a relaxed wakefulness stage wherein the *Alpha* brain wave predominates; this is a lowered wave of from 8 to 12 cycles per second. Most people produce *Alpha* rhythms by simply closing their eyes and relaxing, but it is also true that a small percentage of people never produce such waves.

As we fall off to sleep, a relatively slow eye movement can be picked up. Next, a kind of NREM state occurs in which there are *Theta* waves beginning to be reflected in the record. *Theta* waves are roughly 4 to 7 cycles per second and occur with general drowsiness. The *Delta* brainwave of 4 cycles per second or less predominate during very deep sleep. If a REM period occurs and we awaken the person whose eyes are now moving about rapidly, we may be told that he or she was sleeping very "deeply" and that a dream was taking place. In fact, in the earlier study of dreams using electrode measurements, scientists believed that dreams took place *only* during REM sleep. Further study established that NREM sleep also produces dreams, but these are apparently not so vivid in imagery or dramatic in content as the REM dreams (Farthing, 1992, p. 285).

Van Eeden (1913) coined the phrase *lucid dreaming* to describe a personal experience in which he knew that he was dreaming, but turned this phenomenal state into an interactive event:

> On September 9, 1904, I dreamt that I stood at a table before a window. On the table were different objects. I was perfectly well aware that I was dreaming and I considered what sorts of experiments I could make. I began by trying to break glass, by beating it with a stone. I put a small tablet of glass on two stones and struck it with another stone. Yet it would not break. Then I took a fine claret-glass from the table and struck it with my fist, with all my might, at the same time reflecting how dangerous it would be to do this in waking life; yet the glass remained whole. But lo! when I looked at it again after some time, it was broken. It broke all right, but a little too late, like an actor who misses his cue. This gave me a very curious impression of being in a *fake-world*, cleverly imitated, but with small failures. (Covello, 1984, pp. 81–82; italics in original)

Presumably, what makes the dream lucid in the dictionary sense of being clear, rational, or transparent, is the fact that the person understands that he or she *is* actually engaged in a dream. Such dream experiences have been reported for centuries. Chang (1977) found examples of lucid dreaming in the literature of ancient Tibetan Buddhism. A lucid dream is therefore one in which the person knows that he or she is dreaming while the dream content is being created. There have been disagreements over the precise definition. Some authorities (Tart, 1984) would hold that a dream is not lucid simply because the dreamer knows that it is taking place. The dreamer should also have some memory of his or her waking life (e.g., "I am presently asleep in my bed [a hotel bed, etc.]"), and sense the capacity to intervene and thereby control the course of the dream to some extent. Others have argued that simply being cognizant of dreaming is sufficient and that even control is not essential to meet the definition of lucidity (Alexander, 1988; Hunt, 1989).

Lucid dreams have great visual clarity and, if in color, the hues are rich and bright (Farthing, 1992, p. 265; Green, 1968). Tactile sensation is reduced or nonexistent so that a lucid dreamer can pass through walls (Sparrow, 1976). Natural laws are routinely violated like this; in lucid dreaming the person can leap over tall obstacles and even fly about at will (Green, 1968). Sense of smell, taste, and pain are not frequently reported. As suggested in the Van Eeden example above, demonstratively valid logic is violated in lucid dreaming just as it is in ordinary dreaming. There is some question about whether moral or ethical values can be violated—at least, for certain dreamers. Brown (1936) once tried to strangle another person during lucid dreaming. He found that his clasping hands kept passing through the person's neck so the windpipe could not be cut off. He then concocted a rope to hang the person, but though he did raise the latter's body above ground, all that resulted was a sore neck for the harried victim.

Because of the capacity to influence a dream (at least to some extent) there was a time when lucid dreaming was thought to occur during brief arousal, microawakening, or sleep stage transition rather than genuine sleep (Berger, 1977; Hartmann, 1975). But thanks in large measure to the findings of LaBerge (1985), this interpretation was eventually corrected. Lucid dreaming takes place in genuine sleep, and although it is more likely in REM sleep, it also occurs in NREM sleep (Gackenbach, 1991, p. 120). There is some evidence that lucid dreaming is most likely to appear during an enhanced and intensified REM sleep, in which a higher level of neuronal activation is said to be underway (LaBerge, 1988, p. 139; see also Brylowski, 1986).

The *Bios* emphasis evident in dream research reminds us of the brain theorizing discussed in Chapter 5. The EEG and REM measures help identify when certain levels of sleep are reached, or dreams are being produced, but they do not clarify the phenomenology of dreaming. This is not to disparage such measurement, of course. But we may be mixing apples and oranges when we consider physical measures *and* the purely cognitive aspects of the dream. I see no evidence that the former cause the thematic content of the latter. As with the readiness potential and Libet's (1985) work (see Chapter 5), we are forced to consider that such physiological measures capture some instrumental aspect of the organism's equipment, but the process being tracked in the *Bios* realm is not what fashions and directs the meaningful course of the dream content. If we acknowledge the importance of a *Logos* realm then the explanation shifts from a biophysical (material-efficient cause) process of mediation to that of predication.

Psychologists make theoretical explanations of lucid dreaming on the basis of concepts like *schemata* (LaBerge, 1985), *model* of the self (Blackmore, 1988), and *simulation* of the external world (Tart, 1986). This suggests a considerable reliance on information-processing terminology. But one also finds efforts to explain lucid dreaming in more dynamic terms such as a *phenomenal field* that can be influenced by the *ego* (Tholey, 1990). There are also theorists who consider lucid dreaming a "higher" state of consciousness paralleling the effects to be noted in the meditative traditions (Gackenbach, 1990; Hunt, 1988, 1989).

Lucid dreaming teaches us a lot about the nature of psychic consciousness. Thanks to Freud, the concept of dreaming has been identified with or seen as an aspect of the concept of unconsciousness. People have these hallucinatory experiences when they fall off to an unconscious state known as sleep. There is a clearly altered state going on here. The "lights go out" as biophysical consciousness gives way to unconsciousness. But lucid dreaming forces us to consider the possibility that what we have been calling *psychic* consciousness is not identical to biophysical consciousness —or "wakeful activity" as we termed it in Chapter 1. In other words, just as one can be physically awake and yet unipredicate some aspect of experience so that a state of unconsciousness results (this can include hypnotism), so too can one be asleep and transpredicate in a dream sequence. A review of the research literature establishes that the primary difference between garden-variety and lucid dreaming is that the latter involves reflective self-consciousness and an awareness of dreaming (Gackenbach, 1988). Both of these characteristics suggest transpredication by way of oppositional (dialectical) reasoning. Transpredication and unipredication are obviously not bound by the demands of physical consciousness.

Over half of the adults questioned report that they can recall one or more times in their life when they knew that they were dreaming, and about one third say they experience at least one such lucid dream per month (Farthing, 1992, p. 329). Finding lucid dreaming in sleep laboratories, where subjects are monitored throughout the night (e.g., Snyder, 1970), has been notoriously rare (Farthing, 1992, p. 324); but this paucity seems to be changing as researchers refine techniques for inducing lucid dreaming (p. 324). I believe that we can see LLT principles reflected in the didactic strategies framed to aid in the production of lucid dreams (adapted from Tholey, 1983). First of all, it is clear that in order to dream lucidly the person must be cognizing in a self-reflexive mode. In ordinary dreaming it is rather common for the dreamer to "reflect" on some action going on in the dream (e.g., "I wonder who these people walking past me are?"). But this reflective commentary is not a self-reflexive questioning of whether dreaming itself is occurring, or wondering if the course of dream events can be changed at will (see Farthing, 1992, pp. 261, 324 on this matter). This latter reflexivity demands a transcendent capacity to turn back on the dream theme and put it all to question in that Kantian sense that we discussed in Chapter 1.

A common technique in the training for lucid dreaming is to ask oneself "Am I dreaming?" every time something strange or unusual occurs during the waking day. By asking this question and then carefully analyzing the unusual event (let us say that a plate has mysteriously fallen from a shelf) an analytically reflective attitude is fostered. This same question is asked as close to the time of falling asleep as possible. Eventually, the person will ask it while actually dreaming. If the sleeping individual can answer "yes," the lucid dream is underway. Upon awakening, the sleeper also tries to remember as much of each dream that night (lucid or not) as possible. Forming strong autosuggestions on going to bed is also recommended (e.g., "This is the night I will have a lucid dream"). Role play during the day is encouraged: The person pretends that a dream is taking place while some rather monotonous task like doing laundry or grocery shopping is carried out. Even during such routine activities, the person pays close attention to every aspect of the environment.

Once the person has actually assessed the likelihood that he or she is having a lucid dream, there are various recommendations for how to prove this is true. One widely used test is to attempt to float or fly in the air. By testing the environment of the dream one can also establish the correct dream status. For example, the dreamer may look for a window or a door in the room. Are these portals situated properly? Look out a window, draw back, then look out again. Is the external environment constant or has it changed? Is there a light switch on the wall where it ought to be? Flick the switch to see if a light comes on. Another test is to try putting one's hand through a solid object. Something can be read, and then reread: Does it remain constant in meaning or does the meaning change? If any of the above occurrences deviate from commonsense expectations, the person can be assured that a lucid dream is truly underway.

I think it is fair to say that all of the training practices, the reflexive questioning, intentions to dream lucidly, and capacity to redirect the course of a dream sequence are readily subsumed by the concepts of LLT. To dream lucidly is to transpredicate, which is the other side of unipredicating. To dream lucidly is to willfully intrude on the spontaneous course of thought (commonly subsumed under the concept of "metacognition" by those who study lucid dreaming; e.g., see Kahan & LaBerge, 1994). If we recall that the predicate establishes the context of meaning-extension (see Chapter 2), we might now suggest that when a person falls off to sleep there is a loss of any "particular" context that might even conceivably direct thought. With our eyes open, alert to the environmental requirements of the day, we extend meaning as we behave according to these demands: "Time to get up. Late, late, I'm late. Call immediately! What's that person's name? Is that the retail or wholesale price? How in the world did that happen? Can I get out of this, or am I stuck?" These are the everyday demands put upon us by the environment, an environment that we are always adapting to but also rearranging to our advantage if at all possible. But in a state of sleep such predicating demands on our thought are not specified and therefore are not limited by a set of external circumstances. The formal-cause organization is up to us, to the predicating context that we put on the dream theme. It is for this reason that any of a number of predicating formulations may be entertained, even those that may meld two or more (including oppositional) frameworks together—enabling our uncle in the dream to look like someone else (Freud's "overdetermined" dream image).

What I am suggesting here is that dreams are conceptualized in the same predication-to-target fashion that produces waking thought. The difference between these two states is that the predicating context is "set loose" during the dream state and hence any of a number of possibilities may be entertained no matter how mutually inconsistent or eccentric they are. The principle of contradiction does not hold in a dream production anymore than it may hold in a conscious argument in which the person fails to see a negation of the very point under espousal. We can be and often enough are illogical even when awake and walking around.

It is common to look for symbolic expressions or *symbols* in dreams. If such symbols really take place, they function much like the ex cathedra universals that we discussed in Chapter 4. A symbolic expression in the dream does not draw meaning from other predications. It *is* a predication, a sort of universal claim on meaning that the dream interpreter tries to fathom, often with little success, for it is difficult or impossible to target a symbol through other predications. The symbol always extends meaning "to something other than itself" (Johnston, 1993, p. 63) so it represents a kind of unipredicated meaning that cannot be tapped into. To give an example of what I am driving at, an ordinary dream might be wound around the theme of a huge fish, or a strange light, either of which holds some vaguely implied significance for the dreamer. What can these symbols mean? What archetypal significance can we draw from their arcane manifestations? This is the general approach taken by Jungian analysis (see Chapter 4).

But in the case of lucid dreaming we witness the dreamer bringing into question the symbol-laden images like fish or lights, as dream items that must themselves be targeted. Can the dreamer cut the fish in half? Can the light be made to blink? The transpredication of lucidity enables the dreamer to decontextualize the symbol, altering or destroying its very significance—assuming the presumed symbols actually convey any meaning in the first place. This wrenching apart of the dream contents is not unlike the conscious decision to dismiss all dream symbols as nonsense, due more to digestive disturbances ("something I ate") than to universal meaning expressions. As we are well aware by now, the transpredication that is psychic consciousness can reframe any meaning imaginable. What is remarkable is that transpredication takes place during the biophysiological state of unconsciousness known as sleep. We move next to the altered state of consciousness that some people have found related to lucid dreaming— that is, meditation.

MEDITATION

Meditation is an ancient practice, often carried out in a religious context as prayer, in which through a ritualistic control of attention the person seeks to alter consciousness. For brevity's sake I will combine traditions in the presentation (i.e., Christian, Yoga, Zen, Sufism, etc.), but no great distortion will result thereby in specifying the psychological state they share as "meditation." Some would say that meditation is concerned with the development of *presence*, the spontaneous flow of immediate experience, without the usual concern to fix and direct attention on specific objects in consciousness (Naranjo & Ornstein, 1971, pp. 8–11). This release of contact with *things* in the environment may be described as a detached or transpersonal state of consciousness (p. 24). Indeed, the point of certain meditation practices is to extinguish such dichotomies as it me, subject–object, is–is not, or even life–death in order to achieve a unity of thought—called a "middle path"—that results in enlightenment or *nirvana* (Nikhilananda, 1967, p. 147).

That an altered state is achieved through meditation is said to be supported by the fact that the meditator's brain waves move from Beta to Alpha, and even to Theta, suggesting a deepening state of concentration and relaxation (Johnston, 1993, pp. 39–40). We do not see such changes in hypnotized people (p. 43). Unfortunately for those who make much of such findings, we can get similar brain-wave changes in subjects who are not using meditation techniques but merely "thinking good thoughts" or mentally relaxing (Smith, 1976). Many researchers on meditation suggest that what is important is not the meditation technique per se, but rather the belief that such measures "really work" in some way (Farthing, 1992, p. 438). Of course, beliefs are phenomena of the *Logos*, and in this realm they are important considerations as such. What the brain-wave research surely does establish is that people making the effort to meditate do bring about physically measurable changes. But the relevance of meditation— the very *meaning* of the meditation—need not therefore be limited to the *Bios* realm.

There are two major forms of meditation. The first, and by far the most widely practiced form is termed *concentrative* meditation, where the aim is to restrict attention to an unchanging object or thought in order to attain a "centering" or a "one-pointedness" of mind. The meditator may focus attention on a source of light, a lotus flower, or the cross; alternatively, he or she may repeat a sacred word or *mantra*, over and over again. A famous Indian mantra is OM, but in the Christian tradition the word *Jesus* is also a form of mantra when expressed repetitively in prayer. Sometimes the meditator focuses on a riddle or a paradox, called a *koan* (e.g., the oft-cited "What is the sound of one hand clapping?"). Using the external items or verbalized mantra or koan to restrict attention, the meditator can now reflect on his or her inner being or selfhood ("Who am I?"), which necessarily involves the absence of self as well (Naranjo & Ornstein, 1971, pp. 21–22).

Here is where a parallel with lucid dreaming may be suggested, in that we have both a freeing of the directedness of mind (as in a dream), but also a question posed that has implications for what is to follow. However, such questions in concentrative meditation are not answered in words. A Zen master rejects such rational exploration. Conceptualization in any form, including imagery, is rejected in favor of what is experienced as a deeper level of consciousness known as *san'mai* (or *samadhi*). It is at this level that meditation is sometimes said to encompass a trance state. Here is where that unity or oneness with nature is sensed as nirvana. There is no real awareness of sensations or thoughts in the state of nirvana because the person is "in" nature—an actual part of it—rather than having to frame or conceptualize it as something "other" (Goleman, 1978). On this very point, it is said that there are two stages in Zen meditation. The first is "I am breathing." The second is "The universe is breathing" (Johnston, 1993, p. 91). We see here the separateness of selves being supplanted by the oneness of nature (the many-in-one principle).

The other form of meditation is referred to as *opening-up*, because in this case rather than limiting attention to one observed item or repeated word there is an effort made to maintain complete awareness of all conscious thoughts, perceptions, and actions (Farthing, 1992, p. 424). This form of meditation is found in Zen Buddhism but it would not be practiced by a Yoga master (Johnston, 1993, p. 44). Sometimes the phrase "right-mindedness" is used, which suggests that actions throughout the day are never carried out mindlessly (as a robot, etc.). But this does not mean that the meditator is going to change or actively shape the environment. The attitude taken here is receptive and accepting rather than reactive and challenging. One moves within events as an aspect of them rather than as a manipulator of them.

Returning to the concentration form of meditation, it is fascinating to see how the aim seems to be to move dialectically from "something" in experience to "nothing." Naranjo and Ornstein (1971) summarize the Buddhistic meditative state as "one of awareness-centeredness-emptiness." This emptiness is not a lack of anything but rather a detached freedom from all of those obsessive demands that we place on ourselves, our self-evaluations and artificial distinctions that invariably remove us from a direct sense of who we are. Thus, Naranjo and Ornstein can say, "When he [the meditator] achieves detachment from pleasure and pain, he is not indifferent but free to live and die, and to enjoy the gift of life without caring about gain and loss" (p. 24).

There are other techniques of meditation that we could discuss, such as counting breaths, just sitting, steady gazing, and so on, but now we want to move on to the implications of meditation for our understanding of psychic consciousness. One of the leading analysts of meditation is Robert Ornstein, whom we reviewed in Chapter 5 (see Ornstein, 1977, 1991). Ornstein believes the mind is similar to a computer, and therefore it follows that he would use some such model to describe how meditation works for the person: "This process might be considered in psychological terms an attempt to recycle the same subroutine over and over again in the nervous system" (Naranjo & Ornstein, 1971, p. 161). Anything that enables a focused awareness to take place is suitable for such recycling of information (p. 161). Repetition per se "evokes" a state in which the external world is shut out (pp. 162–163). The mechanism for this separation from reality is to be found in the central nervous system: "It seems that a consequence of the structure of our central nervous system is that if awareness is restricted to an unchanging source of stimulation, a 'turning off' of consciousness of the external world follows" (pp. 167–168).

Naranjo and Ornstein make the intriguing suggestion that a continuous repetition of the same stimulus (looking at the same thing, repeating the same mantra, etc.) is tantamount to "no stimulation at all" (p. 169). Change in stimulation demands a change in the object of attention, from one item or word to another. We must keep in mind that they are not referring to psychic consciousness here. This is not precisely unipredication taking place, but a kind of "mindless" focusing on the physical stimulation per se, whether seen or heard. The aim here is not to focus meaning but to remove all meaning from experience by shutting down or at least greatly restricting the activity of the central nervous system for a time. The resultant experience is that of a void in which presumably no physical stimulation takes place—more a question of nonconsciousness than unconsciousness. This nonconsciousness is experienced positively, as a kind of vacation from the demands of reality. Naranjo and Ornstein sum things up as follows: "The practice of meditation, then, can be considered an attempt to turn off conceptual activity temporarily, to shut off all input processing for a period of time, to get away for a while from the external environment" (p. 193).

And the salubrious outcome of such mental vacationing is that when we return to our reality we "see it differently, 'anew'" (p. 193). This seeing anew takes place in a psychological and not a biological realm. We have shifted locations from the merely sensory shut-down to a change in conceptual outlook. Meditation traditions all express a willingness to allow stimuli to enter consciousness devoid of typical biases (p. 194). This permits the meditator to frame alternative perspectives on things. The "opening-up" form of meditation encourages a similar willingness to see things differently, or to become aware of practices that are carried out "automatically" (p. 211). The meditator's sense of enriched consciousness stems from this getting out of a habitual rut and the consequent generation of useful alternatives in behavioral routine (p. 210).

From the LLT perspective, innovations brought on following a meditational "vacation" are understandable in exclusively psychological terms set in *Logos* groundings. People willfully forego direction of thought for a time, focusing psychically on some repetitive sound or visible object not only to avoid the possibility of transpredication but to limit the very complexity of the resultant unipredicated contents. Meditation therefore involves both the predicational process and the content of this process, each of which can be narrowed. Not all unipredicated contents are simplified and repetitive; some are quite complex, as in unipredicating to focus on an intricate mathematical problem. Slightly modifying Naranjo and Ornstein's explanation, I might suggest that after the meditator experiences this narrowing of both process and content for a time, the individual springs back to psychic functioning with a new slant on things. Shop-worn precedents may then give way to an "opening up" of newly transpredicated alternatives. Of course, we should expect that occasionally the transpredicational effort might produce an unfortunate alternative. The outcome need not always be positive, but there are those who seem to think the "higher state of consciousness" emanating from meditation will, indeed, always be positive (e.g., Dillbeck & Alexander, 1989).

In further support of this LLT explanation, I would point to what meditators have said about their experience after they have maximally limited their consciousness and its contents. The use of oppositional descriptors here is striking. Thus, upon reaching the depths of meditation, a level that is experienced as bottomless, empty, and endless, the meditator may sense this as "the night from which proceeds light, the non-being that sustains being, the absence of self at the heart of selfhood" (Naranjo & Ornstein, 1971, p. 22). These dialectically arrayed comments are common in the meditation literature. I would suggest that this way of expressing things reflects the flow of experience that we have been considering—from initial unipredication to an awareness of alternatives via transpredication. The succession here is from unconsciousness to consciousness by way of generic and delimiting oppositionality (light from night, being from nonbeing, etc.). Meditators probably develop added awareness of the totality of cognition as a "one" (total) among many (possibilities). This richly insightful overview may be what prompts the person to speak of a higher consciousness following the meditation experience.

DOES RESEARCH FIND THE UNCONSCIOUS TO BE WISE?

In both the present and earlier chapters we have noted that meanings extending from the psychic unconscious seem to be conveyed in ex cathedra fashion, striking the person experiencing them as true personal insights, universals, or wisdom from ages past. We might now ask what empirical research there is concerning the wisdom of the unconscious. I do not mean the kinds of studies referred to in the discussion of hypnotism, which usually come down to demonstrations of the phenomenon per se. I am thinking now of studies carried on in academic centers that purport to test unconscious influences on behavior more scientifically. What are these studies like and how are their findings rationalized theoretically?

In approaching the topic more rigorously, academic researchers invariably think of their data in terms of the computer or information-processing models of Chapter 7. For example, Bowers (1984) has presented an excellent analysis of the fact that people can *perceive* and employ "information" without *noticing* certain aspects of what is being conveyed. The quotation marks framing information signify that he is *not* using the term in the strict engineering sense (i.e., sans meaning). Bowers has meaningful information in mind. An example he gives of the difference between perceiving and noticing is "repeatedly checking [perceiving] the time on an unfamiliar clock before noticing that the clock face was inscribed with roman numerals rather than arabic numbers" (p. 230).

Bowers takes the fact that "information can be perceived without being noticed" (p. 229) as evidence of an unconscious influence on behavior. He suggests that to be conscious, information must enter short-term memory, where it is selectively attended or noticed as it is being stored. He believes that "determinants of thought and action that are not noticed or appreciated as such constitute unconscious influences" (p. 228). Bowers is obviously a mediational theorist who considers all information qua meaning under processing to have been patterned into existence by some source external to the cognitive processing of the person. The informational meaning is "there" at input, ready for perception first and noticing second. Bowers sees this linear sequence as the "two stages of information processing" (p. 230). His point is that sometimes the information does not reach the second stage even though it is influencing behavior.

Logical learning theory equates Bowers' noticing with predication in the framing of a conceptualization. According to LLT, when the person looks at a clock the intention is to discern the time, so that a specifying *unipredication* focuses attention on this fact alone. The cognizing individual endows meaning instead of some external source inputting an already patterned meaning. According to LLT, the process here would be as follows: At first, the person looks at the unfamiliar clock with the intention of finding out the time. The meaning-extension concerns an unknown—the pattern of the clock's face. The face is the target and the predicate seeks the pattern of hands and numbers on this face. Once the meaning is extended the targeted time is known, so that the "last" glance at the clock always predicates the "next" glance, and so on. This ongoing enrichment of the target does not stop with the patterning of the numbers and hands on the face of the clock. The initial intention is a unipredication: "What time is it?" But as the former target (clock's face) can now be used as a predicate—that is, it has been *learned*—this original intention is further enriched by predications such as "I had better check that clock again" and "How much time has passed since I first looked at the clock?"

The predicated meaning has changed at this point, so that the person has already established the time frame and may use this knowledge to target the clock in a less unipredicated fashion. Transpredications of the type "What sort of clock face is that, anyway?" are now capable of formulation. In LLT we speak of this human tendency to move from the most to the least understood targets of experience as the *principle of meaning-extension* (Rychlak, 1994, pp. 52–53). So the person, who has already identified the clock's time and comes to know this aspect of the clock's appearance, moves to what is not yet known. I suspect whether the person would come to know the difference between a roman and an arabic clock face would depend upon the level of consciousness in the task being carried out under time pressure. The more unipredicated the task being undertaken, the less likely this noticing would occur. Regardless of how we interpret Bower's "perceive versus notice" distinction, it is clear that there is no profound wisdom that we can attribute to the unconscious.

Another area that researchers usually see as the study of unconscious behavior is that of *subliminal perception*. *Subliminal* means below the level of discerning a perceivable difference—as in not being able to make out a visual image or hear a word because they do not stand out from their context. We have all been told about the sneaky movie theater manager who sends messages on the screen to "Eat Popcorn" or "Drink Coke," flashing them during the regular motion picture so rapidly that we cannot actually see or notice them. Yet, these subliminal messages presumably work because popcorn and coke sales are said to increase if such manipulations are carried out. The implication is, of course, that the unconscious mind received the hint or cue and the person responded as if this were his or her personal decision to eat and drink. This area of research has been much studied and debated over the years (Bruner, 1957; Dixon, 1971; Eriksen, 1960; Merikle, 1982). By the 1970s a consensus developed among researchers that a well-controlled experiment never garnered evidence to support subliminal perception.

Today, the pendulum has swung back and researchers are once again expressing support for subliminal perception or "unconscious cognition" (see, e.g., Greenwald, 1992). Studies using *priming* in human memory have provided the major backing here (Tulving & Schachter, 1990). A typical priming study asks people to look at a series of pictures, and, after a period of time has lapsed, to look at the pictures again and name the object contained in each one. But the unique thing here is that the first exposure is to degraded pictures in which it is unclear what is being depicted. Also, some of the pictures are so faint that the subject matter on them cannot even be seen. Even so, compared with individuals who have not had this previous exposure, participants who have been so primed do a significantly better job of identifying what the pictures contain than those who have not had this experience. Except for the possible influence of affective assessment in such studies, priming research does not seem to involve psychic consciousness so much as it does the physical capacity to sense very low-level visual discriminations. In any case, there is not much evidence here for a wise unconscious. Greenwald flatly states that unconscious processes are quite simple and unsophisticated.

Furthermore, just because a person might sense a subliminal message taking place in cognizance does not mean that he or she would affirm it as an action-understanding and unconsciously carry it out. Such studies have not obviously demonstrated any efficiently caused determinism. There is also a continuing problem in demonstrating comparable unconscious influences in other sensory modalities. For example, a study of the efficacy of self-help audiotapes to raise self-esteem or improve memory, played repeatedly while a participant slept through the night, found no such benefits taking place over a month's exposure (Greenwald, Spangenberg, Pratkanis, & Eskenazi, 1991). Finally, there are still vigorous critics of research on subliminal perception or—as it is now usually referred to—"perception without awareness" (see, e.g., Hollender, 1986).

Another area of research suggesting an unconscious influence on behavior is so-called *blindsight*. This phenomenon occurs in patients with amnesia who have damage to the striate cortex of their brain's occipital lobe. Such patients recognize and recall previously exposed words (table, mountain, apple, etc.) much more poorly than the general population. However, the former perform as well as the latter in completing fragments of words that have been presented before but are now introduced as a new task (Warrington & Weiskrantz, 1970; Weiskrantz, 1986). For example, they accurately complete the fragment *tab* more readily if they have seen the word *table* previously, even though they cannot recall seeing the word. The results of this test are always better than if they have not been "unconsciously" primed in this fashion (for many examples of this phenomenon, see Roediger, 1990).

Given the biological tie-in it would seem that we are dealing more with the *Bios* than the *Logos* realm: But LLT does contend that human beings can know without remembering. We know concepts but cannot recall where we learned them. A person may not remember with certainty which finger is used to hit a specific key on the keyboard even though he or she is an excellent typist. As I have suggested about other habits, such as driving a car (see Chapter 4), what is under predication in typing— once we have learned to type—is the end product of a typed letter or manuscript page. The telos of "what finger hits what key" has long since given way to the more advanced goal of the total process, which is to carry out an action intention relying on the typewriter to meet this goal, and not the former goal of learning to type. The fingers on the board are no longer targets but have patterned into the *known predicating context* that the typist brings to bear at the keyboard. The target is now exclusively the finished page, what it will convey, and so on. The more facile the typist is in using her or his fingers to predicate the task the less likely it is that an error in typing will occur. Conversely, if even a skilled typist begins targeting the fingers, losing the total predicating pattern of motion to concerns about individual fingers, the probability of a typing error increases.

In like fashion, the rudimentary knowledge of letter and word recognition must predicate the patients' (with amnesia) reading capacities or they would be unable to read any words or fragments to begin with. Because the experimental situation is itself a predicating context, finding a former target (i.e., the word *table*) taking meaning from that context so that now the target can be used as a predicate extending to the new target (i.e., *tab*) is no more surprising than finding that the patient with amnesia cannot recall where she or he originally learned the letters that form the word *table*. Of course, there is also a deficit in the brain structure of such patients that handicaps the predicational process in a certain way; but the *Bios* deficit does not explain the *Logos* process so adversely affected.

It is important to keep the process–content distinction clearly in mind in this discussion, because what passes as unconscious knowledge ("wisdom," etc.) is always the meaningful content being processed by the person. It is never the process per se so far as the person is concerned. Contents are what convey the impression of great insight, truth, or wisdom to the person experiencing meaning from some unconscious realm. But due to the requirements of experimental control in the empirical studies, the contents under testing are necessarily simple and innocuous. What is presumably under study is the process known as unconsciousness (see Jacoby, Lindsay, & Toth, 1992). Researchers frankly admit that what they are studying has little to do with Freud's efforts to circumscribe the meanings of unconscious dream symbols and the like (e.g., Kihlstrom, Barnhardt, & Tataryn, 1992, p. 789). This may well account for the fact that there has been little evidence for the wisdom of the unconscious issuing from these studies. One cannot find what one is unable to look for. A major problem with the empirical studies done so far is that they deal in tracings of contextless word meanings so that the predicational influence is very subtle, hence easily minimized in preference to mechanical explanations. In a Freudian account, the life context is everything: it is the ultimate protopoint from which meanings are framed so that they take on the universal quality we discussed in Chapter 4.

Loftus and Klinger (1992) answer the question put by the title of their paper, "Is the unconscious smart or dumb?": "[T]here seems to be a general consensus that the unconscious may not be as smart as previously believed" (p. 764). Unconscious cognition seems quite limited in the sophistication of the analyses that it can accomplish. Even if researchers believe their findings support intelligent learning at the unconscious level, they admit that conscious learning is more flexible and adaptable than unconscious learning (Lewicki, Hill, & Czyzewska, 1992). This meets our understanding of consciousness as framing transpredications that result in alternatives being suggested and then enacted. The unipredication that is unconscious behavior can indeed be rigid and unyielding. Undoubtedly, the final word has not been said concerning the capacity that unconscious processing has to generate truly profound insights. Those who favor the importance of unconscious factors in human affairs can take solace from the fact that at least there is empirical evidence today that unconscious influences on behavior do take place. Not too many decades ago the academic community carrying out so-called rigorous psychological research would not admit that the distinction between conscious and unconscious behavior made much sense.

CONCLUDING COMMENT

The survey of major forms of altered states leaves me with the general conviction that the LLT interpretation of psychic consciousness falls nicely into line. At least, no major anomalies stand in the way of viewing altered states in light of unipredication, transpredication, affective assessment, and so forth. Surely there is much to question about the validity of activities like hypnosis, channeling, or meditation. As a psychologist, however, I cannot dismiss the importance of understanding the invalid, misleading, and deluding actions of people. People behave a certain way psychologically even when they are out to deceive or mislead. I think the role of intention in all human affairs is fundamental, and we can see this teleological side of human behavior clearly showing through the altered states. Altered states are altered for a purpose, and they make greatest sense if understood in this fashion even though this alteration may result in self- or interpersonal deception. Logical learning theory accommodates all such atypical manifestations of human behavior, whether sincere or insincere.

9

COLLECTIVES AND CONSCIOUSNESS

At various points in earlier chapters I have alluded to the fact that consciousness has relevance to anything from two-person interactions to huge social identities. It is not unusual to hear the phrase "group consciousness" used today, especially in terms of attempting to raise the awareness of people belonging to some targeted collective, such as social, ethnic, and racial minorities (or majorities). One might wonder what it means to raise a group's level of consciousness and how this may relate to the consciousness of the individual in the designated collective. Does raising one also raise the other, or can group and individual levels of consciousness take on either a parallel or a reciprocal relationship? What processes and content-meanings are involved in such consciousness raising? Finally and most importantly, how well does the trans- versus unipredication explanation apply to such matters?

As a fundamentally psychological explanation of behavior, LLT focuses on the individual. It postulates a process known as predication that functions in the *Logos* realm where meanings are constantly being patterned and repatterned in the ongoing understanding of individual human beings. These meanings are all-important to the behavior of the individual, of course; even so, they are still separate and distinct from the process that actually frames them and brings them into play. If individual people form together into collectives there are going to be dynamics that can influence the likelihood that people will select or emphasize certain contents over others. People are influenced by the views of others, especially significant others like family, friends, the gang, and religious communities, as well as national, age-group, sexual-orientation, or racial memberships.

But what is the *process* by which such influences take place? Are these supra-individual occurrences happening in an exclusively *Socius* realm, where the individual has nothing to contribute by way of a *Logos* patterning of meaning? Or is what distinguishes one collective from another the meaningful *contents* under affirmation by individual predicators, who find themselves sharing some discernible belief that lends members a "group identity"? The LLT position contends the latter so that, for example, political liberals and conservatives may staunchly defend opposing views on fundamental issues, but the process whereby they affirm their stands is identical. The same is to be seen in cross-cultural studies where, although the premises of diverse cultures may differ, the logical processing used is common to all (Cole & Scribner, 1974; Scribner & Cole, 1981).

We know that a person is influenced by the cultural norms of her or his group. A *norm* has been defined as "a standard or set of standards in a given culture derived from the behavior of the generality of the individual members of that culture" (Chaplin, 1985, p. 113). Norms are expectations that the group frames for its members and against which the latter's individual behavior will be judged (p. 113). The LLT position is that norms are "predications held in common" by a group of individuals who pari passu form an identity under the unifying affirmation of this content meaning. As such they are generally held contents. This is not to deny that to fully understand the behavior of individuals in groups we may require considerations of a *Socius* nature such as social conformity, political advantage, or mutual encouragement and support. The question remains as to whether norms function consciously or unconsciously to influence the behavior of group members.

Traditionally, psychologists have interpreted norms as mediators (i.e., contents), shaped into existence by some kind of sociocultural force. Psychology's commitment to social-influence theorizing was inevitable once it had embraced the mediation model. That is, a process that inputs patterned contents necessarily places its major emphasis on the external sources of such influence (e.g., social shaping, group manipulation, linguistic convention, etc.). All behaviorists and information-processing cognitivists are ultimately social psychologists. In previous chapters we have seen efforts being made in psychology to sweep individualism under the rug—a tendency that has been assisted in recent decades by developments in philosophy, art, and linguistics. As a result of such efforts, the generally held picture is that of the reputed decline—and, indeed, the demise—of characteristics once believed to be at the center of human existence. In Chapter 9 we take up three such characteristics: individuality, authorship, and truth.

DEMISE OF INDIVIDUALITY: GROUP CONSCIOUSNESS AND ITS PARADOXES

One of the themes of Chapter 1 was the role of consciousness in the collective. It was noted that in reaction to the rationalism of modern scientific philosophy, beginning in roughly the 17th century, a countering romantic movement of the 18th century advanced the concept of Zeitgeist, a mystical "spirit of the age" that significantly influenced if not directed the thinking of all people during some period of history as if it were a group mind (Becker & Barnes, 1952, pp. 487–490). Rationalistic philosophers, who were captivated by the rise of natural science during the 17th century (sometimes known as the Age of Reason), tended to frame their conceptions of the group on the basis of the individual. For example, Thomas Hobbes analogized from the single person to the Commonwealth or State, viewing the latter as an "artificial man" consisting of many "natural" men and women (Hobbes, 1651/1952, p. 47). The individuals of this collective form a covenant or social contract among themselves as well as with their leaders to ensure a peaceful existence in which all can benefit from the strength in numbers (p. 101). The language of the covenant expresses the intentions of the individuals who banded together in the first place.

In contrast to Hobbes, we can cite the philosopher of history, Johann Gottfried von Herder (1744–1803). An important forerunner of the romantic criticism of rationalism, Herder believed that history was impelled by a combination of *Geist* (the mind or spirit of a people) and various geographical considerations like location and climate (Becker & Barnes, 1952, p. 489). Herder argued that although God was the creator of all things he did not interfere in the historical forces that shaped their ongoing development. Even so, the core notion of Herder's analysis is that forces outside the control of the individual directed his or her destiny. This shaping influence included the physical environment. But as later theorists elaborated his concept of the *Geist* (or Zeitgeist, as it came to be known), the role of the individual in the group was significantly diminished. Instead of moving in Hobbesian fashion from individual or "self" to the collective, Herder's group-mind emphasis shifted the direction of influence from collective to the individual.

This shift in locus of influence was not lost on the rising social sciences of the late 19th and early 20th centuries. Initially, social influence was cast in a negative vein. For example, in his classic study, *The Crowd*, Le Bon (1903) warned that in face-to-face collectives a spontaneous eruption can occur leading to mob actions such as panic, riot, or lynching. He specifically noted that if individuals homogenize into a crowd it "puts them in possession of a sort of collective mind" (p. 29). McDougall's (1920) later work entitled *The Group Mind* followed Le Bon's lead to describe panic reactions as due to the perception of imminent danger by a face-to-face crowd. Allport (1924) then spelled out how such group actions arise from the spontaneous polarization that occurs if a crowd focuses on some issue and elevates it to a normative demand on everyone to resist, flee, or attack. A unifying identification takes place in which the person reasons "as one" with other members of the group.

Group contexts also easily heighten emotions. McDougall (1920) noted that the "intensification of emotion is the most striking result of the formation of a crowd" (p. 24). Because he believed that such emotional reactions invariably prompted irrational outcomes, Le Bon (1903) concluded that crowds were "always intellectually inferior to the isolated individual" (p. 37). Moreover, due to the anonymity of such irrational crowd actions, the individual can hide all sense of personal responsibility for any irrational actions that might take place. More than one member of a lynch mob has said "I don't remember exactly what happened to me last night" on the morning following an illegal hanging.

Tarde's (1903) *Laws of Imitation* introduced an important concept to the study of collectives, one that facilitated extending such explanations from the negative to the more positive side of the ledger. Drawing on the concepts used in attempts to explain hypnotism, Le Bon spoke of *suggestion* as the underlying process of crowd behavior (see Chapter 8). McDougall's (1920) concept of *contagion* had a related meaning—as the sympathetic acceptance of others' views during spontaneous group formation. Such formulations made it appear that group influences were limited to the accidents of transitory face-to-face contacts. But what of the larger, more permanent social units? Tarde's concept of *imitation* had the potential for explanations at this level, reaching beyond the spontaneity of temporary crowds to capture lasting collectives known as social classes, castes, electorates, and nationalities—groups that are obviously too large to congregate at the face-to-face level. People could be understood to imitate one another, whether prompted by casual encounters on the street or through reading about certain behaviors in books and newspapers.

This concept of copying the patterns of others (i.e., imitation or modeling) enabled social scientists to explain fads and crazes, such as shifting styles in dress and behavior, preferences in music, food, or recreational pursuits. With the invention and development of such marvels as the radio, motion picture, and television, the concept of imitation took on even greater significance. As noted in Chapter 3, Riesman (Riesman, Glazer, & Denney, 1953) distinguished between the other- and inner-directed character structures that seemed to be partialling themselves out at mid-20th century: Whereas inner-directed people are influenced by tradition, other-directed people find their contemporaries as the source of influence (pp. 33, 36). Other-directedness obviously retained the negative connotations of character structures habitually swayed by others and of individuals thoughtlessly affirming (i.e., blindly imitating) the values of the collective (p. 37).

This kind of supra-individual (group) influence was gradually co-opted by the social sciences, which no longer considered it negative (thoughtless, etc.) because it was presumably the way in which all social shaping took place (aided and abetted by the learning of language, as we will discuss). Indeed, in direct parallel to natural sciences like chemistry or biology, such group explanations could be framed extraspectively, so that now psychologists may see the individual as under the control of the stimuli triggering imitation rather than as the framer and selector of such stimuli for purposeful copying. It is no accident that leading behaviorists like Miller and Dollard (1941) or Bandura (1962) founded their views on this imitation model, which interprets behavior as an efficiently caused response that is rewarded in contiguous relation to some external stimulus.

Whereas a classical view such as Aristotle's definition of politics as the "life of the individual completed in society" (Carruthers, 1990, p. 24) assumes the person to be fundamental to the body politic, behaviorism turns Herder's mystical, sociohistorical forces into empirically measurable, normative, efficient causes that fashion behavior from above and beyond such individuality. As social-class values determining the behavioral patterns of individuals, these supra-individual norms are considered worthy of study in their own right. In fact, as I have already noted, socioculturally oriented theoreticians have now concluded that it is no longer necessary to study the person because this concept is nothing more than the product of group forces in any event—hence, the demise of individuality.

There is good reason to believe that individual and group consciousness are not the same thing. A significant difference stems from the fact that it is not really possible to understand group consciousness as a predicational process. Collective explanations are invariably framed extraspectively, whereas predication is an introspective process in which meanings are affirmed and brought forward in pro forma fashion as a point of view, assumption, attitude, and so forth. Recall McLuhan's (1962) suggestion that not until movable type occurred was a "fixed point of view" made possible because this shifted the person's mode of understanding from an auditory to a visual mode. The author's perspective was more appreciated than the scribe's efforts at merely transmitting the oral tradition from one context to another. The author's perspective is introspectively framed, and increasingly departs from traditional repetition to present an individualized slant on things. McLuhan can therefore suggest that movable print intensified the tendency to individualism, that it decollectivized the readership (p. 192).

In LLT terms, what happened here is that the transpredications of the authors overtook the staid unipredications of scribal tradition, which in turn raised the psychic consciousness of the individual reader. There is a direct parallel here with the computer, which is like a scribe unconsciously matching one scripted account to another, whereas only the programmer has a conscious point of view (see Chapter 7). But as the consciousness of readers increased there was always the risk—which was often enough the reality—that the cohesiveness of the group would be called into question. Alternatives to group traditions were being considered. This is why book burnings take place in closed societies. If one is out to solidify a collective's internal strength of identity then it is helpful to raise the *level of unconsciousness* among its members. The usual strategy is to focus unipredications on in-group propaganda detailing the merits of the *insider* group while dismissing consideration of alternatives as the corrupting ideas of trouble-making *outsiders*. One narrows and even weakens the unique identities of the individual members to strengthen the identity of the collective. Meyrowitz (1985) has accurately observed that "Extremely powerful group identities are unconscious and intuitive" (p. 135).

Whyte's (1956) analysis of *The Organization Man* insightfully contrasted individual with group consciousness in the observation that top executives are rarely blind to what company loyalty involves: "Of all the organization men the true executive is the one who remains most suspicious of The Organization" (p. 166). This suspicion involves transpredication because "To be aware of one's conformity is to be aware that there is some antithesis between oneself and the demands of the system" (p. 172). Being conscious of when something is good for the organization and when it is good for oneself (such benefits can coexist, of course) is the mark of true executive quality (p. 182). Only run-of-the-mill executives lose individual consciousness through total identification with the organization.

In Chapter 4 we found Jung contrasting individual with group consciousness. Jung recognized that a certain degree of conformity must always take place in the realm of the collective. Thus, in collective consciousness the person wears a mask that conforms to group expectations of behavior. Usually the person is cognizant of the difference between such social expectations and a personal ego behind the mask. But if the person confuses his or her individual identity with this social facade, a kind of mindless unconsciousness results. Jung (1953b) specifically discusses the loss of personal identity associated with such confusion (p. 191). The mask identifier is an automaton who blindly enacts the unipredications modeled by the mask and never transpredicates to affirm truly personal alternatives.

Jung believed that primitives were under the direction of a group mind and consciousness emerged gradually from such unconsciousness.

Unipredication therefore held total sway in early humanity (a theme we also found in the Jaynesian speculations of Chapter 5). The archetypes are said to be objective because they are lasting remnants akin to McLuhan's scribal traditions. They have quite specific meanings, as in standing for the deity, for the contrasexual, for the family, and so on. Jung finds an important use for such unipredicated formulations because as iconic precedents they can counterbalance any one-sidedness developing in the psyche of a given individual. Although they are unipredications, archetypes can nevertheless facilitate the emergence of transpredicating insights if they balance off the narrowing propensities of the individual's psychic outlook on life.

For example, the first paragraph of this volume (see Chapter 1) quotes Jung's dialogue with a feminine identity who "spoke" to him from the depths of his psyche. The meanings being vocalized presumably came from his anima archetype—the feminine attitude carried by each male in his collective unconscious—but the actual voice was that of a female patient whom Jung was treating at the time. Archetypes have no specific symbolic form so they must borrow shapes from the person's experience to make their meanings known in consciousness. This one-sided female attitude provoked Jung into an internal argument over whether he was engaged in art or science as he worked through his personal analysis. Fortunately, he succeeded in arguing this feminized viewpoint away and thereby negated any one-sided hold that the anima might have gained over his consciousness. But in the dispute he also had to acknowledge certain legitimate points the anima made. This weighing of contradictory views resulted in the formation of Jung's *self* (i.e., a centering point of balanced attitudes in his personality). Something that was totally unconscious helped effect a richer sense of consciousness. The movement here from the unipredication of anima one-sidedness to a balancing selfhood via the alternative transpredications of an internal dialogue is a remarkable demonstration of how to enrich and elevate the personal through use of the collective.

I mentioned above how minority groups in American culture try to raise the level of consciousness regarding their social problems (e.g., racial prejudice, sexual inequities in employment, etc.). However, this group effort, if it is truly consciousness raising and not an insular form of unconsciousness raising, has a paradox associated with it. As Meyrowitz (1985) expressed it,

> Today's minority consciousness is something of a paradox. Many people take renewed pride in their special identity, yet the heightened consciousness of the special group is the result of being able to view one's group from the outside; that is, it is the result of no longer being fully *in* the group. (p. 132)

As the group is singled out from other groups (via transpredicating comparisons), the individual in the group necessarily shifts from a one-sided to a multifaceted understanding. From this broader perspective, there are counterarguments that have been leveled by other groups to consider. Such counters are rarely without some merit (as was true of Jung's anima arguments). They cannot be easily dismissed. All such consciousness raising runs the risk of weakening the commitment of individual members to the group by generating transpredicational understandings of the points at issue. With growing individual awareness, alternative intentions, aspirations, and goals begin to pop up that are not always welcome to the group. As Taylor (1989) has observed, "the atomistic focus on our individual goals dissolves community and divides us from each other" (pp. 500–501). Just as Jung forged a unique self from among conflicting alternatives, true consciousness raising in the collective encourages individuality rather than uniformity. It is not easy for a group to bring cohesion to the conflicting views of individual members.

It is probably for this reason that much of the so-called consciousness raising of collectives is in reality a unipredicating effort to achieve cohesion. This is accomplished through emphasizing the distinctive nature of the group ("Who are we?") or finding some McLuhanian tradition on which to encourage group pride ("What are our common roots?"). The collective gives little credence, distorts, or ignores completely the claims and arguments of nongroup members. All collectives must endorse such unipolar views because this is what lends them cohesiveness and ensures longevity. These are good forms of unconsciousness, from which group members gain confidence and a continuing sense of identity and purpose. Even a delinquent or criminal gang seeks such identity in traditions; although these are good for its unique survival, the broader cultural groupings on which the gang preys would find nothing positive in such cultural solidification.

We come to the interesting conclusion that for a group's identity to be strengthened, the identity of its individual members must be weakened. Group identity is ultimately fashioned on unconsciousness, on unipredications that its members more or less uncritically endorse. There is also a good deal of affection involved here. People copy others in order to be liked and feel appreciated as an active member of the collective. There is no group mind, but there is group consensus on meanings and preferences held in common. The pressure of social expectation cannot be denied. There are such *Socius* considerations in all human behavior.

We also learn from this analysis that the predicational process per se does not stipulate what kinds of meanings are to be affirmed as understanding-intentions and then brought forward into action-intentions. The predicational process is entirely open and arbitrary on this matter. So to select what could, should, or ought to be affirmed, people look to others for the grounds of behavior. Children look to parents, one person looks to another, and in due course some kind of power hierarchy takes shape. Leaders step forward. And here is where a major problem arises for the teleologist because it definitely appears that people cannot be responsible contributors to their behavior in this social conglomerate. The predicational process of the individual is being submerged if not supplanted. If we observe people extrospectively, the process seems to be something other than an individually situated act of predication. Mediational modeling seems a more parsimonious explanation. To speak of selves at this point appears superfluous.

DEMISE OF THE AUTHOR:
LANGUAGE AS SOCIAL CONSTRUCTION

One of the most important sources of the power hierarchy referred to in the previous section is that of language. Language has been so extensively studied and analyzed in the social sciences that it has taken on a life of its own. That is, language has been interpreted by various social-constructionist theories as a supra-individual force that conveys influence in its own right, no matter what a given author may be intending in framing ideas linguistically. This constructionist ideology has great relevance for our understanding of psychic consciousness. In the present section we will first contrast Hegelian with Marxian interpretations of consciousness, and then show how this same issue is manifested today in conflicting interpretations of constructionism as rooted either in the meaningful intentions of the author or the linguistic conventions of the collective.

Hegelian Individual-Consciousness Versus Marxian
Class-Consciousness

There are many current analyses of human consciousness that follow a line of argument used by Karl Marx (1818–1883), who was in turn influenced by Georg Wilhelm Friedrich Hegel (1770–1831). The former took the latter's idealistic speculations and turned them into a materialistic realism (see Marx, 1952a, p. 11). And in doing so, Marx advanced a formidable *Socius* explanation that current theories of social constructionism have adopted. Coulter (1985) has observed that the central intellectual interest of all forms of social constructionism (or constructivism) is "the description of the ways in which cultural–conceptual schemes are deployed in the constitution of phenomena and the way in which the conceptualization of phenomena is socially organized and socially accredited (or *discredited*)" (p. 129; italics in original). We will first review the style of theorizing used by Hegel and Marx and then move into a general discussion of social constructionism to learn how this interpretation of behavior and consciousness has, in effect, postulated the demise of McLuhan's author (see Chapter 3).

Hegelian philosophy analyzes the gradual working out of consciousness by an individual (albeit divine) mind or spirit. History for Hegel is not the unfolding of an efficiently caused sequence of events but is more like a reasoning process—a succession of premises leading to conclusions, which in turn suggest new premises (Stace, 1955, p. 22). In contrast to the computer enthusiasts of today, Hegel rejects the view that humans (much less the deity) reason demonstratively. He states unequivocally that "the essential movement of thought is dialectic" (Hegel, 1821/1952b, p. 53). Following Socrates and Plato (see Chapter 7), Hegel spoke of this dialectical flow in terms of a *thesis* (initial meaning affirmed), *antithesis* (opposite of initial affirmation), and *synthesis* (combining the best of these opposites). All ideas framed by mind are fundamentally dialectical or oppositional; indeed, each idea has within it the seeds of its own contradiction (Hegel, 1857/1952a, p. 182). Resolving such contradictions enables progress in ongoing thought. History is a record of the deity's progress in this regard.

Consciousness for Hegel involved two things: "first, the fact *that I know*; secondly, *what I know*" (p. 161; italics in original). The former refers to a process and the latter to the content of this process. Self-consciousness combines both of these aspects to bring about awareness of "one's own being" (p. 161). The highest form of knowledge is such self-knowledge (p. 186). If self-consciousness is achieved, self-realization can take place because now the identity can "make itself *actually* that which it is *potentially*" (p. 161; italics in original). Becoming actual is experienced as a profound freedom. Hegel focused his analysis on the divine spirit's development from potentiality to actuality (p. 160).

The movement of history is therefore the record of a deity coming to self-consciousness and hence freedom. Each historical epoch has an internal contradiction (thesis–antithesis) that the deity works out as it progresses to self-consciousness, at which point it will transcend the contradictions and establish a balanced unity. For example, Hegel traced the dialectical steps of spiritual development from the spirit of Egypt (thesis) to its contradiction in Persia (antithesis) leading to an entirely new Greek spirit (synthesis; pp. 257–258). And, of course, in due time the Graecian free spirit (thesis) was to prompt its contradiction in the more controlled, legalistic spirit of the Roman Empire (antithesis) calling for yet another synthesis until such time as a perfectly balanced (noncontradictory) collective might take place. There is a dynamic conflict at play in history that brings about change, movement, and ultimately progress as the divine spirit comes to self-consciousness. Even though Hegel is talking about collective states like Egypt and Greece, his basic analysis is of the individual. As he put it, "The principles of the successive phases of spirit that animate the nations, in a necessitated gradation, are themselves only steps in the development of the one universal spirit, which through them elevates and completes itself to a self-comprehending *totality*" (p. 190; italics in original).

The dialectical process is reminiscent of Jung's analysis of the person balancing the psyche into a functioning totality (the self) at the center-point where consciousness and unconsciousness meet. Jung appreciated the singularity of this balancing process for he named it *individuation* (1953b, p. 152). This Hegelian strategy so fascinated me years ago that I wrote to Jung and naively asked him whether he had ever been an advocate of Hegelian philosophy. In his answer (dated April 27, 1959), Jung rejected any direct influence here whatsoever, and referred to Hegel as "not even a proper philosopher, but a misfired psychologist" (Rychlak, 1975c). I therefore concluded that the similarity in theoretical explanation was due to the fact that both Hegel and Jung independently theorized predicationally, which led to a comparable individuality in their formulations.

It is quite different when we come to Marx (1952a), who believed that Hegel had set dialectic on its head (p. 11) by misunderstanding the origin and function of ideas. For Marx also, the dialectic is a world principle, a law of nature manifested in historical change; but he conceived of it as a play of opposites within the means of material production that each society employs. Ideas do not carry the oppositionality of dialectic; they do not create institutions, evolve governments, or distribute economic rewards. Ideas are the *result* and not the cause of such dialectically material aspects of existence. Social institutions, political attitudes, philosophies, and religions are merely the superstructure of society that has been built upon the soil of its own form of material production. The entire purpose of this superstructure is to retain the status quo, which involves the material advantage of some groups and the expropriation of others. In the England of his time, Marx observed the worker, the proletarian, getting a meager return for the amount of actual production he or she contributed to the material rewards enjoyed by society; whereas the capitalist, the bourgeois, who like a "leech" did not work to produce wealth, reaped greater and greater rewards. Capital is therefore not a personal but a social power (Marx, 1952b, p. 426).

Borrowing the Hegelian concept of dialectic, Marx saw in this unfair distribution of material reward for work a *class conflict*, the formation of a triad. One class (bourgeoisie) that had been the synthesis of a bygone era was now facing its antithesis in a new class on which it must prey (the proletariat); consequently, what would most certainly issue from this "tension of opposites" was a revolution (a negation) and the establishment of a classless society (communistic collective). Class conflict would then no longer occur following this final "negation of a negation" because the expropriators (i.e., the bourgeoisie) would disappear from the face of the earth, and peace with plenty for all who actually worked to produce capital would be achieved.

In order for this communistic revolution to occur it is vital for the proletariat to attain self-consciousness as a group identity—also known as *class consciousness*. Instead of a Hegelian divine spirit coming to self-consciousness for freedom's sake, a self-conscious class of people must attain its freedom through such group awareness. Only then can it marshall its forces against the oppressor. Marx therefore stressed that "The proletarian movement is the self-conscious, independent movement of the *immense majority*, in the interest of the *immense majority*" (Marx, 1952b, p. 424; italics added). Ideas are class-linked: "The ruling ideas of each age have ever been the ideas of its ruling class" (p. 428). Education is determined by the social conditions predominant at the time; communism therefore seeks to "rescue education from the influence of the ruling class" (p. 427). And the way such redistribution of power in the society is to be achieved demands that an end be put to class conflict once and for all: "The social consciousness of past ages, despite all the multiplicity and variety it displays, moves within certain common forms, or general ideas, which cannot completely vanish except with the total disappearance of class antagonisms" (p. 428). Of course, in the Marxian worldview, this meant ending class differences altogether.

Individuals might flatter themselves into believing that their thoughts are occasionally entirely their own, free of collective determinants. But according to Marx, the truth is quite otherwise. Every idea in mind is conditioned by the perspective of the class background from which it issues. The same holds for the idea of consciousness. A person's self-consciousness is born in speech, and the language used in speech arises out of the concrete need for social exchange. Consciousness is therefore social before it is individual (Hook, 1962, p. 44). The class struggle always directs things—in philosophy, art, religion, law, medicine, and so on. No aspect of the social life of a people escapes this class logic. Furthermore, everything in life is political because "every class struggle is a political struggle" (Marx, 1952b, p. 423). The very notion of individuality has a class-linked meaning because, as Marx challenged his reader to appreciate,

> You must ... confess that by 'individual' you mean no other person than the bourgeois, than the middle class owner of property. This person must, indeed, be swept out of the way and made impossible [in the future]. (p. 426)

We might ponder whether Marx was really interested in class-consciousness as transpredication. In line with our discussion of the paradoxical aspects of such claims it seems that class-unconsciousness (via unipredication among group members) might suit the Marxian—or any—revolutionary's aims to perfection. It sounds ridiculous to encourage "raising the level of unconsciousness" among group members, but this is what our analysis implies given our terminological usage. Considering his belief that ideas are class-linked, another paradox arises in the fact that as the son of middle-class parents, how is it that Marx could break free of his class identity and frame such anti-bourgeoisie ideas? Did such ideas spring from the "inner contradictions" that Hegel had suggested we might find in ideas shaped initially by the bourgeoisie? Possibly, but this conclusion would go against the Marxian view of people being strictly limited to the ideas of their class. Marx viewed dialectical oppositionality externally (in opposing classes) rather than internally, whereby the individual might willfully contradict his or her class beliefs. Whatever the case, the point of importance is that we appreciate the difference between a Marxian collective analysis and the individualized analysis of consciousness favored by Hegel and Jung.

Individual Versus Collective Forms of Constructionism

It was George A. Kelly who raised the concept of construction to prominence in psychology at mid-20th century, interpreting this as an individual or personal phenomenon (see Chapter 1). Kelly believed that a human being's reasoning process involved the framing and naming of constructs. A construct—which is "construed" into being—involves finding two items (objects, people, actions, etc.) that are alike but yet contrast in some way with a third item (Kelly, 1955, p. 61). For example, the construct of *bossiness* might equate a parent and a teacher as both aggressively telling others what to do, but also contrast this similarity with a close friend who is never intrusive or demanding. Parent and teacher are alike and contrast with the friend on this bossiness construct. The individual doing the construing chooses not only the substance but the names of what Kelly called *personal constructs*. It is important to recognize that Kelly relied on predication in his theorizing, where oppositionality plays a fundamental role in cognition (as in the inside vs. outside of the predicating circles of Figures 2 and 3). And, like Hegel and Jung, Kelly's formulations adapt best to descriptive analysis of the individual.

From the late 1950s to the present, we see an increasing tendency for constructivism in psychology to be co-opted by psychologists with a preference for social theorizing. I have continually been puzzled by the process that is supposed to bring about social constructionism. Of course, as is true of the concept of predication, we can think of construction as either a process (verb usage) or as a content (noun usage) within some process. Social stereotypes are contents in some kind of process; a social stereotype is essentially a construct or a construction. If Whites see Blacks stereotypically, and vice versa, is this racially linked imagery anything more than a predication held in common by an identifiable group—akin to any normative belief? There is no Hegelian individual like the divine spirit framing the stereotype for everyone in the collective. Group members seem to me to be agreeing or accepting a common phenomenal assumption, held to now in an unconscious manner (i.e., lacking in transpredicational criticism to negate the stereotype). Who creates these assumptive predications in the first place? Fortunately the literature on social constructionism has addressed this matter.

Sociologists and psychologists frequently mention Peter L. Berger (1963; with Luckmann, 1966) as one of the "fathers" of social constructionism. Berger analyzed the sociologists Émile Durkheim and Max Weber, whom we noted in Chapter 1 held opposing views on *Socius* theorizing. What makes this contrast especially interesting in the present context is that it parallels our discussion of Hegel and Marx. Durkheim (1961), a so-called "objectivist," thought of society as in a class by itself (see especially p. 16). He wanted to avoid "reducing" the social to the individual because he feared this would permit psychology to swallow up sociology. Durkheim construed society extraspectively, as a supra-individual process. The individual becomes a content of the social process in this view, molded and shaped into identifiable existence by collective forces of some sort (Durkheim, 1933, p. 269). Weber, on the other hand, was considered a "subjectivist," trying to understand the collective from the introspective perspective of the individuals who formed it (Berger & Luckmann, 1966, p. 18). As a consequence, Weber's theory stressed that social actions embodied people's collective intentions, akin to our notion of "predications held in common." Logical learning theory is obviously consistent with the Weberian viewpoint.

Berger and Luckmann tried to bring the objectivist and subjectivist views of society together, claiming both that "*Society is a human product*" and also that "*Man is a social product*" (p. 61; italics in original). There is a kind of dialectical interaction taking place between the individual and society, each influencing the other. But Berger does not really describe two processes interacting. I do not think that Durkheim would be pleased with Berger's interactive social constructionism, for when he comes right down to it, again and again the creative or initiating process is placed in the individual and not in the collective.

Berger and Luckmann (1966) defined social construction as follows: "all social phenomena are *constructions* produced historically through human activity" (p. 106; italics in original). There is an ongoing social content of belief available to the person, who in turn modifies and contributes to such belief so that it changes meaning over time. The initiating source of this change is, as I say, invariably the individual, for at no point is there a supra-individual process or a group mind consciously framing events. The individual human being frames an idea and then conveys it for consideration by others. If it is seen as meaningfully relevant this idea is then *objectified* and *internalized* by others in the collective (pp. 60–61). Thus,

Berger and Luckmann describe how a religious genius might concoct a "new mythology" that will become part of the cultural lore (objectified) and then used as grounds for social action by succeeding generations (internalized; p. 83).

But the individual member of the collective is not a mere pawn to such internalizations. That is, "rebellious constructions of the mind" can "liberate the individual to a considerable extent from the definatory system of his society" (Berger, 1963, p. 133). People as individuals can "say 'no' to society and often have done so" (p. 142). This capacity to negate lends support to the suggestion that Berger has a predication process under consideration. He did not overlook the fact that people can self-reflexively transcend and oppose any meanings that they are now affirming. This individual dynamic is totally consistent with LLT's predicational modeling in the *Logos*. Even so, I am none too pleased with Berger and Luckmann's frequent use of terms like *mechanism* and *mediation* in presenting this version of social construction theory (pp. 55, 76, 109). They may not mean to use these terms in the efficient-cause manner of traditional psychological explanation, but this is how they will undoubtedly be understood in today's social science.

It is not difficult finding Marxian and Durkheimian views manifested in the writings of social constructionists in psychology. For example, Gergen (1989) urged that "we avoid reducing the social world to the psychological" (p. 479). Gergen believes that knowledge issues from a supraindividual, interpersonal source so that "what we take to be knowledgeable propositions about the world are essentially the outcome of social relatedness. What we take to be knowledge bearing propositions are not achievements of the individual mind, but social achievements" (p. 472). Harré (1987) speaks in the same vein: "We should begin with the assumption that the primary location (in both a temporal and logical sense) of psychological processes is collective rather than individual" (pp. 4–5). Sampson (1993) next brings in the Marxian class-conflict theme by suggesting that "every [social] construction has a dominant group—the constructors—and its others, those who are constructed" (p. 4). The LLT advocate would prefer to hear from Berger and Luckmann (1966) at this point, for they say in contradiction to these other social constructionists that "all social constructed universes change, and the change is brought about by the concrete actions of human beings.... Reality is socially defined. But the definitions are always *embodied*, that is, concrete individuals and groups of individuals serve as definers of reality" (p. 116).

The predication process explains how an individual might come to define or construe reality, which, to follow the Berger strategy, is eventually objectified and then identified as *the* reality by others in the group. Logical learning theory can readily embrace this view of social constructionism. What is the comparable social construing process advanced by Gergen,

Harré, and Sampson? These theorists fall back on the functioning of language in social construing, particularly as manifested in dialogues. Such interpersonal (or, "intersubjective") relations are taken as prima facie evidence that something social is occurring, something that transcends the individual or "self." Self-consciousness is never achieved individually, but only as the result of an "immersed interdependence" with others (Gergen, 1991, p. 147). Language is relatedness (p. 157) and we cannot escape the language system in which we are collectively immersed. Indeed, group consciousness erases individual consciousness: "As the category of the individual person fades from view, consciousness of construction becomes focal. We realize increasingly that who and what we are is not so much the result of our 'personal essence' (real feelings, deep beliefs, and the like), but of how we are constructed in various social groups" (p. 170). Hence, "without others there is no self" (p. 178).

This formulation pictures the individual as unable to dialectically transpredicate beyond—and therefore as being locked in by—demonstrative "givens" known variously as inputs, information entry, language signs, and so on. There can be no true authorship here, for there is never the McLuhanian "point of view" being expressed. Nor can Berger's rebellious individual—or Karl Marx, offspring of bourgeoisie parents—break free of the collective's unipredications, which control the person in that blind fashion of Skinnerian conditioning (see Chapter 5). Thoughts may multiply but never through transpredicating efforts of the individual reasoner. In effect, the person is like a computer, living in a constant state of unconsciousness, mediating the unipredications of the collective's linguistic signaling system (see Chapter 7). Harré (1984) adds to this image of the person trapped in language:

> Consciousness ... is not some unique state, but is the possession of certain grammatical models for the presentation to oneself and others of what one knows by inter- and intrapersonal perception. These models provide the structures by which I can know that which I am currently feeling, thinking, suffering, doing and so on, that is, they provide the wherewithal for an organization of knowledge as mine. (p. 214)

The problem with this interpretation of language is that it overlooks the important role played by oppositionality in the formulation of meanings. If, as LLT suggests, language terms, or words, are instrumentalities coined in order to express these meanings, then it follows that oppositionality should be reflected in linguistic systems. The LLT view is in agreement with Hegel that ideas always contain the seeds of their own negation or contradiction. Linguists have recognized the importance of oppositionality in linguistic structure and function. Thus, Trier (1931) essentially defined delimiting oppositionality when he observed that every antonymic word that is uttered implicitly suggests its opposite meaning to both the speaker and hearer. Lyons (1977) has said that "opposition is one of the most important principles governing the structure of language" (p. 271), and Richards (1967) has singled out opposition as an essential principle through which language works (p. 10).

Freud once cited the philologist Karl Abel, who maintained that early human beings had learned their oldest and simplest concepts as "contraries to their contraries, and only learnt by degrees to separate the two sides of an antithesis and think of one without conscious comparison with the other" (1910/1957a, p. 158). Thus, in the Egyptian language "there are a fair number of words with two meanings, one of which is the exact opposite of the other" (p. 156). Vygotsky (1986) has also noted that languages like Chinese, Hebrew, Latin, and Russian have one word signifying opposites —such as high versus low, or night versus day (pp. 128, 131). With one word conveying two meanings it would appear that it is up to the hearer or reader to decide which direction understanding should take concerning the meanings being expressed, and invariably it is the context provided by predication that enables this decision to be made. Logical learning theory finds the rationale for human agency in such oppositional reasoning capacities. I will return to linguistic oppositionality when we take up deconstructionism.

By ignoring the individual's innate capacity to negate what he or she is being linguistically "shaped" to do or believe, the social constructionists find it possible to refer to personhood, selfhood, or individuality as mere linguistic conventions that people have picked up in interpersonal relations through dialogues, imitations, and so forth. Sampson (1993) says: "Not only are we socialized in and through conversations directed toward us and held about us, but we learn those skills requisite to engaging in conversations. We especially learn how to use our talk to account for ourselves to others and to ourselves" (p. 20). Along with the loss of individual identity and authorship there is now a *loss in agency* to consider.

Given the collective determination of all behavior, we cannot hold people responsible for moral violations nor credit them with creative achievements; as Gergen (1991) says, "If it is not individual 'I's who create relationships, but relationships that create the sense of 'I,' then 'I' cease to be the center of success or failure, the one who is evaluated well or poorly, and so on" (p. 157). Harré (1984) adds, "Agency ... is an endowment from theory, permitting the formulation of hypotheses about what I was, am, or could be capable" (p. 214). Because he finds all personal meaning stemming from the collective, Sampson (1993) concludes that "an identity builds upon its relation to other identities; nothing can be itself without taking into consideration the kinds of relationship by which its selfsameness is constituted" (p. 92). The Hegelian form of self-conscious freedom is thus impossible on these versions of social constructionism.

My initial reaction to the social constructionist's claim that language is the source of all belief, creativity, and behavioral responsibility is to think of this as just another example of mediational modeling in the traditional style of behaviorism and information-processing. Language from this perspective is a string of mediated signals, previously input and now directing the course of output-responses in efficient-cause fashion (see Figure 1). As such, the meaning conveyed by these signals reflects the collective's rather than the individual's "point of view." Although a legitimate formulation, I do not think that we can rest with this routine commentary, which is more or less applicable to all psychological theorizing today. Something must be added here about how language learning occurs. Logical learning theory holds that this learning process is predicational, and that meaningful predications occur prelinguistically (Rychlak, 1994, p. 267). The earliest predications of the newborn are surely affective assessments. But at some point the infant is called on to learn language. Language is an extension from the physical sensation to the abstract labeling of such sensations, which in turn can then be extended as knowledge to other realms of experience.

Language, according to LLT, is constructed initially by having the sensory realm predicate the abstract realm of symbols. The symbols are targeted and draw meaning from the predicating feeling-sensations. Once learned, these symbols (words, labels, constructs, etc.) are used as predicates to extend understanding. As I have noted in other chapters, this succession of events is what we mean by *learning*. Learning occurs when the individual is confident enough to use a former target (e.g., word qua meaning) as a predicate (Rychlak, 1994, pp. 49, 129, 130). We develop a sense of what *reliable* means by experiencing others keeping their promise, showing up when they are supposed to, meeting the goal set, and so on. At some point we can then use this word reliable as a predicating meaning to target someone in our experience. What began as an embodied sensation or attitude toward this behavioral pattern symbolized by the word reliable becomes an abstraction that can be intentionally generalized (or not) to different targets in our experience—to people like John of Figure 2. Abstractions (words) then serve a monumental role as predicates in the ever-expanding learning of human beings. We call this growing range of predications *knowledge*. Language terms as symbols are fraught with such meaning (Cassirer, 1944, p. 80). Meaning-extension is the logical patterning of an affirmed predicate to its target (Rychlak, 1994, pp. 15, 99). This extension occurs in a precedent-sequacious fashion.

The initial problem facing the "language-ready" infant—at 10 months or so—is that the infant must achieve a patterning between strictly physical sensations (seeing, hearing, feeling, etc.) and a targeted pattern that the culture identifies as a word-symbol, expressing meaning. A culture can only exist because the collective freezes its valued knowledge into a linguistic symbol-system that can be conveyed across subsequent generations as its social heritage (Barthes, 1986, p. 53). As both Jaynes and Jung have noted (see Chapter 4), primitive thinking finds it impossible to separate the physical from the symbolic, resulting in a reification of the latter. In the primitive mind, words are real entities with palpable powers so that magical changes can be effected in physical reality through the use of certain word combinations (e.g., magical incantations).

This bridging from the physical to the symbolic is difficult for the infant. To begin with, as Polanyi (1964) has noted, "no one can learn a new language unless he first trusts that it means something" (p. 151). Applying this to our infant in the learning of a first language, we see that consciousness must be elevated for such learning to take place. That is, a transpredication must occur in which the infant now realizes that the word-symbol has a significance over and beyond itself—its symbolic role. A word is not simply a collection of letter-signs to be traced or mouthed in rote fashion. Such literal copying of a sign is identical to the unconscious processing of a computer (Chapter 7).

A marvelous, highly dramatic example of what the LLT view of language learning involves may be found in Helen Keller's (1902/1980) autobiography. Blind and deaf from age nineteen months she tells of the "most important day I remember in all my life" (p. 20). This day occurred a few months before her seventh birthday, and involved an interaction with her teacher, Anne Mansfield Sullivan. Ms. Sullivan had been trying to get Helen to understand that words have meaning by placing objects in her right hand and spelling out words in her left hand. Helen had already learned to copy letters like this by simply matching an object placed in one hand with what was traced on the other. For example, when a doll was grasped by her right hand and d-o-l-l spelled out in her left hand, Helen "learned" to copy this sequence by placing the doll in one and tracing this spelling out in the other of her mother's hands. But this was merely a physical-sensory tracing. Helen had not grasped the abstract pattern being suggested between one hand and the other—namely, that objects have names and words have meanings. As a result, she regularly confounded the physical tracings of m-u-g and w-a-t-e-r (p. 22). On the miraculous day in question, Ms. Sullivan gave Helen her hat, preliminary to taking a walk on the family grounds. Helen observes: ". . . I knew I was going out into the warm sunshine. This thought, if a wordless sensation may be called a thought, made me hop and skip with pleasure" (pp. 22–23). I think we see here that Helen *is* reasoning predicationally albeit purely at a sensory level. She knows that the item that is placed on her head (hat) signifies that warm sunshine is soon to follow. Past experience of a walk in the sunshine had served as a predicating sensory meaning, lending this meaning to the targeted hat. The hat was also framed by a highly positive affective assessment. But now the hat is itself a predicate targeting the meaning of *walk* to follow, although neither predicate nor target is yet named. As teacher and student walked down a path to the well house, there were other targeted sensations to assess positively, such as the fragrance of honeysuckle. When they arrived at the well house someone was drawing water, so Ms. Sullivan took Helen's hand and placed it under the well spout, which in turn delighted the child as yet another enjoyable sensation. Here is what Helen had to say about what then took place:

> As the cool stream gushed over one hand she [Ms. Sullivan] spelled into the other the word *water*, first slowly, then rapidly. I stood still, my whole attention fixed upon the motions of her fingers. Suddenly I felt a misty consciousness as of something forgotten—a thrill of returning thought; and somehow the mystery of language was revealed to me. I knew then that "w-a-t-e-r" meant the wonderful cool something that was flowing over my hand. That living word awakened my soul, gave it light, hope, joy, set it free! There were barriers still, it is true, but barriers that could in time be swept away. (p. 23)

Social constructionism would doubtless stress the fact that Helen was engaged in a dialogue of sorts with her teacher, and was thereby being shaped into a certain language structure in the hand printing. Logical learning theory does not deny either of these facts. But note how Helen is able to recall *wordless sensations* as meaningful thoughts, such as the expectation of what it meant to wear her hat. This clearly suggests an active intellect, in the style of Brentano and Husserl (see Chapter 6), bringing to bear predicational assumptions even before there is a cultural language content. As LLT contends, people do not learn to predicate, they predicate in order to learn. I think we see this learning process taking place in Helen's personal experience.

Helen was apparently aided in her learning by the preliminary predication of a positive affection for the water. The gushing water was itself an initial target for affective assessment; it was a much-liked sensation. But it then acted as a predicate for the word being etched on her hand. The positive context established by this much-liked sensation of the water doubtless heightened the concentration she experienced in extending meaning from one hand (the predicate) to the other (the target). Although Helen refers to a "misty consciousness" in deriving her insight, I would suggest that initially she experienced a highly focused, "good" form of unconsciousness. A highly liked, former target (pleasurable water), acting now as a predicate, delimited her attention to such an extent that she effectively tautologized one hand's meaning to the other. In this shift from water as target to water as predicate, Helen reflects learning. Furthermore, once the tracing of w-a-t-e-r had been given a meaning, Ms. Sullivan repeated the process so that Helen learned that this former target could itself be a predicate, tautologically extending meaning to other liquids having a water-like quality. Her ongoing education was now greatly enhanced for she had learned that the hand etchings had a symbolical—that is, meaning-extending—role to play in learning and communication.

Logical learning theory does not eclipse or explain away the author, because it is only through the efforts of such individual cognizing (or construing) that meanings are framed and carried forward to be copied consciously or unconsciously by others. This is what Berger was getting at in his theory of objectification and internalization. Even though we never forget that collectives are populated by individuals, there is no need to deny that collective influences on the individual do occur. It is not easy framing predicated meanings at every turn. People need help in deciding what to affirm in this or that circumstance. As we have already noted, people naturally look to imitate others for how to behave, dress, and even "think" on various matters. Such cultural influences are inevitable. The *Socius* ground has a legitimate role to play in theorizing about human beings.

Logical learning theory has no hidden scenario advocating that people *are* or *ought to be* individualists in the sociopolitical sense. This would be a content issue (i.e., concerning what meanings should be affirmed and enacted) and all LLT is seeking to understand is the process whereby human beings learn and behave. Even in the most conforming society imaginable, where individualism might be punished as a criminal act, the *process* by which such cultural values qua contents are fashioned and enforced must necessarily rest on individual consciousness and unconsciousness. Groups have differing cultural perspectives, of course, in which what is taken to be correct or true is relative to such background differences. Here language plays a major role in shaping such viewpoints (contents) and carrying them forward as cultural artifacts. In this scheme culture, not the individual, creates styles of selfhood. But now, can such sculpted selves actually find truth—even relative truth—in the linguistic formulations of a culture? Or, is there something about language per se that inevitably contradicts the truth that its words convey no matter which culture may be framing such presumed certainties?

DEMISE OF TRUTH: DECONSTRUCTIONISM

Our analysis of social constructionism has, in effect, shifted attention from the individual as framer of meanings to collectives as framers of meanings. This account pictures individuals as trapped within their language system. Social constructionists embrace the Whorfian view that "We [human beings] cut nature up, organize it into concepts, and ascribe significances as we do, largely because we are parties to an agreement to organize it in this way—an agreement that holds throughout our speech community and is codified in the patterns of our language" (Whorf, 1958, p. 5). I am not suggesting that social constructionism was born of the Whorfian hypothesis. A more important influence here was undoubtedly *structuralism*, a school of thought nurtured by the writings of Claude Lévi-Strauss and Ferdinand de Saussure among others (Reese, 1980, p. 553). Structuralism has affected such varied fields as anthropology, architecture, economics, history, linguistics, literary criticism, philosophy, psychoanalysis, and religion.

Structuralism arose in opposition to so-called *essentialism* (Culler, 1982, p. 18). The essentialist believes that there is one and only one aspect of reality to be identified—its free-standing "essence"—whereas the structuralist turns to linguistic practices to see how these culturally fashioned meanings have shaped the presumed structure of reality. Structuralists are therefore relativists (p. 19) and, like the social constructionists, reject the author as creator, believing instead that such creations arise from a context of meaning in which the culture's language actually determines any such innovations (Rosenau, 1992, p. 29). Our essential reality is not free-standing but is fashioned by, hence depends on, the language we use to characterize it.

But note, although the structuralists believe—in what might be termed a Marxian-Durkheimian fashion—that the individual is not *the* creator of what he or she expresses, there is still the expectation that the cultural context itself can be accurately identified, codified, and studied. The account issuing from this effort will always be relativistic, of course. Culture A's language system employs categories to understand reality that culture B's language system finds erroneous. However, within the constraints of these two cultural language systems, truth—albeit a relativistic truth—may still be expressed. Structuralism and social constructionism share this view of language-induced knowledge.

Unfortunately, a problem arises in that it is also true that even within a given culture, disagreements over the truth being expressed can take place. Those who share a language system do not always uniformly understand a written or spoken text. The matter of unipredication versus transpredication intrudes here because one can claim that any meaning being "read" is not *the* meaning actually conveyed. A listener or reader might not find such a unipredicated, "given" meaning clearly expressed by the text in question. The message might be *consciously* transformed through transpredications of one sort or another.

Actually, it had been recognized for centuries that more than one meaning could be conveyed in a written text. In the Middle Ages, theologians believed that they could "decode" such hidden meanings in Biblical tracts. In the 17th century, this form of Biblical exegesis was termed *hermeneutics* (Palmer, 1969, p. 34). The root of this word is from Hermes, the messenger of the Greek gods who conveyed the deity's wishes down from Olympus to the mortals below. The suggestion here is that the Christian

God is also sending hidden, albeit discernible, messages in the Biblical text—and that this is the true message being sent. The text as written is merely a smoke screen for this Divine Truth, which had to be covertly transmitted because of its uniquely esoteric nature. Analogical to the structuralist thesis, the writer of the relevant text was not author of this arcane truth. Writing under divine inspiration, the initial "author" was merely a conduit, entirely unconscious of the alternative transpredications that would later be consciously put to his writings by the hermeneuticist.

Gradually, the term hermeneutics expanded to mean the "interpretation of texts," as in literary analyses that have nothing to do with biblical writings. And with the development of structuralism we find the two fields of literary analysis merging on such points as, for example, the nonexistence of individual authors, language shaping all thought, and the idea that "meaning is a matter of [culturally defined] context" (Palmer, 1969, p. 24). The removal of the text from the author's influence did not stop here. The so-called New Criticism of literary analysis claimed that the written text per se had its own "being" that could be analyzed "without the help of biographical, historical, or psychological background data" (pp. 17–18). This attitude takes Marx and Durkheim out of the picture by holding to an exclusively syntactical thesis: namely, that it is in the arrangement of words alone, as expressed in the existential present, that we find the meaning conveyed—or, if one prefers, *intended*—in the text. This attitude sets the scene for yet another development taking place, in thesis–antithesis fashion.

The new development was *poststructuralism*, a term that has been equated with *postmodernism*. Such doubling of terminological descriptors can become confusing (Sarup, 1989, p. 131). Add to this the fact that there are "probably as many forms of post-modernism as there are post-modernists" (Rosenau, 1992, p. 15) and one wonders what the tie is that binds all of these views together. The binding tie seems to be the conviction that it is impossible to arrive at true knowledge either *between* or *within* cultural language systems. As Culler (1982) sums it up, "Structuralists are convinced that systematic knowledge is possible; post-structuralists claim to know only the impossibility of this knowledge" (p. 22). We have a very pessimistic message here: According to the poststructuralists, not only are we humans locked into a language system, we are locked into an undecidable course of linguistic exchange (i.e., dialogue), discussing all sides of myriad issues without hope of achieving even a relative, arbitrary, culture-bound truth.

The major poststructuralist (postmodernist) approach discussed in the literature today is Jacques Derrida's (1981) *deconstructionism*. Derrida was influenced significantly by Friedrich Nietzsche (1844–1900) and Martin Heidegger (1889–1976), and we will take a few samplings from these philosophers to show what it means to deconstruct a text. Literally any kind of phenomenon that can be delineated for consideration is a text in post-modern writings (Rosenau, 1992, p. xiv). Probably the most interesting feature of deconstructionism for me is its heavy reliance on oppositionality and negation. From Heidegger, Derrida adopted the concept of *sous rature* ("under erasure"). This refers to the fact that sometimes a word will be used in a text that is not really adequate for what it must express, and it should really be negated or erased, but is retained in a text by simply crossing it out. Thus Heidegger often crossed out the word *Being* as a kind of editorial deletion even as he let it stand right alongside another printing of *Being* (Sarup, 1989, p. 35). The point he was making was that the word was not adequate for what he was dealing with, yet it was necessary; it had to remain—warts and all!—under erasure even though it threatened to subvert the meaning of the textual passage.

For Derrida, a word in a textual phrase can always be found that has a similar duality of meaning. All words bring their baggage, a meaningful trace that unhinges what is conveyed to suggest quite the reverse. In the final analysis, a word-signal is never without some such trace of meaning to its opposite (negation, contradiction), a meaning that is not mentioned in the text, but which functions as a trace nevertheless—reminding us of a similar point Hegel made that we referred to above. Thus, to deconstruct a text is to find such traces and note how they influence what is being formulated. And a close reading of the text invariably shows that the distinctions being drawn fail because of the inconsistent and paradoxical use being made of the concepts within the text.

This awareness of oppositionality carries over to universals as well. So-called first principles are defined by what they exclude as much as by what they include. Culler (1982, p. 86) has taken an example of Nietzsche's early deconstruction of such a first principle—that of *causation*—to demonstrate how the deconstructive process takes place. Nietzsche challenged the view that causality is a basic principle of our universe. He analyzed *cause–effect* to show that even though we tend to think of the thrust of causation from the former to the latter, we overlook the important role played by the latter (effect) to the former (cause) in our phenomenal understanding. I feel a pain, look about my person and discover a pin. Instead of following the phenomenal truth, in which effect (pain) preceded cause (pin), we reverse the sequence and give the initiative to the cause. This deconstruction of the cause–effect construct is not done to dismiss this concept. In fact, we have used the notion of cause here to deconstruct the very notion of causation—the experience of pain causes us to discover the pin and frame our conception. We might therefore erase the cause–effect sequence even as we record right next to it the cause–effect sequence that enabled us to frame causation in the first place. Critics find it hard to accept this maneuver, which asserts "the indispensability of causation while denying it any rigorous justification" (p. 88).

Note that in putting the initiation of explanation on the side of the pain we have reversed the sequential thrust of cause–effect, which always seems to originate in the cause (pinprick to pain). Effects seem quite secondary, of no basic importance really because they owe their very existence to causes. Derrida (1981) claims this is a hierarchical influence in which a kind of pecking-order is always implied in oppositional arrangements such as cause–effect, but also, bourgeoisie–proletariat, male–female, or truth–falsehood. The left-hand term in these pairings always takes ascendance over the right-hand term. This hierarchy is not to be minimized, says Derrida, because

> In a classical philosophical opposition we are not dealing with the peaceful coexistence of a *vis-a-vis*, but rather with a violent hierarchy. One of the two terms governs the other (axiologically, logically, etc.), or has the upper hand. To deconstruct the opposition, first of all, is to overturn the hierarchy at a given moment. To overlook this phase of overturning is to forget the conflictual and subordinating structure of opposition. (p. 41)

In a deconstructive analysis we can expect to find a key point in the text relying on some such hierarchical oppositionality (Ellis, 1989, p. 139), which then exposes some paradox or contradiction in the original textual assertion—as in showing that the effect is actually the phenomenal cause of the cause. In Chapter 2, I tried to show that there is usually a precedent context influencing which of the opposite words in such pairings will be considered more salient than (or hierarchically superior to) the other. Derrida can effect a deconstructive analysis by shifting the author's intended context, which then calls for the reverse implications to what was originally stated. Some critics have suggested that Derrida tries to replace the principle of contradiction with a logic in which opposites can coexist (p. 6). In deconstructionism, the reader is held to be more important than the author of a text. Anyone who claims to know the truth is open to challenge by the deconstructionist, who is notorious for aggressive counterarguments (pp. 15, 144–145).

Probably the most common criticism of deconstructionism is that, unlike other forms of analysis, it makes no effort to point to a corrective that might avoid the problems of the deconstructed text in the future (Ellis, 1989, pp. 42, 78–81). Yet, to be fair to Derrida, this seems to be the very point of a textual usage "under erasure." One is limited to working with what one has, even though it may be inadequate (under erasure). It just so happens that all language has such vulnerability. In the final analysis, because the author does not matter, texts converse only with other texts (p. 116) and are always constrained by the language in which they are written (p. 120). Because anything has its oppositional trace of meaning there is no way in which to escape the fact that nothing stands textually free of anything else—including its negation—nor can any text be proven better than any other. The result is a frozen gridlock of alternative points of view known as *intertextuality*; that is, an "endless conversation between the texts with no prospect of ever arriving at or being halted at an agreed point" (Rosenau, 1992, p. xii).

If we extend this argument to psychology it can be quite disconcerting, for as Rosenau (1992) said of the postmodern social sciences, "the search for causes in terms of sources or origins of phenomena must be discontinued in an authorless, totally intertextual world where the agent is omitted" (p. 33). There is no teleology in postmodern (poststructuralist) views like deconstructionism anymore than there is in social constructionism, hermeneutics, or structuralism (p. 32). We seem to have arrived at a consensus in the theories of social science today, holding that the intellect is neither "individual" nor embodied. Logical learning theory, on the other hand, holds that it is possible to explain how the individual author is personally responsible for selective creations, including the collective belief systems and values that are passed on from one generation to the next (for an example, see Berger, 1963). Furthermore, LLT pursues old-fashioned empirical evidence to support the validity of its claims (see Rychlak, 1994). Finally, as a psychological formulation, it is the responsibility of LLT to subsume or explain behavioral manifestations like those of postmodernism. I believe that LLT can actually engage and explain the views now under consideration, something that is unthinkable using the concepts of traditional S-R learning theory or recent information-processing theories.

There is definitely a process–content issue separating certain social constructionists (or structuralists) and a postmodern (poststructuralist) view like deconstructionism. I say "certain" social constructionists because I think Berger is indeed concerned with the process underlying such collective phenomena. Gergen and Harré, on the other hand, are drawn to the *relativism* of cultural content-differences per se without stipulating the process that brings these "social constructions" about. Indeed, in response to my prompt, Harré (1992) specifically denied that social constructionism requires a learning theory to account for how individuals acquire their socially induced beliefs and behavioral patterns (p. 63). All that is important is that we know what the language directs ("socially constructs") people in culture A to believe, relative to people in culture B; a belief that is acceptable in the former milieu may be unacceptable in the latter, and so on. Now, as there is no author to worry about, what are we to make of this sociocultural explanation?

As suggested above, social constructionists are describing an *unconscious* social order in the sense that the culture is unable to see its belief systems from another perspective; that is, the culture cannot transcend. Social constructionists conceive culture here in extraspective terms, as contents being transmitted "over there" from one generation to another. Social constructionists think of each culture as a unipredicated assemblage of such content-beliefs (values, customs, etc.), which flow along without that intrinsic Hegelian negation that the introspectively conceived, individualized deity experienced and worked out through dialectical oppositionality in coming to self-consciousness.

Having accepted this extraspectively framed model for the collective, the social constructionists are emboldened to frame the behavior of individuals in like terms. Ultimately, this means that social constructionists— whether they say so or not—fall back on mediational explanations not unlike those used by information-processing theorists (see Chapter 7). They end up construing people as moving unipredicated signals along in efficient-cause fashion, trapped in their linguistic chains of mediating words. The person who is socially constructed is therefore unidirectionally molded into a pattern that he or she has no capacity to sharpen, enlarge, reduce, or negate altogether—except through further mediation such as dialogue, performed in robot fashion. This person may "think" that he or she can formulate individual alternatives, and even shout these alternatives from the rooftops, but such beliefs are merely illusory linguistic conventions authored by the collective and not the shouter (Harré, 1992, p. 62). As Jung explained so well in his analysis of primitives, the socially constructed person is an *unconscious* being, under the yoke of the collective and therefore unable to frame conscious alternatives.

In deconstruction there is a shift in concern to the process. From the LLT perspective, deconstructionism is actually founded on a predicational model of psychic processing, but this kind of explanation proves awkward if leveled at collectives. Images of a group mind spring to life if we try to apply predicational logic to collectives. It is easier to see such predicational logic if we are considering the individual. For example, when Nietzsche says that the person looks to the pinprick following a sensation of pain, he is actually saying that the latter *predicates* the former. Logical learning theory would suggest that there is a confusion of causation in this example. If the person sensing pain looks around for its cause he is indeed behaving causally—but what causes are actually involved here? In LLT terms, there is a formal-final cause seeking of an efficient-cause explanation because at this point in history causation is limited to or equated with efficient causation. Hence, the pin as cause *must* effect the painful sensation. This is how efficient causes work. But the point of importance for an LLT analysis of such events is that a deconstructive analysis invariably brings the trace of opposite meanings to bear on the target under consideration (see Fish, 1980, p. 349).

Logical learning theory contends that not only the larger, predicating Euler circle lends meaning to the target, but the opposite realm of meaning outside of this circle does so as well. In the predicating alignment of "John is reliable," for example, not only is reliability predicating John but its opposite—unreliability—is lending its meaning to John as well (see Figures 2 and 3). The oppositionality here forms from an even broader range of meaning than is characteristic of the predicating Euler circle. We might say in deconstructive terms that *unreliable* is the trace meaning for *reliable*. Derrida is involved more with generic than delimiting oppositionality, for he is out to explain how language terms or signs function generically and not merely to show how any specific word may delimit its opposite meaning (Sarup, 1989, p. 35).

Now, there is good news and bad news for the LLT enthusiast in the deconstructivist's analysis. The good news is that, due to his appreciation of oppositionality, Derrida (1981) frames a collective that is conscious because of its transpredication of values, beliefs, knowledge, and so on (p. 59). Such transpredication is inevitable thanks to the role of oppositionality in processing language. Unlike social constructionism, which draws our attention to collective unipolarities, deconstructionism presents a picture of a collective actively transpredicating. The group's culture must be directing the transpredication because presumably the individual author is not (Ellis, 1989, p. 13). No culture properly understanding deconstruction could presume to frame even a relative truth, limited strictly to its collective identity. The bad news is that intertextuality traps deconstructive transpredication in an intellectual gridlock where evaluations and selections of alternatives are no longer possible. A sort of nihilistic consciousness is taking place.

Turning now to a consideration of the individual, I think that deconstructionism's commitment to the view that the author is not at least as important as the reader, or signifier, (Sarup, 1989, p. 59) is unfortunate. The logic of predication on which deconstructionism draws is entirely consistent with LLT so far as an understanding of individual cognition is concerned. This is because, as we have already suggested, to predicate there must be a predicator—a reasoning intelligence. Hence, assigning predication to collectives brings on these group-mind formulations that are difficult to sustain. How can there be a collective predication that is actually framed by the collective? In fact, I would suggest that deconstructionists are really addressing individual authors in their analyses (e.g., see Silverman, 1989), which invariably makes sense without bringing in the collective at all.

Whereas social constructionism gives us a collective theory, deconstructionism gives us an individual theory. A deconstructive analysis is friendly to phenomenological theories like Kelly's (1955) constructive alternativism or LLT. The latter views hold that the individual cognitive process is predicational, that it frames meanings one way even as the opposite direction is ever potentially there for consideration—if not frequently (but never mechanically) selected for consideration and enactment. Derrida, as an individual, chooses to follow the opposite direction regularly and thus shows us a kind of humanity that traditional S-R learning theories or current information-processing theories lack the conceptual tools to capture.

Unfortunately, although I would like to construe deconstructionism phenomenologically, I am not at all certain that it could be justified given its emphasis on linguistic texts. In deconstructive analysis intertextuality seems to occur "out there," in an extraspectively framed realm of language gridlock, instead of "in here," within the cognitions of an individual so gridlocked—which would at least be a bad form of consciousness. If we frame our explanations extraspectively we are in danger of turning the individual cognizer into a mere mediator. The paradox resulting, of course, is that once gridlock has been reached we are no longer able to direct our transpredications—which is tantamount to saying that we are forced to sink back into a bad form of unconsciousness.

CONCLUDING COMMENT

Although postmodern formulations like deconstructionism can raise our consciousness concerning the tremendous role that oppositionality plays in cognition, they are not necessarily going to help us increase our level of personal understanding. Unlike Hegelian theory, in which oppositionality was also central, there is no real capacity for transcendence and reflexivity to take place in the postmodern formulations. How can collectives function reflexively? All reflexivity comes down to in this view is just more language expressions framing other language expressions, texts exchanging linguistic signs with other texts, and so forth. As authors, we stand outside this exchange, unable to redirect things because we have no inroads through which we can introduce changes.

From the LLT perspective, language is a content within a *Logos* process. As such, language is an instrumentality, a way of expressing *ideas*— or whatever one wishes to call these formal-cause patterns that are formed in the *Logos* predicationally. We are never trapped or imprisoned in our language, although we can be so ensnared by our assumptions. Languages can be and are regularly enlarged and altered to fit assumptions, which as meaningful grounds are much more difficult to redefine. People often frame idea-intentions under the focused attention we have termed (a good) unconsciousness, which is a proactive effort to remove distractions from thought as we zero in on some line of intellectual insight. But, as Derrida teaches, we always have traceable footprints leading in from certain quarters of the realm outside the larger circle that predicate our targeted items (as symbolized by the Euler circles of Figures 2 and 3). Whether we consider them or not, such opposites lend their meaning to what we are targeting at the moment—and, depending on our reading, can change things or turn them around altogether.

Languages belong to cultures. Languages are tools, formed and modified to meet changing circumstances, passed down as cultural artifacts to succeeding generations. Thought belongs to individuals, who may form into sociocultural units for any number of reasons. To conclude that the tool directs the toolmaker is a deconstruction that LLT counter-deconstructs through negation. The tool may influence the toolmaker's outlook, as by lending confidence and encouragement to use it in various ways. But it never can break out of its signified purpose in the way that the person can transcend—and, yes, deconstruct—meanings for the sake of which life's purposes are continually enacted. In the language of this volume, tools cannot—but people can and do—achieve psychic consciousness. The author and the reader are not mere pawns in a language game. As both authors and readers we can predicate affectively, which means that we continually are evaluating the meanings under linguistic formulation. Thanks to our dialectical or oppositional reasoning capacity, we are evaluating organisms. We cannot evade evaluating although we may pretend to avoid or repress it. Fortunately, the evaluative process never quite reaches gridlock because it is not tied to words, which can change affective quality from moment to moment even though their meaning remains the same.

10

SUNDRY POINTS FOR FURTHER CONSIDERATION

I would like to cover a handful of points that we have dealt with or alluded to throughout the book that deserve elaboration. Some aspects of the material I will cover may be considered a summary review; other aspects will be a more detailed examination of what we have covered, with various educated guesses advanced for future consideration and investigation. Sections are headed by questions that introduce the issue at hand. As these are not rhetorical questions, they will all be answered. I aim to demonstrate some of the further reaches of LLT, and hopefully encourage the reader to begin thinking about human behavior in terms of the concepts of this volume, which are by no means provided as unipredicated truisms. Open speculations and suggestions are important beginnings in the revision of the human image that LLT is trying to effect in the social sciences.

WHICH IS MORE IMPORTANT TO THE ACTUAL FUNCTIONING OF PSYCHIC CONSCIOUSNESS: PROCESS OR CONTENT?

The fact that LLT approaches psychic consciousness from the view of process and not content is very important. We have seen how instructive this assumption proved to be in reviewing many different topics throughout this volume. And yet, when we are actually thinking or reasoning, it is the meaningful contents of our thoughts that absorb us and not the process by which we are turning such thoughts over in mind. We do not give the digestive process a second thought as we bite into a slice of pizza, so why should we be concerned with the thought process when we think? It is what we are thinking about, the meaning under processing that matters. As I noted in Chapter 2, in reasoning we intend the meaning under processing and are conceptually extending it to a target of some sort. Whether we have pictorial images or actual words in mind, they have reference value. They point to things. From a process viewpoint, these meanings are predications (formal causes). They serve as the *that* in the "that, for the sake of which" phrase defining final causation.

Recall from Chapters 2 and 6 that the concept of *determinism* refers to setting limits on alternatives, and that each of the Aristotelian causes fashions its own brand of determinism. As a telic theory, LLT relies on formal and final causation to explain thought. *Intentionality* is a final-cause form of determinism. If the person intends to get a suitable night's rest he or she negates the late-night movie, thereby limiting the alternatives open for the evening. In Chapter 2 we referred to this intentional influence on behavior as psychic determinism or *will*. In this example it is akin to a proactive unipredication because the person wishes or wants to limit the evening's activity. But it would be possible for a psychic causation to be reactive, in which case the determinism would involve avoidant intentions.

For example, a person might ask a psychologist "Why do I so fear leaving my home that I can't go shopping anymore?" This is a meaningful statement expressing an unfortunately disturbing life circumstance. Assuming there is no realistic threat, this person is probably predicating affectively negative meanings in life and forming reactive unipredications. Now, surely to the person concerned, the most important aspect of this agoraphobic symptom is the meaningful content—home, street, crowds, terror, helplessness, and so on. What is it in the person's life history that has brought this about? It is at this point that the therapist or patient may fashion all manner of explanations to "account for" the disturbance. I have no quarrel with this effort to understand and then rectify unhealthy life circumstances. For those of us who believe that humans are telic organisms, the problem arises when we hear that the person's agoraphobia stems from past shapings, a reinforcement history, or informational input. Such mechanical processes can even become a model for the framing of contents, so that people literally begin speaking of themselves as "programmed" to perform, "storing" information, or being "positively reinforced" to behave in a certain way.

The teleologist finds it not only incorrect but often downright harmful to characterize human behavior in this manner. No matter how badly the person with agoraphobic symptoms might require certain insight-producing contents in psychotherapy (i.e., interpretations), for the teleologist there is always a problem with the characterization of what is taking place. In fact, we might even ask just what an insight in psychotherapy really is. Could it be that the insights that supposedly cure a neurosis in psychotherapy may actually benefit more from the process per se than from the specific content meanings encompassed by the interpretation? Do these content meanings have to be "true" to effect a helpful personal adjustment for the person being treated, or might they benefit from a Jamesian pragmatism no matter what transpires?

Freud's interpretations of unconscious (unipredicated) ideas relied on offering patients meaningful alternatives to what they might otherwise be thinking about concerning their neurosis. In LLT terms, what Freud as interpreter did was suggest certain transpredications—affectively charged, meaningful contents that confronted the defensive or reactive unipredications of the patient. He offered insight by tying together meanings that were not initially seen as relatable, particularly in the context of self-reflexive examination. He did a fair amount of deconstructing here as well. The resultant cohesive pattern (i.e., meaning) centered on the plausibility of the procedural evidence applied to dreams, memories, and free associations. Yet, clearly, the interpretation did *not* have to be true. Just so long as it had a Jamesian cash-value for the patient's conscious outlook, a therapeutic outcome was possible. I might now suggest that it was not the *specific* meaning-content that effected the cure—this could have been otherwise—but rather the conceptual force of transpredication.

There is a sense in which meaningful insights have an impact on the individual who experiences them. The "weight" of logic is a *Physikos* metaphor that makes greatest sense if we appreciate that such forceful "aha" experiences occur at the logical point of affirmation when a new predication or a new slant on things takes place. An insight pops into mind shrouded in affective assessments of one sort or another. Freud found it necessary to concoct a mental energy (the libido) to explain such mental processing to his scientific colleagues, but I think we can now appreciate that such insightful "wallops" take place exclusively in the patterning, meaning-creating, meaning-extending realm of the *Logos*. This too is psychic or final-cause determinism.

As mechanistic formulations of behavior, traditional S-R and modern computer models also do not place great emphasis on content meaning. In fact, a concept like meaning and the consciousness to which it is tied is something of an embarrassment to such approaches. In Chapters 5 and 7 we covered mechanistic theories, which are grounded in the *Physikos* and *Bios* and are consequently ill-suited to the formal- and final-cause concept of meaning. From these perspectives, the person is never a source of meaning creation. Even when the social constructionists of Chapter 9 rely on language to explain things, the person is so heavily immersed in linguistic directives sent as efficient-cause mediators that she or he is never a true creator of meaning. Indeed, there is no "person" at all. There is only a socially constructing process taking place, which shapes the linguistic mediators to be carried along in efficient-cause fashion sans true formal- or final-cause meaning. Social dialogues may exist, but they never express intended meanings.

In answer to the question of this section, I think it correct to say that from the point of view of the person who meaningfully winds his or her way through life, it is the content of psychic consciousness that is paramount. Psychodynamic clinicians, who work with people in therapeutic contexts, must engage their clients in terms of specific meanings—things that make sense as they seek improved adjustment. In this regard, all of the many self-help efforts we see in bookstores today have the same goal of working at the level of content. But from the point of view of the psychological scientist trying to understand what is taking place in basic human cognition, the process must also be targeted. Thus, in LLT, we can make general assumptions about a predicational process and study it without suggesting *specific* concepts (meaningful contents) in the manner of a personality theory. However, it is also true that teleologists like myself frequently believe that it would be salutary for a culture to have a psychological theory that is scientifically sound yet non-mechanistic. This attitude follows from the belief that human beings are not mere machines (computing or otherwise), and to claim so not only poisons but eventually empties a rich reservoir of humanity.

DOES HUMAN THOUGHT ACTUALLY BEGIN IN UNCONSCIOUSNESS?

Jaynes and Jung suggested that primitive humans were unconscious organisms, taking direction from a group mind (Jung) or a "deity" embedded in the brain structure (Jaynes). Jung held that modern humanity's heritage from such group-mind thinking was the collective unconscious and the mask that people wear in public. Personal consciousness is born when the infant begins drawing conceptual distinctions on the basis of a principle of oppositionality (e.g., here–there, me–not me, etc.). Freud also held that the infant is totally unconscious, and that it takes some time for consciousness to arise conjointly with the development of the ego portion of the personality structure.

Many advocates of psychoanalysis take the claim that human life begins in unconsciousness—or "the" unconscious—to mean that this is a deeper portion of mind in which clever strategies are concocted to get around the censorship points of mental repression (leading to the notorious

Freudian slips). Freud eventually found it necessary to turn the censor into the ego, which then opposed the totally unconscious id, as well as other sources of influence on the psyche. Freud claimed that the ego traverses levels of mind so that it could both confront the external world in con ociousness and parry with the id in unconsciousness. Actually, in Freud's theorizing it is sometimes difficult to distinguish clearly between the unconscious and the id, for they both take on attributes of a homunculus. But when in 1923 Freud (1923/1961a) clarified the ego and the id as distinctive *actors* (homunculi) in the psyche, consciousness and unconsciousness became more like contrasting regions (levels, spheres, etc.) within which such action took place. In Chapter 4, I noted this tendency of Freud and Jung to treat psychic consciousness and unconsciousness as regions.

Incidentally, I should note that in Chapter 2 when I presented the LLT view of an infant's first manifestation of predication—in which a target is predicated of itself (e.g., "a nipple is a nipple")—I was effectively outlining an unconscious process of learning. The infant's learning of a "nipple" (or, "nippleness") was unipredicated, and not until this meaning was extended to other targets (e.g., "a thumb is a nipple"), was psychic consciousness born. The infant was then forced to rely on generic oppositionality to break out of the confining (large) Euler circle (see Figures 2 and 3) to learn that a thumb was only partially nipple-like. Thumbs are analogical and not tautological to nipples. It is in this disanalogous extension that transpredication takes root and learning extends through new meaning formations. The nontautological and disanalogous features of experience demand that psychic consciousness be extended, resulting in growing awareness as maturation proceeds. We learn a great deal from what is not true or not possible in life. Even though new content will be engaged during maturation, the process remains the same. In line with the conclusion of the first section of this chapter, it is this process that LLT is out to explain and not the specific contents that are being processed by it.

The focus on process is not always true of Freudian or Jungian theorizing, where we observe the suave moving back and forth between process and content (see Chapter 4). For example, libido is sometimes a process impelling behavior and at other times it is an instrumentality born of specific ego-intentions, cathecting certain objects or intentionally being removed from others. I am reminded here of Freud's letter to Jung in February of 1912, where he says of himself "I took myself in hand and quickly turned off my excess libido" (McGuire, 1974, p. 488). How could Freud consciously or willfully achieve this outcome if libido initiated and directed mentation? As I said in Chapter 4, this theoretical shifting about of the libido concept stemmed from the fact that Freud found it necessary to combine *Bios* and *Logos* groundings in his theorizing in order to satisfy his medical colleagues. But if the unconscious employs a process, what sort of process is this? Freud tells us explicitly that in the unconscious "no process that resembles 'judging' occurs" (Freud, 1905/1960a, p. 175). This would imply that only unipredications are found in the unconscious region of the psyche because there is never a preliminary weighing of alternatives in such cases, as transpredication would demand.

In answer to the question of this section, I suggest that thought begins in unconsciousness because it is initially unipredicational. This answer might be rejected because it appears to be founded exclusively on psycho-analysis, a problematic theory of human nature. But I can arrive at the same answer from another direction, one that does not touch upon personality dynamics but relies on a rigorous examination of assumptive reasoning. Thus, it is often said that strictly on the basis of logical re-quirements, it is not possible to be reflexively conscious of one's basic assumptions. The Gödelian theorems that we discussed in Chapters 2 and 7 address this point. No consistent mathematical system can prove that it is consistent, for this would require the capacity for self-consciousness via self-reflexivity. Hence, another more broadly conceived system must be employed to subsume the initial one and thereby account for it. Here again, this even broader system cannot self-reflexively account for its own con-sistency. As we have seen in previous chapters, self-reflexivity is dependent on transpredication, the capacity to remove oneself from the predicating Euler circle of Figure 2 and turn back to judge or evaluate the meaning of this broader context. Unlike mathematical systems, people can indeed self-reflexively explore and prove their own consistency, or lack of it, even if this involves a so-called vicious circle in logic (see Lucas, 1961).

The problem of universals is also relevant to the question of this sec-tion. In LLT terms, a universal is a content, not a process. The universal captures some comprehensive meaning completely and can therefore stand alone as an unquestioned assertion having relevance (extending) to other, less abstract meanings. A universal is a unipredicated content that resists compromise, that is, transpredication (see Chapters 2 and 4). The human's introspectively inclined, philosophical intellect searches for truths that have fundamental, universal validity. Socrates pressed to find the common nature of things in existence. Plato fashioned a realm of Being in which universally unchanging "perfect" idea-forms existed. Aristotle enumerated a series of universal categories (relation, time, position, etc.) that presumably fashioned and organized substantial experience. And there were many other such ef-forts over the history of thought. In answer to the question posed, we can again conclude, as the psychoanalysts had done from another angle, that human thought begins in unipredication and hence is initially unconscious.

WHY DID PSYCHIC CONSCIOUSNESS DEVOLVE FROM CONSCIENCE? IS THERE STILL A MEANINGFUL TIE HERE?

If there is one truth, one significant point to be made following our extensive survey of psychic consciousness in terms of a predicational model, it is that human beings are evaluating organisms. A quick answer to the first question of this section is therefore that consciousness was once *conscience-ness* because these terms are variations on the same theme: namely, that human experience is intrinsically evaluative. By evaluation I mean judgmentally placing a value of like–dislike, good–bad, right–wrong, and so forth on the meanings being fashioned in cognition. Even if we intentionally avoid judging, this is done on the basis of a judgment. As for the second question of this section, the answer would seem to be "yes," because human nature has not changed these past 2,000 years. A conscience is suggested if the evaluations of experience being made are framed in terms of right and wrong (as opposed to, e.g., true and false), particularly because these judgments are deeply wound into one's personal identity and therefore rely on a transcending self-examination.

As Taylor (1989) expressed it, "My identity is defined by the commitments and identifications which provide the frame or horizon within which I can try to determine from case to case what is good, or valuable, or what ought to be done, or what I endorse or oppose. In other words, it is the horizon within which I am capable of taking a stand" (p. 27). We cannot take a personal stand—as a "self"—unless there is first some range of alternative possibilities to consider along our horizons, leading to an affirmation that we are likely to call *choice*. We will consciously go "this way" and not "that way" because after a transpredicating analysis we determine that it is the right thing to do.

But if we are correct that our most basic assumptions are unconscious, then how can we delude ourselves into believing that we *are* making a conscious choice of right over wrong from some universal stance, which must itself be unconsciously predicated by an even more universal stance? Maybe a religious belief is expected to be unconscious or unipredicated. Jaynes's suggestion (see Chapter 5) that morality issued from a biologically based deity, sending directives to the person from within the brain, is consistent with the view that religious beliefs are not to be transpredicated. This willingness to stand by a unipredication in the face of transpredicating understandings that challenge such unconscious commitments is what we mean by faith. Mowrer (1961) expressed this another way: "Religion, at its best, is always concerned with the unconscious, conceived as conscience and the Voice of God" (p. 32).

The Garden of Eden story fits in here nicely. While Adam and Eve followed God's unipredicated demands, all went well. No choice was required for the perfect life. But once these unipredications were violated (i.e., transpredicated), which is symbolized in the eating of the apple, psychic consciousness was raised—as when Adam and Eve were made aware of their nakedness—and existence changed from the universally positive to a range of possibilities, both positive and negative. Choice was born.

Responsibility was born. Indeed, in dire need of God's help to resume the path of righteousness, *grace* was born.

Even so, the moral or ethical search for universal grounds on which to behave has been pursued for centuries, resulting in such practical rules of thumb as the Golden Rule and the Categorical Imperative. If followed, these universal guides will direct our conduct to do what is right and good. Now, in LLT terms, moral universals are contents—exceedingly important unipredications that one presumably cannot violate if right and good conduct is to result. This suggests a question: Is morality always a matter of finding such universal content-meanings on which to found our choices to do what is right and good; or, is it possible to focus more directly on the process of moral behavior?

I think it is possible to distinguish between what we might term *content morality* on the one hand, and *process morality* on the other. This is not exactly an either–or division because obviously there is always a process creating or conveying the content, so we cannot split things totally in half. What I am driving at here is that some people establish their morality on certain unassailable content meanings which take them in the direction of unipredication, for they are unwilling to contemplate transpredicating these universals. Others who are more open to transpredications in weighing moral alternatives according to circumstances give their morality a process coloration. Now, all people are capable of, and probably practice, both forms of morality at one time or another over their lifetime. But it seems that there is a tendency to lean in one direction or the other at any one time, and some people actually become fully committed to only one of these approaches for all occasions. Also, each approach has its strong and weak points.

By a content morality I mean the approach that seeks to find a clear, universal basis on which to guide life. This might be some form of humanism, in which a universal assertion like the "dignity of life" is affirmed, or a more traditional religion in which something like God's Ten Commandments are the universal influences that ground moral decisions. On the positive side, content morality is clear, dependably consistent, and often considered the basis of good character formation (*ethos*, in Greek). We admire people who stick to their moral guns like this "no matter what." On the negative side, people who commit to content morality are often said to be rigid, unrealistic, and even internally hollow because they seem to live by the dictates of external rules rather than by their personal evaluations of unique circumstances that may arise in any moral dilemma. Piaget (1965) referred to this commitment to the external as *moral realism* (p. 191), and he was critical of such an attitude because it did not emanate from "within" (p. 196) the way he believed a more cooperative kind of morality does. Piaget viewed moral realism as immature, more likely to be found in children than adults. The emphasis here is on psychic unconsciousness, an unstudied acceptance of rules, and so on, much as we characterized the Freudian superego in Chapter 4. But many religions of the world highly prize the attitude of coming to the deity "as a child" in complete faith, realizing that the human intellect is limited and must rely on something greater than the self.

A process morality is not irretrievably rooted in universals, or, to put it another way, one of its universals is that accommodation in ethical decision making is sometimes necessary (a view that the content moralist rejects). A person following a process morality places emphasis on the fact that although our moral decisions are grounded in "ideal" universal principles, such content meanings are not beyond negotiation on the basis of present circumstances. There are always exceptions to prove the rule. There are always alternative ways of looking at the same fact pattern. What is our position given the present fact pattern? Knowledge of cultural differences provided by the social sciences establishes that alternative content beliefs about behavior abound, and are therefore processed to various ends depending on the culture under consideration. This process emphasis need not be construed as teleological. That is, a process moralist might rely on a predicational model like LLT does, or on some mechanistic interpretation of behavior in which ethical principles are believed to be socially constructed and handed to the person as directing mediators. It makes no difference to the process moralist, because all such theories have stated that the contents being carried by the process can vary, be different, and even be in conflict at the level of universal assumptions.

In truth, psychology, as all social sciences, has done much to enhance process morality by analyzing cognitive evaluation in moral behavior and development (see Kurtines & Gewirtz, 1991). Even if the focus is on a Piagetian "morality from within," the theories of learning in psychology have emphasized process over content for the reasons I have discussed in the first section of this chapter. On the positive side, a process morality is admirable because it takes into consideration the unique characteristics of any given fact pattern under evaluation. Process morality gives each instance of moral evaluation a uniquely individual assessment, which is sometimes demanded as when two universal assumptions come into conflict (e.g., "Thou shalt not kill" versus "An eye for an eye"). Because there is a recognition that the process must inevitably have such conflicts, considerations other than universal assertions come into play in judging the specific instance ("Do we take a life here or not?"). In LLT terms, transpredications are brought to bear (raising consciousness) to arrive at a moral course of action.

On the negative side, process morality may provide so many extraneous considerations involved in each instance that one who adheres to it cannot render a satisfactory, final, moral judgment. This morality appears to be inconsistent, makes excuses, and can thereby erode its own moral authority. Social critics today are concerned about the apologies being made for those who violate traditional moral precepts. Concepts of "sin" no longer hold; there are only "mistakes in judgment" that "anyone might make." As I have already suggested, both process and content morality have always been with us. Even before the advent of social science, people knew that they could change ultimate groundings for the sake of which they rendered evaluations. Probably when people began equating consciousness with conscience, the moral code of a society was heavily on the side of content—as when words were reified (see Chapter 3). This is the morality of isolated regions, of people who have not seen much of the world—stereotyped today in our image of rural fundamentalism. But as people followed trade routes to other locations and saw other viewpoints being espoused, the resultant elevation of consciousness via transpredicating alternatives served the same role that the social sciences have served in more recent times. With the combined recognition of cultural relativism and the philosophical insight that it is impossible to be entirely conscious of one's most fundamental assumptions, the scene is set for a sophisticated process morality in modern times.

I must mention an important distinction at this juncture concerning how one might arrive at a unipredicated, content morality. A person can take on a moral belief unipredicationally without giving preliminary consideration to alternatives. Or, a person can take on such a belief after first giving it serious thought, including many transpredications in which he or she examines alternative possibilities. In the latter case, the person would become convinced through the transpredicating efforts, and then commit to the sole viewpoint from that time onward. But as this rigid commitment has followed a more "enlightened" initiation than merely affirming a position without such forethought, it is a different kind of unconscious belief than the case in which transpredication is never attempted. A content morality of this enlightened sort would probably be the one reflecting the strongest level of character for those individuals who manifest it. Their confidence in knowing "the" truth is born of personal effort and not mere imitation. This certainly suggests a proactive form of unconsciousness.

There are those who believe that, although the older content moralities required tempering, the pendulum has swung too far in the opposite direction of a relativistic process morality. In the United States and other economically advanced societies a veritable *authoritophobia* has arisen. Those holding this perspective consider any critical evaluation of behavior that might be leveled in terms of a content morality virtually inhumane. Judgment of others must be avoided at all costs, and in many instances it is not even acceptable to judge oneself. This does not pertain to negative assessments alone, for even assigning a positive value to some action or person is considered unethical—or at least improper—because this must inevitably detract from another person or action by comparison. This kind of moralizing appears to have permeated many school systems in the United States, where it is now common to promote inadequately prepared students from one grade level to the next, whereas previously they would have been judged solely on poor performance and held back.

The ironic thing about today's authoritophobia is that, although it has developed from process-morality beginnings, it seems now to be taking on a content-morality posture. We see this in the so called politically correct recommendations of recent years, which were initially framed to raise consciousness by highlighting the damage that can be done if we use certain mindless characterizations of people rather than others (e.g., referring to people as "mentally retarded" when "mentally challenged" is less condescending, etc.). However, as more and more of these suggested changes in description were advanced, they seemed increasingly to take on the character of unyielding universals in the style of traditional content morality. At least this is how many critics have viewed things—in LLT terms, as moving from an initial effort to increase the level of consciousness regarding the feelings of others to one of reducing consciousness by mindlessly accepting a host of new terms on tenuous and even questionable grounds.

The lesson would appear to be that one should carefully examine (i.e., transpredicate) various grounds before one takes an initial stand, keep in mind the alternative arguments to one's affirmed position, have their rebuttals ever available, and then live by one's freely arrived-at convictions. A person might even select the teachings of some established moral system (religion, philosophy, etc.) as a position. It is still hard to carry out this latter strategy of personal action, particularly if one's culture or subculture considers such authoritarian stands as morally indefensible per se. It would take us far afield to examine all of the influences here, but doubtless the experience we have had in the 20th century with dictatorial political regimes and unpopular wars has biased many against anything smacking of judgmentalism. Whatever the case, it is fascinating to see that moralities can cover a wide range, encompassing both psychically conscious and unconscious aspects of the human experience.

CAN FREE WILL BE UNCONSCIOUS?

I reviewed several interpretations of free will in Chapter 6. I noted there that willful action is pointed to some end. There is undoubtedly a *Bios* process that has to be engaged in order to carry out some overt action, as in dressing oneself or dialing a telephone. To *act* or *behave* requires some instrumental physico-biological process enabling the actor to get the job done. But the question that free will brings up is can we direct and redirect this instrumental process voluntarily, altering it to suit our intentions? The free-willist says we can, and the mechanist says we cannot. The position that LLT takes is that human beings do indeed have a free will, because they can select the predicating grounds for the sake of which they behave. Indeed, as we have been reviewing in this chapter, humans are literally forced to frame these groundings albeit ultimately, at the most abstract levels, in a unipredicational manner.

Now this would seem to present a problem: If thought actually begins at the most abstract levels in unconsciousness (unipredication), and if we hold that people have free wills, then it would seem that a free will must be unconscious. Yet, the very notion of being free to do otherwise, all circumstances remaining the same, implies that transpredication is involved. That is, free will seems to demand transpredication, so how can we be free if our thought begins in unipredication?

I think the problem here arises from the fact that when we think of free will we think it has to occur at the point of initiation when an idea or intention is first expressed—as what Hegel termed the *thesis*. The assumption seems to be that free will must occur in the selection of this initiating meaning. This is probably where the notion of a homunculus arises. The little person inside the brain decides what idea will be thought today and then sends it forward as a thesis. But if we look at human reason as fundamentally oppositional or dialectical, then the *antithesis* (Hegel, 1857/1952a, p. 165) is just as important as the thesis, because meanings invariably reach for their opposite expression (a fact that we found Derrida capitalizing on; see Chapter 9).

What if our understanding of free will is that it arises in weighing antithesis against thesis, settling thereby on either alternative "as such" or concocting some other alternative that would borrow from both sides? This uniting of opposite meanings is what Hegel termed the *synthesis*. And before coming to some grounding for the sake of which behavior would then be carried forward (telosponded), this same thesis–antithesis examination of possibilities could be repeated many times over. Each synthesis can serve as a new thesis, delimiting yet another antithetical alternative, and so on, until such time as the reasoning individual settles on (or affirms) the meaning. Note that we are describing ongoing transpredication here.

This is the view of free will advanced by LLT. Thus, in life, it is not necessary for the person to "think up" the initial meaning about which a freewill decision is to be made. This initiating thesis might be suggested by others, arise in unexpected life circumstances, or just "pop into mind" via some randomly drawn analogy. It is not in the initiation of the meaning that agency is born, but in a consideration of the ramifications of this meaning in relation to its opposite (including affective assessments of the opposed sides) that a freely willed decision would arise. This antithetical examination would, of course, involve transpredication.

We do not have to make this out to be some ponderous activity in every instance. That is, much of so-called freewill expression is routine. The person awakes in the morning, glances at the clock and then rolls out of bed to get dressed for the day. But now, the initial assumptions here—the theses—are that the clock time is not in error, that it is a work day, that it is therefore worthwhile getting out of bed at this time (e.g., in order to earn a living), and so forth. None of these presumptions need be questioned and decided at the moment in order for a freewill course of action to take place. We are in the "will" phase of the freewill course of action. We have already affirmed these presumptions; we have considered them in the past and they now frame a context within which behavior is willfully unfolding. The person is committed to meeting assigned responsibilities, to be on time, to meet the day's challenges, and to reap the financial reward on payday. This is a psychic determinism, a formal-final cause line of behavior that could always be different, all circumstances remaining the same, but the person has decided to go "this way" and not "that way" in his or her life's course—and now carries this out as a uniprediction. It is not necessary to be making a decision at every turn once this context of meaning has been framed. The *will* term of the *free will* phrase takes into consideration that a determinism is involved here.

I once heard a vignette from the life of Mohandas (Mahatma) Gandhi (1869–1948) that I cannot vouch for as I have forgotten the source, and it may be apocryphal. But it so beautifully demonstrates what free will is about that I would like to present it here even though it may not actually have taken place (however, if it didn't it should have!). As I heard the story, once when he was imprisoned unjustly, instead of being hostile to his guards, Gandhi thanked them politely and suggested that he really appreciated the time they made available for him to confront his long-overlooked correspondence. The guards promptly responded by taking away his pen and paper. He again politely thanked his guards, affirming that they were perfectly correct in removing his writing materials for he had been lax in doing his reading and studying. The guards quickly took away his books. Gandhi again thanked his guards for so forcefully reminding him that he had been ignoring his meditation. He then assumed the lotus position and settled into a deep meditation as the guards looked on in frustration.

Whether true or not, this story epitomizes free will as the interplay of thesis–antithesis directed into an intentional synthesis. It was what Gandhi did with what was presented to him that reflected his agency, no matter how sparse the transpredicated alternatives might be. Imprisonment did not remove his free will. Being denied his correspondence and reading materials did not remove his free will. He would not accept the determined efforts of his guards to quash his agency. He would set the grounds for the sake of which his prison time was to be spent, even though this involved diminishing alternatives concerning what content-meanings were possible to affirm and what were not. He exerted his will as freely as was possible, given the circumstances, and thus never forfeited his human agency.

Most people tend to think of free will as tied to reality, and especially the reality that is coming up in the future. Human agency has been so identified with purpose, expectancy, and goals that the idea of free will in retrospect seems a contradiction. Because in LLT the emphasis is on affirming certain grounds for the sake of which meaning is extended and behavior is intended, it does not matter whether the intention is projected into the future or attributed to the past. As we saw in Chapter 8, individuals following out a posthypnotic suggestion are likely to make up a scenario to explain why they are doing something odd. Suddenly, the person under posthypnotic suggestion rises to stand on one leg. If asked why by the hypnotist, the person says, "My foot just 'fell asleep,' and I'm trying to shake it off." This capacity to frame a predicating justification or rationalization for what is already underway, or distant in the past for that matter, is reflective of the same conceptual ability that we in other contexts consider to be free will. But is the person "free" to not carry out the posthypnotic suggestion? The answer here is that when this person agreed to be a participant, and submitted to the hypnotist's unipredication, *that* was the point at which a free choice was made—a willful commitment to play the good participant to the very end in precedent-sequacious fashion.

There is another way in which the question of this section can be understood. For some people unconsciousness is a realm of activity—a "psychic region," as I have referred to it earlier in this chapter (see also Chapter 4). In the psychodynamic tradition, for example, the assumption is that identities such as the id, ego, and superego populate this region. Do they have free will if they are working out compromises in the unconscious region (level of mind), particularly if this negotiation involves neurosis? There is an opinion in the analytical school of thought that holds that to the extent consciousness is influenced by unconsciousness, human agency is comparably diminished. Hospers (1961) reflects this view in suggesting that "a person's freedom is present in *inverse proportion to his neuroticism*: in other words, the more his acts are determined by a *malevolent* unconscious, the less free he is" (p. 43, italics in original). Menninger (1966) has suggested that some of the basic assumptions of modern psychiatry contradict legal assumptions like having the freedom to choose right from wrong, or being able consciously to resist unconscious impulses (p. 118).

In discussing free will in Chapter 6, I argued that this capacity is born of the ability to negate or contradict a thesis by way of an antithesis. James's second-event argument could be co-opted at this point, where the contradicting antithesis would be seen as a kind of second event, although I do not mean to introduce a time factor here. The first-to-second alignment is purely logical—a logic of what the Greeks called dialectical reasoning (see Chapter 7). Thanks to this oppositional (thesis–antithesis) reasoning capacity, an agent always has the potential to step outside of the predicating meaning under extension (the larger Euler circle of Figure 2) and come to some position inside, outside, or in between. In this view, both Gandhi and his jailers were reasoning oppositionally. Looked at from the jailers view, Gandhi would cite a thesis, and they would negate it (antithesis), leading to an alternative in which Gandhi affirmed *that* (reading) in place of *this* (correspondence), followed by another antithetical maneuver on the part of the jailers and a further oppositional counter by Gandhi.

Logical learning theory claims that psychic consciousness involves transpredication. It would seem to follow that to enact a freewill course of behavior the person must be psychically conscious. It looks as though Hospers and Menninger are correct. There can be no such thing as unconscious free will. The person suffering from some neurotically rooted, irresistible impulse is surely not being directed by psychic consciousness.

But things are not quite this clear-cut. When Freud increased his psychic residents from just id and ego to id, ego, and superego, he also made it possible for the ego to be in the unconscious region of the mind yet at the same time behave in what I am calling a transpredicational manner. As was noted in Chapter 4, this occurred because of the need for the ego to frame compromises among its three "tyrannical masters ... the external world, the super-ego and the id" (Freud, 1932/1964b, p. 77). Because it ranges across all levels of the psyche, the ego can actually know at one level (unconsciously) what it *does not know* at another (consciously). Thus, Freud could say that an unconscious wish (hoped-for intention) or a conflict between such wishes (e.g., to love and hate someone at the same time) is *always known* by the person in such a dilemma: It is known unconsciously (see Breuer & Freud, 1893–1895/1955, p. 117; Freud, 1915/1957b, p. 168).

The meaning of unconscious at this point shades over into something like "the unadmitted." There is an unadmitted cognizance of what is known in one region (psychic unconsciousness) but not known in the other region (psychic consciousness). Freud more than once referred to that "strange state of mind in which one knows and does not know a thing at the same time" (Breuer & Freud, 1893–1895/1955, p. 117). The id, ego, and superego would be unable to work out compromises if such a paradoxical mental capacity did not exist in the psyche. These homunculi go through elaborate mental gyrations *quite intentionally* to keep unconscious wishes out of the conscious region (Freud, 1925/1959a, p. 162). This is why Freud could say that the essence of repression is that it is an intentional act (Breuer & Freud, 1893–1895/1955, p. 116).

When Freud spoke of what he sometimes called the illusion of free will, he was actually suggesting that what one side of mind (consciousness) claims is a decision freely made is in fact the outcome, compromise, conclusion, implication, and so forth of the other side of mind—which was *also freely made*. Psychic determinism of the most rigid and unyielding sort is always founded on final-cause determinism and not efficiently caused determinism (which often springs from chance occurrences). Here is a core statement from Freud's writings on this matter:

> According to our analyses it is not necessary to dispute the right to the feeling of conviction of having a free will. If the distinction between conscious and unconscious motivation is taken into account, our feeling of conviction informs us that conscious motivation does not extend to all our motor decisions.... But what is thus left free by the one side receives its motivation from the other side, from the unconscious; and in this way determination in the psychical sphere is still carried out without any gap. (1901/1960b, p. 254)

Freud's treatment of determinism here is clear. He views the mind as *always* under a psychic determination—that is, under a formal- or final-cause determinism and *not* an efficient-cause determinism (see Cameron & Rychlak, 1985, pp. 123–134). Whether conscious or unconscious, the mind intends its ends, ends that have been chosen in the formation of compromises. But who contemplated, suggested, and negotiated such compromised solutions from a bevy of alternatives? The ego, of course. The ego continually works to arrange things amidst the pressures of id, superego and "reality" (i.e., the external environment). The ego must follow a reality principle whereas the id and superego can make extreme, conflicting, and unrealistic demands. Freud obviously has the ego dealing in transpredications during these negotiations, even though the working-out of such compromises may be taking place in an unconscious region of mind. The id follows an amoral pleasure principle and the superego follows an unforgiving content morality. The id and superego are not only in an unconscious region of mind, they are limited to unipredications during the negotiations. The ego is transpredicating in this unconscious region, following a free-wheeling process morality, and it is from this source that freewill determination issues.

Probably the clearest example of Freud placing psychic consciousness within the region of unconsciousness is his explanation of how anxiety could be used to achieve specific ends in the personality system. Freud interpreted anxiety as an emotional reaction serving as a warning signal that something was amiss in the psyche, either realistically or as an imagined threat. Sometimes this signal is automatic, an emotional reflex that arises as when we find ourselves in a situation of immediate threat like losing control of an automobile while driving on a slippery road. At other times, however, Freud believed that anxiety could be brought on intentionally:

> One [way of anxiety generation] was involuntary, automatic and always justified on economic grounds, and arose whenever a danger situation analogous to birth had established itself. The other [way of anxiety generation] was produced by the ego as soon as a situation of this kind merely threatened to occur, in order to call for its avoidance. In the second case the ego subjects itself to anxiety as a sort of inoculation, submitting to a slight attack of the illness in order to escape its full strength. It vividly imagines [at an unconscious level] the danger-situation, as it were, with the unmistakable purpose of restricting that distressing experience to a mere indication, a signal. (1925/1959a, p. 162)

So, what is imagined unconsciously by the ego as a threat has its impact on the conscious portion of the ego as a slight dose of anxiety inoculating it against letting down its defenses. The personality system girds itself all the more to continue its repressive efforts. The malevolent impulses that Hospers referred to, playing themselves out at the unconscious level, must be kept out of consciousness at all costs. And although it looks like the Freudian unconscious (*qua* region or level) is directing consciousness at the expense of free will, the deeper truth is that the intention of an ego in the unconscious region of mind has transpredicated to bring about a freewill decision to submit to inoculation in the conscious region.

Returning to the question posed by this section, the LLT view is that if we are limiting this strictly to the predicational process, then no, there can be no unconscious free will. The very meaning of free will is to transpredicate, to reply to theses with antitheses, to negate and redirect the course of events according to purpose. On the other hand, if the unconscious is pictured as a region of mind within which certain identities (id, ego, superego) are located, and one or more of these identities is transpredicating in an effort to effect compromises among them, then yes, it is possible to have unconscious free will.

Logical learning theory views the phrase "freedom of the will" as a nontechnical reference to agency. Predicating organisms have the free will to precedently affirm grounds or assumptions for the sake of which they will be determined. Before affirmation occurs we can speak of freedom, and after affirmation occurs we can speak of will (or willpower) in the meaning-extension to follow sequaciously. Settling on the direction of such free will invariably involves transpredication.

WHAT IS THE ROLE OF LANGUAGE IN PSYCHIC CONSCIOUSNESS?

Logical learning theory professes to explain the actions and behaviors of individual human beings in terms of a process known as predication.

We have, throughout this volume, addressed psychic consciousness in light of this process and avoided detailing specific contents that might be carried along by it. Of course, as learning proceeds, as predications extend over the course of life, the individual acquires a language system that names and helps pattern myriad aspects of experience including the very processes we have been considering (i.e., mediation vs. predication). Obviously, this acquisition of language greatly extends the person's grasp of things, enables memory to be enriched, and increases the probability of influencing or being influenced by others in social relations. Indeed, it is through linguistic terminology that we come to characterize our "selves" (see Chapter 6).

Given this broad significance for the use of language, does it follow that increasing language can increase psychic consciousness? Well, yes, if we take the view that language terms *symbolize* meanings (see Chapter 8 on dream symbols). If language terms are merely *signs*, then I would suggest that language does not facilitate consciousness and in fact, limits it. As Cassirer (1944) noted, signs are attached to certain elements of experience and come to stand proxy for these elements in thought and communication; but symbols have meaning even though they may not relate to anything existing in reality except themselves (pp. 80–84). Symbols are predicational; they have a meaning that can be extended to a target. Signs are not meaning-endowing in this fashion; they merely match-up with that for which they stand. Thus, as a sign the word *seven* stands surrogate for "1 + 1 + 1 + 1 + 1 + 1 + 1," but as a symbol it expresses "luck." The demonstratively reasoning computer (see Chapter 7) mediates signs by matching one to another on the basis of certain algorithmic rule patternings. The computer generates no meaning for it has no capacity to use the occasional sign analogically and thus generate an alternative that takes on meaning transpredicationally. As Langer (1948) once observed, "Symbols are not proxy for their objects, but are *vehicles for the conception of objects*" (p. 61; italics in original). This vehicular role is predicational in nature.

Lakoff (1987; with Johnson, 1980) has shown us the immense role that such linguistic usages as similes and metaphors play in our lives, and the vast reliance we place on categories (i.e., predicates [noun usage]). We take the meaning of one item in experience and use it to frame another, such as "Stephanie is a rock" (positive) or "Stephanie is a box of rocks" (negative). The language here serves a symbolic role in the thinking of the transpredicating reasoner who is using it creatively, forming different contexts for the specific meaning of a word (such as *rock*) and so on. But we are considering language now in terms of a predicational model. Switching to a mediational model, does it follow that by plugging in more linguistic terminology to a machine its consciousness is increased? Obviously not. The necessary transpredication *of the process* is not taking place.

Language as manifested in a transpredicational process is an instrumentality, a content used to further meaning and thereby generate, record, and carry out alternatives. Language in a mediational process is a signal system, used to blindly match one item with another. Load a computer with thousands upon thousands of chess moves, write a program that encompasses hopefully all possible alternatives (transpredications), and then arrange a contest between the computer and the best chess player in the world. This contest was actually arranged when, in February 1996, an IBM computer ("Deep Blue") squared off against Garry Kasparov (Krauthammer, 1996). Kasparov won the match, but not every game. Possibly in time, when programs are perfected, the computer will be the consistent winner. Does the fact that the computer won one game mean it was consciously selecting moves—that it was transpredicating? Of course not. The computer is mediating, and just as our example from Gandhi's life demonstrates that free will is not simply a question of "how many" alternatives are open to the mediating organism, we can now say that even though a computer program might survey every imaginable play in the closed system of chess, this does not mean that it is reasoning transpredicationally (see Chapter 7).

It is not the alternatives being mechanically moved forward in a signaling system that define free will. It is the capacity to behave symbolically for the sake of an intention, given even minimal options, that encompasses free will (qua consciousness). Intentions are predications framing targets, and they are always "taken on" because there is the cognizance that things could be otherwise all circumstances remaining the same. Kasparov knew each time that he moved a chess piece on the board this selection could be other than what he chose. The machine never had such consciousness of alternative possibilities. Once the calculation as to the statistically proper move was made, the machine blindly followed such programmed directives. The selection was no selection at all; the move was a fait accompli.

As discussed in Chapter 9, the collectivists in psychology rely a great deal on language to explain behavior. Humans can predicate entirely through imagery, without words (not to mention affectively assess in this manner). But in the social sciences it is helpful to think of language as a sort of "grand manipulator" of individual consciousness. The theoretical strategy here is Durkheimian. People are thought of in collective terms as the recipients of linguistic signals that move them along, influenced by these inputs to talk one way in situation X and another in situation Y. Insofar as this kind of mediated signalizing has relevance for our topic, I would say it manifests unconsciousness. According to this view, the person is locked into his or her cultural signals unable to transpredicate. Self-reflexivity is also not possible, because there is no instruction given on how to step outside of one's biasing assumptions to examine the opposite—a problem that Hofstadter wrestled with at great length (see Chapter 7).

Logical learning theory makes the assumption, on the basis of a thorough examination of the evidence (see Rychlak, 1994, pp. 267–273), that we use language instrumentally. People use—and misuse—words to express meanings. But these words always extend from a meaningful context that targets them to send forward a Jamesian cash-value in ongoing experience. A meaningful context always relates to or intends its targeted end (telos). In LLT we call this meaning-extension (see Chapter 2). Meanings extend from the broader to the narrower range of significance, but this is not because of the words (i.e., the contents) per se. Once again, it is the underlying predicational process that makes it possible for the human being to frame all kinds of meaningful relations, including some reasonably sensible relations of words (A school is a ladder, A school is a prison, etc.) and some not so reasonable (A trunk is a shoe horn, A trunk is a shoe tree, etc.). Predication is at work in all such sentences as it would be at work if we were visualizing these unusual relations in a dream (see Chapter 8).

The role of language in social influence has always been considered important in psychology. Even Wilhelm Wundt (1832–1920), arguably the first experimental psychologist, relied heavily on such an analysis of language in his folk psychology (Wundt, 1900/1920, Vol. 1). But it was Wiener (1954) who, in his cybernetics (or information processing) analysis, gave a clear rationale for linguistic influence when he equated social communication with social control:

> When I communicate with another person, I impart a message to him, and when he communicates back with me he returns a related message which contains information primarily accessible to him and not to me. When I control the actions of another person, I communicate a message to him, and although this message is in the imperative mood, the technique of communication does not differ from that of a message of fact. (p. 16)

Given a signalizing mechanism such as this, if we now multiply such communications millions of times, we have a collective of intercontrolling mechanisms like Minsky's society of mind or Hofstadter's ant hill (see Chapter 7). So what we end up with, if language is merely a string of signals inputting and outputting according to some naturally selected conglomeration of neurons, is an unconscious organism that is under the unidirectional (nondialectical) control of a collective.

In contrast to this view, LLT follows more of a neo-Hegelian view of language. Words are selected and expressed to extend meanings, and always in relation to the opposite possibilities. Thanks to this trail of oppositionality a series of words can be transpredicated by the listener, resulting in what Derrida would call an alternative reading (see Chapter 9). Indeed, the words can form an alienating context of meaning "all their own," one that the author did not intend (Heinemann, 1958, p. 10). Not that the words are speaking for themselves, but they can be used transpredicationally by the listener or reader and come to mean something totally different and often in direct contradiction to the intention of the person who initially framed them. Language as a symbol system is a uniquely human process of continual meaning-extension, of affirming, contradicting, and winding its way from one intention to another. This is the complete, teleological role that language plays in psychic consciousness.

AS PREDICATIONS, ARE AFFECTIVE ASSESSMENTS CONSCIOUS, UNCONSCIOUS, OR BOTH?

Affective assessment is a capacity to transcend and reflexively evaluate the likability of whatever it is that the evaluating organism is predicating at the moment (including both predicate and target contents). This capacity—technically termed a *transcending telosponse*—stems from a reasoner's innate generic oppositionality (see Chapter 2). To affectively assess—or experience an affection—is to render an additional predication of whatever is under unipredication *or* transpredication at the moment. These assessments can be readily reported as liked, disliked, or ambivalent (i.e., equally liked and disliked). For purposes of analysis we might distinguish between *conceptual* and *affective* predications as two kinds of contents (actually, they are different aspects of the same content). Claire gets off work very late, cancels an appointment with her attorney, calls her friend Mary Helen for a dinner date at a favorite restaurant, and then after eating drives her car home while thinking over the next day's work demands. All of these conceptually predicated events are also being predicated affectively at the same time.

Of course, Claire does not verbalize her likes and dislikes as she goes through the day; they are leveled as unipredications. There is a parallel here with the concept of a universal in framing what we are calling conceptual predications. In the same way that conceptions draw on universal assumptions that are unipredicational, so too does affection draw on unipredicated judgments that do not require any further rationale. A liked item is a liked item in thought, which proceeds smoothly without having to stop and consider the reasons why it is liked. At times, as when ordering a restaurant meal, Claire might indeed target her capacity to like and dislike per se in conjunction with her efforts to make a decision. The very process of liking and disliking might serve as dinner conversation for a time, and a search for the grounds in making affective assessments might then be attempted. At such moments I think it would be appropriate to say that affection is conscious, as the discussion reviews times when it is easy to accomplish the decision and times when it is not. Of course, I would still expect Claire to be affectively assessing this effort at understanding the nature of affective assessment—and this would in all probability be in the form of a unipredication, ergo unconscious.

As noted in Chapter 2, it is not necessary to have a ground in mind in order to render an affective assessment. We often make up reasons why we like something after we have sensed this preference for the item in question. One can pretend to like something if it is really disliked by thinking up such grounding "reasons," but this play-acting never takes genuine effect. In order to make a disliked into a liked target, one must consider alternative conceptual predications—get to know more about the target in question—at which time a totally new affective predication is rendered. Things can also go in the other direction, as when one person likes another until increasing familiarity breeds a certain contempt.

Logical learning theory holds that in earliest experience—even before language has been acquired—the infant begins to form patterns in the *Logos* on the basis of affective assessment (see Chapter 2). To know is to be capable of drawing such "knowledgeable" distinctions, thereby orienting oneself to upcoming events. The infant distinguishes likes from dislikes as it extends specific meanings tautologically in the first fumbling attempts at conceptual predication (e.g., "nipple is a nipple" vs. "hunger pain is a hunger pain"). In time, these meanings will target words through which they will be symbolically expressed, including the subjectively affective rendering on which each infant settles. Here is where Freudian insights become relevant, for it surely can be true that one child likes the feeding (nipple-sucking) experience a lot, thanks to the mother's warm acceptance in the relationship, whereas another child confronting a rejecting mother hates it. It is also possible that the mother is neither especially accepting nor rejecting, but the infant affectively predicates her as one or the other. Human behavior is difficult to capture because of such unique capacities to frame experience subjectively.

One frequently hears it said that machines are not conscious because they cannot experience emotions. In LLT we tend to avoid such arguments because they really do not clarify anything. In a sense, they are themselves emotionalized complaints. If tomorrow some kind of mechanism were constructed to give off varying levels of vibration or heat, and this was then called an "emotional reaction" for it accompanied other mechanical responses of the machine, this argument would fall on its face. Feeling per se is nonconscious, occurring outside the predicational process in the *Bios* realm. In any case, it is through the meaning-lending predication of such feelings that we name the emotion ("Let's see, am I really angry or just tensely excited?"). Similar nonconscious events arise in the *Physikos* realm as well. We walk outside to meet a brisk breeze, bright sunshine, or a heavy snowfall. Each of these physical events has an effect on our being, and depending on circumstances and our general attitude concerning these events, we assign them meanings accordingly. It is the same with emotions. Emotions can be easy and relaxing like a stroll in the park on a beautiful day, or jarring and threatening like crashing thunder and lightning at midnight. Of course, some people dislike parks and love the thrill of a thunderstorm. All of which means that either an emotion or a natural force like sunshine or rain must be made plausible in terms of a context of meaning, which includes what we have been calling both conceptual and affective predications.

Concepts drawing on the *Bios* as the source of reflexes, drives, traits, and other such notions were once very important in psychology. If explanation of behavior is totally extraspective, so that one is observing the motions of an organism "over there" and must account for its actions without appealing to an introspectively understood self-determination, these reductive conceptions prove very inviting. There is no need to divide affect from emotion in such models. Insofar as it may be said that an evaluation is taking place, the assumption is that some biologically released emotion or other feeling state (e.g., a drive) is determining what eventuates. If the person dislikes parks and likes thunderstorms then this cannot be due to an inherent capacity to render uniquely individual preferences. It must be that such individuals are predetermined by an atypical heredity, or they have been emotionally shaped as children by eccentric parents who met their drive for love only if they behaved in some peculiar manner. With the rise of computer modeling in psychology the older drive theories have waned. Of course, there is a remnant of drive theory today, masquerading as social drives like group conformity, the need for group identity, and so forth. There are also individual quasi-drives, such as achievement motives of one sort or another.

So, all in all, I think it most correct to suggest that affective assessments are predominantly unipredications, and not until called upon to do so is a person likely to consider—or make up—the grounds for the sake of which such judgments are rendered. These may or may not be the actual groundings, but once an affection is clear to the person there is no doubt that this preference can exert a psychic determination on subsequent behavior. It is not necessary for people to render a specific affective assessment for each item in a situation confronting them. It is the total situation that matters, and it can usually be subsumed with a predicating word symbol. Thus, in attending a party (social context) it is not necessary for the person to go about tabulating specific likes and dislikes (party games disliked, singing liked, dancing both liked and disliked, etc.) to render an affective assessment of a party. The overall situation is what may be given a rendering with little thought devoted to details. And if the person says or possibly merely senses "I dislike parties" the formulation here is unipredicational. Even so, if forced to attend a disliked party the person may, through this experience, find things quite different than expected, calling in turn for a new affective assessment—which may in this case be positive or at least ambivalent.

Even if the person does not consciously give consideration to some item in experience, if we force him or her to assess such items we can empirically demonstrate a role for affection in both learning and memory (see Rychlak, 1994, Chapter 7). People will learn a list of words or quasiwords more quickly if these items are liked than if they are disliked. But if people predicate the learning context negatively (dislike memorizing things), consider themselves inadequate (have low confidence), or are seriously maladjusted (suffering from neurosis, psychosis, depression, alcoholism, etc.), we find them learning words or quasiwords that they dislike *more readily* than those they like. There are no emotional reactions or drive-states involved in such experiments. People are rating words for likability on one day and then learning them several days later. Similar findings occur if we use recognition of paintings, designs, or faces as learnable items. Students attain higher IQ scores on tests they like than on those they dislike. In 30 years of research on learning and memory, I have rarely found the influence of affective assessment entirely lacking in the data of over 100 such experiments.

There is definitely something going on of an affectively unconscious (i.e., unipredicated) variety in the way that people frame their understanding and organize their memories. We have not taken up in detail the myriad studies on affective assessment because they essentially deal in the same predicational process employing different contents. It is this common process that I have sought to clarify in this volume. The circumspect answer to the question of this section is that affective assessments are usually, and doubtless for some people always, unipredications. But occasionally, and surely in principle, they can be involved in transpredication as well.

IS IT POSSIBLE TO HAVE TOO MUCH CONSCIOUSNESS?

In most cases this question probably refers to what we have been calling a bad kind of psychic consciousness, in which the person is flooded with alternatives in life and pushed to the wall with the demands of too many possibilities. In some cases, however, the question deals with the full range of consciousness and unconsciousness. In this latter sense, the questioner is likely to be a mediation modeler who uses extraspective formulations that do not require consciousness because the account rests on nonconscious *Bios–Physikos* mechanisms. A grudging allowance for certain mediators (e.g., linguistic cues) may be granted as effecting a quasi-awareness. However, the main attitude of mediation modelers is that too much emphasis on consciousness in human behavior waters down scientific explanation.

This is, of course, the standard behavioristic line trailing back through Skinner and Hull to Watson. We scientists can study people without considering their predicational capacities whatsoever. We can view their behavior as supposedly under continual efficient cause shaping. But it is also incontrovertibly true that if we look a little closer we find that our so-called behavioral conditioning of their behavior "depends" on their grasping (predicating) what we are trying to get them to do, and their willingness to go along with our manipulative efforts (Brewer, 1974; Page, 1972; Rychlak, 1994, p. 139). To understand really what behavioral manipulation or shaping involves, we must view things from the person's (introspective) perspective, where we learn that such controls are voluntary and follow from preliminary transpredications (qua awareness) by the person who is supposedly being unconsciously influenced.

I do not suggest that it is impossible in principle to control others unconsciously via unipredicated formulations. We have already suggested that affection works in this way, and people are surely influenced by their likes and dislikes. But if it comes to actually influencing behavior, the fact is that participants under shaping often try to figure out what is going on, and in the process lay down a predicating scenario for themselves. I am reminded here of a young woman who was in one of our operant-conditioning experiments some years ago. We were giving her a contingent reinforcement each time she voiced a certain type of word (plural noun). The reinforcement was *good*, as I recall, so only when she spontaneously voiced a plural noun (e.g., clouds, shoes, etc.) did the experimenter follow with the encouraging word ("good"). Although initially it appeared that she was being shaped—she was coming up with plural nouns—she abruptly switched exclusively to singular nouns. Afterwards, we asked her about this sudden shift in her shaping pattern and, in a righteous tone she said something like, "I'm not going to be a party to unethical research. You were 'hinting' to get me to give you the experimental results you want!" She was referring here to the "good" reinforcement, of course. In an interesting way she had revived the historic tie of consciousness to conscience and predicated our manipulative intentions as trying to covertly influence the outcome of a scientific experiment.

From the LLT perspective, although this young woman was not shaped in the direction called for by the experiment, the process she used to behave as she did was no different from the one that she would have used had she actually been verbally shaped to produce plural nouns. It is always a matter of predication in psychic determination, and the evidence suggests that transpredication is invariably involved in such shaping. The shaping here is therefore founded on formal-final causation and not on material-efficient causation as the "shaper" likes to pretend (see Brewer, 1974, for ample evidence in this regard). We are now in the *Logos* realm, relying on its predicational process, so we can hardly drop psychic consciousness from consideration because it is simply a further elaboration of this process.

Returning to the initial interpretation of this question, I do think that there is a problem with the great emphasis placed on consciousness in modern times. Gergen (1991) points out how the media has so expanded the range and variety of relationships available to the population of modern society that there is a possibility of socially oversaturating the self. Recall from Chapter 9 that, as a social constructionist, Gergen believes that there is no such thing as a "personal essence" (p. 170) found in selfhood. Selfhood is born of language usage because selves are defined by others (p. 178). Communities are more fundamental than private inner resources, so it is in the patterns of relationship with others, and the flowing discourse that takes place in such contact, that we find our selves. We should no longer be concerned about what Riesman called the other-directed character structure (see Chapter 3). The problem is not one of "me" against the group, but one of conflict over the "form of relatedness" to be followed (p. 242).

Gergen believes in the relativity of languages, but not in the relativity of individual reasoning (p. 253). Logical learning theory can agree with Gergen that there is "no transcendent reality, rationality, or value system with which to rule between competitors" (p. 253). That is, there is no such system unless all parties to the discussion over such a possibility can come to agreement on one (both individually and as groups in discourse). Where LLT differs from Gergen is in believing that human beings *must* seek such universal groundings, which they make unipredicationally. This logical necessity is not born of social influence but of human nature. If people lack some such basis for their conviction they are made uneasy, lose confidence, and become vulnerable to all kinds of demagoguery.

Here is the source of so-called "identity" for individuals and groups alike—those universal groundings that somehow reassure and encourage. Here is also the source of altruistic causes that people are moved to support. A cause that evokes energetic commitment can organize and direct even the most disoriented person or anomic group. Causes are fundamentally confrontations of what the group members assume to be the right against the wrong, or the good against the bad (expressed introspectively as "me against the world," "us against them," and so forth). As previously noted in this chapter, religious commitments reflect the same kind of reaching for universal certitude. When Gergen tells us that there are no selves but only those linguistic conventions about selfhood given to people in dialogue, he is no different than anyone else who holds to a conviction. He has his ex cathedra universals at work in this argument. He may elect to ignore the influence of such logically affirmed universals, of course. Because they are ultimately rooted in unconsciousness it is easy to do so.

Interestingly, there is another way in which "too much" transpredication can be manifested in the very dialogue that Gergen espouses. It stems from the deconstructive strategy of rereading, rephrasing, or otherwise twisting what is said into opposite implications, sometimes with considerable humor—on the order of a "straight line" followed by a Woody Allen gag. Gergen tells of a luncheon that he once attended with a group of postmodernist colleagues. Although there was hope for sincere dialogue on Gergen's part, one of the participants at the luncheon took every opportunity to use puns, wordplay, and ironic caricature to essentially deconstruct what was being submitted to discourse by the group members. In LLT terms, this person was not focusing into a useful form of unipredication over the topic at hand, but was playfully transpredicating whatever came up. Gergen (1991) gives us his reaction to this matter:

> For a time the deconstructive antics [of the colleague] were enjoyed by all. But slowly, as the luncheon bore on, it became clear that no "serious discussion" was possible. This customary form of pursuit, while fulfilling to many scholars, was "out of bounds." To underscore the postmodern dilemma most poignantly, it became apparent that should all participants "go postmodern" in this way, we would be reduced to an empty silence. (p. 194)

The paradox here is that through transpredicating, however humorously, Gergen's colleague was countering (via free will) the possibility of a productive unconsciousness to develop in the group. The group could not narrow and fix its grounds to get on with its business because a deconstructionist in its midst had run amuck. But now, does this not prove that there is a difference between the individual and the group? Here was a deconstructionist maverick who was not playing the dialogue game according to the group's rules. His self-image might indeed be that of the eccentric cut-up, the Woody Allen of academia. But his capacity to deconstruct by way of transpredication was something different from and in addition to this self-image. I think this vignette supports the Riesman thesis that not everyone is readily other-directed in group relations. Individuals do make a difference.

In answer to this final question, yes, there are probably times when there is just too much consciousness going on, and a little psychic unconsciousness would doubtless prove beneficial. In the same way that humans sometimes need to break free of the ordinary to move into new alternatives, so too do they need on occasion to narrow their alternatives, fix on a cause, engage in a solitary pursuit, or be moved by a singular obsession. Having too many alternatives can take away the luster from any one course of action. Those individuals who are bored, or who cannot commit to any goal in life (e.g., marriage, a career, etc.) probably suffer from something of this nature. Too many alternatives seem to pop up, so that either there is a fear of missing something "new" to enrich existence—or the affective sense is that there really is nothing to choose. Once again, LLT cannot offer any single content—*the* solution—to such empty lives. But the hope is that by more accurately capturing the process through which people achieve consciousness, we might facilitate a more fruitful search for meaningful contents tailored to the individual. At the very least, as predicational modelers we will begin our search introspectively rather than extraspectively, take into consideration subjective affective assessments, and count on the fruits of reflexive self-examination.

FINAL CONCLUDING COMMENT

Hopefully, the handful of questions and answers covered in Chapter 10 will leave the reader with a sense of the kinds of issues and alternative viewpoints that LLT encourages. For an extensive review of the empirical research in support of LLT see Rychlak (1994). I am of the opinion that the social sciences are now well-positioned to allow some colleagues to propose theories departing from the mechanistic, efficient-cause views of traditional science. Indeed, many—and I think most—modern scientists have already departed from relying exclusively on such Newtonian precepts. For some reason, probably because they are working so close to the vulnerabilities of the human mind, experimental psychologists are among the leading theoretical reactionaries in the scientific community. Caution is therefore understandable.

However, I also believe that we psychologists have exercised caution at the expense of garnering new ideas. We have, in the terminology of this volume, limited our image of humanity to unipredications issuing from the biological and inanimate realms. We have been slow to transpredicate the resultant mechanistic image of humanity, and to find thereby equally instructive conceptions in the phenomenal realm. Such teleological conceptions can be readily subjected to empirical validation, and those that pass this scientific test can be very helpful in the never-ending quest for an understanding of human beings. I hope this volume has raised the psychic consciousness of those who respect both human nature and psychological science, which up to this point in time have been ill-suited associates.

The attitude that psychologists and other social scientists must view every phenomenon under study as a machine if they are to fulfill their role as scientists is surely passé. This Newtonian attitude limits what can be brought to test in the scientific method, and it is also the source of the arrogance mentioned in the preface to this volume regarding the possible validity of the nonmechanistic folk psychology. Foisting a mechanistic conception onto a teleological organism is not only bad science, it is dangerously misleading and can prove disastrous to the lives of those so labeled. I would like now to suggest that the social sciences move into a *post-*

mechanism phase of their development. There are vastly different inferences and implications to be drawn if we begin with the assumption that people are agents as opposed to being mechanical robots. Our legal systems presume that people have free will, from which flows personal responsibility. Religio-ethical precepts are predicated on the same assumption. Aesthetic endeavours of all sorts stem ultimately from the capacity that people have to evaluate their environment and select or create the more beautiful alternative. Finally, there is a continuing sense of intentionality and purpose in everything that people do. To treat this ubiquitous cognizance as if it were a serendipitous outcome of evolution or a mediating illusory belief is to rob the human image of its very humanity.

As we move into the 21st century, we are in an era of increasing emphasis on human rights. In my opinion, one of the most basic of these rights is that people be given the dignity of possessing free will and the psychic consciousness on which it is founded. The only way we can accomplish this, in my estimation, is for a fundamental change to occur in how we think about human behavior. Logical learning theory, and the predicational model on which it rests, is one such suggested change. It is now in its formative years, and there are undoubtedly many developmental changes ahead. In the meantime, I hope that its application to the topic of psychic consciousness has proven stimulating if not completely satisfying to the reader.

GLOSSARY
THE TERMINOLOGY OF LOGICAL
LEARNING THEORY

ACONSCIOUS   An unintended outcome of conscious or unconscious acts.
The person intends one meaning-extension but is charged with, blamed,
or criticized for intending another.

ACTION-INTENTION   A form of telosponse in which the target is to carry
out an observable action sequence that is typically referred to as "behavior." All action-intentions begin as understanding-intentions. *See also*
Intention, Telosponse, Understanding-Intention.

AFFECTIVE ASSESSMENT, AFFECTION   A transcending telosponse; that is,
an innate capacity to reflexively target and thereby evaluate the meanings of one's cognitive contents (premises, concepts, predicates, etc.),
characterizing them as either *liked* (positive evaluation) or *disliked* (negative evaluation) in quality. Logical learning theory holds that affection
is the most basic and abstract cognition carried on by a human being.
See also Reflexivity, Telosponse, Transcendence.

AFFIRMATION   An aspect of telosponsivity in which a point anywhere
along a bipolar dimension of meaning is affirmed as being the grounds
for the sake of which understanding or action will be furthered in cognition. Affirmation is the psychic equivalent of drawing the Euler circle
of a predication, for it delimits the specific realm of meaning that will
be extended to the target. *See also* Euler Circles, Telosponse

AFFIRMING THE CONSEQUENT   A logical error growing out of an "If,
then" course of reasoning. It takes place if we reason "If A then B" and
subsequently affirm B to conclude "therefore A." In science it arises if
we reason "If my theory is true then my experimental data will array as
predicted" and subsequently affirm "My experimental data array as predicted" to conclude "therefore, my theory is [necessarily] true." The latter conclusion is technically incorrect: The theory is only "true" with

293

the proviso that an alternative theory might in principle also be validated by the observed data.

AGENCY   The capacity that an organism has to behave or believe in conformance with, in contradiction of, in addition to, or without regard for what is perceived to be environmental or biological determinants. *See also* Freedom of the Will.

APODICTIC   Refers to the belief that some item of knowledge is absolutely certain, and therefore not open to alternative or contradictory interpretations.

APPOSITION   The state of being "side by side." In Boolean formulations, apposition replaces opposition. Because the items in apposition do not delimit each other, there is no intrinsic tie between them as there is in an opposition. *See also* Opposition.

ASSUMPTIONS   Highly abstract understanding-intentions that work as a prememory to frame what can then be known. They can be examined via reflexivity, but usually are not because they are taken as unquestionably plausible, self-evident, and so forth. *See also* Ground, Knowledge, Prememory.

AWARENESS   A cognitive state occurring when the person knows that something other than what is now occurring might or could take place. Thus, some subjects who are aware in a conditioning experiment occasionally fail to comply with the instructions (i.e., behave as agents). They know that it is possible to "do otherwise," and actually do so. *See also* Agency, Conscious, Transpredication.

BACONIAN CRITICISM   The charge that adding telic conceptions into the description of natural processes adds nothing to our understanding of these processes. Bacon did *not* level this charge against final-cause descriptions of human beings.

BEHAVIOR   A global reference to the overt and covert actions of living organisms, including their physiological and biological functions.

BIOS   One of the four major grounds used in psychology on which to base explanations. *Bios* grounds draw from the chemical and tissue substances of animate nature to explain events on the basis of such processes as mediation, organic systems, and genetics. *See also Logos, Physikos, Socius.*

CATEGORIZATION   Another term for the predicational process. This process results in a category, or what is often termed a "cognitive representation." *See also* Predication, Process.

CAUSES   Derived from the Greek word *aitía*, which means "the responsible factor" in any descriptive understanding of the nature of things, including behaviors, physical bodies, and thoughts. The four causes include the material, efficient, formal, and final. These meanings—singularly or in combination—serve as the predicates of literally anything in existence. They are highly abstract precedents in human thought from which meaning-extension occurs sequaciously. *See also* Efficient Cause,

Final Cause, Formal Cause, Material Cause, Meaning-Extension, Precedent.

CHOICE In LLT, this refers to a relatively difficult affirmation. In telosponding, the person is continually taking a position in ongoing experience, but this is not perceived as making choices. It is only when ambivalence or complexity arises during premise-affirmation that the person senses the telosponsive process as involving "choice." *See also* Affirmation, Taking a Position, Telosponse.

COGNITION According to LLT, this is simply an alternative term for "telosponsivity." Cognition is evaluational at its core because of the capacity to render affective assessments of the targets under predication. *See also* Affective Assessment, Telosponsivity.

CONSCIOUSNESS, CONSCIOUS A concept describing behavior that has several interpretations depending on the grounds used to define it. The most common description of conscious behavior is that it involves awareness. Biological interpretations emphasize wakeful activity in behavior. In LLT the focus is on the framing and extension of predicating meanings to alternative targets, resulting thereby in understanding- and action-intentions. Logical learning theory finds awareness stemming from the capacity to transpredicate. *See also* Action-Intention, Awareness, Predication, Psychic Consciousness, Transpredication, Understanding-Intention, Unipredication.

CONSTRUCTION This term has both a Kantian and a Lockean usage. In the Kantian sense, this means "to interpret" that which is under observation in top–down fashion. In the Lockean sense, this means "to heap together" as in building a structure from small, brick-like units in bottom–up fashion.

CONTENT An ingredient that is produced, conveyed, or otherwise employed by a process. *See also* Process.

CONTEXT According to LLT, the meaning framed by a context is tantamount to predication. The predication process is what always ensures that there will be contextual meanings at play in human cognizance. *See also* Predication, Process.

CONTRADICTION, LAW OR PRINCIPLE OF Also known as noncontradiction. This principle holds that A is not *non*-A. It underwrites demonstrative reasoning and was used by Boole as the law of duality in framing the either–or logic later embraced by computer modelers. *See also* One and Many.

DELIMITING OPPOSITIONALITY Bounds a specific meaning that stands in relation to its bipolar counterpart, as when *injustice* delimits *justice* and vice versa. Delimiting oppositionality involves the *contents* of the predicational process, enabling the reasoner to draw implications. Thus, certain opposites lend a direction to thought, as when saying "John is not reliable" implies he "is" unreliable. *See also* Generic Oppositionality, Implication, Oppositionality.

DEMONSTRATIVE REASONING   Cognition in which oppositionality is dismissed in favor of the either–or distinctions of the law of contradiction. The "inside the Euler circle" is focused on as if it were the only alternative framing reasoning. Aristotle claimed that demonstrative reasoners affirmed their major premises on the basis of the fact that these premises were primary and true, hence not open to dispute or negation. *See also* Dialectical Reasoning.

DETERMINE, DETERMINISM   Refers to the limitation or setting of limits on events, including behavior. Each of the four Aristotelian causes involves a distinctive form of determinism. *See also* Causes.

DIALECTIC, DIALECTICAL   From the Greek word *dialektos*, which refers to discourse, talk, exchanging ideas (*dia* = between; *legein* = talk). Among other uses, this concept was used to describe the exchange that Socrates had with his students, whereby there was an initial expression of a thesis, a countering antithesis, resulting in a synopsis (modern term "synthesis"). The fundamental idea here is that knowledge is tied together through oppositionality (i.e., the "one and many" thesis). There are many dialectical theories in the history of ideas. Logical learning theory views dialectic as a special case of oppositionality in which the union of bipolar meaning is being emphasized. *See also* Dialectical Reasoning, One and Many, Oppositionality.

DIALECTICAL REASONING   Cognition in which oppositionality is employed, so that the "outside the Euler circle" region of meaning is not dismissed as irrelevant or erroneous. Aristotle claimed that dialectical reasoners affirmed the major premise on the basis of opinion (point of view, arbitrary choice, bias, etc.) rather than on a fixed, primary and true basis. *See also* Demonstrative Reasoning, Dialectic, Oppositionality.

DIFFERENCE   One of the outcomes of generic oppositionality, in which the "sameness" of a target framed by a predicate (category, attribution, etc.) is negated. For example, if "John is German" is negated ("John is not German"), removing "John" from the predicating meaning of "German," we have a difference taking place. John is different in nationality from German people. *See also* Delimiting Oppositionality, Generic Oppositionality, Predication, Sameness.

EFFICIENT CAUSE   A predication used to account for the nature of things (including behavior) founded on the impetus in a succession of events over time. Explanations of behavior relying on energy pushes, gravity attractions, and the machine-like flow of motion are under predication by efficient causation. *See also* Causes.

EMOTION   According to LLT, this refers to a pattern of physiological feelings in a certain life situation, the sum total of which is targeted and thereby organized into meaning by the predications of the person experiencing these feelings and living through the circumstances of the situation involved. Emotions are not telosponses, but are affectively assessed via such transcending telosponses. Emotions are not arbitrarily generated through oppositional cognition, but occur in unidirectional fashion as do all biological and physical promptings in experience. Emotional feelings can be stimulated by certain drugs, or by having the person recall an emotion-provoking life circumstance. *See also* Affective Assessment.

EULER CIRCLES A means of representing class or categorical relations through spatial figures that was introduced by the Swiss mathematician, Leonhard Euler (1707–1783). Circles of various sizes depict the relations. For example, "All A is B" would be represented by a smaller circle labeled A situated within a larger (predicating) circle labeled B. Logical learning theory employs the Euler circles (or, Euler Diagrams) as a model to depict the predicational process.

EXTRASPECTIVE PERSPECTIVE, THEORY OF Framing theoretical explanations of things or events in the third person ("that, it, him, her," etc.), from the convenience of an observer (i.e., on the outside, looking in). Extraspection is the natural outlook for validation—where we look "at" our experimental data unfolding—but it is always possible to test introspective theory through validation if we just keep a clear distinction between method and theory. *See also* Affirming the Consequent, Introspective Perspective, Theory of.

FINAL CAUSE Any concept used to account for the nature of things (including behavior) on the basis of the assumption that there is a reason, end, or goal for the sake of which things exist or events are carried out. Explanations that rely on the person's intentions, aims, or aspirations are final-cause descriptions of behavior. *See also* Causes, Teleology.

FORGETTING Occurs if the organism is unable to frame a predication in which the target to be recalled is lent relevant meaning—with *relevance* involving the reason why the target is to be brought into current cognizance. A target that has been poorly organized is likely to be forgotten. *See also* Knowing, Memory as Process, Remembering.

FORMAL CAUSE Any concept used to account for the nature of things (including behavior) on the basis of their patterned organization, shape, design, or order. Explanations of behavior emphasizing the style or type of behavioral pattern taken on are formal-cause descriptions. Often these explanations are said to involve the quality or essence of the item in question. *See also* Causes.

FREEDOM OF THE WILL A non-technical reference to agency. The person has *free will* who is capable of precedently affirming the ground or assumption for the sake of which she or he will be determined. Before affirmation we can speak of freedom, and, after affirmation we can speak of will (or willpower) in the meaning-extension to follow sequaciously.

See also Affirmation, Assumption, Final Cause, Ground, Sequacious, Telosponse.

GENERIC OPPOSITIONALITY   A general aspect of the predicational process in which targets fall either under or beyond the meaning being extended by the predicate. In the Euler-circle model, this would involve falling either inside or outside of the framing circle. Generic oppositionality is intrinsic to the predicational *process*, and is most clearly reflected in negations of predicate meanings that fail to extend a delimiting oppositionality—as in the case of "John is not German." In this case, although we cannot draw any implication as to John's actual nationality (content), we are nevertheless involved in an oppositional process of negation. *See also* Delimiting Oppositionality, Oppositionality

GROUNDS   The basis on which a theory is being framed. There are four major groundings to consider in psychology: *Bios, Logos, Physikos,* and *Socius.* Each of these grounds has its own process and thereby specific contents that are under processing.

HOMUNCULUS   The "little person" who supposedly must be concocted to explain how it is that agency can occur in human behavior. The homunculus is needed because of the mechanism that is postulated as an explanation of human behavior: Since the mechanism is without intention, it requires a "driver" or "director." In LLT, the person *is* the homunculus, because the person is conceptualized from the start as teleological.

IDEA   Another term for the content that is either created or mediated by a mental process. *See also* Content, Process.

IMPLICATION   A line of cognition in which the premises under affirmation are considered by the person to be uncertain—possibly true but possibly false—resulting in conclusions that are not experienced as confidently or as certainly the case, really true, and so forth. *See also* Affirmation, Inference.

INFERENCE   A line of cognition in which the person considers the premises under affirmation to be true, so that he or she accepts any conclusions reached as soundly justified. *See also* Affirmation, Demonstrative Reasoning, Implication.

INTENTION   Behaving for the sake of purposive meanings as encompassed in images, language terms, affections, and so on, all of which are encompassed as premises in the act of predication. Purpose and intention combine to form telosponsivity. Intentionality is as pure an expression of final causation as possible. Logical learning theory also distinguishes between (a) *understanding-intentions,* in which the meanings under affirmation are restricted to the logical ordering of cognizance, and (b) *action-intentions,* in which the meanings under affirmation are extended into readily observable, overt behavior. *See also* Affirmation, Final Cause, Predication, Premise, Purpose, Telosponse.

INTROSPECTIVE PERSPECTIVE, THEORY OF   Framing theories of things or events in the first person, from the view of an identity acting within them (i.e., on the inside, looking out). Introspective theory refers to "I, me" rather than to "that, it." *See also* Extraspective Perspective, Theory of.

JUDGMENT   Another way of referring to the evaluations—including of fictive assessments—entering into the affirmations of predications. *See also* Affective Assessment, Affirmation, Choice, Predication.

KNOWING, KNOWLEDGE   Refers to the organization of meanings that predicate targets in top–down fashion. At the highest level of abstraction, knowledge is organized as universals that are rarely themselves targeted for awareness. In trying to remember a target, *knowing* refers to the predicating context involved in this process. It is possible to remember a target without remembering the context-setting knowledge used. But if knowing does not occur, remembering cannot occur. *See also* Assumption, Prememory, Remembering.

LAW, LAWFULNESS   A law is a presumably inviolate (i.e., nonarbitrary) regularity emanating from the *Physikos* or *Bios*. Lawfulness is a stable and generalizable relationship obtaining between an independent and dependent variable of an experiment. At its base, the law concept borrows from the meaning of formal causation, with the addition of material and efficient causation that stamps laws as necessary patterns. Logical learning theory holds that those human beings who frame "laws" observe a stable, reliable relationship among variables in an experimental format and at some point place enough confidence in it to term it a law. *See also* Rule.

LEARNING   May be said to occur when the "learner" is confident enough to use a former target as a predicate. *See also* Predicate, Target.

LOGIC, LOGICAL   In LLT, this refers to the concern with meaningful patterns in cognition as well as the patterning of these meanings in ongoing experience. Both demonstrative and dialectical logic are involved. The focus is not on accuracy, precision, or correctness, but solely on how meanings are patterned into other meanings. Logical explanations stress formal and final causation relying on demonstrative and dialectical rule-following.

LOGICAL LEARNING THEORY   A teleological formulation of cognition and behavior that draws heavily on the concepts of predication and opposition to picture the human being as a telosponding organism, one that is continually "taking a position" on life as an active agent. *See also* Agency, Logic, Oppositionality, Predication, Telosponse.

LOGOS   One of the four major grounds used in psychology as a basis of explanations. *Logos* grounds draw from the patterned order of events to explain according to processes like predication, construing, or mental acts. *See also* Bios, Physikos, Socius.

MATERIAL CAUSE   Any concept used to account for the nature of things (including behavior) on the basis of an assumed underlying, unchanging substance that constitutes things. Explanations of behavior founded on genetic transmission or chemical elements are examples of material-cause descriptions. *See also* Causes.

MEANING   In traditional associationistic theory, the joining of independent units through frequency and contiguity over time, relying primarily on efficient causation. LLT interprets meaning as the logical relationship organized between an affirmed predicate and its target, relying primarily on formal or final causation. Hence, LLT holds that meaning is an organization or pattern that intends its significance to some relevant target. *See also* Efficient Cause, Final Cause, Formal Cause, Meaning-Extension.

MEANING-EXTENSION   The precedent-sequacious flow of meaning in the conceptualizations of telosponsivity, commonly referred to as the inductive and deductive knowledge of experience. As meaning-extension continues, the knowledge framed by the predications of telosponsivity extends its range. *See also* Meaning-Extension, Principle of.

MEANING-EXTENSION, PRINCIPLE OF   Holds that if all other considerations are equal, the pattern of meaning forming in a predication extends to the least understood or poorest known targets relevant to the predicating meaning. *See also* Meaning-Extension, Predication.

MEANINGFULNESS   As used in LLT, the extent of personal significance that a particular meaning has for the individual concerned.

MECHANISM   An explanation of behavior founded predominantly on efficient causation, with occasional use of material causality. In no case do these explanations employ a final-cause concept. Hence, mechanism is essentially the opposite of teleology. *See also* Efficient Cause, Material Cause, Teleology.

MEDIATION, PROCESS OF   As used in this volume, this is a mechanical process in which something that is produced elsewhere and taken in or input comes to play a role in the process that was not initially a part of or intrinsic to it. *See also* Predication.

MEMORY, AS CONTENT   A target that has been extended meaning several predications previously, and is then reconceptualized in the present.

MEMORY, AS PROCESS   According to LLT, memory is a concept describing the cohesiveness and clarity of a tightly organized, relevant precedent meaning that is extended sequaciously in ongoing experience. The tighter this organization, the better the memory.

METHOD   The means or manner of determining whether a theoretical construct or statement is true or false. There are two broad types of method: (a) cognitive or conceptual method, which makes use of procedural evidence, and (b) research method, which uses validating evidence in addition to procedural. *See also* Procedural Evidence, Theory, Validating Evidence.

MODEL   A distinctive conceptual pattern, used in the study of some topic as a standard to generate, organize, and communicate knowledge. Models are, in effect, predicates.

MOTIVATION   According to LLT, this is an evaluation of the relative advantage that an affirmed premise, encompassing a predicated target, makes possible in the telosponder's life. This advantage can be leveled by the telosponding individual or by an observer who presumes to know what the intentions enacted comprise, and what they will therefore result in relative to the telosponder's total life situation.

NONCONSCIOUS   A process that does not involve predication, hence is neither conscious nor unconscious. *See also* Aconscious, Conscious, Unconscious.

ONE AND MANY   The principle holding that all experience is organized meaningfully through opposition, so that *same* delimits the meaning of *different*, and vice versa. This principle underwrites dialectical reasoning and soft disjunction, and can be opposed to the law of contradiction. *See also* Contradiction, Law of.

OPPOSITION, OPPOSITIONALITY   A "double predication" in which one predicate of a duality intrinsically delimits its target as being a contrary, contradiction, contrast, or negation of the meaning under extension, and, pari passu, the target in question—serving now as a reverse predicate—returns the favor. *See also* Apposition, Delimiting Oppositionality, Generic Oppositionality.

PERCEPTION   In LLT, this refers to the predication of sensory input, thereby organizing it into meaning. To perceive is to capture the patterns of sensations that align themselves in the *Logos*. Perception has a logic to it, which is employed in a problem-solving effort continually made by the perceiver qua telosponder.

PHYSIKOS   One of the four major grounds used in psychology as a basis for explanations. *Physikos* grounds are drawn from the material and energic substances of inanimate nature. Examples of the processes of the *Physikos* realm are gravitation, or the principles of constancy, and conservation. *See also* Bios, Logos, Socius.

PRECEDENT (Pre-cee'-dent)   Refers to the ordering of meaning without regard for time's passage; that is, a precedent meaning is one that goes before others in order or arrangement, as the major premise always precedes the minor premise of a syllogism, framing its general meaning so that the minor premise can only extend the meaning that is contained therein. *See also* Sequacious.

PREDICATE, PREDICATION   Can be understood in either a verb or a noun sense. In the verb meaning this refers to a process of affirming or denying, and in the noun sense it refers to that which is affirmed or denied (i.e., a meaningful content). Logical learning theory holds that cognitive representations such as schemata, plans, scripts, prototypes, and so on, are predicate contents of a predication process ("to predicate"). If a predicate is used to frame a target in the process of predication it is known as the context meaning. *See also* Affirmation, Predication, Process of.

PREDICATION, PROCESS OF   The logical process of affirming, denying, or qualifying precedently broader patterns of meaning in sequacious extension to narrower or targeted patterns of meaning. The target is the point, aim, or end (telos) of the meaning-extension. *See also* Meaning-Extension, Precedent, Sequacious.

PREMEMORY   The assumptive framework that gradually forms in the course of learning and is therefore known although it need not be remembered. Prememory organizes what is to be remembered. Affective assessment can also serve as prememory because it serves as an organizer of cognition from its very inception. The amnesiac patient may be unable to recall the name of an item, but can still understand or read the question put to him or her concerning this item. This capacity to read is a reflection of prememory. Knowing and remembering are not identical. *See also* Affective Assessment, Assumption, Knowing.

PREMISE   A statement of meaning (including assumption, belief, point of view, argument, etc.) that is put forward at the outset of a line of reasoning. Premises always encompass predication, and are affirmed at the protopoint. In the traditional syllogistic formula, premises embody precedent major and minor affirmations of meaning that are extended sequaciously to the increasingly focused conclusion that follows. *See also* Affirmation, Predication, Protopoint.

PROACTIVE   In LLT, this term is used to identify a telosponsive affirmation of predicating meaning that is perfectly acceptable to the person's general psychic outlook (i.e., belief system, attitudes, morals, etc.). A proactive unipredication leading to a period of unconsciousness in the thinking or behavior of an individual is entirely normal and psychologically healthy. Proactive unconsciousness might be seen in a person greatly focusing on some activity like reading an affectively positive novel, or concentrating on the less liked but necessary need to fill out income tax forms. *See also* Reactive, Unipredication.

PROCEDURAL EVIDENCE   A basis for belief in a theory because of its plausibility or consistency with common sense. This is sometimes called face validity or theoretical proof.

PROCESS   A discernible, repeatable course of action on the basis of which some items under description are believed to be sequentially patterned. *See also* Content.

PRO FORMA   For the sake of a precedent form, organization, or order that is extended sequaciously to the target of interest. In LLT this phrase is used to suggest that human mentation, rather than being tabula rasa and hence ordered exclusively by experiential input, extends meaning "to" experience. *See also* Tabula Rasa.

PROTOPOINT Refers to the anchoring point of meaning-extension at which affirmations and negations are made. The terms precedent and sequacious refer to the ordering of meaning-extensions at any point in the course of intentional behavior—for example, over the full course of a deductive or inductive line of thought. But the *initiating* point at which a pro forma intelligence grounds its understanding or intends its purposes is the protopoint. In one sense this is the "first precedent" for any one line of intentionality, but all protopoint affirmations are sequaciously extended from ever more abstract meanings. Universals represent the ultimate protopoints of reason. *See also* Meaning-Extension, Pro Forma.

PSYCHIC CONSCIOUSNESS In LLT, this refers to an explanation of consciousness entirely in the realm of the *Logos*, as framed in terms of the predicational process. To the extent that there is cognizance of meanings outside of or beyond the scope of the larger Euler circle in the predicational model, the person is experiencing psychic consciousness. Awareness in cognition is made possible through such transpredication. (Note: This phrase is frequently used as a global reference to the full range of both consciousness and unconsciousness.) *See also* Consciousness, Euler Circles, Predication, Psychic Unconsciousness, Transpredication, Unconsciousness, Unipredication.

PSYCHIC UNCONSCIOUSNESS In LLT, this refers to an explanation of unconsciousness entirely in the realm of the *Logos*, framed in terms of the predicational process. To the extent that meaning-extension is confined to the largest Euler circle of the predication model, with no appreciation or acceptance of meaningful realms beyond this limiting point, the person is experiencing psychic unconsciousness. Awareness is therefore narrowed through such unipredication. *See also* Consciousness, Euler Circles, Predication, Psychic Consciousness, Transpredication.

PURPOSE The "aim of the meaning" of a concept, which is brought to mental existence by the intentional behavior of a telic organism. Purpose focuses on the formal-cause aspect of telosponsive behavior. If such patterned organizations that have an aim (point, significance, end, etc.) are intended by a conceptualizing organism, we can speak of the combined process as a telosponse. *See also* Intention, Telosponse.

REACTIVE In LLT, this term is used to identify a telosponsive affirmation of predicating meaning that is not acceptable to the person's general psychic outlook (i.e., belief system, attitudes, morals, etc.). The person "reacts" to the affectively negative threat of such meanings to deny them contact with the broader realm of meanings in the mind. A reactive unipredication leading to a period of unconsciousness in the thinking or behavior of an individual is psychologically unhealthy. Reactive unconsciousness might be seen in a person seeming to "not hear" when spoken to on certain threatening topics. In extreme forms of such reactivity the person may actually dissociate aspects of his or her personality or take on so-called multiple personalities. *See also* Proactive, Unipredication.

RECOGNITION   The tautologizing of a cognitive content with itself. *See also* Tautology.

REFLECTIVITY, SELF-REFLECTIVITY   The capacity to "look at" the resultant contents of cognitive processing in an extraspective manner. Unlike reflexivity, which is an introspective examination of one's assumptions, biases, and convictions, reflectivity is going over and elaborating what a thought sequence has already accomplished or "arrived at." We "reflect" on what has occurred or is the case in thought. We "reflexively examine" what otherwise might have been the case in thought. *See also* Extraspection, Introspection, Reflexivity.

REFLEXIVITY, SELF-REFLEXIVITY   The introspective capacity for mentation to turn back on itself by transcending the process taking place, and thereby realizing that it "is" involved in the pro forma framing of experience. Reflexivity always leads to the appreciation that the meanings presently under affirmation could be otherwise. Reflexivity is made possible through oppositionality, in which there is always a sense that the meanings under affirmation could be brought into question, rejected, revised, reaffirmed, and so on. *See also* Affirmation, Oppositionality, Pro Forma, Reflectivity, Transcendence.

REINFORCEMENT   In LLT terms, this occurs when understanding- or action-intentionality flows from a premise that successfully (effectively, helpfully) conceptualizes a life circumstance for the individual employing it. The meaning-extension has "cash-value," it works for the person concerned as evidently "true" (although objectively it may be false). Positive reinforcements successfully extend meanings that are rooted in positive predications, and negative reinforcements successfully extend negative premises.

REMEMBERING   Places emphasis on the target in cognitive efforts to affirm the same predication that was affirmed initially some time ago. To remember a past event or object is to extend meaning from an approximation of the initial predication to the target being remembered. The "better" the organization of this initial predication, the greater the likelihood that the target will be remembered. *See also* Knowing, Predication, Prememory.

REPRESENTATION   Another term for the content of a cognitive process. Representations can be signs or symbols, depending on the process producing them. Predicational models consider their representations to be symbols (i.e., meaning-producing organizations). Mediational modelers consider their representations to be signs (i.e., learned cues that act as surrogates for something else).

RESPONSIBILITY   A recognition that the person plays a role in the telosponsive affirmation of premises, encompassing the grounds for the sake of which the person furthers thoughts and enacts behavior.

RULES Fundamentally arbitrary proscriptions that must be conformed to if they are to retain their integrity. Rules are formal-cause regularities having an internal consistency that dictates a pattern of thought or action. Rules also have a final-cause aspect in that they are subject to change depending on the intentions of those who are to follow, obey, or submit to them. *See also* Law, Lawfulness.

SAMENESS When a target is subsumed by the meaning of a predicate (category, attribute, etc.). In the case of "John is German," the target *John* is the same as all other members of the category *German*, so far as this specific meaning is concerned. *See also* Difference.

SELF In LLT, this refers to the predications concerning personal identity as framed telosponsively during maturation. The telosponding person arrives first on the scene in life, but in time can (a) reflexively target an introspective viewpoint as an "I, me," lending it meaning through predications drawn from personal experience as well as the opinions and impressions of others ("I am smart"); (b) become increasingly conscious of doing so ("I know myself better now"); and (c) seek to improve on the advantages gained from the use of further premises in which the "I, me" serves as a self-enhancing predicate ("That is mine"), or in which the identity is targeted for enhancement ("I can be even smarter").

SEMANTICS Having to do with meaning. *See also* Syntax.

SEQUACIOUS (See-kway'-shus) Refers to the ordering of meaning without regard for time considerations. A sequacious meaning is one that follows or flows logically from the meanings of precedents, extending these as understanding- or action-intentions in a *necessary* fashion once they have been affirmed. Sequacious meaning-extensions can be entirely or partially tautological of their precedents. Partial sequacious extensions of a precedent meaning include analogies, metaphors, and so on. *See also* Meaning-Extension, Precedent, Tautology.

SIGNS, SIGNALS Surrogate designations for that to which they are related—as when the number 7 stands for a specific number of single markers. Non-telic theories rely on signs, as associated "stand ins" for environmental influencers. On the basis of the frequency and contiguity of past experience, such environmentally produced surrogates are bonded together and "input" cognitively, totally without intention. *See also* Symbol.

SOCIUS One of the four major grounds used in psychology on which to found explanations. The *Socius* ground draws from the supra-individual organizations that influence through such processes as socialization, historicism, and political collectivism. *See also* Bios, Logos, Physikos.

SYMBOLS Vehicles for the creation of meaning, acting like predications because they are pregnant with meanings, not all of which are clearly delimited in any one target. In linguistic theory, a symbol employs words instrumentally to convey the meaning symbolized. *See also* Sign.

SYNTAX   Having to do with the grammatical structure of word usage in a language. *See also* Semantic.

TABULA RASA   The view that mind is as a "blank sheet" at birth and that all it subsequently contains is penciled upon it from external sources. *See also* Pro Forma.

TAKING A POSITION   Affirming a meaning for the sake of which behavior is intended, given that there is always an alternative meaning that could be the grounds for understanding or action. This is merely a recognition that any meaning under affirmation in telosponsivity can be transcended hence reflexively put to question, rejected, and so forth. *See also* Affirmation, Reflexivity, Transcendence.

TARGET   Essentially the "telos" or aim (reason, goal, etc.) of meaning-extension. The target is an integral aspect of predication. Meanings framed in predication are extended to targets. *See also* Predication, Process of.

TAUTOLOGY   A relation of identity in meaning, considered either extraspectively as redundant, analytically true statements or introspectively as the premised meaning being extended from what is known to what can be known.

TELEOLOGY, TELIC   The view that events are predicated according to plan, design, or assumption—that is, on the basis of purposive meanings or reasons—and therefore directed to some intended end. Teleologies can be natural, divine, or human in formulation. Telic accounts rely on final causation and thus are the very opposite of mechanistic accounts. *See also* Mechanism.

TELOS   Greek word for end, goal, or grounding reason for the sake of which things exist or an event or behavior is taking place. *See also* Final Cause, Teleology, Telosponse.

TELOSPONSE, TELOSPOND   To affirm a premise (encompassing a predication) and behave covertly or overtly for the sake of the meaning affirmed rather than its opposite. Telosponsivity can be intentionally halted or negated, but a complete telosponsive act involves taking a position that then willfully determines the course of thought (understanding-intention) or behavior (action-intention). *See also* Affirmation, Intention, Predication, Purpose.

THEORY   A series of two or more schematic labels (words, visual images that we name, etc.) that have been hypothesized, presumed, or even factually demonstrated to bear a meaningful relationship with one another. Theories are, in effect, predications having specific targets to be endowed with meaning. *See also* Method.

THOUGHT   Essentially synonymous with predication; the taking of a position relating to a target given the grounding context of a framework, as well as the continuing meaning-extension to follow. *See also* Meaning-Extension, Predication.

TIGHTNESS OF ORGANIZATION   Refers to the internal consistency and clarity of the meaning (content) under extension in predication. If a predicate content is tightly organized, the likelihood of retention in memory is increased. The predicating context must also have a relevant organization if memory is to be facilitated. *See also* Content, Predicate.

TIME   A unit of measurement employed to array (organize, pattern, plan, etc.) life events logically. Time can thus serve as a standard—a "that" —for the sake of which life events are evaluated according to rate of progress, completion, and so forth.

TRANSCENDENCE   The capacity that all humans have to rise above their ongoing predicational process even as it is taking place. Because human cognition involves affirmation and the taking of a position within oppositional possibilities, there is always this capacity to extend meanings away from the "given" to a realm of awareness that is "not given." Transcendence is closely tied to reflexivity. *See also* Affirmation, Reflexivity, Taking a Position.

TRANSPREDICATION   Crossing over the boundary limits of a framing predication. To transpredicate is to be cognizant that the framing meaning of one's line of thought (symbolized by the largest Euler circle in the predicational model) can be transcended, leading to wider realms of meaning having relevance for the target under consideration. To transpredicate is therefore to reason for the sake of not only what is being affirmed, but of what is being implied, inferred, rejected, negated, contradicted, and contrasted in ongoing thought. This sense of alternative possibilities is the source of the awareness attributed to consciousness. *See also* Awareness, Consciousness, Euler Circles, Predication, Psychic Consciousness, Transcendence.

UNCONSCIOUSNESS, UNCONSCIOUS   A term loosely used to describe thoughts or behaviors which seem to occur outside of awareness. In LLT there is an effort made to be more explicit by interpreting this concept according to the way that predications are affirmed and enacted. *See also* Consciousness, Psychic Unconsciousness, Unipredication.

UNDERSTANDING-INTENTION   A telosponse in which the meaning affirmed frames understanding but is not necessarily going to be manifested in overt action. Understanding-intentions can be fleeting impressions as well as deep-seated convictions. *See also* Action-Intention, Intention.

UNIPREDICATION   Restricting thought to the boundary limits of a framing predication. To unipredicate means that no cognizance is taken of a realm of possible meaning outside of the course that thought is taking at the moment (symbolized as remaining entirely within the largest Euler circle in the predicational model). The restricted awareness of such possible alternatives is what is meant by psychic unconsciousness. *See also* Euler Circles, Transpredication, Psychic Unconsciousness, Unconsciousness.

VALUE   The relative worth of an object or action, in comparison to possible alternatives. The judgment rendered here places great emphasis on affective assessment, because values are essentially positive predications that can be wound into a social group's mores or norms. *See also* Affective Assessment.

VALIDATING EVIDENCE   Believing in something only after it has been put to test in a prearranged course of events designed specifically to show what it relates to meaningfully. This is how scientists prove things, relying on the control of events and the prediction of an observable outcome. *See also* Procedural Evidence.

WILL   A term capturing the determinism of sequacious meaning-extension that follows the affirmation of a premise. This concept encompasses a psychic (final-cause) determinism. *See also* Determine, Freedom of the Will, Sequacious.

REFERENCES

Alexander, C. N. (1988). A conceptual and phenomenological analysis of pure consciousness during sleep. *Lucidity Letter, 7,* 39–43.

Alexander, F. G., & Selesnick, S. T. (1966). *The history of psychiatry: An evaluation of psychiatric thought and practice from prehistoric times to the present.* New York: Harper & Row.

Allport, F. H. (1924). *Social psychology.* Cambridge, MA: Houghton Mifflin.

Anderson, J. R. (1983). *The architecture of cognition.* Cambridge, MA: Harvard University Press.

Aristotle. (1952a). Categories. In R. M. Hutchins (Ed.), *Great books of the western world* (Vol. 8, pp. 5–21). Chicago: Encyclopedia Britannica.

Aristotle. (1952b). Metaphysics. In R. M. Hutchins (Ed.), *Great books of the western world* (Vol. 8, pp. 499–626). Chicago: Encyclopedia Britannica.

Aristotle. (1952c). On generation and corruption. In R. M. Hutchins (Ed.), *Great books of the western world* (Vol. 8, pp. 409–441). Chicago: Encyclopedia Britannica.

Aristotle. (1952d). On memory and reminiscence. In R. M. Hutchins (Ed.), *Great books of the western world* (Vol. 8, pp. 690–695). Chicago: Encyclopedia Britannica.

Aristotle. (1952e). Posterior analytics. In R. M. Hutchins (Ed.), *Great books of the western world* (Vol. 8, pp. 95–137). Chicago: Encyclopedia Britannica.

Aristotle. (1952f). Topics. In R. M. Hutchins (Ed.), *Great books of the western world* (Vol. 8, pp. 143–223). Chicago: Encyclopedia Britannica.

Aristotle. (1952g). Rhetoric. In R. M. Hutchins (Ed.), *Great books of the western world* (Vol. 9, pp. 593–675). Chicago: Encyclopedia Britannica.

Asch, S. E. (1952). *Social psychology.* New York: Prentice-Hall.

Augustine. (1961). *Confessions.* (R. S. Pine-Coffin, Trans.). New York: Penguin Books.

Ayer, A. (1946). *Language, truth and logic.* New York: Dover.

Baars, B. J. (1988). *A cognitive theory of consciousness.* Cambridge, England: Cambridge University Press.

Bacon, F. (1952). Advancement of learning. In R. M. Hutchins (Ed.), *Great books of the western world* (Vol. 30, pp. 1–101). Chicago: Encyclopedia Britannica.

Baenninger, R. (1994). A retreat before the canon of parsimony. *Contemporary Psychology, 39,* 805–807.

Bandura, A. (1962). Social learning through imitation. In M. R. Jones (Ed.), *Nebraska Symposium on Motivation* (Vol. 10, pp. 211–274). Lincoln: University of Nebraska Press.

Bandura, A. (1979). Self-referent mechanisms in social learning theory. *American Psychologist, 34,* 439–442.

Bandura, A. (1986). *The social foundations of thought and action: A social cognitive theory.* Englewood Cliffs, NJ: Prentice-Hall.

Barber, T. X. (1969). *Hypnosis: A scientific approach.* New York: Van Nostrand Reinhold.

Barber, T. X., Spanos, N. P., & Chaves, J. F. (1974). *Hypnosis, imagination and human potentialities.* Elmsford, NY: Pergamon Press.

Barthes, R. (1986). The death of the author. In R. Barthes (Ed.), *The rustle of language* (pp. 49–55). Berkeley: University of California Press.

Becker, H., & Barnes, H. E. (1952). *Social thought from lore to science* (2 vols., 2nd ed.). Washington, DC: Harrén Press.

Bendix, R. (1962). *Max Weber: An intellectual portrait.* Garden City, NY: Doubleday Anchor.

Berger, P. L. (1963). *Invitation to sociology: A humanistic perspective.* New York: Doubleday Anchor.

Berger, P. L., & Luckmann, T. (1966). *The social construction of reality: A treatise in the sociology of knowledge.* New York: Doubleday Anchor.

Berger, R. (1977). *Psychosis: The circularity of experience.* San Francisco: Freeman.

Berlyne, D. (1960). *Conflict, arousal, and curiosity.* New York: McGraw-Hill.

Blackmore, S. (1988). A theory of lucid dreams and OBEs. In J. Gackenbach & S. LaBerge (Eds.), *Conscious mind, sleeping brain: Perspectives on lucid dreaming* (pp. 48–67). New York: Plenum.

Boden, M. A. (1977). *Artificial intelligence and natural man.* New York: Basic Books.

Bohm, D. (1957). *Causality and chance in modern physics.* Philadelphia: University of Pennsylvania Press.

Bohm, D. (1987). *Unfolding meaning: A weekend of dialogue with David Bohm.* New York: Ark Paperbacks.

Bohr, N. (1934). *Atomic theory and the description of nature.* Cambridge, England: Cambridge University Press.

Boneau, C. A. (1974). Paradigm regained? Cognitive behaviorism restated. *American Psychologist, 29,* 297–309.

Boole, G. (1958). *An investigation of the laws of thought on which are founded the mathematical theories of logic and probabilities.* New York: Dover. (Original work published 1854)

Boring, E. G. (1950). *A history of experimental psychology.* New York: Appleton-Century-Crofts.

Bowers, K. S. (1984). On being unconsciously influenced and informed. In K. S. Bowers & D. Meichenbaum (Eds.), *The unconscious reconsidered* (pp. 227–271). New York: Wiley.

Bowers, K. S. (1992, November 2). *Preconscious processes: How do we distinguish mental representations that correspond to perceived events from those that reflect imaginal processes?* Paper presented at National Institute of Mental Health workshop "Basic behavioral and psychological research: Building a bridge," Rockville, MD.

Bowers, P. G., Laurence, J. R., & Hart, D. (1988). The experience of hypnotic suggestions. *International Journal of Clinical and Experimental Hypnosis, 36,* 336–349.

Bradley, J. (1971). *Mach's philosophy of science.* London: Athlone Press.

Brentano, F. (1973). *Psychology from an empirical standpoint.* New York: Humanities Press. (Original work published 1874)

Breuer, J., & Freud, S. (1955). Studies on hysteria. In J. Strachey (Ed. and Trans.), *The standard edition of the complete psychological works of Sigmund Freud* (Vol. II). London: Hogarth. (Original work published 1893–1895)

Brewer, W. F. (1974). There is no convincing evidence for operant or classical conditioning in adult humans. In W. B. Weimer & D. S. Palermo (Eds.), *Cognition and the symbolic processes* (pp. 1–42). Hillsdale, NJ: Erlbaum.

Broglie, L. A. de. (1949). A general survey of the scientific work of Albert Einstein. In P. Schlipp (Ed.), *Albert Einstein, philosopher scientist* (Vol. 1, pp. 38–51). New York: Harper & Row.

Bronowski, J. (1958). *The common sense of science.* Cambridge, MA: Harvard University Press.

Brown, A. E. (1936). Dreams in which the dreamer knows he is asleep. *Journal of Abnormal and Social Psychology, 31,* 59–66.

Brown, R. H. (1987). Personal identity and political economy. In R. H. Brown (Ed.), *Society as text: Essays on rhetoric, reason, and reality* (pp. 28–63). Chicago: University of Chicago Press.

Bruner, J. (1957). On perceptual readiness. *Psychological Review, 64,* 123–152.

Brylowski, A. (1986). H–reflex in lucid dreams. *Lucidity Letter, 5,* 116–118.

Bunge, M. (1980). *The mind–body problem: A psychobiological approach.* New York: Pergamon Press.

Burtt, E. A. (1955). *The metaphysical foundations of modern physical science* (Rev. edition). Garden City, NY: Doubleday.

Calkins, M. W. (1906). A reconciliation between structural and functional psychology. *The Psychological Review, 13,* 61–81.

Cameron, N., & Rychlak, J. F. (1985). *Personality development and psychopathology: A dynamic approach.* Boston: Houghton Mifflin.

Carruthers, M. (1990). *The book of memory: A study of memory in medieval culture.* Cambridge, England: Cambridge University Press.

Cassirer, E. (1944). *An essay on man: An introduction to a philosophy of human culture.* Garden City, NY: Doubleday.

Cassirer, E. (1950). *The problem of knowledge.* New Haven, CT: Yale University Press.

Chang, G. C. (1977). *Teachings of Tibetan yoga.* Secaucus, NJ: The Citadell Press.

Chaplin, J. P. (1985). *Dictionary of psychology* (2nd rev. ed.). New York: Bantam Doubleday Dell.

Cole, M., & Scribner, S. (1974). *Culture and thought: A psychological introduction.* New York: Wiley.

Coulter, J. (1985). Two concepts of the mental. In K. J. Gergen & K. E. Davis (Eds.), *The social construction of the person* (pp. 129–144). New York: Springer-Verlag.

Cousins, N. (Ed.). (1985). *Nobel prize conversations with Sir John Eccles, Roger Sperry, Ilya Prigogine, & Brian Josephson.* San Francisco: Saybrook.

Covello, E. (1984). Lucid dreaming: A review and experimental study of waking intrusions during stage REM sleep. *The Journal of Mind and Behavior, 5,* 81–98.

Cranston, M. W. (1957). *John Locke: A biography.* New York: Macmillan.

Crevier, D. (1993). *AI: The tumultuous history of the search for artificial intelligence.* New York: Basic Books.

Crick, F. (1984). Function of the thalamic reticular complex: The searchlight hypothesis. *Proceedings of the National Academy of Sciences, USA, 81,* 4586–4593.

Culler, J. (1982). *On deconstruction: Theory and criticism after structuralism.* Ithaca, NY: Cornell University Press.

Daro, D. (1988). *Confronting child abuse.* New York: Free Press.

Darwin, C. (1952a). The descent of man. In R. M. Hutchins (Ed.), *Great books of the western world* (Vol. 49, pp. 253–600). Chicago: Encyclopedia Britannica.

Darwin, C. (1952b). The origin of species by means of natural selection. In R. M. Hutchins (Ed.), *Great books of the western world* (Vol. 49, pp. 1–251). Chicago: Encyclopedia Britannica.

Darwin, C. (1989). The expression of the emotions in man and animals. In P. H. Barrett & R. B. Freeman (Eds.), *The works of Charles Darwin* (Vol. 23). New York: New York University Press.

Davies, P. C. W., & Brown, J. R. (Eds.). (1986). Interview with John Bell. *The ghost in the atom* (pp. 45–57). Cambridge, England: Cambridge University Press.

Dennett, D. C. (1984). *Elbow room: The varieties of free will worth wanting.* Cambridge, MA: Bradford.

Dennett, D. C. (1991). *Consciousness explained.* Boston: Little Brown.

Derrida, J. (1981). *Positions* (A. Bass, Trans.). Chicago: The University of Chicago Press.

Dewey, J. (1893). *Psychology* (3rd ed.). New York: Harper.

Dillbeck, M. C., & Alexander, C. N. (1989). Higher states of consciousness: Maharishi Mahesh Yogi's vedic psychology of human development. *The Journal of Mind and Behavior, 10,* 307–334.

Dittrich, A., von Arx, S., & Staub, S. (1981). International study on altered states of consciousness (ISASC), Part 1: Theoretical considerations and research procedures. *Revue Suisse de Psychologie, 40,* 189–200.

Dixon, M., & Laurence, J.-R. (1992). Two hundred years of hypnosis research: Questions resolved? Questions unanswered! In E. Fromm & M. R. Nash (Eds.), *Contemporary hypnosis research* (pp. 23–41). New York: Guilford.

Dixon, N. F. (1971). *Subliminal perception: The nature of a controversy.* New York: McGraw-Hill.

Dollard, J., & Miller, N. E. (1950). *Personality and psychotherapy: An analysis in terms of learning, thinking, and culture.* New York: McGraw Hill.

Dreyfus, H. L. (1979). *What computers can't do: The limits of artificial intelligence* (Rev. ed.). New York: Harper & Row.

Durkheim, É. (1933). *The division of labor in society.* New York: Macmillan.

Durkheim, É. (1961). *Elementary form of the religious life.* New York: Macmillan.

Eccles, J. C. (1977). In K. R. Popper & J. C. Eccles (Eds.), *The self and its brain,* part 2 (pp. 225–421). London: Springer International.

Edelman, G. M. (1987). *Neural Darwinism: The theory of neuronal group selection.* New York: Basic Books.

Edelman, G. M. (1992). *Bright air, brilliant fire: On the matter of the mind.* New York: Basic Books.

Edwards, P. (Editor-in-chief). (1967). *The encyclopedia of philosophy* (Vol. 1). New York: Macmillan; and Free Press.

Einstein, A. (1934). *Essays in science.* New York: Philosophical Library.

Ellis, J. J. (1989). *Against deconstruction.* Princeton, NJ: Princeton University Press.

Engelberg, E. (1972). *The unknown distance.* Cambridge, MA: Harvard University Press.

Eriksen, C. W. (1960). Discrimination and learning without awareness: A methodological survey and evaluation. *Psychological Review, 67,* 279–300.

Farthing, G. W. (1992). *The psychology of consciousness.* Englewood Cliffs, NJ: Prentice-Hall.

Feuer, L. S. (1974). *Einstein and the generations of science.* New York: Basic Books.

Fish, S. (1980). *Is there a text in this class? The authority of interpretive communities.* Cambridge, MA: Harvard University Press.

Fraser, J. T. (1987). *Time: The familiar stranger.* Amherst: University of Massachusetts Press.

Freud, S. (1953). The interpretation of dreams (2nd part) and On dreams. In J. Strachey (Ed.), *The standard edition of the complete psychological works of Sigmund Freud* (Vol. V). London: Hogarth. (Original work published 1900)

Freud, S. (1955a). An infantile neurosis and other works. In J. Strachey (Ed.), *The standard edition of the complete psychological works of Sigmund Freud* (Vol. XVII). London: Hogarth. (Original work published 1917)

Freud, S. (1955b). Beyond the pleasure principle, group psychology, and other works. In J. Strachey (Ed.), *The standard edition of the complete psychological works of Sigmund Freud* (Vol. XVIII). London: Hogarth. (Original work published 1920–1921)

Freud, S. (1955c). Totem and taboo and other works. In J. Strachey (Ed.), *The standard edition of the complete psychological works of Sigmund Freud* (Vol. XIII). London: Hogarth. (Original work published 1913)

Freud, S. (1957a). Five lectures on psycho-analysis, Leonardo da Vinci, and other works. In J. Strachey (Ed.), *The standard edition of the complete psychological works of Sigmund Freud* (Vol. XI). London: Hogarth. (Original work published 1910)

Freud, S. (1957b). On the history of the psycho-analytic movement, papers on metapsychology, and other works. In J. Strachey (Ed.), *The standard edition of the complete psychological works of Sigmund Freud* (Vol. XIV). London: Hogarth. (Original work published 1915)

Freud, S. (1958). The case of Schreber, Papers on technique and other works. In J. Strachey (Ed.), *The standard edition of the complete psychological works of Sigmund Freud* (Vol. XII). London: Hogarth. (Original work published 1911)

Freud, S. (1959a). An autobiographical study, inhibitions, symptoms, and anxiety, The question of lay analysis, and other works. In J. Strachey (Ed.), *The standard edition of the complete psychological works of Sigmund Freud* (Vol. XX). London: Hogarth. (Original work published 1925)

Freud, S. (1959b). Jensen's "Gradiva" and other works. In J. Strachey (Ed.), *The standard edition of the complete psychological works of Sigmund Freud* (Vol. IX). London: Hogarth. (Original work published 1906)

Freud, S. (1960a). Jokes and their relation to the unconscious. In J. Strachey (Ed.), *The standard edition of the complete psychological works of Sigmund Freud* (Vol. VIII). London: Hogarth. (Original work published 1905)

Freud, S. (1960b). The psychopathology of everyday life. In J. Strachey (Ed.), *The standard edition of the complete psychological works of Sigmund Freud* (Vol. VI). London: Hogarth. (Original work published 1901)

Freud, S. (1961a). The ego and the id, and other works. In J. Strachey (Ed.), *The standard edition of the complete psychological works of Sigmund Freud* (Vol. XIX). London: Hogarth. (Original work published 1923)

Freud, S. (1961b). The future of an illusion, Civilization and its discontents, and other works. In J. Strachey (Ed.), *The standard edition of the complete psychological works of Sigmund Freud* (Vol. XXI). London: Hogarth. (Original work published 1929)

Freud, S. (1962). Early psycho-analytic publications. In J. Strachey (Ed.), *The standard edition of the complete psychological works of Sigmund Freud* (Vol. III). London: Hogarth. (Original work published 1894)

Freud, S. (1963). Introductory lectures on psycho-analysis (Part III). In J. Strachey (Ed.), *The standard edition of the complete psychological works of Sigmund Freud* (Vol. XVI). London: Hogarth. (Original work published 1916)

Freud, S. (1964a). Moses and monotheism, An outline of psycho-analysis, and other works. In J. Strachey (Ed.), *The standard edition of the complete psychological works of Sigmund Freud* (Vol. XXIII). London: Hogarth. (Original work published 1939)

Freud, S. (1964b). New introductory lectures on psycho-analysis and other works. In J. Strachey (Ed.), *The standard edition of the complete psychological works of Sigmund Freud* (Vol. XXII). London: Hogarth. (Original work published 1932)

Freud, S. (1966). Pre-psycho-analytic publications and unpublished drafts. In J. Strachey (Ed.), *The standard edition of the complete psychological works of Sigmund Freud* (Vol. I). London: Hogarth. (Original work published 1892)

Fromm, E. (1962). *Beyond the chains of illusion: My encounter with Marx and Freud.* New York: Pocket Books.

Gackenbach, J. (1988). Psychological content of lucid versus nonlucid dreams. In J. Gackenbach & S. LaBerge (Eds.), *Conscious mind, sleeping brain: Perspectives on lucid dreaming* (pp. 181–219). New York: Plenum.

Gackenbach, J. (1990). Is lucid dreaming naturally female? In S. Krippner (Ed.), *Language of the night* (pp. 32–51). Los Angeles: Tarcher.

Gackenbach, J. (1991). Frameworks for understanding lucid dreaming: A review. *Dreaming, 1,* 109–128.

Galton, F. (1971). Measurement of character. In L. D. Goodstein & R. I. Lanyon (Ed.), *Readings in personality assessment* (pp. 4–10). New York: Wiley. (Original work published 1884)

Gardner, H. (1985). *The mind's new science: A history of the cognitive revolution.* New York: Basic Books.

Gergen, K. J. (1989). Social psychology and the wrong revolution. *European Journal of Social Psychology, 19,* 463–484.

Gergen, K. J. (1991). *The saturated self: Dilemmas of identity in contemporary life.* New York: Basic Books.

Ghiselin, B. (1952). *The creative process.* New York: Mentor.

Gleick, J. (1988). *Chaos: Making a new science.* New York: Penguin Books.

Goleman, D. (1978). A taxonomy of meditation-specific altered states. *Journal of Altered States of Consciousness, 4,* 203–213.

Green, C. (1968). *Lucid dreams.* London: Hamish.

Greenwald, A. G. (1992). New Look 3: Unconscious cognition reclaimed. *American Psychologist, 47,* 766–779.

Greenwald, A. G., Spangenberg, E. R., Pratkanis, A. R., & Eskenazi, J. (1991). Double-blind tests of subliminal self-help audiotapes. *Psychological Science, 2,* 119–122.

Gruber, H. E. (1974). *Darwin on man: A psychological study of scientific creativity.* New York: Dutton.

Harré, R. (1984). *Personal being: A theory for individual psychology.* Cambridge, MA: Harvard University Press.

Harré, R. (1987). Enlarging the paradigm. *New Ideas in Psychology, 5,* 3–12.

Harré, R. (1992). On being taken up by others. In D. N. Robinson (Ed.), *Social discourse and moral judgment* (pp. 61–74). San Diego, CA: Academic Press.

Hartmann, E. (1975). Dreams and other hallucinations: An approach to the underlying mechanism. In R. K. Siegal & J. L. West (Eds.), *Hallucinations* (pp. 26–42). New York: Wiley.

Hastorf, A. H., & Cantril, H. (1954). They saw a game: A case study. *Journal of Abnormal and Social Psychology, 49,* 129–134.

Hawking, S. W. (1988). *A brief history of time: From the big bang to black holes.* New York: Bantam Books.

Hayes, P. J., Ford, K. M., & Adams-Webber, J. R. (1992). Human reasoning about artificial intelligence. *Journal of Experimental and Theoretical Artificial Intelligence, 4,* 247–263.

Hebb, D. O. (1972). *A textbook of psychology* (3rd ed.). Philadelphia, PA: W. B. Saunders.

Hebb, D. O. (1974). What psychology is about. *American Psychologist, 29,* 71–79.

Heer, F. (1962). *Medieval world: Europe 1100–1350* (J. Sondheimer, Trans.). New York: World Publishing.

Hegel, G. W. F. (1952a). The philosophy of history. In R. M. Hutchins (Ed.), *Great books of the western world* (Vol. 46, pp. 151–369). Chicago: Encyclopedia Britannica. (Original work published 1857)

Hegel, G. W. F. (1952b). The philosophy of right. In R. M. Hutchins (Ed.), *Great books of the western world* (Vol. 46, pp. 1–150). Chicago: Encyclopedia Britannica. (Original work published 1821)

Heinemann, F. H. (1958). *Existentialism and the modern predicament.* New York: Harper & Row.

Hilgard, E. R. (1973). A neodissociation interpretation of pain reduction in hypnosis. *Psychological Review, 80,* 396–411.

Hilgard, E. R. (1992). Dissociation and theories of hypnosis. In E. Fromm & M. R. Nash (Eds.), *Contemporary hypnosis research* (pp. 69–99). New York: Guilford Press.

Hilgard, E. R., Morgan, A. H., & Macdonald, H. (1975). Pain and dissociation in the cold pressor test: A study of hypnotic analgesia with "hidden reports" through automatic key pressing and automatic talking. *Journal of Abnormal Psychology, 84,* 280–289.

Hobbes, T. (1952). Leviathan. In R. M. Hutchins (Ed.), *Great books of the western world* (Vol. 23, pp. 41–283). Chicago: Encyclopedia Britannica. (Original work published 1651)

Hodges, A. (1983). *Alan Turing: The enigma.* New York: Simon & Schuster.

Hofstadter, D. R. (1980). *Gödel, Escher, Bach: An eternal golden braid.* New York: Vintage Books.

Hollender, D. (1986). Semantic activation without conscious identification in dichotic listening, parafoveal vision, and visual masking: A survey and appraisal. *Behavioral and Brain Sciences, 9,* 1–23.

Holton, G. (1973). *Thematic origins of scientific thought: Kepler to Einstein.* Cambridge, MA: Harvard University Press.

Hook, S. (1962). *From Hegel to Marx: Studies in the intellectual development of Karl Marx.* Ann Arbor: The University of Michigan Press.

Hospers, J. (1961). Free will and psychoanalysis. In H. Morris (Ed.), *Freedom and responsibility* (pp. 35–47). Stanford, CA: Stanford University Press.

Howe, M. L., & Courage, M. L. (1993). On resolving the enigma of infantile amnesia. *Psychological Bulletin, 113*, 305–326.

Hull, C. L. (1937). Mind, mechanism, and adaptive behavior. *Psychological Review, 44*, 1–32.

Hull, C. L. (1952). *A behavior system.* New Haven, CT: Yale University Press.

Hunt, H. T. (1988). The multiplicity of dreams. *Lucidity Letter, 7*, 5–14.

Hunt, H. T. (1989). *The multiplicity of dreams: A cognitive psychological perspective.* New Haven, CT: Yale University Press.

Immergluck, L. (1964). Determinism–freedom in contemporary psychology: An ancient problem revisited. *American Psychologist, 19*, 270–281.

Jacoby, L. L., Lindsay, D. S., & Toth, J. P. (1992). Unconscious influences revealed: Attention, awareness, and control. *American Psychologist, 47*, 802–809.

James, H., Jr. (Ed.). (1920). *The letters of William James* (2 vols.). Boston: Atlantic Monthly Press.

James, W. (1943). *Pragmatism.* New York: The World Publishing Co. (Original work published 1907)

James, W. (1952). The principles of psychology. In R. M. Hutchins (Ed.), *Great books of the western world* (Vol. 53). Chicago: Encyclopedia Britannica. (Original work published 1890)

James, W. (1958). *The varieties of religious experience: A study in human nature.* New York: The New American Library. (Original work published 1902)

James, W. (1967). Does "consciousness" exist? *Essays in radical empiricism and A pluralistic universe* (pp. 1–38). Glouster, MA: Peter Smith. (First appeared in the *Journal of Philosophy, Psychology and Scientific Methods, 1*, 1904, 477–491).

Janet, P. (1924). *Principles of psychotherapy.* New York: Macmillan.

Janet, P. (1965). *The major symptoms of hysteria.* New York: Hafner Publishers. (Original work published 1929)

Jaynes, J. (1976). *The origin of consciousness in the breakdown of the bicameral mind.* Boston: Houghton Mifflin.

Johnston, W. (1993). *The mystical way.* London: Fount Paperbacks.

Jung, C. G. (1953a). Psychology and alchemy. In H. Read, M. Fordham, & G. Adler (Eds.), *The collected works of C. G. Jung* (The Bollingen Series, Vol. 12). New York: Pantheon Books.

Jung, C. G. (1953b). Two essays on analytical psychology. In H. Read, M. Fordham, & G. Adler (Eds.), *The collected works of C. G. Jung* (The Bollingen Series, Vol. 7). New York: Pantheon Books.

Jung, C. G. (1954a). The development of personality. In H. Read, M. Fordham, & G. Adler (Eds.), *The collected works of C. G. Jung* (The Bollingen Series, Vol. 17). New York: Pantheon Books.

Jung, C. G. (1954b). The practice of psychotherapy. In H. Read, M. Fordham, &

G. Adler (Eds.), *The collected works of* C. G. *Jung* (The Bollingen Series, Vol. 16). New York: Pantheon Books.

Jung, C. G. (1956). Symbols of transformation. In H. Read, M. Fordham, & G. Adler (Eds.), *The collected works of* C. G. *Jung* (The Bollingen Series, Vol. 5). New York: Pantheon Books.

Jung, C. G. (1957). Psychiatric studies. In H. Read, M. Fordham, & G. Adler (Eds.), *The collected works of* C. G. *Jung* (The Bollingen Series, Vol. 1). New York: Pantheon Books.

Jung, C. G. (1958). Psychology and religion: West and east. In H. Read, M. Fordham, & G. Adler (Eds.), *The collected works of* C. G. *Jung* (The Bollingen Series, Vol. 11). New York: Pantheon Books.

Jung, C. G. (1959). The archetypes and the collective unconscious. In H. Read, M. Fordham, & G. Adler (Eds.), *The collected works of* C. G. *Jung* (The Bollingen Series, Vol. 9,1). New York: Pantheon Books.

Jung, C. G. (1960a). The psychogenesis of mental disease. In H. Read, M. Fordham, & G. Adler (Eds.), *The collected works of* C. G. *Jung* (The Bollingen Series, Vol. 3). New York: Pantheon Books.

Jung, C. G. (1960b). The structure and dynamics of the psyche. In H. Read, M. Fordham, & G. Adler (Eds.), *The collected works of* C. G. *Jung* (The Bollingen Series, Vol. 8). New York: Pantheon Books.

Jung, C. G. (1961). Freud and psychoanalysis. In H. Read, M. Fordham, & G. Adler (Eds.), *The collected works of* C. G. *Jung* (The Bollingen Series, Vol. 4). New York: Pantheon Books.

Jung, C. G. (1963). *Memories, dreams, reflections.* New York: Pantheon Books; and London: William Collins Sons, Ltd.

Jung, C. G. (1964). Civilization in transition. In H. Read, M. Fordham, & G. Adler (Eds.), *The collected works of* C. G. *Jung* (The Bollingen Series, Vol. 10). New York: Pantheon Books.

Jung, C. G. (1966). The spirit in man, art, and literature. In H. Read, M. Fordham, & G. Adler (Eds.), *The collected works of* C. G. *Jung* (The Bollingen Series, Vol. 15). New York: Pantheon Books.

Jung, C. G. (1967). Alchemical studies. In H. Read, M. Fordham, & G. Adler (Eds.), *The collected works of* C. G. *Jung* (The Bollingen Series, Vol. 13). New York: Pantheon Books.

Kahan, T. L., & LaBerge, S. (1994). Lucid dreaming as metacognition: Implications for cognitive science. *Consciousness and Cognition, 3,* 246–264.

Kant, I. (1952). The critique of pure reason. In R. M. Hutchins (Ed.), *Great books of the western world* (Vol. 42, pp. 1–250). Chicago: Encyclopedia Britannica. (Original work published 1788)

Kapp, E. (1942). *Greek foundations of traditional logic.* (No. 5 in Columbia Studies of Philosophy). New York: Columbia University Press.

Keller, H. (1980). *The story of my life.* Mahwah, NJ: Watermill Press. (Original work published 1902)

Kelly, G. A. (1955). *The psychology of personal constructs: A theory of personality* (2 vols.). New York: Norton.

Keyes, D. (1981). *The minds of Billy Mulligan.* New York: Bantam Books.

Kihlstrom, J. F. (1985). Hypnosis. In M. S. Rosenzweig & L. W. Porter (Eds.), *Annual Review of Psychology, 36,* (pp. 385–418). Palo Alto, CA: Annual Reviews.

Kihlstrom, J. F., Barnhardt, T. M., & Tataryn, D. J. (1992). The psychological unconscious: Found, lost, and regained. *American Psychologist, 47,* 788–791.

Kihlstrom, J. F., & Harackiewicz, J. (1982). The earliest recollection: A new survey. *Journal of Personality, 50,* 134–148.

Kirsch, I., & Lynn, S. J. (1995). The altered state of hypnosis: Changes in theoretical language. *American Psychologist, 50,* 846–858.

Klein, D. B. (1984). *The concept of consciousness: A survey.* Lincoln: University of Nebraska Press.

Klimo, J. (1987). *Channeling: Investigations on receiving information from paranormal sources.* Los Angeles: J. P. Archer.

Krauthammer, C. (1996, February 26). Deep blue funk. *Time,* pp. 60–61.

Kuhn, T. S. (1970). *The structure of scientific revolutions* (2nd ed.). Chicago: The University of Chicago Press.

Kurtines, W. M., & Gewirtz, J. L. (Eds.). (1991). *Handbook of moral behavior and development* (3 vols.). New York: Erlbaum.

LaBerge, S. (1985). *Lucid dreaming.* New York: Ballantine.

LaBerge, S. (1988). The psychophysiology of lucid dreaming. In J. Gackenbach & S. LaBerge (Eds.), *Conscious mind, sleeping brain: Perspectives on lucid dreaming* (pp. 128–147). New York: Plenum.

Lakoff, G. (1987). *Women, fire, and dangerous things: What categories reveal about the mind.* Chicago: University of Chicago Press.

Lakoff, G., & Johnson, M. (1980). *Metaphors we live by.* Chicago: University of Chicago Press.

Langer, S. K. (1948). *Philosophy in a new key.* New York: Penguin Books.

Langer, S. K. (1964). *Philosophical sketches.* New York: New American Library.

Le Bon, G. (1903). *The crowd.* London: F. Unwin Publishers.

Lefcourt, H. M. (1973). The function of the illusions of control and freedom. *American Psychologist, 28,* 417–425.

Lewicki, P., Hill, T., & Czyzewska, M. (1992). Nonconscious acquisition of information. *American Psychologist, 47,* 796–801.

Lewis, M., & Brooks, J. (1974). Self, others, and fear: Infants' reactions to people. In M. Lewis & L. Rosenblum (Eds.), *Fear: The origins of behavior* (Vol. 2, pp. 54–73). New York: Wiley.

Libet, B. (1985). Unconscious cerebral initiative and the role of conscious will in voluntary action. *The Behavioral and Brain Sciences, 8,* 529–566.

Locke, J. (1952). An essay concerning human understanding. In R. M. Hutchins (Ed.), *Great books of the western world* (Vol. 35, pp. 85–395). Chicago: Encyclopedia Britannica. (Original work published 1690)

Loftus, E. F. (1993). The reality of repressed memories. *American Psychologist, 48,* 518–535.

Loftus, E. F., & Klinger, M. R. (1992). Is the unconscious smart or dumb? *American Psychologist, 47,* 761–765.

Lorayne, H., & Lucas, J. (1974). *The memory book.* New York: Ballantine Books.

Lucas, J. R. (1961). Minds, machines, and Gödel. *Philosophy, 36,* 112–127.

Ludwig, A. M. (1966). Altered states of consciousness. *Archives of General Psychiatry, 15,* 225–234.

Ludwig, A. M., Brandsma, J. M., Wilbur, C. B., Bendfeldt, F., & Jameson, D. H. (1972). The objective study of a multiple personality. *Archives of General Psychiatry, 26,* 298–310.

Lyons, J. (1977). *Semantics* (Vol. I). Cambridge, England: Cambridge University Press.

Mandler, G. A. (1984). *Mind and body: Psychology of emotion and stress.* New York: Norton.

Marcel, A. J. (1983). Conscious and unconscious perception: Experiments on visual masking and word recognition. *Cognitive Psychology, 15,* 197–237.

Marx, K. (1952a). Capital. In R. M. Hutchins (Ed.), *Great books of the western world* (Vol. 50, pp. 1–393). Chicago: Encyclopedia Britannica. (Original work published 1867)

Marx, K. (1952b). Manifesto of the communist party. In R. M. Hutchins (Ed.), *Great books of the western world* (Vol. 50, pp. 413–434). Chicago: Encyclopedia Britannica. (Original work published 1847)

May, R. (1977). Freedom, determinism, and the future. *Psychology* (April, Trial issue), 3–8.

McCulloch, W., & Pitts, W. (1943). A logical calculus of the ideas immanent in nervous activity. *Bulletin of Mathematical Biophysics, 5,* 115–133.

McDougall, W. (1920). *The group mind.* Cambridge, England: Cambridge University Press.

McGuire, W. (Ed.). (1974). *The Freud/Jung letters: The correspondence between Sigmund Freud and C. G. Jung.* Princeton, NJ: Princeton University Press.

McLuhan, M. (1962). *The Gutenberg galaxy: The making of typographic man.* New York: Signet Books.

Menninger, K. (1966). *The crime of punishment.* New York: Viking Press.

Merikle, P. M. (1982). Unconscious perception revisited. *Perception and psychophysics, 31,* 298–301.

Meyers, R. E., & Sperry, R. W. (1953). Interocular transfer of a visual form discrimination habit in cats after section of the optic chiasm and corpus callosum. *Anatomical Record, 115,* 351–352.

Meyrowitz, J. (1985). *No sense of place: The impact of electronic media on social behavior.* New York: Oxford University Press.

Mill, J. S. (1974). A system of logic: Ratiocinative and inductive (Books I–III). Toronto: University of Toronto Press; and London: Routledge & Kegan Paul. (Original work published 1843)

Miller, G. A., Galanter, E., & Pribram, K. H. (1960). Plans and the structure of behavior. New York: Holt, Rinehart & Winston.

Miller, N. E., & Dollard, J. (1941). Social learning and imitation. New Haven, CT: Yale University Press.

Minsky, M. (1986). The society of mind. New York: Simon & Schuster.

Mountcastle, V. B. (1975). Modality and topographic properties of single neurones of cat's somatic sensory cortex. Journal of Neurophysiology, 20, 408–434.

Mowrer, O. H. (1961). The crisis in psychiatry and religion. New York: D. Van Nostrand.

Mumford, L. (1934). Techniques and civilization. London: Routledge.

Nagel, E., & Newman, J. R. (1958). Gödel's proof. New York: New York University Press.

Naranjo, C., & Ornstein, R. E. (1971). On the psychology of meditation. New York: The Viking Press.

Nash, M. (1987). What, if anything, is regressed about hypnotic age regression? A review of the empirical literature. Psychological Bulletin, 102, 42–52.

Natsoulas, T. (1983). Concepts of consciousness. The Journal of Mind and Behavior, 4, 13–59.

Needleman, J. (1963). Introduction. In L. Binswanger, Being–in–the–world (pp. 1–6). New York: Basic Books.

Neisser, U. (1992). The development of consciousness and the acquisition of self. In F. S. Kessel, P. M. Cole, & D. L. Johnson (Eds.), Self and consciousness: Multiple perspectives (pp. 1–18). Hillsdale, NJ: Erlbaum.

Newell, A., & Simon, H. A. (1972). Human problem solving. Englewood Cliffs, NJ: Prentice-Hall.

Nikhilananda, S. (1967). Concentration and meditation as methods of Indian philosophy. In C. A. Moore (Ed.), The Indian mind: Essentials of Indian philosophy and culture (pp. 136–151). Honolulu: University of Hawaii Press.

O'Connor, D. J. (1971). Free will. Garden City, NY: Anchor.

Orne, M. T. (1959). The nature of hypnosis: Artifact and essence. Journal of Abnormal and Social Psychology, 86, 543–552.

Orne, M. T. (1979). The use and misuse of hypnosis in court. International Journal of Clinical and Experimental Hypnosis, 27, 311–341.

Ornstein, R. E. (1977). The psychology of consciousness (2nd ed.). New York: Harcourt.

Ornstein, R. E. (1991). The evolution of consciousness. New York: Simon & Schuster.

Page, M. M. (1972). Demand characteristics and the verbal operant conditioning experiment. Journal of Personality and Social Psychology, 23, 304–308.

Palmer, R. E. (1969). *Hermeneutics: Interpretation theory in Schleiermacher, Dilthey, Heidegger, and Gadamer.* Evanston, IL: Northwestern University Press.

Penfield, W. (1975). *The mystery of the mind: A critical study of consciousness and the human brain.* Princeton, NJ: Princeton University Press.

Penrose, R. (1989). *The emperor's new mind: Concerning computers, minds, and the laws of physics.* New York: Oxford University Press.

Penrose, R. (1994). *Shadows of the mind: A search for the missing science of consciousness.* New York: Oxford University Press.

Perry, R. B. (1948). *The thought and character of William James.* Cambridge, MA: Harvard University Press.

Piaget, J. (1965). *The moral judgment of the child.* New York: Free Press.

Piaget, J. (1973). *The child and reality: Problems of genetic psychology.* New York: Grossman.

Plato. (1952a). Philebus. In R. M. Hutchins (Ed.), *Great books of the western world* (Vol. 7, pp. 609–639). Chicago: Encyclopedia Britannica.

Plato. (1952b). The republic. In R. M. Hutchins (Ed.), *Great books of the western world* (Vol. 7, pp. 295–441). Chicago: Encyclopedia Britannica.

Plato. (1952c). Sophist. In R. M. Hutchins (Ed.), *Great books of the western world* (Vol. 7, pp. 551–579). Chicago: Encyclopedia Britannica.

Polanyi, M. (1964). *Personal knowledge: Towards a post-critical philosophy.* New York: Harper & Row.

Polanyi, M. (1968). Logic and psychology. *American Psychologist, 23,* 27–43.

Popović, V. (1991). Ascetic body—lustful soul: An archetypal approach to the psychology of anorexia nervosa. In J. Ryce-Menuhin (Ed.), *Harvest* (pp. 112–121). Oxford, England: Joshua Associates Ltd.

Potts, T. C. (1980). *Conscience in medieval philosophy.* Cambridge, England: Cambridge University Press.

Pressley, M., Borkowski, J. G., & Schneider, W. (1987). Cognitive strategies: Good strategy users coordinate metacognition and knowledge. In R. Vasta (Ed.), *Annals of Child Development* (Vol. 4, pp. 89–129). Greenwich, CT: JAI.

Prigogine, I., & Stengers, I. (1984). *Order out of chaos: Man's new dialogue with nature.* New York: Bantam Books.

Reese, W. L. (1980). *Dictionary of philosophy and religion.* Atlantic Highlands, NJ: Humanities Press.

Richards, I. A. (1967). Introduction. In C. K. Ogden, *Opposition: A linguistic and psychological analysis* (pp. 7–13). Bloomington: Indiana University Press.

Rickaby, J. (1906). *Free will and four English philosophers.* London: Burns and Oates.

Riesman, D., Glazer, N., & Denney, R. (1953). *The lonely crowd: A study of the changing American character.* Garden City, NY: Doubleday Anchor.

Roediger, H. L., III. (1990). Implicit memory: Retention without remembering. *American Psychologist, 45,* 1043–1056.

Rosenau, P. M. (1992). *Post-modernism and the social sciences: Insights, inroads, and intrusions.* Princeton, NJ: Princeton University Press

Rosenblueth, A., Wiener, N., & Bigelow, J. (1943). Behavior, teleology, and purpose. *Philosophy of Science, 10,* 18–24.

Rosenthal, P. (1984). *Words & values.* New York: Oxford University Press.

Ruch, J. C. (1975). Self-hypnosis: The result of heterohypnosis or vice versa? *International Journal of Clinical and Experimental Hypnosis, 23,* 282–304.

Russell, B. (1959). *Wisdom of the west.* Garden City, NY: Doubleday.

Rychlak, J. F. (1966). Reinforcement value: A suggested idiographic, intensity dimension of meaningfulness for the personality theorist. *Journal of Personality, 34,* 311–335.

Rychlak, J. F. (1975a). Affective assessment in the recognition of designs and paintings by elementary school children. *Child Development, 46,* 62–70.

Rychlak, J. F. (1975b). Affective assessment, intelligence, social class, and racial learning style. *Journal of Personality and Social Psychology, 32,* 989–995.

Rychlak, J. F. (1975c). A letter from C. G. Jung. In G. Adler & A. Jaffe (Eds.), *C. G. Jung letters* (Vol. 2, pp. 500–502). Princeton, NJ: Princeton University Press.

Rychlak, J. F. (1981). *A philosophy of science for personality theory* (2nd ed.). Malabar, FL: Krieger.

Rychlak, J. F. (1982). Logical learning theory applications to psychotherapeutic practice. In L. E. Abt & I. R. Stuart (Eds.), *The newer therapies: A workbook* (pp. 96–116). New York: Van Nostrand Reinhold.

Rychlak, J. F. (1988). *The psychology of rigorous humanism* (2nd ed.). New York: New York University Press.

Rychlak, J. F. (1991). *Artificial intelligence and human reason: A teleological critique.* New York: Columbia University Press.

Rychlak, J. F. (1993). A suggested principle of complementarity for psychology. *American Psychologist, 48,* 933–942.

Rychlak, J. F. (1994). *Logical learning theory: A human teleology and its empirical support.* Lincoln, NE: University of Nebraska Press.

Rychlak, J. F., & Barnard, S. (1993). Depth of processing versus oppositional context in word recall. A new look at the findings of "Hyde and Jenkins" as viewed by "Craik and Lockhart." *The Journal of Mind and Behavior, 14,* 155–177.

Rychlak, J. F., & Barnard, S. (1996). The role of negation in implication versus inference. *Journal of Psycholinguistic Research, 25,* 483–505.

Rychlak, J. F., Barnard, S., Williams, R. N., & Wollman, N. (1989). The recognition and cognitive utilization of oppositionality. *Journal of Psycholinguistic Research, 18,* 181–199.

Rychlak, J. F., Carlsen, N. L., & Dunning, L. P. (1974). Personal adjustment and the free recall of material with affectively positive or negative meaningfulness. *Journal of Abnormal Psychology, 83,* 480–487.

Rychlak, J. F., Flynn, E. J., & Burger, G. (1979). Affection and evaluation as logical processes of meaningfulness independent of associative frequency. *Journal of General Psychology, 100,* 143–157.

Rychlak, J. F., Galster, J., & McFarland, K. K. (1972). The role of affective assessment in associative learning: From designs and CVC trigrams to faces and names. *Journal of Experimental Research in Personality, 6,* 186–194.

Rychlak, J. F., Hewitt, C. W., & Hewitt, J. (1973). Affective evaluation, word quality, and the verbal learning styles of black versus white junior college females. *Journal of Personality and Social Psychology, 27,* 248–255.

Rychlak, J. F., & Marceil, J. C. (1986). Task predication and affective learning style. *Journal of Social Behavior and Personality, 1,* 557–564.

Rychlak, J. F., McKee, D. B., Schneider, W. E., & Abramson, Y. (1971). Affective evaluation in the verbal learning styles of normals and abnormals. *Journal of Abnormal Psychology, 77,* 247–257.

Rychlak, J. F., & Rychlak, L. S. (1991). Evidence for a predication effect in deciding on the personal significance of abstract word meanings. *Journal of Psycholinguistic Research, 20,* 403–418.

Rychlak, J. F., & Saluri, R. E. (1973). Affective assessment in the learning of names by fifth- and sixth-grade children. *Journal of Genetic Psychology, 123,* 251–261.

Rychlak, J. F., Stilson, S. R., & Rychlak, L. S. (1993). Testing a predicational model of cognition: Cueing predicate meanings in sentences and word triplets. *Journal of Psycholinguistic Research, 22,* 479–503.

Rychlak, J. F., & Tobin, T. J. (1971). Order effects in the affective learning styles of overachievers and underachievers. *Journal of Educational Psychology, 62,* 141–147.

Rychlak, J. F., Tuan, N. D., & Schneider, W. E. (1974). Formal discipline revisited: Affective assessment and nonspecific transfer. *Journal of Educational Psychology, 66,* 139–151.

Rychlak, J. F., & Williams, R. N. (1984). Affective assessment and dialectical oppositionality in the cognitive processing of social descriptors. *Personality and Social Psychology Bulletin, 10,* 620–629.

Rychlak, J. F., Williams, R. N., & Bugaj, A. M. (1986). The heuristic properties of dialectical oppositionality in predication. *Journal of General Psychology, 113,* 359–368.

Sampson, E. E. (1993). *Celebrating the other: A dialogic account of human behavior.* San Francisco: Westview Press.

Sarbin, T. R. (1950). Contributions to role-taking theory: I. Hypnotic behavior. *Psychological Review, 57,* 255–270.

Sarbin, T. R., & Coe, W. C. (1972). *Hypnosis: A social psychological analysis of influence communication.* New York: Holt, Rinehart & Winston.

Sarup, M. (1989). *An introductory guide to post-structuralism and postmodernism.* Athens: University of Georgia Press.

Schacter, D. L. (1977). EEG theta waves and psychological phenomena: A review and analysis. *Biological Psychology, 5,* 47–82.

Schreiber, F. R. (1974). *Sybil.* New York: Warner Publications.

Scribner, S., & Cole, M. (1981) *The psychology of literacy.* Cambridge, England: Cambridge University Press.

Searle, J. R. (1985). *Intentionality: An essay in the philosophy of mind.* Cambridge, England: Cambridge University Press.

Searle, J. R. (1990). Is the brain's mind a computer program? *Scientific American, 263,* 26–31.

Searle, J. R. (1992). *The rediscovery of the mind.* Cambridge, MA: The MIT Press.

Shannon, C. E. (1938). A symbolic analysis of relay and switching circuits. Master's thesis, Massachusetts Institute of Technology; published in *Transactions of the American Institute of Electrical Engineers, 57,* 1–11.

Shannon, C. E., & Weaver, W. (Eds.). (1962). *The mathematical theory of communication.* Urbana: University of Illinois Press.

Sheldrake, R. (1988). *The presence of the past: Morphic resonance and the habits of nature.* New York: Viking Press.

Silverman, H. J. (1989). *Derrida and deconstruction.* New York: Routledge.

Simon, H. A. (1985). *The science of the artificial* (2nd ed.). Cambridge, MA: MIT Press.

Skinner, B. F. (1948). *Walden two.* New York: Macmillan.

Skinner, B. F. (1957). *Verbal behavior.* New York: Appleton-Century-Crofts.

Skinner, B. F. (1961). The design of cultures. *Daedalus, 90,* 534–546.

Skinner, B. F. (1971). *Beyond freedom and dignity.* New York: Knopf.

Skinner, B. F. (1974). *About behaviorism.* New York: Knopf.

Skinner, B. F. (1977). Why I am not a cognitive psychologist. *Behaviorism, 5,* 1–10.

Skinner, B. F. (1987). *Upon further reflection.* Englewood Cliffs, NJ: Prentice-Hall.

Slife, B. D. (1993). *Time and psychological explanation.* Albany, NY: SUNY Press.

Slife, B. D., Stoneman, J., & Rychlak, J. F. (1991). The heuristic power of oppositionality in an incidental memory task: In support of the construing process. *International Journal of Personal Construct Psychology, 4,* 333–346.

Smith, J. C. (1976). Psychotherapeutic effects of transcendental meditation with controls for expectation of relief and daily sitting. *Journal of Consulting and Clinical Psychology, 44,* 630–637.

Snell, B. (1953). *The discovery of the mind: The Greek origins of European thought.* Oxford, England: Blackwell.

Snyder, F. (1970). The phenomenology of dreaming. In L. Madow & L. H. Snow (Eds.), *The psychodynamic implications of the physiological studies on dreams* (pp. 124–151). Springfield, IL: Thomas.

Spanos, N. P. (1986). Hypnotic behavior: A socio-psychological interpretation of amnesia, analgesia, and "trance logic." *The Behavioral and Brain Sciences, 9*, 449–502. [Includes peer commentary.]

Spanos, N. P., & Coe, W. C. (1992). Social-psychological approach to hypnosis. In E. Fromm & M. R. Nash (Eds.), *Contemporary hypnosis research* (pp. 102–130). New York: Guilford Press.

Spanos, N. P., Gwynn, M. I., & Stam, H. J. (1983). Instructional demands and ratings of overt and hidden pain during hypnotic analgesia. *Journal of Abnormal Psychology, 92*, 479–488.

Spanos, N. P., & Hewitt, E. C. (1980). The hidden observer in hypnotic analgesia: Discovery or experimental creation? *Journal of Personality and Social Psychology, 39*, 1201–1214.

Sparrow, G. S. (1976). *Lucid dreaming: Dawning of the clear light.* Virginia Beach, VA: A. R. E. Press.

Sperry, R. W. (1961). Cerebral organization and behavior. *Science, 133*, 1749–1757.

Sperry, R. W. (1976). Changing concepts of consciousness and free will. *Perspectives in biology and medicine, 20*, 9–19.

Sperry, R. W. (1985). *Science & moral priority: Merging mind, brain, and human values.* New York: Praeger.

Sperry, R. W. (1992). Turnabout on consciousness: A mentalist view. *The Journal of Mind and Behavior, 13*, 259–280.

Sperry, R. W. (1993). The impact and promise of the cognitive revolution. *American Psychologist, 48*, 878–885.

Spielberger, C. D. (1962). The role of awareness in verbal conditioning. In C. W. Eriksen (Ed.), *Behavior and awareness: A symposium of research and interpretation* (pp. 73–101). Durham, NC: Duke University Press.

Stace, W. T. (1955). *The philosophy of Hegel.* New York: Dover.

Stapp, H. (1975). Bell's theorem and world process. *Nuovo Cimento, 29*, 270–278.

Stone, I. F. (1989). *The trial of Socrates.* New York: Doubleday Anchor.

Straus, E. W. (1958). Aesthesiology and hallucinations. In R. May, E. Angel, & H. F. Ellenberger (Eds.), *Existence: A new dimension in psychiatry and psychology* (pp. 138–156). New York: Basic Books.

Sulloway, F. J. (1979). *Freud, biologist of the mind: Beyond the psychoanalytical legend.* New York: Basic Books.

Sutcliffe, J. P., & Jones, J. (1963). Personal identity: Multiple personality and hypnosis. *Journal of Clinical and Experimental Hypnosis, 40*, 231–269.

Tarde, G. (1903). *Laws of imitation.* (E. Parsons, Trans.). New York: Holt.

Tart, C. (1984). Terminology in lucid dream research. *Lucidity Letter, 3*, 82–84.

Tart, C. (1986). *Waking up: Overcoming the obstacles to human potential.* Boston: New Science Library.

Taylor, C. (1989). *Sources of the self: The making of the modern identity.* Cambridge, MA: Harvard University Press.

Thigpen, C., & Cleckly, H. (1954). *The three faces of Eve*. New York: McGraw-Hill.

Tholey, P. (1983). Techniques for inducing and manipulating lucid dreams. *Perceptual and Motor Skills, 57*, 79–80.

Tholey, P. (1990). Applications of lucid dreaming in sports. *Lucidity Letter, 9*, 6–19.

Tolman, E. C. (1967). *Purposive behavior in animals and men*. New York: Appleton-Century-Crofts.

Trier, J. (1931). *Der deutsche wortschatz im sinnbezirk des verstandes* [A glossary of German terms relevant to the subject matter of understanding]. Heidelberg: Winter.

Tulving, E., & Schachter, D. L. (1990). Priming and human memory systems. *Science, 247*, 301–306.

Turing, A. (1950). Computing machinery and intelligence. *Mind, 59*, 433–460.

Ulasevich, A. (1991). *Affective predication in memory for sentences: Anticipating meaningfulness before meaning*. Unpublished master's thesis, Loyola University of Chicago.

Ultan, R. (1969). Some general characteristics of interrogative systems. *Working papers in language universals* (Stanford University), *1*, 41–63.

Valle, R. S., & Halling, S. (Eds.). (1989). *Existential-phenomenological perspectives in psychology*. New York: Plenum Press.

Van Eeden, F. (1913). A study of dreams. *Proceedings of the Society for Psychical Research, 26*, 431–461.

Velmans, M. (1991). Is human information processing conscious? *Behavioral and Brain Sciences, 14*, 651–669.

Vygotsky, L. (1986). *Thought and language* (revised and edited by A. Kozulin). Cambridge, MA: MIT Press.

Wagstaff, G. F. (1981). *Hypnosis, compliance and belief*. New York: St. Martin's Press.

Warrington, E. K., & Weiskrantz, L. (1970). Amnesic syndrome: Consolidation or retrieval? *Nature, 228*, 628–630.

Watson, J. B. (1913). Psychology as the behaviorist views it. *Psychological Review, 20*, 158–177.

Watson, J. B. (1924). *Behaviorism*. New York: Norton.

Watson, R. I., & Evans, R. B. (1991). *The great psychologists: A history of psychological thought* (5th ed.). New York: Harper Collins.

Weiskrantz, L. (1986). *Blindsight: A case study and implications*. Oxford, England: Oxford University Press.

Weitzenhoffer, A. M. (1957). *General techniques of hypnotism*. New York: Grune & Stratton.

Weizenbaum, J. (1976). *Computer power and human reason: From judgment to calculation*. San Francisco: Freeman.

White, A. R. (1964). *Attention*. Oxford, England: Blackwell.

White, L. (1962). *Medieval technology and social change*. Oxford, England: Oxford University Press.

Whorf, B. L. (1958). Language and stereotypes. In E. E. Maccoby, T. M. Newcomb, & E. L. Hartley (Eds.), *Readings in social psychology* (3rd ed., pp. 1–9). New York: Holt.

Whyte, L. L. (1960). *The unconscious before Freud*. Garden City, NY: Doubleday.

Whyte, W. H., Jr. (1956). *The organization man*. Garden City, NY: Doubleday.

Wiener, N. (1954). *The human use of human beings: Cybernetics and society*. Boston: Houghton Mifflin.

Wittels, F. (1924). *Sigmund Freud: His personality, his teaching, and his school*. New York: Dodd, Mead.

Woody, E. Z., Bowers, K. S., & Oakman, J. M. (1992). A conceptual analysis of hypnotic responsiveness: Experience, individual differences, and context. In E. Fromm & M. R. Nash (Eds.), *Contemporary hypnosis research* (pp. 3–33). New York: Guilford Press.

Wundt, W. (1920). *Volkerpsychologie: Eine Untersuchung der Entwicklungsgesetze von Sprache, Mythus, und Sitte* [Folk psychology: A study of the laws of development of language, myth, and morality] (10 Vols.). Leipzig: Engelmann. (Original work published 1900)

Yartz, F. J. (1984). *Ancient Greek philosophy: Sourcebook and perspective*. Jefferson, NC: MacFarland.

Zukav, G. (1979). *The dancing wu li masters: An overview of the new physics*. New York: Bantam Books.

AUTHOR INDEX

SUBJECT INDEX

extraspective theory, 180
　as Newtonian, 180
　rejected consciousness, 179
Bicameral mind, Jaynes
　collapsed with rise of consciousness,
　　141
　initially unconscious, 139
　language aided consciousness, 139
　signal-bound and binary, 140
Binary, bit
　either–or and never both, 139
　halving signals, 174
Bios
　biological reductionism, 89, 105
　closely tied to *Physikos* grounds, 20–
　　21
　concepts like reflex, drive, trait, 285
　definition of, 20
Boolean algebra
　demonstrative formulation, 195
　disjunction in, 196
　fundamental to computer processing,
　　191, 195
　law of duality, 196
　principle of contradiction, 195–196
Brain
　Cartesian theater lacking, Dennett,
　　183
　executive versus follower, Jaynes,
　　139
　as instrumental organ, 135, 144
　mental events caused by, Searle, 190
　multiple drafts of, Dennett, 188
　readiness potential, Libet, 136–137
　reentry in, Edelman, 129–130
　reflexive actions in, James, 154
　software enhances, Dennett, 189
　splitting of, Sperry, 125
　waves, in altered states, 204

Category, categorization
　framed internally, LLT, 134
　innate capacity, Edelman, 130–131
　as predication, 39, 134
　shaped externally, Edelman, 134
Cause, Causation
　definition of, 3
　downward, Sperry, 127
　relation to determinism, 3
　in rise of science, 80–82
　two-way, Sperry, 125–127
Censor

early Freudian concept, 96–97
　superego as, 102
Channeling
　definition of, 213
　usually positive content in, 213
Charisma, individual's influence on col-
　　lective, Weber, 22
Choice
　birth of, 269
　as emphasis, James, 156
Claparede's law, 93
Class
　conflict, as always political, 244
　consciousness, as group awareness,
　　244
　-linked ideas, 244
Collective
　charismatic influence on, 22
　class consciousness, 13
　influence, negation of, Berger, 247
　Leviathan, Hobbes, 13
　versus predicational explanation, 259
　print decollectivizes, McLuhan, 79
Complementarity, principle of in psychol-
　　ogy, 19
Complex, Jungian theory, 99, 101, 115
Computer model
　as dialectical "reasoner" someday,
　　200
　firmware, 199
　hardware versus software, 174
　information, two forms of, 175
　neural networks, McCulloch and
　　Pitts, 175
　processing without meaning, 176
　simulation of mind, 135, 184
　unconsciousness in, 184, 198, 281
　virtual machine as consciousness,
　　Dennett, 189
Conscience
　Confessions, St. Augustine, 67
　as conscious awareness, 8
　initially, identical to consciousness,
　　66, 141, 269
　intention in, 148
　personal, 103
　repression an aspect of, 102
Conscious, Consciousness
　altered states of, definition, 203–204
　awareness, 3
　class-consciousness, 13, 244
　collective, as mask, Jung, 238

natural selection, 122
  popular in AI theorizing, 184
  survival of fittest, 122
Ex cathedra views
  of bicameral mind, Jaynes, 140–141
  make unconscious appear wise, 117
  seemingly infallible, 117
Experiment, experimentation
  furthered efficient causation, 80–81
  independent versus dependent varia-
    bles, 80
Explanation
  level grounding in, 17
  in traditional psychology, 5
Extraspective, extraspection
  brain theory as, Sperry, 127
  as "looking at," 8
  natural selection theory as, 125
  a third-person theoretical analysis, 8

Feedback
  negative, as teleological action, 176
  positive versus negative, 175–176
Final cause
  in brain action, Sperry, 127
  definition of, 4
  libido as, Jung, 110
  makes best sense in *Logos* realm, 134
  meaning-extension as, 264
  in teleological theory, 4
Forgetting
  due to poor initial predication, 56,
    214
  begun at protopoint, 214
Formal cause
  as basic form of causation, 83
  in brain theory, Sperry, 126
  definition of, 4
  in natural selection, 125
  organization, in dreams, 221
Free will, freedom of the will
  as agency, 7, 61
  can have harmful ends, 165
  changes in brain set, Sperry, 127
  confound of process and content in,
    James, 150
  Darwin did not favor, 122
  definition of, LLT, 61, 160, 279
  determinism in, 275
  example of in life of Gandhi, 277
  and grace, 148
  as human right, 291

as illusion, 148, 162
as insoluble problem, James, 151
introspective versus extraspective,
  160
James versus LLT, 166
in legal systems, 291
Lockean "hang fire" interpretation,
  163
as number of mediating alternatives,
  162
occurs at antithesis, 274
in psychic determinism, 278
Renouvier's definition of, 150
in retrospection, 276
as second event, James, 164
as setting grounds, 275
as statistical unpredictability, 161
sustained fixing of attention, James,
  164
synthesis in, 275
as time of mediational influence,
  162
transpredication in, 148, 274
in unconsciousness, 277, 279
Future, in teleology, 72

Generic oppositionality
  contradictions result from, 167
  deconstructionism relies on, 260
  free will in, 150, 163
  model of, Figure 3, 43
  a process, 42
  transcendence in, 283
Gödel's Theorems
  demands self-conscious thought, 187
  Hofstadter's answer to, 187
  predication involved, 54, 188, 268
  transcendence in, 54
Grace
  birth of, 270
  submission to God's will, 67, 142
Grounds
  Bios, 20
  Logos, 23
  Physikos, 19
  Socius, 21
Guilt, via transpredication, 118
Gutenberg Galaxy, McLuhan, 76

Hermeneutics
  interpretation of texts, 255
  transpredication in, 254

in repression, 277
seeks ends, 6
unconscious form of, 277
understanding versus action, 45
wish as, 98
Introspective, Introspection
basic to self theory, 156
First-person theoretical analysis, 9
Freud's use of, 94–95
as "looking with," 8

Knowledge
dialectical theory of, 191
as extending range of predication,
LLT, 250
must know in order to know, LLT,
30
as not-knowing, 13
pluralism in, James, 169
as social achievement, 247

Language
consciousness aided by, Jaynes, 139
constrains the text, Derrida, 257
content within a *Logos* realm, LLT,
261
efficient causation in, 266
facilitates emergence, Edelman, 131
facilitates mediation, 7
facilitates transpredication, 77
influence on individual, 280
innate categories of, Edelman, 130
as an instrumentality, LLT, 248, 282
learning of, Keller, 251–253
life of its own, 241
as manipulator of behavior, 281–282
is metaphorical, 77
oppositionality important to, 248–
249
predication in, 249
as relatedness, 248
shapes behavior, 10, 133
social constructionism greatly relies
on, 248
as transpredicational process, 280–
282
Whorfian hypothesis, 253
words as contents of a process, 37
words as tools, 36, 262
Learning
definition of in LLT terms, 47, 250
as emergence, 132

Hullian explanation of, 131
unconscious, 267
Libido
cathexis of, 106
élan vital, Jung, 110
Freud–Jung conflict over, 108–110
not a physical concept, 106, 108
psychic energy, Freud, 106
used as both process and content,
Freud, 267
Logic
extraspective formulation of, 31
Port Royal, 31
rules for syllogism, 31, 42
traditional, seeks truth, 30
weight of, is unyielding, 120
Logical learning theory
consciousness viewed as process, 263
deconstruction consistent with, 260
definition of logos, 30
formal-final causation in, 32
free will is accepted and explained,
274
individual is main interest, 233
introspective formulation, 38
a *Logos* formulation, 26, 30
process explanation of cognition, 32
teleological theory, 26
Weber's sociology consistent with,
246–247
Logos
cannot be reduced to *Bios*, 155
complements *Bios*, 121
definition of, as grounds, 23
formal-cause emphasis, 23
meaning-extension in, 265

Many in one, a dialectical principle, 191
Match, matching
versus mismatch, 181
versus predicate, 135
as remembering, Minsky, 186
Material cause
artificial intelligence use of, 199
definition of, 3
as evolving brain structure, Jaynes,
139
Meaning
in cultural context, 255
information lacks, 36
intention basic to, 58
directs course of thought, 118

versus meaningfulness, 49
oppositionality in, 37
psychic consciousness relies on, 138
as syntax, 255
teleological conception, 36
Meaning-extension
definition of, LLT, 250
in language, 282
in *Logos* realm, 265
precedent-sequacious nature of, 41
principle of, 57
as therapeutic insight, 265
Mechanism, machine
ether as, Newton, 83
individuality lacking, 157
less emphasized in modern physical
science, 290
as non-telic, no final causation, 72,
81, 144–145
not favored by James, 160
people are not, LLT, 266
postmechanism, 290
rise of mechanical world view, 17th
century, 71
signals in, 282
virtual, as conscious, Dennett, 189
Mediation
in bicameral mind theory, Jaynes,
143
cue-producing responses in, 35
definition of, mechanical, 33
efficient causation in, 5
frequency and contiguity in, 35
in hypnotism, 208–209
language facilitation in, 7
model, Figure 1, 34
via neurons, Edelman, 134
as process of social constructionism,
250, 259
purpose lacking in, 35
as shaping influences, 5
telic versus mechanical, 33
Medical model, 107–108
Meditation
brain waves in, 223
concentration in, 223
as detached consciousness, 223
dialectical reasoning in, 224, 226
as focused awareness, 225
mantra, 223
Nirvana, 223
opening-up, 224

transpredication in, 226
turning off conceptual activity, 225
unipredication in, 225
Memory
cause of consciousness, Minsky, 186
false, 213
important to consciousness, 15, 131
initial organization of, 75–76
involved in thought, 68
method of loci, 75
two models of, 74
Metaphors, related to analogy, 48
Method, definition of, 17
Mind,
anthill metaphor as, Hofstadter, 183
of computer, 135
The Group Mind, McDougall, 236
mentalism accepted, Sperry, 127
as selecting signals, 137
society of, Minsky, 183
Moral, Morality
consciousness related, Jaynes, 141
content, definition of, 270
content, enlightened form of, 272
content, political correctness as, 273
process, definition of, 270
process, prevalent modern view, 272
process, and sin, 272
realism, Piaget, 270
Multiple personality
case history of, 215–217
definition of, 212, 215
type of hysteria, 214

Natural selection
as extraspective formal causation,
125
in Skinnerian theory, 122, 133
Negation
as affirmation of meaning, 57
of collective influence, Berger, 247
innate human capacity, 249
oppositional reasoning in, 72
of software programs, 137
Neuronal group selection
AI theories and, 184
versus natural selection, 129
parallels Hullian learning theory,
131
Nonconscious
as bottom–up processing, Sperry, 127
does not involve predication, 59

inanimate objects as, 59
    meditation as, 225
Norms
    as mediators, 234
    predications held in common, LLT,
        234

Oedipus complex
    influence on superego formation,
        102
    as mental heritage, Freud, 117
Operant response
    via efficient causation, 133
    not purposive, 132
Oppositionality
    in ancient Greece, 191
    of belief, LLT, 166
    in dialectical reasoning, 37
    is dimensional, 196
    in external events, Marx, 245
    generic versus delimiting, 42
    hierarchy in, 257
    in implication, 38, 41
    lacking in logic of a computer, 198
    in language, 248–249
    many in one, 196
    one pole delimits the other, 37
    in origin of personal consciousness,
        266
    pecking order of, Derrida, 257
    in psychoanalysis, 100–102
    in same versus different, 44
The Organization Man, Whyte, 238

Paradigm, in science, Kuhn, 14
Pelagianism, 67
Person
    absent in mechanistic theories, 266
    basic to psychology, James, 156
    as framer of self, 118
    not a machine, LLT, 201
    personal construct, Kelly, 245
    product of group forces, 237
    as telosponder, 60
Physikos, definition of, 19
Plans and the Structure of Behavior, Miller,
        Galanter, and Pribram, 177
Postmodernism
    claims truth is impossible, 255
    denies transpredication, 261
    many forms of, 255
    as poststructuralism, 255

Pragmatism, James, 153
Precedent
    extend meaning to targets, 41
    meanings, come first in logical order,
        41
Preconscious
    also called foreconscious, Freud, 95
Predicate, predication
    broad to narrow realm of meaning,
        39
    as category, 39
    complete, 38
    conceptual versus affective, 283
    in conditioning, 287
    context as, 57
    definition of, LLT, 41
    in dreams, 221–222
    Euler circles and, 39–40, 259
    examples of, James, 167–168
    in hypnosis, 208
    immediate, not mediate, 40
    as introspective concept, 237
    makes learning possible, 251
    model, Figure 2, 39
    not matching, 135
    noun versus verb usage, 42
    occurs prelinguistically, 250
    in semantics, not syntax, 38
    taking a position, 167
    target in, 38
    of time as concept, 71
    time's passage irrelevant, 41
    Whorfian hypothesis as, 253
Premise
    definition of, 45–46
    different types of, 194
The Principles of Psychology, James, 149
Process
    confounded with content, 95
    definition of, 5–6
    does not change with different con-
        tents, 6
    of group versus individual, 234
    logical, 31
Pro forma
    active framing of meaning, 237
    process not content, 47
Project for a Scientific Psychology, Freud,
        108
Protopoint
    attention fixes, James, 156
    in Freudian interpretations, 230

definition of, 60
exists only with others, Gergen, 248
as externally shaped, 10
many forms of, James, 158
-fulfilling prophecy, 31, 60
introspective concept, 156
as linguistic convention, 10
me and not-me, James, 158
sameness in behavior, 9–10, 60
saturated, Gergen, 288
selfless, 169
as social product, 248
soul, as inner, 67, 69
as subjective, 69
Sequacious
following necessarily in logical order,
41
as formal-cause determinism, 41
versus instrumental meaning-extension, 201
Simulation, 176–177, 179
Society
extraspective view of, Durkheim,
246
introspective view of, Weber, 246
LLT consistent with Weber, 246
Socius
can detract from selfhood, 79
definition of, 21–22
importance to human behavior, 240
in Jaynesian theory, 139
Marxian theory grounded in, 241
Sophistry, 191
Soul, as inner self, 67, 69
Strange loop, 187–188
Structuralism
as essentialism, 254
founded on linguistics, 254
relativistic view, 254
Suggestion, Janet, 90
Superego, Freud, 102
Survival of fittest, 123
Syllogism
definition of, 42, 46
introduced by Aristotle, 192
Symbols
in dreams, 222
language in, 280
as predicates, 280
versus signals, 174, 280
word-, transpredication in learning,
251

Systematic doubt
Descartes's method, 69
search for truth, 70
Tabula rasa
blank sheet of paper, 34
used in mediation theory, 34–35
Target
meaning-extension and, 38
in predication, 38
Tautology
analogy as partial, 47
in demonstrative reasoning, 194
in learning, Keller, 252
principle of, 46
Teleology, telic
final causation basic to, 4
future important to, 72
Hull and Skinner versus Edelman,
132
negative feedback accounts for, 176
postmodernism lacks, 258
problems with extraspection, 127
intention in, 6
vitalism, 21
Telosponse
definition of, LLT, 46
as fiat of the will, 155
transcending, 283
Theory, definition of, 17
The Three Faces of Eve, Thigpen and
Cleckly, 215
Thought, thinking
begins in unconsciousness, 268
computer, is never purposive, 185
brain influences on, 128, 143–144
demonstrative and dialectical, 194
individual and, 262
Logos ground necessary, 201
machine, 173
as unconscious, 198
parallels consciousness, James, 156
predication directs, 118
protopoint fixes context, 54
stream of, James, 155
wordless, Keller, 251
Time
absolute, Newton, 71
consciousness and, James, 157
efficient causation and, 81
imaginary, Hawking, 72
irrelevant to predication, 41

Wish
    as intention, 98
    as the reason for action, 98
Will
    blocking of in thought, James, 155
    confer or withhold assent, 68
    definition of, James, 161
    fiat of, James, 155
    follows affirmation, 61
    generic oppositionality in, 150
    ideo-motor theory of action, James,
      155

    loss of, in hysteria, 91
    in movement, definition of, 155
    as proactive unipredication, 264
    as psychic determinism, 264
    teleological concept, 91
    telosponsivity in, 155

Zeitgeist
    Geist, Herder, 235
    as group mind, 15
    as paradigm, 14
    spirit of the age, 235

ABOUT THE AUTHOR

Joseph F. Rychlak, PhD, is the Maude C. Clarke Professor of Humanistic Psychology at Loyola University of Chicago, where he also holds an appointment in philosophy. In addition to teaching for 40 years at five universities, Rychlak has distinguished himself as a psychotherapist, author, theorist, and researcher. He is a fellow of both the American Psychological Association and the American Psychological Society. He has twice been elected president of the APA Division of Theoretical and Philosophical Psychology. Rychlak is known as a rigorous humanist because he submits his non-mechanistic theoretical claims to the traditional scientific test. His wife, Lenora, assists him, and they both take great pleasure in their grandchildren—to whom this book is dedicated.